Lecture Notes in Computer Science 14689

Founding Editors

Gerhard Goos
Juris Hartmanis

Editorial Board Members

The series Lecture Notes in Computer Science (LNCS), including its subseries Lecture Notes in Artificial Intelligence (LNAI) and Lecture Notes in Bioinformatics (LNBI), has established itself as a medium for the publication of new developments in computer science and information technology research, teaching, and education.

LNCS enjoys close cooperation with the computer science R & D community, the series counts many renowned academics among its volume editors and paper authors, and collaborates with prestigious societies. Its mission is to serve this international community by providing an invaluable service, mainly focused on the publication of conference and workshop proceedings and postproceedings. LNCS commenced publication in 1973.

Hirohiko Mori · Yumi Asahi
Editors

Human Interface and the Management of Information

Thematic Area, HIMI 2024
Held as Part of the 26th HCI International Conference, HCII 2024
Washington, DC, USA, June 29 – July 4, 2024
Proceedings, Part I

Editors
Hirohiko Mori
Tokyo City University
Tokyo, Japan

Yumi Asahi
Tokyo University of Science
Tokyo, Japan

ISSN 0302-9743 ISSN 1611-3349 (electronic)
Lecture Notes in Computer Science
ISBN 978-3-031-60106-4 ISBN 978-3-031-60107-1 (eBook)
https://doi.org/10.1007/978-3-031-60107-1

This Springer imprint is published by the registered company Springer Nature Switzerland AG
The registered company address is: Gewerbestrasse 11, 6330 Cham, Switzerland

If disposing of this product, please recycle the paper.

Foreword

This year we celebrate 40 years since the establishment of the HCI International (HCII) Conference, which has been a hub for presenting groundbreaking research and novel ideas and collaboration for people from all over the world.

The HCII conference was founded in 1984 by Prof. Gavriel Salvendy (Purdue University, USA, Tsinghua University, P.R. China, and University of Central Florida, USA) and the first event of the series, "1st USA-Japan Conference on Human-Computer Interaction", was held in Honolulu, Hawaii, USA, 18–20 August. Since then, HCI International is held jointly with several Thematic Areas and Affiliated Conferences, with each one under the auspices of a distinguished international Program Board and under one management and one registration. Twenty-six HCI International Conferences have been organized so far (every two years until 2013, and annually thereafter).

Over the years, this conference has served as a platform for scholars, researchers, industry experts and students to exchange ideas, connect, and address challenges in the ever-evolving HCI field. Throughout these 40 years, the conference has evolved itself, adapting to new technologies and emerging trends, while staying committed to its core mission of advancing knowledge and driving change.

As we celebrate this milestone anniversary, we reflect on the contributions of its founding members and appreciate the commitment of its current and past Affiliated Conference Program Board Chairs and members. We are also thankful to all past conference attendees who have shaped this community into what it is today.

The 26th International Conference on Human-Computer Interaction, HCI International 2024 (HCII 2024), was held as a 'hybrid' event at the Washington Hilton Hotel, Washington, DC, USA, during 29 June – 4 July 2024. It incorporated the 21 thematic areas and affiliated conferences listed below.

A total of 5108 individuals from academia, research institutes, industry, and government agencies from 85 countries submitted contributions, and 1271 papers and 309 posters were included in the volumes of the proceedings that were published just before the start of the conference, these are listed below. The contributions thoroughly cover the entire field of human-computer interaction, addressing major advances in knowledge and effective use of computers in a variety of application areas. These papers provide academics, researchers, engineers, scientists, practitioners and students with state-of-the-art information on the most recent advances in HCI.

The HCI International (HCII) conference also offers the option of presenting 'Late Breaking Work', and this applies both for papers and posters, with corresponding volumes of proceedings that will be published after the conference. Full papers will be included in the 'HCII 2024 - Late Breaking Papers' volumes of the proceedings to be published in the Springer LNCS series, while 'Poster Extended Abstracts' will be included as short research papers in the 'HCII 2024 - Late Breaking Posters' volumes to be published in the Springer CCIS series.

I would like to thank the Program Board Chairs and the members of the Program Boards of all thematic areas and affiliated conferences for their contribution towards the high scientific quality and overall success of the HCI International 2024 conference. Their manifold support in terms of paper reviewing (single-blind review process, with a minimum of two reviews per submission), session organization and their willingness to act as goodwill ambassadors for the conference is most highly appreciated.

This conference would not have been possible without the continuous and unwavering support and advice of Gavriel Salvendy, founder, General Chair Emeritus, and Scientific Advisor. For his outstanding efforts, I would like to express my sincere appreciation to Abbas Moallem, Communications Chair and Editor of HCI International News.

July 2024   Constantine Stephanidis

HCI International 2024 Thematic Areas
and Affiliated Conferences

- HCI: Human-Computer Interaction Thematic Area
- HIMI: Human Interface and the Management of Information Thematic Area
- EPCE: 21st International Conference on Engineering Psychology and Cognitive Ergonomics
- AC: 18th International Conference on Augmented Cognition
- UAHCI: 18th International Conference on Universal Access in Human-Computer Interaction
- CCD: 16th International Conference on Cross-Cultural Design
- SCSM: 16th International Conference on Social Computing and Social Media
- VAMR: 16th International Conference on Virtual, Augmented and Mixed Reality
- DHM: 15th International Conference on Digital Human Modeling & Applications in Health, Safety, Ergonomics & Risk Management
- DUXU: 13th International Conference on Design, User Experience and Usability
- C&C: 12th International Conference on Culture and Computing
- DAPI: 12th International Conference on Distributed, Ambient and Pervasive Interactions
- HCIBGO: 11th International Conference on HCI in Business, Government and Organizations
- LCT: 11th International Conference on Learning and Collaboration Technologies
- ITAP: 10th International Conference on Human Aspects of IT for the Aged Population
- AIS: 6th International Conference on Adaptive Instructional Systems
- HCI-CPT: 6th International Conference on HCI for Cybersecurity, Privacy and Trust
- HCI-Games: 6th International Conference on HCI in Games
- MobiTAS: 6th International Conference on HCI in Mobility, Transport and Automotive Systems
- AI-HCI: 5th International Conference on Artificial Intelligence in HCI
- MOBILE: 5th International Conference on Human-Centered Design, Operation and Evaluation of Mobile Communications

List of Conference Proceedings Volumes Appearing Before the Conference

1. LNCS 14684, Human-Computer Interaction: Part I, edited by Masaaki Kurosu and Ayako Hashizume
2. LNCS 14685, Human-Computer Interaction: Part II, edited by Masaaki Kurosu and Ayako Hashizume
3. LNCS 14686, Human-Computer Interaction: Part III, edited by Masaaki Kurosu and Ayako Hashizume
4. LNCS 14687, Human-Computer Interaction: Part IV, edited by Masaaki Kurosu and Ayako Hashizume
5. LNCS 14688, Human-Computer Interaction: Part V, edited by Masaaki Kurosu and Ayako Hashizume
6. LNCS 14689, Human Interface and the Management of Information: Part I, edited by Hirohiko Mori and Yumi Asahi
7. LNCS 14690, Human Interface and the Management of Information: Part II, edited by Hirohiko Mori and Yumi Asahi
8. LNCS 14691, Human Interface and the Management of Information: Part III, edited by Hirohiko Mori and Yumi Asahi
9. LNAI 14692, Engineering Psychology and Cognitive Ergonomics: Part I, edited by Don Harris and Wen-Chin Li
10. LNAI 14693, Engineering Psychology and Cognitive Ergonomics: Part II, edited by Don Harris and Wen-Chin Li
11. LNAI 14694, Augmented Cognition, Part I, edited by Dylan D. Schmorrow and Cali M. Fidopiastis
12. LNAI 14695, Augmented Cognition, Part II, edited by Dylan D. Schmorrow and Cali M. Fidopiastis
13. LNCS 14696, Universal Access in Human-Computer Interaction: Part I, edited by Margherita Antona and Constantine Stephanidis
14. LNCS 14697, Universal Access in Human-Computer Interaction: Part II, edited by Margherita Antona and Constantine Stephanidis
15. LNCS 14698, Universal Access in Human-Computer Interaction: Part III, edited by Margherita Antona and Constantine Stephanidis
16. LNCS 14699, Cross-Cultural Design: Part I, edited by Pei-Luen Patrick Rau
17. LNCS 14700, Cross-Cultural Design: Part II, edited by Pei-Luen Patrick Rau
18. LNCS 14701, Cross-Cultural Design: Part III, edited by Pei-Luen Patrick Rau
19. LNCS 14702, Cross-Cultural Design: Part IV, edited by Pei-Luen Patrick Rau
20. LNCS 14703, Social Computing and Social Media: Part I, edited by Adela Coman and Simona Vasilache
21. LNCS 14704, Social Computing and Social Media: Part II, edited by Adela Coman and Simona Vasilache
22. LNCS 14705, Social Computing and Social Media: Part III, edited by Adela Coman and Simona Vasilache

47. LNCS 14730, HCI in Games: Part I, edited by Xiaowen Fang
48. LNCS 14731, HCI in Games: Part II, edited by Xiaowen Fang
49. LNCS 14732, HCI in Mobility, Transport and Automotive Systems: Part I, edited by Heidi Krömker
50. LNCS 14733, HCI in Mobility, Transport and Automotive Systems: Part II, edited by Heidi Krömker
51. LNAI 14734, Artificial Intelligence in HCI: Part I, edited by Helmut Degen and Stavroula Ntoa
52. LNAI 14735, Artificial Intelligence in HCI: Part II, edited by Helmut Degen and Stavroula Ntoa
53. LNAI 14736, Artificial Intelligence in HCI: Part III, edited by Helmut Degen and Stavroula Ntoa
54. LNCS 14737, Design, Operation and Evaluation of Mobile Communications: Part I, edited by June Wei and George Margetis
55. LNCS 14738, Design, Operation and Evaluation of Mobile Communications: Part II, edited by June Wei and George Margetis
56. CCIS 2114, HCI International 2024 Posters - Part I, edited by Constantine Stephanidis, Margherita Antona, Stavroula Ntoa and Gavriel Salvendy
57. CCIS 2115, HCI International 2024 Posters - Part II, edited by Constantine Stephanidis, Margherita Antona, Stavroula Ntoa and Gavriel Salvendy
58. CCIS 2116, HCI International 2024 Posters - Part III, edited by Constantine Stephanidis, Margherita Antona, Stavroula Ntoa and Gavriel Salvendy
59. CCIS 2117, HCI International 2024 Posters - Part IV, edited by Constantine Stephanidis, Margherita Antona, Stavroula Ntoa and Gavriel Salvendy
60. CCIS 2118, HCI International 2024 Posters - Part V, edited by Constantine Stephanidis, Margherita Antona, Stavroula Ntoa and Gavriel Salvendy
61. CCIS 2119, HCI International 2024 Posters - Part VI, edited by Constantine Stephanidis, Margherita Antona, Stavroula Ntoa and Gavriel Salvendy
62. CCIS 2120, HCI International 2024 Posters - Part VII, edited by Constantine Stephanidis, Margherita Antona, Stavroula Ntoa and Gavriel Salvendy

https://2024.hci.international/proceedings

Preface

Human Interface and the Management of Information (HIMI) is a Thematic Area of the International Conference on Human-Computer Interaction (HCII), addressing topics related to information and data design, retrieval, presentation and visualization, management, and evaluation in human computer interaction in a variety of application domains, such as learning, work, decision, collaboration, medical support, and service engineering. This area of research is acquiring rapidly increasing importance towards developing new and more effective types of human interfaces addressing new emerging challenges, and evaluating their effectiveness. The ultimate goal is for information to be provided in such a way as to satisfy human needs and enhance quality of life.

The related topics include, but are not limited to the following:

- *Service Engineering:* Business Integration; Community Computing; E-commerce; E-learning and E-education; Harmonized Work; IoT and Human Behavior; Knowledge Management; Organizational Design and Management; Service Applications; Service Design; Sustainable Design; User Experience Design
- *New HI (Human Interface) and Human QOL (Quality of Life):* Electronics Instrumentation; Evaluating Information; Health Promotion; E-health and Its Application; Human-Centered Organization; Legal Issues in IT; Mobile Networking; Disasters and HCI
- *Information in VR, AR and MR:* Application of VR, AR, and MR in Human Activity; Art with New Technology; Digital Museum; Gesture/Movement Studies; New Haptics and Tactile Interaction; Presentation Information; Multimodal Interaction; Sense of Embodiment (SoE) in VR and HCI
- *AI, Human Performance and Collaboration:* Automatic Driving Vehicles; Collaborative Work; Data Visualization and Big Data; Decision Support Systems; Human AI Collaboration; Human-Robot Interaction; Humanization of Work; Intellectual Property; Intelligent System; Medical Information System and Its Application; Participatory Design

Three volumes of the HCII 2024 proceedings are dedicated to this year's edition of the HIMI Thematic Area. The first focuses on topics related to Information and Multimodality, and Information and Service Design. The second focuses on topics related to Data Visualization, and User Experience Design and Evaluation. Finally, the third focuses on topics related to Information in Learning and Education, Information in Business and eCommerce, and Knowledge Management and Collaborative Work.

The papers in these volumes were accepted for publication after a minimum of two single-blind reviews from the members of the HIMI Program Board or, in some cases, from members of the Program Boards of other affiliated conferences. We would like to thank all of them for their invaluable contribution, support, and efforts.

July 2024

Hirohiko Mori
Yumi Asahi

Human Interface and the Management of Information Thematic Area (HIMI 2024)

HCI International 2025 Conference

The 27th International Conference on Human-Computer Interaction, HCI International 2025, will be held jointly with the affiliated conferences at the Swedish Exhibition & Congress Centre and Gothia Towers Hotel, Gothenburg, Sweden, June 22–27, 2025. It will cover a broad spectrum of themes related to Human-Computer Interaction, including theoretical issues, methods, tools, processes, and case studies in HCI design, as well as novel interaction techniques, interfaces, and applications. The proceedings will be published by Springer. More information will become available on the conference website: https://2025.hci.international/.

General Chair
Prof. Constantine Stephanidis
University of Crete and ICS-FORTH
Heraklion, Crete, Greece
Email: general_chair@2025.hci.international

https://2025.hci.international/

Contents – Part I

Contents – Part II

Contents – Part III

Information in Business and eCommerce

Knowledge Management and Collaborative Work

Information and Multimodality

Agent "Nah": Development of a Voice-Driven Embodied Entrainment Character with Non-agreeable Responses

Yutaka Ishii[1]([✉]), Masaki Matsuno[2], and Tomio Watanabe[1]

[1] Okayama Prefectural University, Kuboki 111, Soja, Okayama, Japan
{ishii,watanabe}@cse.oka-pu.ac.jp
[2] Graduate School, Okayama Prefectural University, Kuboki 111, Soja, Okayama, Japan
masaki716@hint.cse.oka-pu.ac.jp

Abstract. Herein, we demonstrated the effectiveness of a communication support system by developing a voice-driven embodied entrainment character "InterActor", which automatically generates body movements, such as nodding, based on a user's speech. As nodding is generally perceived as a positive and an agreeability gesture, the system evaluation in previous studies may have been more favorable. Therefore, in this study, we developed a character that automatically generates non-agreeable reactions, such as "the terrible twos" to examine the relationship with the degree of entrainment. Additionally, the effectiveness of the developed system was evaluated, based on the result of a user test at a science experience event for children as well as a speech experiment.

Keywords: Embodied entrainment character · Non-agreeable response · Interaction enhancement

1 Introduction

In face-to-face communication, non-verbal information, such as nodding and gestures promotes smooth information sharing [1]. In previous studies, communication support systems were based on voice-driven embodied entrainment systems, that would automatically generate body movements, such as nodding, based on a user's speech [2–5]. Additionally, the effectiveness of such systems was confirmed through communication experiments. However, nodding is a response that is generally received in a positive and agreeable manner, and consequently, the system evaluations in previous studies may have been evaluated more favorably. Children, also known as "the terrible twos", may repeatedly disagree with whatever their parents say to them. Although the parents are very confused, the interaction is successful because the child responds properly to the conversation. Furthermore, although there has been extensive research and development on consensual body movements, such as nodding, there have been no studies focusing on the relationship between the activation level of entrainment and agreeability in communication [6].

H. Mori and Y. Asahi (Eds.): HCII 2024, LNCS 14689, pp. 3–11, 2024.
https://doi.org/10.1007/978-3-031-60107-1_1

In this study, to investigate the influence of listeners' agreeableness on communication, we developed a computer generated (CG) character that automatically generates non-agreeable reactions. The CG character is a voice-driven embodied entrainment character based on the interaction model that was developed in a previous research [3]. In this study, we treat nonconsensual responses, such as shaking one's head to the side as "negation" and tilting one's head as "questioning".

2 Related Research

With regard to past research on listener responses, such as backchannels and nods in communication, Mori et al. focused on the co-occurrence relationship between the backchannels and nods, and investigated the differences in the ease of co-occurrence with nods and the timing [7]. As a result, similar to nodding, response-based interjections expressing acceptance, approval, understanding, and agreement and lexical responses tend to co-occur with nodding; on the other hand, state-change interjections expressing differences in perception between speaker and listener, and lexical responses tend to co-occur with nodding. Moreover, it has been reported that evaluation responses from a position different from that of the speaker are difficult to co-occur [7].

Takasugi et al. reconstructed the timing mechanism of speech and gestures as a human-robot interaction, and evaluated its impact [8]. As a result of analyzing how the timing control affected the impression of a dialogue, it was revealed that interaction with a robot equipped with a timing control model yielded a more favorable impression. This shows that the temporal structure of the timing mechanism of speech and gestures plays an important role in a dialogue.

As mentioned above, the communication support systems in previous studies [2–5] relied on developing a voice-driven embodied entrainment systems that automatically generates body movements, such as nodding based on the user's speech. Examples of these systems are shown in Fig. 1.

Fig. 1. Interaction agents/robots with nodding in previous studies [2, 3].

3 System Overview

3.1 Interaction Model for Auto-generated Entrained Motion

A listener's interaction model of a slave avatar includes a nodding reaction model called InterRobot Technology (iRT) [3] that estimates the nodding timing from a speech ON-OFF pattern and a body reaction model linked to the nodding reaction model. A hierarchy model consisting of two stages, macro and micro (Fig. 2), predicts the timing of the nodding. The macro stage estimates whether a nodding response exists or not in a duration unit that consists of a talk-spurt episode $T(i)$ and the following silence episode $S(i)$ with a hangover value of 4/30 s. The estimator $M_u(i)$ is a moving-average (MA) model, expressed as the weighted sum of unit speech activity $R(i)$ in (1) and (2). When $M_u(i)$ exceeds the threshold value, the nodding $M(i)$ is also an MA model, estimated as the weighted sum of the binary speech signal $V(i)$ in (3). The body movements are related to the speech input at a time instance above the body threshold. The body threshold is set lower than that of the nodding prediction of the MA model, that is expressed as the weighted sum of the binary speech signal to nodding. The mouth motion is realized by a switching operation, synchronized with the burst-pause of the speech. In other words, when the InterActor works as a listener for generating body movements, the relationship between nodding and other movements is dependent on the threshold values of the nodding estimation.

$$M_u(i) = \sum_{j=1}^{J} a(j)R(i-j) + u(i) \tag{1}$$

$$R(i) = \frac{T(i)}{T(i) + S(i)} \tag{2}$$

Here,
   $a(j)$: linear prediction coefficient.
   $T(i)$: talk-spurt duration in the i-th duration unit.
   $S(i)$: silence duration in the i-th duration unit.

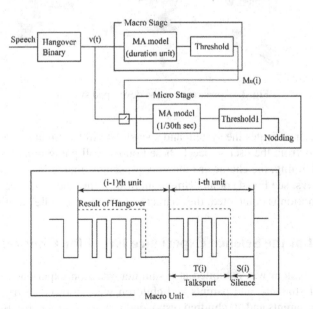

Fig. 2. Interaction model for auto-generated motions by iRT.

$u(i)$: noise

$$M(i) = \sum_{k=1}^{K} b(k)V(i-k) + w(i) \tag{3}$$

Here,

b(j): linear prediction coefficient.
$V(i)$: voice.
$w(i)$: noise.

3.2 Nah: "No" and "hmm" Reaction Agent

Figure 3 shows the appearance of the system. Here, we developed Nah ("No" and "hmm" reaction agent), a prototype of a voice-driven entrainment character that automatically generates nonconsensual reaction actions with timing predicted by the iRT reaction agent). This system assumes the "no" stage of infants as a situation, in which listeners show nonconsensual reactions. For this reason, the appearance of the character is modeled as a prototype, after a 2- to 3-year-old child.

Fig. 3. Appearance of the developed system.

When the user activates the system and speaks, the iRT estimates the timing of the response actions from the user's speech, based on the call paragraph classification. At each estimated timing, the character randomly presents either a "No" motion (shaking the head sideways, see Fig. 4) or an "Hmm" motion (tilting the head, see Fig. 5). After the presented motion is completed, the character performs the "idle" motion.

4 User Test at the Science Experience Event for Children

The developed system was exhibited at a summer vacation experience event for elementary school students, and parents and children were allowed to try out the same (Fig. 6). Eleven parents and 40 children responded to the questionnaire. Figure 7 shows the results of the questionnaire. The opinions obtained at that time from the parents and

Fig. 4. "No" motion (shaking the head).

Fig. 5. "hmm" motion (tilting the head).

the children are presented in Tables 1 and 2, respectively. Although a number of children responded that it was difficult to talk, many of them said that they had fun or that they wanted to talk more.

Fig. 6. Example of a user interaction at the science experience event.

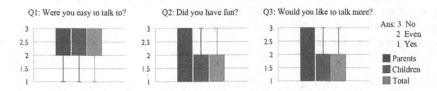

Fig. 7. Summary of responses to the questionnaire.

Table 1. Examples of comments from parents.

Positive comments

- As I got used to it, it seemed like I understood how to steer the conversation
- I wanted to, somehow, make the character nod
- Since she looked like a small child, it was easy to talk to her
- Depending on the child's feelings, it might react in that fashion
- With a cute face and those gestures, it was easy to accept her as a child
- The character's movements were cute
- It was fun for a first-time experience

Negative comments

- No matter what I said, the character would not respond
- The conversation did not continue because the character did not nod
- Since the responses seemed negative, I became anxious
- I did not like it; it was like dealing with a child in its terrible twos
- The character appeared to be in a gloomy mood; so I could not talk to her for long
- I would not even bother talking if it were not for their small appearance and reactions

Other

- It would be easier to continue the conversation if there were a few more types of emotions
- I was reminded of my own child's terrible twos
- I did not like the reaction; however, I thought the impression changed with appearance
- With various characters, such as boys and older people, I think we can use them for practicing communication

Table 2. Examples of comments from children.

Positive comments

- I felt the character was cute and quiet
- They did not speak, however, it was interesting
- They did not nod; however, they were cute
- It was interesting that they did not speak at all
- Cute, why was the background Christmas-themed?
- It was interesting that they absolutely did not nod; however, if there really were a child who did not nod, it might be a bit difficult to talk to it
- I did not dislike them because they did not ignore me
- I was happy that they responded

(*continued*)

Table 2. (*continued*)

Negative comments

- They would definitely seem unpopular at school
- They were cute; however, it was sad that they did not talk
- Since they did not nod, I could not understand what they wanted
- This child was cute; however, since they did not respond, I did not want to be friends with them
- I wanted them to say more than "uh-huh, uh-huh."
- The conversation did not continue much, if they did not nod
- If these children w ere in my school class, they might end up being disliked
- I am not sure what to talk about; it was a bit sad because they did not nod
- It was difficult to talk because they did not respond
- The conversation did not flow and it was quiet
- I wanted them to increase their reactions

5 Speech Experiment

5.1 Experimental Setup

In this study, we conducted an evaluation experiment using this system to examine the effect of agreeability on automatically generated reaction actions to user utterances. Figure 8 shows an example of the experimental scenario. He participants were asked to read a manuscript of approximately 150 Japanese characters to the system. Two types of manuscripts to be read out were created using ChatGPT3.5, and a total of six sets were created using three types of operation modes as follows: (A) no reaction; (B) nodding; and (C) "No" motion (shaking the head). After the reading was completed, the participants would respond to each mode by speaking freely and using a questionnaire form on the web. No restrictions were imposed on the content of the utterances during the free speech, and the timing at which the utterances ended was left to the participants' discretion. The number of evaluation items of the questionnaire was set to seven, based on previous research as follows: (1) "This character is likable." (2) "I can talk to this character easily." (3) "This character is listening." (4) "I feel safe when this character responds." (5) "This character understands the story." (6) "It would be fun to talk to this character." (7) "I would like to use this character." We also obtained free-text responses. To confirm and evaluate the usability of the system while speaking, the participants were allowed to use the system, while answering the questionnaire. Furthermore, we conducted the experiment after changing the presentation order to eliminate any bias caused by the presentation order of each mode. The participants in the experiment were 12 university students (six men and six women).

5.2 Results of Sensory Evaluation

Figure 9 shows the results of the 7-point bipolar rating. Statistical tests were performed using the Friedman test and Wilcoxon signed-rank test for multiple comparisons. Significant differences were observed for all the items at a significance level of 1% between

Fig. 8. Example of the experimental scenario.

modes A and B, and at a significance level of 5% between modes B and C. Furthermore, between Modes A and C, Item (3) "This character is listening." and Item (6) "It would be fun to talk to this character." had a significance level of 1%; furthermore, Item (2) "I can talk to this character easily." and Item (5) "This character understands the story." had a significant level of 5%.

Overall, the results showed that the evaluations of agreeable responses were higher than those of non-agreeable responses, and suggest that agreeable reactions give a more favorable impression than non-agreeable reactions. The comparison between non-responsive and non-agreeable reactions indicated that the presence or absence of a response behavior affects the "ease" and "enjoyment" of communication, regardless of the agreeableness of the response.

In the free description section, many participants responded that they felt lonely because there was no reaction in mode A; on the other hand, some others opined that it was easier to talk to them in mode C because there was a reaction.

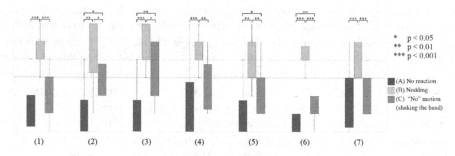

Fig. 9. Result of the sensory evaluation.

6 Conclusion

In this research, we developed a speech system using "Nah", an agent that automatically generates actions based on non-consensual responses to a speaker's speech. Additionally, effectiveness of the developed system was evaluated from user testing at the science experience event for children and the speech experiment. In the future, we intend to consider evaluation experiments on the interaction between entrainment and non-consensual responses using this system.

Acknowledgments. This work was supported by JSPS KAKENHI Grant Number JP20H04232.

References

1. Watanabe, T.: Human-entrained embodied interaction and communication technology. In: Fukuda, S. (ed.) Emotional Engineering, pp. 161–177. Springer, London (2011). https://doi.org/10.1007/978-1-84996-423-4_9
2. Watanabe, T., Okubo, M., Ogawa, H.: An embodied interaction robots system based on speech. J. Rob. Mechatron. **12**(2), 126–134 (2000)
3. Watanabe, T., Okubo, M., Nakashige, M., Danbara, R.: InterActor: speech-driven embodied interactive actor. Int. J. Hum.-Comput. Interact. **17**(1), 43–60 (2004)
4. Sejima, Y., Sato, Y., Watanabe, T., Jindai, M.: Speech-driven embodied entrainment character system with pupillary response. Bull. JSME Mech. Eng. J. **3**(4), 1–11 (2016). Paper No. 15-00314
5. Ishii, Y., Kurokawa, S., Kitamura M., Watanabe, T.: Development of a web-based interview support system using characters nodding with various movements. In: Proceedings of the 24th International Conference on Human-Computer Interaction (HCI International 2022), pp. 76–87 (2022)
6. Nishida, M., Ishii, Y., Watanabe, T.: A speech-driven embodied entrainment character system with a delayed voice back-channel based on negative emotional expression utterances. Trans. Japan Soc. Mech. Eng. **87**(897), 1–12 (2021). (in Japanese)
7. Mori, T., Den, Y.: Co-occurrence relations between forms of response tokens and nods. In: Proceedings of the Japanese Society for Artificial intelligence SIG-SLUD-C002-30, pp. 1–6 (2021)
8. Takasugi, S., Yamamoto, T., Muto, Y., Abe, H., Miyake, Y.: Analysis of timing control mechanism of utterance and body motion using dialogue between human and communication robot. Trans. Soc. Instrum. Control Eng. **45**(4), 215–223 (2009)

Interaction Between Environment and Embodiment Using a Biped Robot

Tomowa Kobayashi$^{(\boxtimes)}$, Ryo Takeba, and Hirohiko Mori

Tokyo City University, Setagaya City, Japan
g2381426@tcu.ac.jp

Abstract. Recent research has claimed that incorporating bodily functions added to physical sensors, such as touching, smelling, and tasting will create AI that is able to classify and think based on its multisensory information. Using an apple as an example, AI recognizes an apple as a symbol, while humans recognize it based on multiple factors such as color, texture, and smell. Based on the idea that human body enables grasping the concept of things in detail, current studies have indicated that a physical body is essential for the establishment of advanced intelligence. This paper identifies differences between AI and human cognitive functions and discusses necessary means of recognizing AI. We reproduce the cognition of things by having the robot perform reinforcement learning of bipedal walking. In the experiment, the two robots reproduced object recognition by performing reinforcement learning of bipedal walking. By having virtual robots of the same mass and size as the actual robots learn to walk, we examine how their learning process, and the results differ between the robots with physical substance and simulators without it. Comparing physical and simulated robots allows us to examine the effects of robot's physicality. We determine the environmental factors (friction, vibration, etc.) that vary the learning process and results, and suggest human-like cognitive functions the robots need to acquire.

Keywords: Embodiment · Robot · Reinforcement Learning

1 Research Background

1.1 Interaction Between Brain, Body, and Environment

In recent years, several studies have been conducted on brain-body interactions. Examples include the idea of "mobiligence" in which knowledge is gained from interaction with the environment through active movement, and the concept of "affordance," proposed by psychologist James Gibson, in which elements of the environment themselves influence humans and animals, causing emotions and behavior [1].

So, we know that interacting with the environment is especially important to how human beings behave.

H. Mori and Y. Asahi (Eds.): HCII 2024, LNCS 14689, pp. 12–24, 2024.
https://doi.org/10.1007/978-3-031-60107-1_2

1.2   Robots and the Environment Embodiment

The interaction between the body and the environment is also considered important for robots. In the old view of robotics, robots first perceive and recognize their environment, and then plan and execute actions based on that environment. In the mobiligence view, on the other hand, the robot first moves actively, perceives, and recognizes feedback from its environment, and learns adaptive behaviors based on this feedback.

Rolf Pfeiffer [2] proposed the idea that only systems that have an embodiment, so that their behavior can be observed when they interact with their environment, are intelligent, and that in order to create an intelligent system, or AI, it is essential to use systems that have physical entities, such as robots.

2   Related Research

2.1   The Body Creates the Brain: A Constructivist Approach to Science Using Robots as a Subject

Research was conducted to determine whether even quite simple neural circuits could discover and acquire different methods of locomotion through interactions between the body and the environment. A model of a human fetus was added to a model of the cranial nerves, and a model with minimal functionality was constructed, incorporating the mechanisms of spinal reflexes and spinal cord oscillations [3]. By moving the body, they found one quasi-stable movement after another, were drawn in, and explored other movements again, confirming the prototypical movements of rolling over and crawling.

2.2   Toward Deep Reinforcement Learning of Robots in the Real World. -Prototyping of a Simulation Environment "Re:ROS"-

Focusing on the differences between real and virtual environments, research is also being conducted to reproduce real environments in virtual environments. Virtual environments differ from real-world environments in that physical conditions are simplified and changes in behavior, states, rewards, processing latency, etc. are discrete [4]. Based on these points, we aim to construct an environment that is close to the real world in a virtual environment by developing simulators and controls. Specifically, the physical conditions are made close to those of the real environment, and the data necessary for the computation of rewards and states are obtained independently and transmitted without synchronization after the computation process to reproduce the real environment.

While this study attempts to create a highly reproducible model that approximates the conditions of the virtual environment to the real environment, it does not aim to reproduce the environment itself, but rather to study the differences.

3 Research Objectives

Although a number of papers have been published on robots and physicality, such as behavior acquisition through reinforcement learning, there are few studies on differences in robot behavior depending on the perceived environment of the robot. The purpose of this study is to investigate whether small differences between virtual and real environments, such as friction, air pressure, and vibration which cannot be reproduced by simulation, affect the robot's learning.

4 Experiment

4.1 Experiment Purpose

The purpose of this experiment is to investigate the changes in behavior caused by the difference between the actual robot and the robot in the virtual space, when the robot is prepared in the actual space and in the virtual space, respectively, and is made to learn the behavioral system. In addition, we will consider what factors influence the results when changes occur.

4.2 Experimental Method

A real NAO [5], a small biped humanoid robot, and a NAO reproduced in virtual space are used. The size, mass, center of gravity, etc. of the two NAOs are reproduced identically. The same code for reinforcement learning of behavioral systems is used for the two robots, and differences in behavior are observed. Specifically, we prepared and trained a reinforcement learning program in which the robot holds a cup filled with BB bullets in its left hand and walks without spilling it, using Python to adjust NAO's joint bending angle, speed, and execution interval, and created a walking motion with the cup in its left hand. In the reinforcement learning, three points were used for learning: speed, foot lifting position, and arm angle. The three points of the learning target were each determined from the values of three steps. The detailed values are explained in the implementation method.

The reinforcement learning method uses a reinforcement learning algorithm called Q-Learning [6]. Biped-related reinforcement learning, which is frequently used in research, was excluded as a method because it has a high risk of failure because the robot falls over many times in the process, and NAOV5 is no longer accepted for repair at the end of February 2021.

The number of BB bullets dropped after walking was measured and penalties were given to update the Q_table. The experiment was repeated until learning converged (Fig. 1).

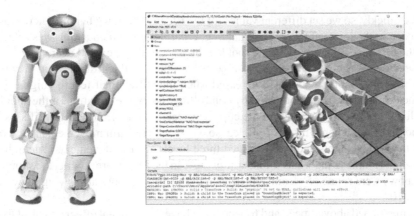

Fig. 1. NAO Robots (left: real NAO, right: NAO in virtual)

4.3 Mounting Method

It was implemented using PythonSDK (NAOqiforPython), an SDK for remote control of NAO, Coregraphe, which displays NAO's movements in a virtual environment, and Webots, a 3D robot simulator. The programming language used was Python.

In the Webots physics simulator, we created a cup for NAO to hold. The size of the cup was adjusted so that NAO could hold it with one hand. The cup was made using a 3D printer to reduce the difference between reality and simulation. To reduce the load on NAO's arms and shoulders, 0.12 g BB pellets were used.

NAO's legs have a total of twelve joints, and values can be specified for each joint. In the basic walking motion, the joints were moved every 0.03 s when the robot was on the ground, and when one leg was in the air, the joint movements were adjusted every 0.018 s to achieve a stable walking motion that would not cause the robot to fall over.

4.4 Reinforcement Learning

For speed, we adjusted the time it takes to move the next joint while one leg is in the air. We implemented three levels of "0.014 s," "0.016 s," and "0.018 s," respectively. When both feet are in contact with the ground, the joints move uniformly every 0.03 s, so there is no difference depending on the choice of action. Although it varies with the number of steps, it takes about eighteen steps from lifting the foot to landing and about eight steps to lifting the next foot. If the interval was too short, the subject fell due to violent movements, and if the interval was too long, the subject fell due to a shift in the center of gravity.

In the foot position, the height of the foot was adjusted by controlling the rotation axes of the hip and knee joints. Rotation of the hip joint adjusted the height of the thigh, and rotation of the knee joint adjusted the position of the shin. The user could select one of three leg height levels: low, normal, or high. In the low case, the hip joint was rotated $-2.8°$ and the knee joint was rotated $+2.8°$ compared to the normal gait motion. In the high phase, the hip joint was rotated $+5.8°$ and the knee joint was rotated $-5.8°$. The actual machine was found to be less tolerant of a low leg lift and tended to lose its balance quickly, so we set different values for the lift and lower leg height. There was no difference in the joints at takeoff and landing, regardless of which action was selected, with the difference increasing as the foot height went to the apex and decreasing as the foot landed. It was confirmed that the subjects stumbled on the ground when they were slip-footed and that their stability decreased when they lifted their feet too high.

The arm angle was implemented by controlling the axes of rotation of the shoulder and elbow of the left arm holding the cup. NAO leans to the right when it lifts its left leg and to the left when it lifts its right leg, so we considered arm movements that would offset these movements and implemented three levels of arm movements: "default (no arm swing)", "arm swing", and "more arm swing". In the case of arm swing, the shoulders and elbows were rotated 5° from default, and in the case of more arm swing, they were rotated 10°.

As mentioned above, speed and foot position have a significant effect on gait stability and were therefore used as learning targets. Preliminary experiments showed that the falling ball had a strong effect up to about the fourth step, and we set the number of steps to four because we believed that as the number of steps increased, stability and the risk of falling increased. There were two patterns for the state, one with the right leg raised and the other with the left leg raised, twenty-seven patterns with three^3 actions, and fifty-four patterns with 2 * 27 Q-values. Table 1 summarizes the behavior patterns and their contents.

Table 1. Behavior by Action selection

Height to raise feet	wave robot's arms	Seconds to move joints
hip joint -2.8° hip joint +2.8° (low)	default	0.014
default	Shoulder and elbow +5°	0.016
hip joint +5.8° hip joint -5.8° (high)	Shoulder and elbow +10°	0.018

In the case of a robot in a virtual environment, the number of trials can be increased if time is available. However, in the case of a real robot, the robot may fail if it is forced to perform bipedal walking, which is a heavy load, for a long period of time. Therefore, the number of trials should be kept as low as possible. Although it is possible to perform transfer learning after training in the virtual environment and compare the results with those of the real robot, we did not do so because we wanted to check not only the number of falling balls, but also the differences in optimal parameters between the virtual and real robots and the transition of penalties throughout the training process.

4.5 Reinforcement Learning Parameters

In Q-learning, it is necessary to set the learning rate and the discount rate, with most learning rates around 0.1–0.2 and discount rates around 0.9. The learning rate is a trade-off for convergence stability, and the discount rate can determine the degree to which immediate and future rewards are considered. In many cases, a low learning rate and a high discount rate will reproduce stable learning, but in this experiment, it is difficult to increase the number of trials in terms of both time and persistence because a real robot is used. Therefore, it is necessary to determine an appropriate learning rate and discount rate. Considering the burden on the real robot, we decided to use $\alpha = 0.2$ and $\gamma = 0.5$, since it is desirable to obtain results in 150 trials.

To reduce the number of learning cycles, we started with a negative initial Q value. Since the number of BBs dropped by the robot in the preliminary phase was at least six, we started learning with a Q value of -11.

The tau of the sigmoid function used to select actions was initially set to a high value of 0.9, so that the robot learned with a high degree of randomness. When the learning frequency was fifty times, the tau was set to 0.8, 75 times to 0.75, and one hundred times to 0.7. The randomness was gradually reduced so that the robot acted with reference to the Q value in the second half of the learning period.

4.6 Virtual Environment

In this experiment we used "webots", an OSS application for robot simulators. We chose webots because it is presented in the Aldebaran document as a simulator that can be used with NAO, and because it can be developed using Python. In addition, we used the R2018a version of webots to work with Choregraphe, the application used to run NAO.

We used the existing sphere model in webots, set the radius and mass to the same values as the BB pellets (radius 3 mm, mass 0.12 g), and prepared the same number of pellets as in the actual device.

5 Result

5.1 Results on Actual Machine

Figure 2 shows the variation of the Q-values for the right and left legs. Since the purpose of this experiment is not to converge the Q-values, but to find the best behavior and compare it with a hypothetical one, the learning was stopped after 130 trials. The right foot converged faster than the left foot. In this experiment, the first step was taken with the right foot, and it is possible that the behavior in the first step is significantly related to the penalty.

Figure 3 shows the penalty values for each number of trials. The value of the penalty is the number of BBs dropped*-1. In the early stages of learning, penalties are often around -10 to -20, sometimes -5 to -10, and sometimes -20 to -25, showing that there is a large variation in penalties.

Table 2 summarizes the behavior of the top three combinations with the highest Q values on the right foot of the actual machine. All three pairs have a speed of 0.018 s, suggesting that stability and speed are most closely related. The "Height of foot lift" was low for the first and second pair, but high for the third pair, so it cannot be said to be related to stability. Arm swing is considered to have a low association with stability.

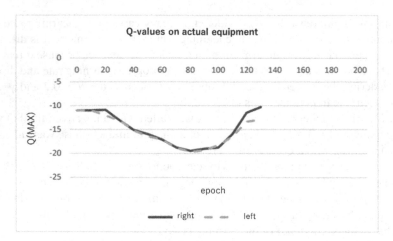

Fig. 2. Transition in Q value on actual machine

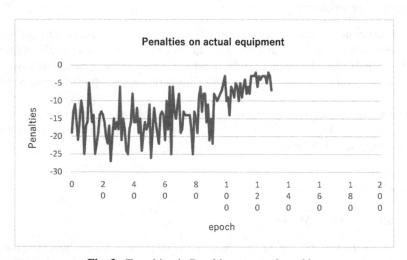

Fig. 3. Transition in Penalties on actual machine

Table 2. Actual right foot top three action selection

order	Height to raise feet	wave robot's arms	Seconds to move joints
1	low	Shoulder and elbow +10°	0.018(slow)
2	low	default	0.018(slow)
3	high	Shoulder and elbow +5°	0.018(slow)

Table 3. Actual left foot top three action selections.

order	Height to raise feet	wave robot's arms	Seconds to move joints
1	low	Shoulder and elbow +5°	0.018(slow)
2	default	Shoulder and elbow +5°	0.018(slow)
3	high	Shoulder and elbow +10°	0.018(slow)

Table 3 summarizes the TOP 3 combinations of actions with the highest Q-value values on the left foot of the actual machine. All three pairs had a velocity of 0.018 s, suggesting that stability and velocity are most closely related. The results for "foot lift height" and "arm swing" are scattered.

Comparing the right foot to the left foot, "speed" was 0.018 s (slow) for both top three pairs and is considered the most important choice among the factors that can be changed by reinforcement learning in this experiment. The next most important choice was "low" for "height of foot lift", which was the first and second most important choice for the right foot and the first most important choice for the left foot, respectively. The item "swinging arms" was considered to have little influence on penalties.

5.2 Virtual Results

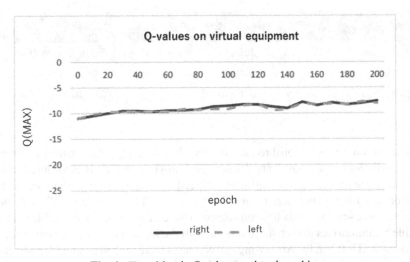

Fig. 4. Transition in Q value on virtual machine

Figure 4 shows the variation of the Q values of the right and left feet. There was no significant difference in Q between the left and right feet.

There was no significant difference in Q between the left and right feet.

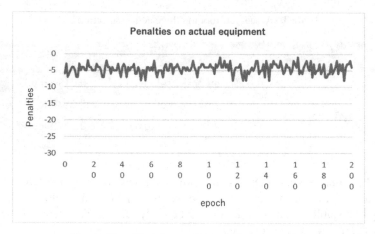

Fig. 5. Transition in penalties on virtual machine

Figure 5 shows a graph of penalties for each number of virtual trials. After 140 trials, there appears to be a slight decrease in the number of penalties below −6, but the penalties did not vary much from the beginning and remained similar throughout the trial. Since the walk was stable from the beginning, there was not much difference in the results.

Table 4. Virtual right foot top 3 action selection

order	Height to raise feet	wave robot's arms	Seconds to move joints
1	low	default	0.016(norcmal)
2	high	default	0.016(normal)
3	high	default	0.018(slow)

Table 4 summarizes the top three actions with the highest Q values in the hypothetical right leg. All "Swinging Arms" are defaults (not moving), which is considered to have a large influence on the virtual results. For "Speed", the fast case is not ranked, and the normal or slow case is considered better. In the case of "Height of foot lift", both "low" and "high" were selected, which is considered to have little relevance for stable students.

Table 5 summarizes the top three actions with the highest Q-value combinations for the hypothetical left leg. In "Arm swing" all elements were ranked as shoulder and elbow +5°. In "Speed" all elements were included and their influence on the virtual walking was considered low. In "Height to raise the foot", none of the options were ranked as "high", suggesting that other options would be better.

Comparing the right foot and the left foot, in "Arm swing" there is no "Shoulder and elbow +10°" in the top 3, and it is considered that the gait is more stable when the arms are not swung very much. The next most important choice for the right foot was

Table 5. Virtual left foot top 3 action selection

order	Height to raise feet	wave robot's arms	Seconds to move joints
1	low	Shoulder and elbow +5°	0.014(fast)
2	normal	Shoulder and elbow +5°	0.018(slow)
3	low	Shoulder and elbow +5°	0.016(normal)

"low", followed by "low" for "height of foot lift", which was the first and third most important choice for the left foot. The "high" option was the second and third choice for the right foot, but the Q value was far from the first, suggesting that the "low" option was more stable. The item "speed" is considered to have a small influence on penalties. However, in the hypothetical experiment, there was little variation in penalties and Q-values with the number of trials, and as can be seen from the graph, the differences in Q-values were small, so it is impossible to say which factors are important for a stable gait. Although there was not much difference between the top three, most of the Q values were concentrated around −9 and −10, which can be said to be large Q values in comparison.

6   Considerations

In the real machine, there were large fluctuations in the Q-value and differences in the convergence speed between the left and right sides of the body, but this tendency was not observed in the virtual machine. The combination of actions clearly affected the stability of the gait in the real machine, but in the virtual machine all combinations of actions were relatively stable and had no effect on the Q-value. In addition, in the virtual case, each action had an independent effect on the penalties, whereas in the real case the first step had an effect on the second, third, and fourth steps, and this is thought to be the reason why there were no differences between the left and right sides.

Like the Q-value, there was a difference in penalties between the number of training sessions on the real machine, but not on the virtual machine. On the real machine, the penalties varied from −5 to −25, while on the virtual machine, the penalties were mostly in the range of −2 to −7, and there was little difference in the fluctuating values. Therefore, it can be assumed that there was not much difference in the choice of actions, and no fluctuation was observed even as the number of training sessions increased.

Both the real and virtual machines tended to perform better when "foot lift height" was "low", but the results for the other items were different. In the real machine, "speed" was significantly related to stability, and "arm swing" showed no relationship, while in the virtual machine "arm swing" was related, but the effect of "speed" was not significant. In the real machine, the vibration was transmitted to the arms when the feet landed on the ground, and this tendency was more obvious when the "speed" was higher. It is believed that the virtual machine is not able to reproduce the vibration caused by speed and ground contact well. This suggests that the effect of vibration on the arms may have been greater for "speed" than for "arm swing" in real walking, and not just on the body as a whole. On the other hand, the virtual gait was stable from start to finish regardless of the choice of action, and the trunk was stable, which may have increased the influence of "arm swing".

Assuming that the first step is important for the stability of walking, what kind of behavior can be called good behavior is discussed. The results of this study showed that the first step is good when the "speed" is slow, followed by the second step when the "height" of the foot is low. Therefore, the same results are expected when the penalties are small, and the opposite results are expected when the penalties are large. From the data before learning converged (i.e., before 80 trials), we extracted the top seven behaviors when the penalty was high and when the penalty was low and compared them. The results are summarized in Table 6.

Table 6. Penalties Top and bottom 7 "height of raising feet" and speed.

low penalties Height to raise feet	Low penalties Seconds to move joints	High penalties Height to raise feet	High penalties Seconds to move joints
default	slow	low	**slow**
default	**default**	high	**slow**
high	**default**	low	fast
low	slow	low	**slow**
default	**default**	high	**slow**
low	**default**	low	**slow**
low	**default**	default	**slow**

Table 6 shows that there was no correlation in "foot lift height", but there was a clear bias in "speed". When the penalty was small, the results were biased towards "default", and when the penalty was large, the results were biased towards "slow", which was very different from the optimal behavior in the convergence phase of reinforcement learning. The high proportion of "slow" when the penalty was large, and the high proportion of "slow" even in the final optimal behavior, suggested that the actual walking of the machine was vulnerable to the change in speed from "slow" to "fast".

Table 7 summarizes the speed of the first and second steps for the top and bottom seven penalties. As hypothesized, the second step was "slow" or "standard" for the less punished group, and the overall trend was toward slower movement. On the other hand, the second step of the more punished group was mostly "fast," and the change in speed from the first step was also large. In the second group with higher penalties, the first and second steps were both "slow", but the third step was "fast", indicating an increase in speed. From these hypotheses and considerations, it is clear that penalties are likely to increase when a sudden change in speed from "slow to fast" occurs in the real machine, while in the virtual machine penalties are always less than 10, suggesting that such a change has little effect. By examining these differences, it is possible to see the differences between the virtual and real machines.

Table 7. Penalty "Speed" of the first and second steps of the top and bottom seven

low penalties first step	Low penalties second step	High penalties first step	High penalties second step
slow	**slow**	slow	**fast**
default	**slow**	slow	slow
default	**slow**	fast	**fast**
slow	default	slow	**fast**
default	**slow**	slow	default
default	**slow**	slow	**fast**
default	**slow**	slow	**fast**

In the first step, the penalties were large for "slow" and small for "fast", and in the second step, the penalties were small for "slow" and large for "fast". In this case, it appears that the convergence of the second step, i.e., the left foot, is faster because the penalties are clearly defined according to speed, but actually the convergence of the first step, i.e. the right foot, is faster. The reason for this may be the effect of "vibration", which was also hypothesized at the time of the center of gravity. If the first step is stable, the subsequent steps are likely to be stable as well. On the other hand, if the first step is unstable, the second, third, and fourth steps will also be affected by the instability, and the randomness of the vibration will increase the penalties. Therefore, it is assumed that the first step is very important, and its high relevance to the penalties may have led to early convergence.

7 Conclusion

We confirmed that there was a significant difference in learning when the interaction with the environment was strong (real) and when it was weak (virtual). In light of mobile intelligence and physicality, external factors such as changes in speed and vibrations upon contact with the ground are thought to be related to learning. The external factors are thought to have physical effects such as hand swing and overall body balance.

8 Future Works

8.1 Consideration of Further Elements Using Virtual Environments

In this experiment, we eliminated the differences between the real and virtual environments as much as possible, performed reinforcement learning in both environments, and discussed the results. However, since there are many differences between the real and virtual environments, it is difficult to clarify the influencing factors. Therefore, we would like to conduct a contrasting experiment by changing the environment in the virtual environment in detail, and from the differences in the results that appear in the experiment, we would like to further discuss the factors that influence learning.

8.2 NAO's Performance

In this study, we performed reinforcement learning by making NAO, a humanoid robot, perform actions. However, it was difficult to maintain constant performance due to overheating caused by controlling the actual NAO for an extended period of time. Therefore, it would be possible to conduct a more in-depth study by developing a device that enables stable performance or by attaching sensors to NAO's arms and other parts and collecting data on its movements.

References

1. Gibson, J.J.: The Ecological Approach to Visual Perception, 332 p. Houghton Mifflin, Boston (1979)
2. Pfeifer, R., Bongard, J.: How the Body Shapes the Way We Think a New View of Intelligence (2010)
3. Kuniyoshi, Y.: The body creates the brain: a constructivist approach to science using robots as a subject. Karada ga nou wo tukuru – robot wo daizai tosita kouseironntekikagaku no apuro-ti (in Japanese). Cogn. Neurosci. 11(1) (2009)
4. Ueno, S., Osawa, M., Imai, M., Kato, T.: Toward deep reinforcement learning of robots in the real world. -Prototyping of a Simulation Environment "Re:ROS"-", SIG-AGI-004-06 (2016)
5. NAO: Personal Robot Teaching Assistant | SoftBank Robotics America
6. Watkinsand, C.J., Dayan, P.: TechnicalNote: QLearni. Mach. Learn. 8, 279/292 (1992)

Research on Sound Production Considered from the Effects of Natural Wave Sounds on Physiological and Emotional Factors

Yukina Sato[1]([☒]), Keiko Kasamatsu[1]([☒]), and Takeo Ainoya[2]([☒])

[1] Tokyo Metropolitan University, 6-6 Asahigaoka, Hino-shi, Tokyo, Japan
yukina.animando.084@gmail.com
[2] Tokyo University of Technology, 1404-1 Katakuracho, Hachiohji-Shi, Tokyo, Japan

Abstract. In this study, I analyzed the characteristics of the sound of waves that affect the psychological and physiological evaluation of the sound of waves, using EEG as a physiological evaluation index. Based on the results of this analysis, an attempt was made to create a simpler sound pattern, using electronic sounds with high reproducibility, that would have the same effect on humans as the sound of waves. In the first experiment, an impression evaluation questionnaire and EEG measurements were used to determine which sounds of waves produced the most pleasant sensations. I also considered the acoustic characteristics of the sound of waves that influence these measures; in the second experiment, based on the results of the first, I focused on the first characteristic of the sound of waves that is most effective in inducing pleasant emotions. The sound of waves is considered to consist of two major components: a sustained sound with a long period due to the push and pull of the waves, and a short sound due to the bubbles caused by the breaking waves in the sound of waves. The randomness of the rhythm and melody of the latter short sound and its relationship to the sound of waves were considered in the same way as in the first experiment.

Keywords: Sound of waves · Brain waves · Psychological · Sound

1 Introduction

1.1 Background

We often listen to various types of natural sounds in our daily lives and sometimes consciously seek out those sounds. Particularly for us Japanese, who live in an island nation, the sea is a very familiar presence, and most Japanese people have likely visited it at least once. Personally, I have always been deeply drawn to the sea and have been interested in its factors for some time. According to a survey conducted by the Nippon Foundation (2019), approximately 70% of respondents expressed a desire to visit the sea when asked whether they wanted to go to the sea or not. Across different age groups, the results showed consistent responses, with over 70% of individuals expressing an interest in visiting the sea. This indicates a generally positive attitude towards the sea and its sounds among the Japanese population.

H. Mori and Y. Asahi (Eds.): HCII 2024, LNCS 14689, pp. 25–41, 2024.
https://doi.org/10.1007/978-3-031-60107-1_3

1.2 Previous Studies and Case Studies

Nadaoka and Tokumi [1] revealed the importance of the role of the sound of waves from a human psychological perspective and elucidated the factors contributing to the "pleasantness" of the sound of waves. They also specifically analyzed the characteristics of the sound of waves. In a questionnaire survey selecting the natural environmental elements that constitute the attractiveness of the coast, the score for "the sound of waves" ranked second after "sandy beaches" indicating the significant role of "the sound of waves" in coastal environments. Additionally, the survey conducted by Kamitsuki et al. among residents of Tokushima Prefecture regarding the "likeness of the sea" received the highest evaluation for "the sound of waves" From these surveys, it is evident that "the sound of waves" are considered a major element constituting the sea. This study focused on this aspect and selected it as the research subject.

Furthermore, Nadaoka et al. investigated the relationship between the "rhythmicity" of natural sounds and the "pleasantness" of sounds from an acoustic psychological perspective. They used a total of 10 natural sounds, including the sound of waves, river murmurs, and waterfall sounds, and found that the "rhythmicity" of natural sounds is closely related to the "pleasantness" of the sounds.

Murakami et al. used EEG α waves as a physiological evaluation index of comfort, and attempted to examine the characteristics of changes in α waves with changes in the intensity P (Pav; average sound pressure level, Pmax; average maximum sound pressure level), period T of the sound of waves, variation range dP (Pmax - Pav), and various factors of the index expressing the tone of waves, as shown in Fig. 1 and the various indices that express the timbre of the sound of waves [2]. The results showed that the feeling of comfort changes from pleasant to unpleasant when the intensity of the sound of waves exceeds a certain value, and that changes in the alpha waves of the brain waves are observed depending on the intensity of the sound of waves, affecting psychological and physiological pleasantness. The comfort decreased with shorter period of the sound of waves, and the power of the α waves tended to increase in the sound of waves of 8 to 10 s.

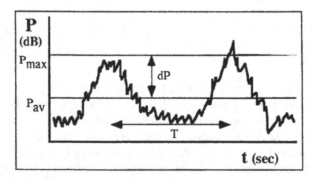

Fig. 1. Indicators **for Describing the Sound of Waves**

As described above, there have been many reports on the effects of the sound of waves. Healing music using the sound of waves is now widely available and used in the field of music therapy. In addition, music inspired by the sound of waves has been produced in various genres for a long time.

1.3 Objectives of This Study

Although research on the sound of waves and the use of the sound of waves in music production has been actively conducted, methods of utilizing the sound of waves in music have mostly relied on the sounds themselves or the sensibility of musicians. It can be speculated that there is potential for the transferability of their effects. Therefore, in this study, with the aim of applying the effects of the sound of waves on humans to music production, we analyze not only the psychological effects of the sound of waves on humans but also their effects on physiological indicators using brain waves as an evaluation index. Based on these indicators and considering the characteristics of the sound of waves that influence them, we attempt to create sounds that resemble the effects of the sound of waves on humans using electronic sounds with higher reproducibility. We then discuss their acoustic characteristics.

2 Experiment I

2.1 Objective of the Experiment

To analyze the effects of the sound of waves on humans, we conducted an experiment to select the benchmark sound of waves. As this study operates under the premise that the sound of waves induces pleasure in humans, we prepared five different types of the sound of waves with distinct characteristics. Through a combination of subjective impression evaluations and brainwave measurements during listening, we aimed to determine which the sound of waves induces the most pleasure and influences brainwaves the most, as well as to examine the acoustic characteristics of these sounds.

2.2 Experimental Method

Evaluation Sounds. Based on Nadaoka et al.'s report [1], which suggests that the pleasantness and "waviness" of the sound of waves primarily depend on the rhythmicity of the waves, we selected five types of the sound of waves (Sounds A to E) from YouTube. These sounds had clear rhythmic variations in acoustic power and varied in their sonic characteristics. To ensure consistency in perception regardless of volume differences among the evaluation sounds, we converted them to mono and normalized the volume using editing software.

Participants. Eleven healthy male and female participants aged 21–23, currently enrolled in the Systems Design Department at Tokyo Metropolitan University, took part in the experiment (2 male students and 9 female students).

Psychological Evaluation. To assess the psychological effects of the evaluation sounds, we conducted a psychological evaluation survey using the Semantic Differential (SD) method, consisting of two themes: (a) subjective awareness of mind and body while listening to music, and (b) impressions of sound quality. Both themes were rated on a 7-point scale. (a) Subjective awareness of mind and body while listening to music: The adjective pairs used were selected from items in reports by Takayama [3] and Matsui et al. [4], resulting in five pairs: "Unpleasant - Pleasant," "Tense - Relaxed," "Discomfortable - Comfortable," "Alert - Drowsy," and "Dislike - Like." (b) Impressions of sound quality: Like theme (a), the adjective pairs were selected from the reports, resulting in six pairs: "Weak - Strong," "Dark - Bright," "Noisy - Calm," "Muddy - Clear," "Dirty - Clean," and "Soft - Hard."

Brainwave Measurement. Electrodes were fixed to the Cz area according to the international 10–20 system, with earlobes connected as reference electrodes, to record brainwaves during wakefulness. Participants were instructed to close their eyes during the experiment to account for the effects of eyelid closure and light stimulation. Additionally, due to the individual differences in the magnitude and power values of brainwaves, the data of each participant were standardized for analysis.

Experimental Procedure. Figure 2 presents the time chart of the measurements. Initially, brainwaves during rest were measured, followed by the presentation of evaluation sounds via headphones at approximately 60 dB for 120 s for auditory perception brainwave measurement. Simultaneously, to consider the psychological effects of changes in the sound of waves, a psychological evaluation questionnaire survey was conducted after listening to the evaluation sounds. The questionnaire responses took about 3–5 min, and participants were asked to evaluate each of the five types of evaluation sounds. The order of presenting the five evaluation sounds was randomized for each participant.

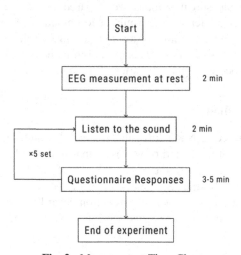

Fig. 2. Measurement Time Chart

2.3 Experimental Results and Analysis

Psychological Evaluation. Figure 3 shows the average profile of psychological evaluations for all participants. To visualize the characteristics of each evaluation sound, a principal component analysis was performed using statistical analysis software SPSS with varimax rotation. As a criterion for selecting factors, factors with eigenvalues greater than 1 were obtained. From adjective pairs with high factor loadings for each factor, the first factor was named the "comfort" factor, the second factor the "clarity" factor, and the third factor the "power" factor concerning the impression evaluation of sounds. Furthermore, scatter plots were created by plotting the scores of each evaluation sound on the first factor × second factor, first factor × third factor, and second factor × third factor dimensions (Fig. 4). From the scatter plot in Fig. 4, Sounds A and E tend to be similar, as also inferred from Fig. 3. From each scatter plot, it can be observed that Sound D has high positive values in the "comfort" factor and "clarity" factor, Sound C has significantly low values in the "power" factor, and B has low values in the "comfort" factor.

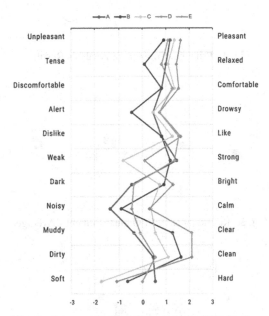

Fig. 3. Average Profile of Psychological Evaluation

Brainwave Measurement. Figure 5 shows the mean values and their standard deviations of the expression of θ waves, α waves, and β waves (standard scores) of all participants at rest and during the listening to each sound of waves. Figure 6 shows the mean values of the α/β ratios at rest and during listening to each sound. These results show that α waves increase when listening to Sound D compared to the resting state, that the value of α/β ratio is the highest when listening to Sound D, and that the value of α/β ratio increases for all sounds except Sound E compared to the resting state.

	1	2	3
Q5. Dislike-Like	.850	.381	.062
Q2. Tense-Relaxed	.847	.059	-.185
Q3. Discomfort-Comfort	.781	.482	-.100
Q1. Unpleasant-Pleasant	.769	.464	-.092
Q4. Alert-Drowsy	.735	-.038	-.242
Q8. Noisy-Calm	.728	.206	-.531
Q9. Muddy-Clear	.200	.865	-.154
Q10. Dirty-Clean	.220	.863	-.141
Q7. Dark-Bright	.123	.806	-.250
Q6. Weak-Strong	-.107	-.131	.920
Q11. Soft-Hard	-.231	-.332	.781

The 1st Factor : **Comfort**

▶ The 2nd Factor : **Clarity**

The 3rd Factor : **Power**

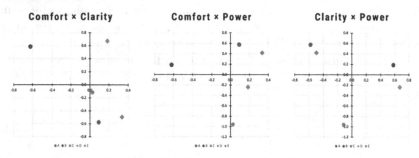

Fig. 4. Principal Component Analysis Result

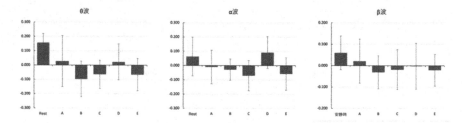

Fig. 5. Results of each EEG measurement - Average

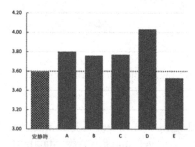

Fig. 6. Alpha/Beta Ratio - Average

Sound Source Analysis. In order to examine the relationship between the characteristics of the sounds of waves and the results of the psychological evaluation and EEG measurement, a sound source analysis of the evaluation sounds was conducted using editing software. The results are shown below as spectrograms of each evaluation sound (Fig. 7). The left spectrogram shows the change in sound pressure of each frequency band within the minimum unit of waves (approximately 4–7 s), while the right spectrogram shows the change in sound pressure of each frequency band when viewed over a longer period

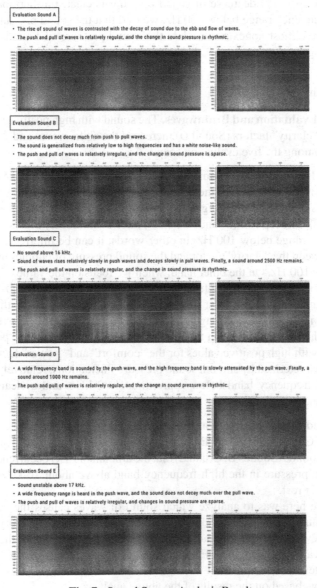

Fig. 7. Sound Source Analysis Result

of 15 s. The results of the spectrograms are shown in the figure, along with the timbre characteristics of the evaluation tones.

In the spectrograms of Sounds B, C, and D, vertical streaks can be seen more clearly in some places than those of Sounds A and E. These streaks are caused by bubbles generated by breaking waves. This is the sound of bubbles generated by the breaking of waves, and the spectrogram clearly shows that the bubbles are larger than those of Sounds A and E. The spectrograms of Sounds A and E show that the sound pressure in the frequency range of 100–2 kHz is continuously higher than that of the other sounds, and that the increase and decrease of sound pressure is clear. Furthermore, when we focus on the frequency range below 100 Hz, we find that the sound pressure of Sounds A, C, and E are almost nonexistent, while the sound pressure of Sounds B and D is continuously high.

2.4 Discussion

Psychological Evaluation and Brainwaves. The sound with high positive values for the "comfort" and "clarity" factors (Sound D) increased the alpha waves and the alpha/beta ratio the most among the five evaluation sounds.

Psychological Evaluation and Sound Source Analysis. The top three Sounds B, C, and D, which have high values for the "clarity" factor, are characterized by the presence of large bubbles created by breaking waves and the clear sound of these bubbles (e.g., popping sounds). The top two (Sounds B and D) have continuously high sound pressure in the frequency range below 100 Hz. In other words, it can be inferred that there is a correlation between the "clarity" factor and the sound pressure of bubbles and sounds in the range below 100 Hz. On the other hand, when we focus on the value of the "power" factor and the sound pressure in the frequency range of approximately 100–2 kHz in the sound source analysis, we can infer that there is a positive correlation: the higher the sound pressure in the frequency range of 100–2 kHz, the higher the "power" factor is, and the lower the sound pressure in this frequency range, the lower the "power" factor is. The sounds with high positive values for the "comfort" and "power" factors (Sounds A and E) are characterized by smooth sound pressure fluctuations, relatively high sound pressure in the frequency band below approximately 2 kHz, and a clear increase or decrease in sound pressure.

Brainwaves and Sound Source Analysis. On the other hand, there was no similarity between the EEG of Sounds A and E. In this respect, it can be inferred from the source analysis of the sounds (Sounds B, C, and E) that the amount of EEG occurrence decreased when the sound pressure in the high-frequency band above about 16 kHz was clearly lower than that at rest.

The purpose here was to analyze which sound of waves causes the most pleasant feelings and influences the EEG, and what characteristics the sound has, by conducting an impression evaluation questionnaire and EEG measurement. From the analysis of the psychological evaluation and EEG measurements, we can say that Sound D is the sound that causes the most pleasant feelings. The acoustic characteristics of the sound are shown below, based on the results of the above analysis.

1. The sound of bubbles produced by wave breaking is large and clear.
2. High-frequency sounds above approximately 16 kHz are included.
3. The sound pressure in the frequency range below approximately 100 Hz is consistently high.

In the next Experiment II, we will compare the electronic music created based on the above analysis and discussion with Sound D, and investigate a method to express the elements of the sound of waves musically and abstractly.

3 Experiment II

3.1 Experiment Objective

In this experiment, we assume that the sound of waves consists of two major components: a sustained sound with a long period due to the pushing and pulling of waves, and a short sound caused by bubbles created by breaking waves in the sound of waves. Based on the results of Experiment I, we will use the sound D as the standard sound of waves in this experiment, and compare our own electronic sound with the sound of waves to analyze what kind of sound has a similar effect on humans as the sound of waves. As in Experiment I, the results of the impression evaluation questionnaire and the EEG measurement will be used to discuss the results.

3.2 Experimental Method

Evaluation Sounds. Based on the results obtained from Experiment I and preliminary experiments, two types of sounds, (a) sustained tones and (b) short tones, are produced using modular synthesizers (Marbles random sampler: Mutable Instruments and Poly Cinematic: KNOBULA).

(a) A sustained sound with a high sound pressure in the range of about 100 Hz or lower, with a periodicity of sound pressure change equivalent to the push and pull of a standard sound of waves (one cycle in about 5 s)
(b) Six types of short tones produced using string tones (Pluck), with the parameter controlling the randomness of rhythm (JITTER in Fig. 8) varied in three steps and the parameter controlling the randomness of pitch (SPEAD in Fig. 8) varied in two steps.

(a) and (b) are synthesized to form the evaluation sounds B-G (Fig. 9). The reference sound of waves (Sound D in Experiment I) is used as Sound A in this experiment, and a total of seven types of evaluation sounds are used in the experiment. Figure 10 shows the spectrogram of each evaluation sound. As in Experiment I, the sounds were converted to monaural using editing software and the volume was equalized using a normalizing function to avoid differences in the impression caused by differences in the loudness of each sound.

Participants. Twelve healthy male and female participants aged 23–24, currently enrolled in the System Design Department at Tokyo Metropolitan University, took part

Fig. 8. Parameter Settings

Pitch \ Rhythm	None	Slightly Yes	Yes
None	B	C	D
Yes	E	F	G

Fig. 9. Evaluation Sounds B-G: Randomness

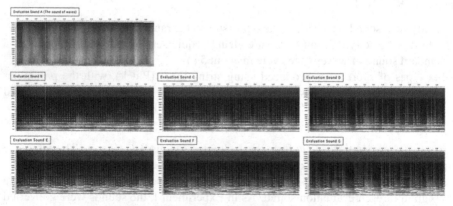

Fig. 10. Spectrograms of Evaluation Sounds A-G

in the experiment (six male students and six female students). Half of the participants underwent both brainwave measurements and psychological evaluation surveys, while the other half only completed psychological evaluation surveys.

Psychological Evaluation. Conducted similarly to Experiment I. (Refer to Sect. 2.2.3 in this paper).

Brainwave Measurements. Conducted similarly to Experiment I. (Refer to Sect. 2.2.4 in this paper).

Experimental Procedure. The measurement time chart is shown in Fig. 11 Initially, brainwaves during rest were measured with participants in a closed-eye state. Subsequently, as in Experiment I, evaluation sounds were presented for 90 s through headphones (Audio-technica ATH-M20x) at approximately 60 dB. Additionally, psychological evaluation surveys were conducted simultaneously to assess participants' psychological responses to changes in the sound of waves. The questionnaire required approximately 3–5 min to complete, and participants evaluated each of the seven evaluation sounds. The order of presentation for the seven evaluation sounds was randomized for each participant.

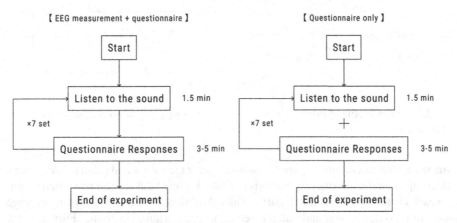

Fig. 11. Measurement Time Chart

3.3   Experimental Results and Analysis

Psychological Evaluation. Figure 12 shows the average profile of psychological evaluations for all participants. Similarly to Experiment I, principal component analysis using varimax rotation was conducted using the statistical analysis software SPSS. By selecting factors with eigenvalues greater than 1 as the selection criterion, three factors related to impression evaluations of sounds were obtained, as in Experiment I. Scatter plots were created by plotting the principal component scores of each evaluation sound on two-dimensional axes: Factor 1 × Factor 2, Factor 1 × Factor 3, and Factor 2 × Factor 3 (Fig. 13). Furthermore, to investigate sounds with characteristics like wave sounds in impression evaluations, hierarchical cluster analysis using the Ward method was performed (Fig. 14).

From Fig. 13, it can be observed that Sound A (wave sound) exhibits high positive values in all factors, and Evaluation Sound F demonstrates high positive values in the "comfort" factor. Additionally, from Fig. 14, Sounds B, C, and D are grouped together, while Sounds A, E, F, and G form another group. Sound G appears to have the closest trend to Sound A. However, it is apparent that there is significant variability in the data, making it difficult to identify evaluation sounds with similar characteristics.

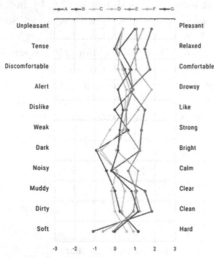

Fig. 12. Average Profile of Psychological Evaluation

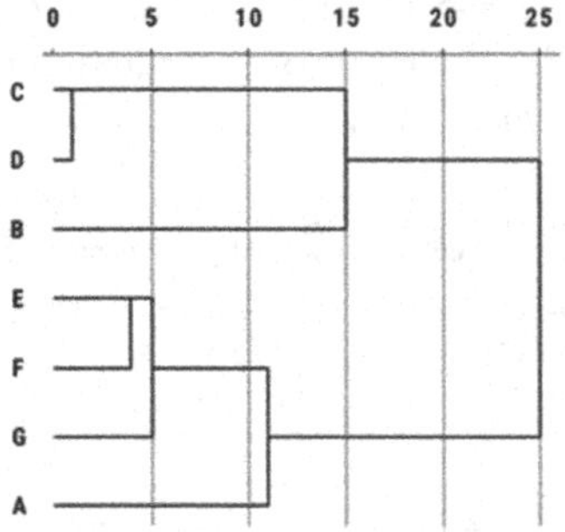

Fig. 13. Cluster Analysis Results

Brainwave Measurements. Figure 15 shows the average values and standard deviations of theta, alpha, and beta wave expressions (standard scores) during rest and when listening to each evaluation sound for all participants. Additionally, Fig. 16 shows the average alpha/beta ratio during rest and when listening to each evaluation sound. Furthermore, hierarchical cluster analysis using the Ward method was performed to investigate sounds with characteristics similar to the sound of waves in brainwave measurements (Fig. 17). From these results, it can be observed that the alpha wave and alpha/beta ratio values are highest when participants listened to Sound F, and the alpha wave expressions and alpha/beta ratios are lower for Sounds B, C, and D compared to other sounds. Moreover, Sound G appears to have the closest trend to Sound A.

3.4 Discussion

Psychological Evaluation and Brainwaves. Looking at the results of the average brainwaves, there is considerable individual variation, making trends difficult to discern. To investigate the relationship between brainwave expressions and impression evaluations, participants were classified into four groups using hierarchical cluster analysis by the Ward method (Fig. 18). The results for each group are shown in Figs. 19 and 20. When examining the results with Sound A as the axis, Sounds in Groups 1, 2, and 3 show tendencies to have alpha wave expressions similar to Sound A in the graph of the "comfort" × "power" factor.

	1	2	3
Q2.Tense-Relaxed	.862	.144	.067
Q4.Alert-Drowsy	.857	-.056	-.056
Q1.Discomfort-Comfort	.715	.490	-.021
Q5.Dislike-Like	.687	.505	-.039
Q3.Unpleasant-Pleasant	.663	.550	-.057
Q8.Noisy-Calm	.620	.065	-.587
Q9.Muddy-Clear	.149	.828	-.040
Q10.Dirty-Clean	.248	.790	-.137
Q7.Dark-Bright	.068	.747	.277
Q1.Weak-Strong	-.052	-.481	.470
Q6.Soft-Hard	.060	.111	.844

The 1st Factor : **Comfort**

▶ The 2nd Factor : **Clarity**

The 3rd Factor : **Power**

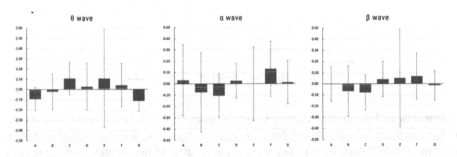

Fig. 14. Principal Component Analysis Results

Fig. 15. Results of each EEG measurement - average

Psychological Evaluation and Acoustic Characteristics. As sounds with high values for the "power" factor are Sounds A, B, and E, there seems to be a correlation between rhythm randomness and the "power" factor. When the rhythm is constant, the value tends to increase, approaching values similar to those of the sound of waves. Additionally, from the cluster analysis results (Fig. 15), it can be inferred that in impression evaluations, the influence of changes in pitch (melody) is more significant than changes in rhythm. Furthermore, since sounds with low values for the "clarity" factor are Sounds B, C, and D, it can be speculated that there is a correlation between pitch (melody) randomness and the "clarity" factor. Overall, although there were no sounds that exhibited characteristics close to Sound A (wave sound), the possibility of the influence of middle-range sounds (approximately 1000–3000 Hz), which were weak in self-produced sounds based on the spectrograms of each evaluation sound (Fig. 10), is suggested.

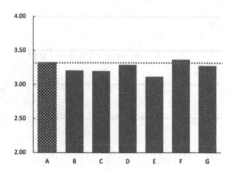

Fig. 16. Alpha/Beta Ratio – Average

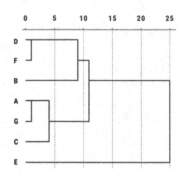

Fig. 17. Cluster Analysis Results

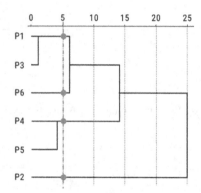

Fig. 18. Participant Cluster Analysis Results

Brainwaves and Acoustic Characteristics. Sounds B, which lack randomness in both rhythm and pitch, Sound C, which has some randomness in rhythm but no randomness in pitch, and Sound E, which has randomness in pitch but lacks randomness in rhythm, have lower alpha/beta ratio values and alpha wave expressions compared to other sounds. This suggests that comprehensive randomness in both rhythm and pitch affects brainwaves.

The objective here was to conduct psychological evaluation surveys and brainwave measurements similar to Experiment I to examine the relationship between the randomness of short tones' rhythms and pitch (melody) and the sound of waves, analyzing which sounds have effects similar to those of the sound of waves. From the analysis of psychological evaluation surveys and brainwave measurements, it can be said that Sound G likely has the closest influence on the sound of waves (Sound A). Below are the acoustic characteristics of this sound based on the aforementioned analysis:

1. Possesses randomness in the rhythm of short tones.
2. Possesses randomness in the pitch (melody) of short tones.

Based on the above results, the assumption that the sound of waves is composed of a sustained sound with long periods and short tones is useful. Introducing randomness

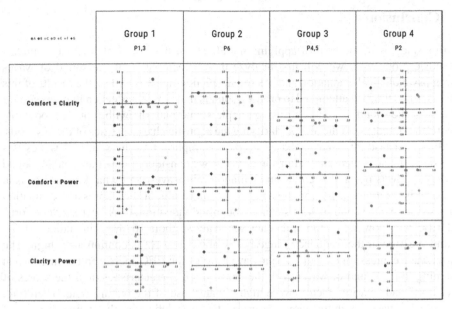

Fig. 19. Group-wise Principal Component Analysis Results

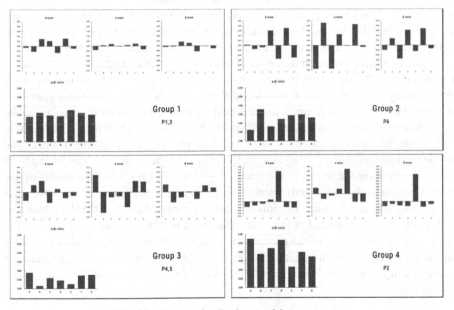

Fig. 20. Group-wise Brainwave Measurements

in rhythm and pitch (melody) to these short tones suggests that they can have effects on humans similar to those of the sound of waves.

4 Conclusion

In this study, with the goal of applying the effects of the sound of waves on humans to music production, we will first analyze the characteristics of the sound of waves using psychological evaluation and electroencephalography. Based on the results of this analysis, this time we attempted to produce sounds that have an effect on humans similar to that of the sound of waves by using simple sound patterns with more reproducible electronic sounds, with the aim of clarifying the acoustic characteristics of these sounds.

First, because this study is based on the assumption that the sound of waves is a sound that induces pleasant feelings in humans, we considered how the standard sound of waves affects psychological evaluation and brain waves, and what kind of acoustic characteristics it has. Based on the analysis of the results of the impression evaluation questionnaire, the sound of waves can be roughly divided into three factors: "comfort," "clarity," and "power. (2) High frequency sound above about 16 kHz is included. (3) The sound pressure in the frequency range below about 100 Hz is continuously high. The alpha wave expression and alpha/beta wave ratio of the EEG increased the most when listening to the sound of waves with the above three characteristics, and the scores of "comfort" and "clarity" factors were higher than those of the resting state. Therefore, the sound of waves with the above characteristics was defined as the standard sound of waves in this study. Next, we focused on the first of the three characteristics, assuming that the sound of waves is composed of a sustained sound with a long period due to the pushing and pulling of waves and a short sound due to bubbles created by breaking waves in the sound of waves. As a result, it was inferred that the influence of changes in pitch (melody) was greater than that of changes in rhythm in psychological evaluation, and that there was a correlation between the randomness of pitch and the "clarity" factor. In addition, (1) The randomness of the rhythm of short tones. (2) Randomness in the pitch (melody) of short tones. It was found that sounds with these two characteristics have the closest effect on humans to the sound of waves. Furthermore, it is suggested that these two complex randomnesses affect the brain waves. Therefore, it is useful to assume that the sound of waves is composed of short tones and a sustained sound, and that the randomness of the rhythm and pitch (melody) of the short tones can be expected to have an effect similar to that of the sound of waves. However, since the results of this study did not show that the sound of waves has the same effect as the sound of waves, it is necessary to consider the effect of sounds in the mid-range of 1000–3000 Hz, which was weak in the sounds produced in this study, the effect of harmony and timbre, the EEG appearance characteristics of the participants in the experiment, and whether they have had musical or coastal environmental experiences. Based on the results of this study, we plan to investigate a method to express the elements of the sound of waves in a musically abstract manner.

References

1. Nadaoka, K., Tokumi, T.: Fundamental study on coastal sound environment. In: Proceedings 35th Coastal Engineering Conference, pp. 757–761 (1988)
2. Murakami, H., Ito, S., Hosoi, Y., Araki, H., Koyabu, T.: Fundamental study on the comfortability of the sound of waves by taking into account the variability characteristics of EEG. J. Coast. Eng. **42**, 1156–1160 (1995)

A Speech-Driven Embodied Listening System with Mirroring of Pupil Response

Yoshihiro Sejima[1]([✉]) [iD], Shota Hashimoto[2], and Tomio Watanabe[3]

[1] Faculty of Informatics, Kansai University, 2,1,1 Ryozenji-cho, Takatsuki-shi 569-1095, Osaka, Japan
sejima@kansai-u.ac.jp
[2] Graduate School of Informatics, Kansai University, 2,1,1 Ryozenji-cho, Takatsuki-shi 569-1095, Osaka, Japan
[3] Faculty of Computer Science and Systems Engineering, Okayama Prefectural University, 111 Kuboki, Soja-shi 719-1197, Okayama, Japan

Abstract. It is known that human pupils are related to own interest and motivation, and the pupil dilation increases attractiveness. Focusing on the effect of pupil response, we analyzed the relationship between a speaker's speech and his/her own pupil response, and confirmed that pupils dilate in synchronization with speech. Furthermore, we developed a pupil response system that expresses various pupil responses and demonstrated its effectiveness. In particular, the pupil dilation can convey strong interest and high motivation to the speaker. Therefore, it is expected to develop an advanced system that actively engages the speaker by expressing pupil response as a listener. In this study, we developed a speech-driven listening system that mirrors the pupil response in synchronization with the speaker's speech. This system can express positive listening attitudes such as pupil responses and nodding responses. The effectiveness of this system was demonstrated by sensory evaluations.

Keywords: Nonverbal Communication · Human-Robot Interaction · Acceptability

1 Introduction

As information devices have become more smaller and faster in recent years, social robots have been widely developed. Furthermore, with the improvement of large language models, social robots that can estimate verbal features from speech and engage to continue conversation with humans are developed [1]. In terms of nonverbal features, affinitive behaviors such as a tail wagging or an adorable voice have been designed [2]. Thus, rich interactions that enhance familiarity through verbal and nonverbal features will be introduced into social robots. However, an interaction design in terms of listening attitudes that be accepted with empathy is essential in human-robot interaction.

Listening attitudes are defined as an important behavior for building friendly relationships with others. In counseling, where a relationship of trust is required, there are

H. Mori and Y. Asahi (Eds.): HCII 2024, LNCS 14689, pp. 42–50, 2024.
https://doi.org/10.1007/978-3-031-60107-1_4

techniques such as "mirroring," "pacing" and "backtracking" [3]. Among them, mirroring is a technique that creates a sense of synchronization by imitating other's behaviors and actions, and plays an important clue in the visualization of nonverbal cue. Various research has been conducted to evaluate impressions on the conversation partner through mirroring [4] and to develop cognitive robot that imitate body movements [5]. These approaches examined the effects of synchrony by imitating visible physical actions. However, excessive imitation may lose trust and relationship, because physical actions include voluntary movements with his/her intention. Therefore, it is desired to express mirroring by involuntary movements as unconscious behaviors.

Focusing on the pupil as unconscious behaviors in communication, we analyzed the relationship between a speaker's speech and his/her own pupil response, and confirmed that pupils dilate in synchronization with own speech [6]. Based on the results of this analysis, we developed a pupil response system that expresses pupil response as a substitute for the speaker, and demonstrated that pupil dilation increases familiarity, empathy, etc. [7]. Thus, controlling pupil response during human-robot interaction has a high possibility of generating synchrony and empathy. Additionally, in previous research, it was suggested when the conversational partner's pupils were enlarged, the feeling of trust in the partner was enhanced [8]. Therefore, it is expected to design a positive listening attitude by introducing unconscious and highly reliable pupil response.

In this paper, we developed a speech-driven embodied listening system that generates the listener's pupil response by mirroring the speaker's pupil response. This system mirrors the pupil response generated based on the speaker's speech input, and expresses an active listening attitude as a listener. In addition, we carried out communication experiment by using sensory evaluations. The results demonstrated that the developed system is effective for active listening.

2   Speech-Driven Embodied Listening System

2.1   Concept

The concept of a speech-driven embodied listening system is shown in Fig. 1. In such situations where a speaker desires to be listened to, complaining or loneliness, the system expresses active listening attitudes [9]. This system generates listening attitude in real

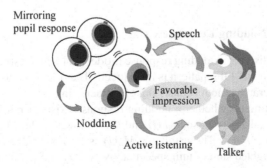

Fig. 1. Concept of the developed system.

time based on the ON/OFF pattern of the speaker's speech input. Specifically, the pupil dilation response creates a positive impression of interest [10]. Furthermore, the nodding response creates a comfortable interaction rhythm. It is expected that the system's active listening attitude will encourage the speaker more to speak and enjoy the conversation.

2.2 Development of the System

Figure 2(a) shows the configuration of the developed system. This system consists of a desktop PC equipped with Windows 10 (CPU: Corei-7 1.8 GHz, Memory: 8 GB, Graphics: Intel(R) HD Graphics Family 10.18.10.3325), a hemispherical display (Gakken WORLDEYE), and a video distributor (SANWA 400-VGA003 TSL). The size of the hemispherical display is 250 mm in diameter, and the resolution is 480 × 480 pixels. Human eyeballs are simulated by projecting a 3D CG model consisting of the pupil and iris arranged in the virtual space shown in Fig. 2(b) onto this hemispherical display. In addition, the background color of the virtual space is white to represent the sclera (white of the eye) in the human eyeball. The pupil response is implemented by moving a black 3D CG model representing the pupil in the front and back directions with respect to the Z-axis direction. The gaze direction, including the nodding response, is realized as vertical and horizontal movement of the human eyeball by simultaneously moving both the pupil and iris models on the X-Y plane. The frame rate which expresses the pupil CG is 30 fps. The voice is sampled using 16 bits at 11 kHz using a microphone.

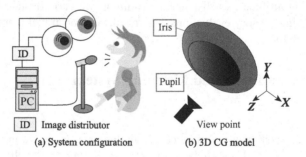

(a) System configuration   (b) 3D CG model

Fig. 2. Setup of the developed system.

2.3 Design of the Nodding Response

In this research, the listener's nodding response model [11] which estimates the nodding timing from a speech ON-OFF pattern is introduced. The timing of nodding response is predicted using a hierarchy model consisting of a macro stage and a micro stage (Fig. 3). The macro stage estimates whether a nodding response exists or not in a duration unit which consists of a talkspurt episode $T(i)$ and the following silence episode $S(i)$ with a hangover value of 4/30 s. The estimator $M_u(i)$ is a moving-average (MA) model, expressed as the weighted sum of unit speech activity $R(i)$ in Eq. (1) and Eq. (2). When

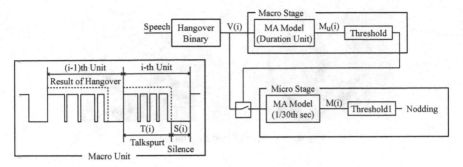

Fig. 3. Outline of the nodding response model.

$M_u(i)$ exceeds a threshold value, nodding $M(i)$ is also a MA model, estimated as the weighted sum of the binary speech signal $V(i)$ in Eq. (3).

$$M_u(i) = \sum_{j=1}^{J} a(j)R(i-j) + u(i) \tag{1}$$

$$R(i) = \frac{T(i)}{T(i) + S(i)} \tag{2}$$

$a(j)$: linear prediction coefficient

$T(i)$: talkspurt duration in the i th duration unit

$S(i)$: silence duration in the i th duration unit

$u(i)$: noise

i : number of frame

$$M(i) = \sum_{j=1}^{K} b(j)V(i-j) + w(i) \tag{3}$$

$b(j)$: linear prediction coefficient

$V(i)$: voice

$w(i)$: noise

The nodding motion was realized by moving the 3D CG model of the iris and pupil in virtual space downward and upward. This vertical motion of the 3D CG models is generated on a hemispherical display as the "tilt forward and return" motion shown in previous research [12]. Figure 4 shows an example of generating a nodding motion. The nodding can be confirmed by moving downwards compared to normal state.

Fig. 4. Example of nodding motion.

2.4   Design of the Mirroring in the Pupil Response

In this study, in order to realize active listening attitudes, the speaker's pupil response is represented as the mirrored listener's pupil response. Regarding the design of mirroring, there is two methods: one is to reflect the speaker's pupil diameter directly as it is measured, and the other is to represent the pupil response based on an estimated value of the model. The method that reflects the measured value can represent the actual pupil size of the speaker, however it is difficult to measure the pupils during blinking. In addition, a pupil measurement device is required. In the type of contact device, the speaker needs the device to be always worn on the head. In the type of non-contact device, the speaker's activities and interactions may restrict due to the limited range of measurement.

On the other hand, in the modeling the speaker's pupil response, it needs an algorithm that generates the speaker's pupil response. In our previous research, it was indicated that speaker's pupil response was synchronized with own speech. In addition, we developed an estimation model for interaction-activated communication based on the speech input [13]. Therefore, in this research, we adopted a method that the listener's pupil response is generated by mirroring the estimated speaker's pupil response based on the model.

The model assumes the real communication space as the virtual temperature space and can estimate the temperatures of talkers in the virtual temperature space. Figure 5 shows an example of time changes the speaker's speech and the estimated temperature. Figure 5 (a) shows the ON-OFF of the speaker's speech, and Fig. 5(b) shows the estimated speaker's own temperature. Since the speaker's own temperature is based on the ON/OFF of the speech, a steep rise is possible. Furthermore, when the speech input finished, it is observed that a certain temperature was maintained, and gradually attenuates. Therefore, in this study, the estimated speaker's temperature was related to the pupil size as a mirrored listener's pupil response. Specifically, the minimum and maximum values of the estimated values were mapped in the Z-axis direction of the black 3DCG model and linearly transformed as the amount of movement. In this way, the mirroring of the pupil response automatically generates from the speaker's speech. Figure 6 shows the dilated pupil response using the model. It is observed that the pupils are dilated compared to normal state.

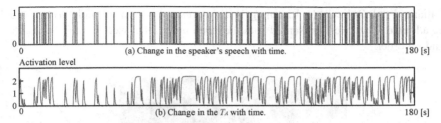

Activation level

(a) Change in the speaker's speech with time.

(b) Change in the T_A with time.

Fig. 5. Example of time changes in the speaker's speech and estimated temperature in the interaction-activated communication model.

Fig. 6. Example of mirroring of pupil response.

3 Communication Experiment

In order to evaluate the effectiveness of the developed system, a communication experiment was conducted under the condition that the system acts as a listener.

3.1 Experimental Method

In this experiment, participants spoke to the developed system that acted as a listener (Fig. 7). The previous study confirmed that a visualizing listener's nodding response supports embodied interactions [11]. Therefore, the following three modes were compared: (A) a mode in which the pupil did not react regardless of the speaker's speech input (no response mode), (B) a mode in which the pupil response is generated in synchronization with the speaker's speech input (mirroring mode), and (C) a mode in which the pupil response is generated randomly regardless of the speaker's speech input (random mode). The participants were 30 Japanese students (15 females and 15 males) who have never seen the system from 20 to 24 years old.

The experimental procedure was as follows. First, the participants used the system in each mode to understand the difference of modes. Next, they were instructed to perform a paired comparison of modes for 30 s. In the paired comparison experiment, based on their preferences, they selected the better mode. Finally, the participants were told to talk on general conversational topics to system for 90 s. The conversational topics were the content of well-known fairy tales. After the conversation, they evaluated each mode using a seven-point bipolar rating scale ranging from −3 (not at all) to 3 (extremely): 0 denotes the moderation. In this experiment, as important elements for listening attitude that forms deep relationship between human and robot, "(a) Enjoyment," "(b) Interaction," "(c)

Familiarity," "(d) Relief," "(e) Listening," "(f) Interest," "(g) Charm" and "(h) Intention" were adopted. They were presented with the three modes that were counterbalanced in a random order.

Fig. 7. Example of experimental scene in the communication experiment.

3.2 Experimental Result

The results of the paired comparison are summarized in Table 1. In this table, the number of winners is shown. For example, the number of mode (A)'s winner is ten for mode (B), and the number of total winners is twenty. Figure 8 shows the calculated results of the evaluation provided in Table 1 based on the Bradley-Terry model given in Eq. (4) and (5) [14].

$$p_{ij} = \frac{\pi_i}{\pi_i + \pi_j} \tag{4}$$

$$\sum_i \pi_i = const.(= 100) \tag{5}$$

π_i : Intensity of i

p_{ij} : probability of judgment that i is better than j

Table 1. Result of paired comparison.

	(A)	(B)	(C)	Total
(A)		10	10	20
(B)	20		19	39
(C)	20	11		31

The consistency of mode matching was confirmed by performing a goodness of fit test ($x^2(1, 0.05) = 3.84 > x_0{}^2 = 0.67$) and a likelihood ratio test ($x^2(1, 0.05) = 3.84$

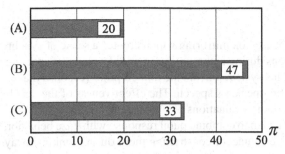

Fig. 8. Comparison of the preference π based on the Bradley-Terry model.

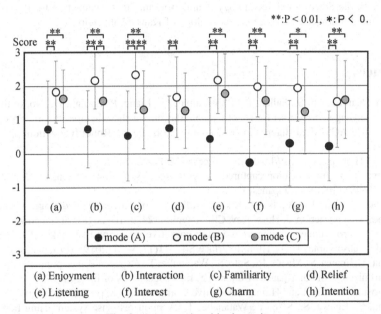

Fig. 9. Seven-points bipolar rating.

$> x_0^2 = 0.67$). The proposed mode (B), mirroring pupil response, was evaluated as the best; followed by mode (C), random mode; and mode (A), no response mode.

The questionnaire results are shown in Fig. 9. From the results of the Friedman signed-rank test and the Wilcoxon signed rank test, all items had a significance level of 1% between modes (A) and (B). "(a) Enjoyment," "(b) Interaction," "(c) Familiarity," "(e) Listening," "(f) Interest" and "(h) Intention" had a significance level of 1%, and "(g) Charm" was at 5% between modes (A) and (C). In addition, "(c) Familiarity" was at the significant level of 1%, and "(b) Interaction" was at 5% between modes (B) and (C).

In both experiments, mode (B) of the proposed mode was evaluated as the best for active listening attitudes. These results indicate the effectiveness of the developed system.

4 Conclusion

In this paper, we focused on mirroring which creates a sense of synchrony by imitating behaviors and actions during communication and developed a speech-driven embodied listening system. This system mirrors the dilated pupil response that estimates the temperature based on the speaker's speech. The effectiveness of the developed system was demonstrated by sensory evaluations.

In the future, we plan to combine pupil response with gaze behavior, such as dilating the pupils during eye contact or constricting them during looking away.

Acknowledgments. This work was supported by JSPS KAKENHI Grant Numbers JP 22H04871, 20H04232, Tateisi Science and Technology Foundation and the Organization for Research and Development of Innovative Science and Technology of Kansai University.

References

1. Cui, Y., Karamcheti, S., Palleti, R., Shivakumar, N., Liang, P., Sadigh, D.: No, to the right: online language corrections for robotic manipulation via shared autonomy. In: Proceedings of the 2023 ACM/IEEE International Conference on Human-Robot Interaction, pp. 93–101 (2023)
2. LOVOT Homepage. https://lovot.life/. Accessed 2 Feb 2024
3. Nozawa, T.: Communication captured by multimodal synchronized sensing, Jpn. J. Appl. Phys. **89**(12) (2020). (in Japanese)
4. Uchida, S., Terasaka, A., Ikeda, K.: The influence of mirroring in dialogic situation on interpersonal attraction. J. Hum. Dev. Clin. Psychol. **24**, 9–16 (2018). (in Japanese)
5. Nagai, Y.: From understanding to assisting: cognitive mirroring that makes developmental disorders observable. Trans. Hum. Interface Soc. **21**(1), 5–10 (2019). (in Japanese)
6. Sejima, Y., Egawa, S., Maeda, R., Sato, S., Watanabe, T.: A speech-driven pupil response robot synchronized with burst-pause of utterance. In: Proceedings of the 24th IEEE International Symposium on Robot and Human Interactive Communication, pp. 285–290 (2015)
7. Sejima, Y., Egawa, S., Sato, Y., Watanabe, T.: A pupil response system using hemispherical displays for enhancing affective conveyance. J. Adv. Mech. Des. Syst. Manuf. **13**(2), jamdsm0032 (2019)
8. Kret, M.E., Fischer, A.H., De Dreu, C.K.: Pupil mimicry correlates with trust in in-group partners with dilating pupils. Psychol. Sci. **26**(9), 1401–1410 (2015)
9. Sejima, Y., Watanabe, T.: Development of a speech-driven embodied listening system by mirroring of pupil response. In: Proceedings of the Symposium on Human Interface 2021, pp. 560–564 (2021). (in Japanese)
10. Hess, E.H.: The role of pupil size in communication. Sci. Am. **233**(5), 110–119 (1975)
11. Watanabe, T., Okubo, M., Nakashige, M., Danbara, R.: InterActor: speech-driven embodied interactive actor. Int. J. Hum.-Comput. Interact. **17**(1), 43–60 (2004)
12. Yoshida, M., Watanabe, T., Yamamoto, M.: Development of a speech-driven embodied entrainment system with 3DCG objects. Trans. Hum. Interface Soc. **9**(3), 87–96 (2007)
13. Sejima, Y., Watanabe, T., Jindai, M.: Estimation model of interaction-activated communication based on the heat conduction equation. J. Adv. Mech. Des. Syst. Manuf. **10**(9), jamdsm0103 (2016)
14. Takeuchi, K.: Mathematical Statistics in Phenomenon and Behavior, pp. 133–148, Shin-Yo-Sha Ltd. (1978). (in Japanese)

Optimizing Reading Experience: An Eye Tracking Comparative Analysis of Single-Column, Two-Column, and Three-Column Formats

Ana Rita Teixeira[1,2,3]([⊠]), Sónia Brito-Costa[1,3], and Hugo de Almeida[4,5]

[1] Coimbra Education School, Polytechnic University of Coimbra, Coimbra, Portugal
ateixeira@ua.pt
[2] Institute of Electronic Engineering and Telecommunications of Aveiro, (IEETA, UA), Aveiro, Portugal
[3] InED - Center for Research and Innovation in Education, Coimbra Education School, Polytechnic University of Coimbra, Coimbra, Portugal
[4] CNL-Consumer Neuroscience Lab, University of Aveiro, Aveiro, Portugal
hugodealmeida@ua.pt
[5] Imagine for Life - A Neuroscience Enterprise, Lisbon, Portugal

Abstract. This study explores the pivotal role of eye-tracking technology and physiological and behavioral signal recording in diverse research domains, notably cognitive science, and human-computer interaction (HCI). Addressing various aspects such as usability testing, user experience research, accessibility, neuroadaptive interfaces, virtual and augmented reality, and user interface design, eye-tracking technology emerges as a crucial tool for garnering nuanced insights into human behavior and cognition. The research specifically focuses on conducting a comparative analysis of single-column, two-column, and three-column document formats using the Gaze Point eye tracker. This integration of quantitative data and qualitative user feedback aims to enhance reading experiences by aligning document formats with user needs and preferences. The study employs eye-tracking technology to capture and analyze readers' eye movements across different column formats, utilizing measures such as fixation time, number of fixations, blinking frequency, and pupil dilation. The comprehensive analysis delves into readers' interactions with text, measuring reading speed and assessing comprehension and information retention. Results reveal that a single-column layout optimizes reading performance, enhancing comprehension, and reducing visual fatigue. However, the study acknowledges the context-specific appropriateness of each layout. The research methodology involves 20 participants reading texts in different layouts while their eye movements are tracked, the study provides insights into reading complexities associated with distinct layouts, emphasizing the importance of eye-tracking technology in understanding visual attention patterns. Ultimately, the study contributes to the development of guidelines for creating clear and accessible printed and digital documents, with the goal of improving written communication efficiency based on readers' experiences.

Keywords: Eye-tracking · attention · reading experience · HCI · usability

H. Mori and Y. Asahi (Eds.): HCII 2024, LNCS 14689, pp. 51–59, 2024.
https://doi.org/10.1007/978-3-031-60107-1_5

1   Introduction

In the dynamic realm of information consumption, the organizational structure of content plays a pivotal role in shaping the overall reading experience. This comprehensive review amalgamates insights from cognitive science, human-computer interaction (HCI), and design principles to delve into the factors influencing the optimization of reading experiences across Single-Column, Two-Column, and Three-Column formats [1].

Research findings [2] suggest that a three-column layout is most effective for repeated reading, while a one-column layout is optimal for standard reading tasks. Emphasizing the importance of interface design, another research underlines its role in enhancing the reading experience [3].

Further insights from another study highlights the impact of line length on readability, proposing a recommended limit of 70 characters per line [4]. Additionally, the necessity for a cognitive fit between information format and reading tasks, particularly within the evolving landscape of information consumption [5, 6].

This synthesis presents a nuanced perspective, incorporating theoretical foundations from cognitive science and Human-Computer Interaction (HCI), along with specific research findings. It underscores the importance of considering diverse factors, such as column format, interface design, line length, and cognitive fit, in optimizing the reading experience [6–8]. This holistic approach contributes to a more profound understanding of how these elements interact to shape the dynamics of reading experiences in various columnar layouts. The insights underscore the significance of considering both content and design elements in shaping the reading experience.

1.1   Design Elements and Cognitive Processing

The relationship between design elements and cognitive processing during reading has been extensively explored in cognitive science. This exploration includes human perceptual and brain activation indicators when interacting with display objects. Some research found that optimizing page layout for onscreen viewing can decrease mental workload [9], while other studies observed that reading in a two-column format can reduce cognitive load and increase visual performance [2, 6]. Another study discussed the impact of hypertext features on cognitive processing during text navigation and comprehension [10]. These studies collectively underscore the importance of tailoring design elements to minimize distractions and cognitive workload for an enhanced reading experience.

1.2   Reading Speed and Comprehension

Research has shown that the layout of text, particularly the number of columns and line length, can significantly impact reading speed and comprehension and that a three-column layout was most effective for repeated reading, while a one-column layout was best for normal reading [2, 11]. Another research emphasized the importance of line length, with the number of characters per line being a critical variable [6, 12–14], and another study highlighted the role of text coherence and readability in matching texts to readers, suggesting that signaling can ease readability for certain readers [15]. These findings underscore the need for a nuanced understanding of the interplay between text layout, reading speed, and comprehension.

1.3 Eye-Tracking Technology in Reading Research

The integration of eye-tracking technology has transformed reading research, providing a dynamic tool to capture and analyze readers' eye movements across different layouts. Gaze patterns, encompassing measures such as time fixation, number of fixations, blinking frequency, and pupil dilatation, offer quantitative insights into how individuals interact with text. This technology enables a granular examination of visual and cognitive responses [16, 17] to varied column formats. Studies utilizing eye tracking have demonstrated its efficacy in understanding how readers process information visually, found a strong link between eye movements during reading and subsequent comprehension of long connected texts, with more, but shorter fixations predicting better comprehension [18]. This is consistent with another study who observed that eye movements reflect mental looking along an abstract timeline during language comprehension [19]. While other researchers have investigated the utility of eye tracking in various fields and environments, such as examining the impact of eye tracking on the description of a healthy product in marketing and its subsequent acceptance and desirability [20], the eye-tracking approach serves as a bridge between design aesthetics and human cognitive processes and offers a method to unravel the complexities of visual attention, information retention, and comprehension.

2 Methodology

A total of twenty-seven participants were recruited within an age range of 18 to 23 years (M = 19,3, SD = 1.3). Exclusion criteria encompassed visual impairments exceeding ± 0.5 diopters and the use of any form of corrective visual assistance. Within the controlled laboratory environment, participants were given precise instructions to diligently complete a meticulously designed online questionnaire aimed at evaluating their adherence to the established exclusion criteria. The thorough questionnaire had the specific objective of identifying potential confounding variables that could significantly impact the precision and reliability of the eye-tracking data. These variables included ocular and physiological conditions, such as neurodegenerative diseases, eye ailments, the physical use of glasses or lenses, respiratory conditions, inflammation, nasal congestion, or the potential influence of psychotropic or psychoactive medications, among other specifics. All participants underwent thorough testing to ensure compliance with these conditions.

2.1 Analyzed Parameters

Considering diverse protocols, distinct parameters will be analyzed, categorized as either independent of the eye tracker or reliant on the device. Among the parameters independent of the eye tracker, particular attention will be given to reading time and speed, error count, and pauses. Concerning the eye tracker, an evaluation will be conducted on information comprehension and retention at two levels: behavioral and physiological. Within the array of parameters, specific emphasis will be placed on horizontal pupil movement, pupil dilation, blinking frequency, ocular fixations, and the duration of gaze on designated areas. This scrutiny aims to infer which format promotes superior comprehension and retention of information.

2.2 Stimuli and Setup

Eye trackers were calibrated using Gazepoint Control software version 6.7.0, set to a sampling frequency of 150 Hz with default configurations. The Gazepoint GP3 remote infrared eye tracker recorded data acquisition during the experiment at the same 150 Hz sampling frequency. To ensure consistent conditions and eliminate external lighting interference, the experimental setup maintained artificial lighting at a constant intensity of 500 lx in a room devoid of strong shadows and pronounced contrasts. The temperature was rigorously controlled at a stable 19 degrees Celsius.

The testing protocol was individually executed for each eye tracker, with the sequence of tracker usage randomized to minimize potential bias. Before each session, the eye tracker underwent calibration using a 9/9 nine-point calibration procedure, repeated until successful calibration was achieved for all nine targets for both eyes. Participants who did not meet this calibration threshold were still assigned the experimental tasks; however, data from such instances were subsequently excluded from the results analysis.

2.3 Procedures

The protocol consists of seven screens that begin and end with a black cross on a hit background (its purpose is to redirect the viewer's gaze) with the screens with text interspersed with those with the cross. The first and last screens have a duration of three seconds, the text screens last fifty seconds and the remaining screens, those with crosses, last two seconds. The total duration of the test is two minutes and forty seconds. As for the test screens, different texts were shown of the same difficulty level, organized in one, two and three columns. The first text has 154 words, the second 138 and the third has 165 words. The participants were asked to read aloud and to ensure the texts were read in their entirety, the tests were audio recorded (Fig. 1).

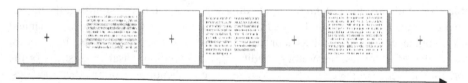

Fig. 1. Protocol Experiment

3   Results and Discussion

The results provide a detailed exploration of the study's findings, offering a thorough examination of both voice recordings and eye-tracking parameters. Through a comprehensive analysis, valuable insights into participants' performance are uncovered, based on the dynamics of verbal expression and visual attention during the study tasks.

3.1 Voice Recording Analysis

Analyzing voice recordings involves a comprehensive examination of various parameters, including errors, pauses, the number of words read, and reading speed, to gain valuable insights into participants' performance, Table 1. In the realm of linguistics, education, and psychology, this practice is common and aids in understanding language processing and cognitive abilities [21]. To evaluate errors, a clear definition is established, encompassing mispronunciations, omissions, substitutions, or additions of words. The total number of errors made by each participant is then counted, and subsequent calculations yield average, maximum, and minimum error values. Pauses in speech are also scrutinized, with durations categorized based on predefined criteria. The total number and durations of pauses for each participant are tallied, leading to average, maximum, and minimum pause duration values. Transcribing recordings allow the determination of the number of words read. This metric is crucial for assessing participants' engagement and comprehension. Reading speed, calculated by dividing the total number of words by the time taken to read them, provides insights into participants' efficiency. The time taken by each participant to complete the reading task is measured, and mean, maximum, and minimum reading speeds are computed. The findings indicate that three-column texts exhibit a higher susceptibility to errors and pauses, leading to slower reading speeds, with an average of 2.9 words per second. Consequently, it can be concluded that the most conducive layout for reading is a single-column text. The impact of reading aloud is evident through the low completion rates for various layouts, as it restricts the ability to read diagonally or skip words for expediting the process. This observation underscores the general challenges that young people face in reading, given their inclination towards consuming content in short formats with minimal text, favoring images or videos. The unexpected result challenges our initial expectation that the two-column layout, aligning with the digital content consumption habits of Generation Z, would be the most efficient. Particularly, we anticipated this efficiency due to the prevalence of narrow text formats on mobile phones, where our participants are accustomed to engaging with digital content.

Table 1. Voice Recording Parameters: Errors, Pauses, Reading Time, Reading Speed. The parameters mean, maximum and minimum are considered.

Columns	Parameters	Errors	Pauses	Reading Time	Reading Speed
1	Mean	1,65	0,8	45,3	3,4
	Max	5	3	50	4,1
	Min	0	0	37,4	2,7
2	Mean	2	1,1	44,4	3,1
	Max	4	4	50	3,8
	Min	0	0	35,8	2,2
3	Mean	2,2	1,5	49,2	2,9
	Max	5	4	50	3,5
	Min	0	0	46,5	2,3

3.2 Eyetracking Parameters

In this study, a comprehensive analysis of eyetracking parameters, specifically focusing on Time View, Fixations, and Revisitations is done. The Time View parameter provides insight into the duration of participants' focus, while Fixations revels the number and distribution of visual fixation points. Furthermore, the Revisitations parameter explores how often participants return to specific content. By scrutinizing these eyetracking metrics, the goal is obtaining details about participants' visual behaviors and discern the impact of design variations, ultimately contributing to a more profound understanding of user interaction with visual stimuli. The Time View parameter is greater for three columns compared to one column, Fig. 2. A Mann-Whitney U test, with a 95% confidence level, revealed a statistically significant difference between the first and third columns ($p = 0.00256$). This indicates that participants spent a significantly different amount of time viewing content when presented in these two column configurations.

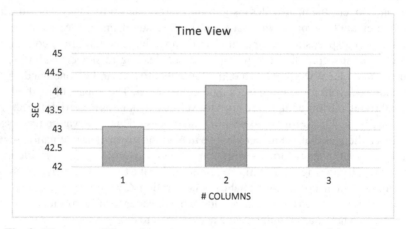

Fig. 2. The mean of Time view parameter considering one, two and three columns

Considering the fixations parameter and by analyzing the Fig. 3, the average number of fixations is higher for three columns and lower for two columns. According to a Mann-Whitney U test with a 95% confidence level, there is a statistically significant difference between the second and third columns ($p = 0.01689$). This suggests that participants made a significantly different number of fixations when presented with these two column configurations.

In the other hand, revisitations are more frequent with one column and less frequent with three columns. A Mann-Whitney U test, at a 95% confidence level, indicates a statistically significant difference between the first and third columns ($p = 0.02569$). This implies that participants exhibited a significantly different pattern of revisiting content when presented with these two column configurations (Fig. 4).

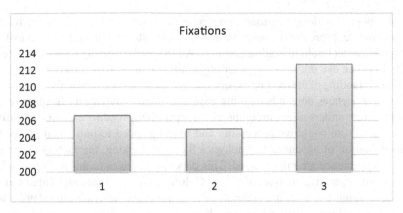

Fig. 3. The mean of fixations parameter considering one, two and three columns

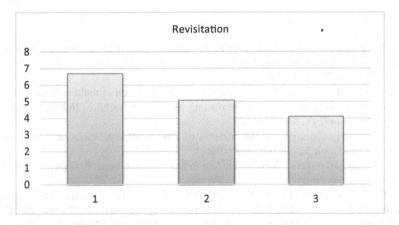

Fig. 4. The mean of revisitations parameter considering one, two and three columns

The findings highlight the significance of column layout in shaping participants' eye movement behaviors, providing insights into the visual attention distribution across various design configurations. In summary, the eyetracking results suggest that, overall, the three-column layout attracts more extended viewing time and a higher number of fixations, while the one-column layout encourages more frequent content revisitations. These findings offer valuable insights into user engagement and visual attention, providing implications for the design and optimization of content layouts based on user behavior.

4   Research Gaps and Future Directions

While existing research provides valuable insights into the impact of column layouts on reading experiences, certain gaps persist. The literature acknowledges limitations in studying the role of columniation in mediating the relationship between design and visual attention. The features of text design can be further manipulated to assess the impact of typography design elements on reading accuracy and speed. Future research endeavors could explore the dynamic nature of visual attention in response to evolving design trends and technological advancements. Additionally, investigations into potential synergies between eye tracking and other physiological indicators could provide a more holistic understanding of the reading experience. As technology evolves, the optimization of reading experiences demands ongoing exploration and adaptation. In summary, the existing literature underscores the complexity of optimizing reading experiences through layout design. From cognitive processing and reading speed to individual preferences and the integration of advanced technologies like eye tracking, the factors influencing the reading experience are multifaceted. This paper contributes to this dynamic field by conducting a comparative analysis of Single-Column, Two-Column, and Three-Column formats, leveraging eye-tracking technology to unravel the intricate interplay between design choices and the optimization of reading experiences.

References

1. Al-Samarraie, H., Eldenfria, A., Zaqout, F., Price, M.L.: How reading in single- and multiple-column types influence our cognitive load: an EEG study. Electron. Libr. **37** (2019). https://doi.org/10.1108/EL-01-2019-0006
2. Al-Samarraie, H., Sarsam, S.M., Umar, I.N.: Visual perception of multi-column-layout text: insight from repeated and non-repeated reading. Behav. Inf. Technol. **36** (2017). https://doi.org/10.1080/0144929X.2016.1196502
3. Muter, P.: Interface design and optimization of reading of continuous text. In: Cognitive Aspects of Electronic Text Processing (1996)
4. Nanavati, A.A., Bias, R.G.: Optimal line length in reading–a literature review. Visible Lang. **39** (2005)
5. Tsai, T.-M., Chou, S.-C., Liu, B.-F., Lin, Y.: The effects of information format and reading task on mobile user's reading behavior: a cognitive fit perspective. In: Stephanidis, C. (ed.) HCI International 2013 - Posters' Extended Abstracts. CCIS, vol. 373, pp. 422–426. Springer, Heidelberg (2013). https://doi.org/10.1007/978-3-642-39473-7_84
6. Teixeira, A.R.O., Brito-Costa, S., Antunes, M., Espada, S.: The influence of line length: a pilot study. In: Proceedings of the 9th World Congress on Electrical Engineering and Computer Systems and Science. Avestia Publishing (2023). https://doi.org/10.11159/mhci23.107
7. Espada, S., Teixeira, A., Antunes, M., Brito-Costa, S.: Natural and artificial lighting: influence on readability. In: Human Dynamics and Design for the Development of Contemporary Societies (2023). https://doi.org/10.54941/ahfe1003538
8. Teixeira, A., Brito-Costa, S., Espada, S., Antunes, M.: Tonal contrast: influence of text background color on the comfort and time of reading. In: 5th Euro Mediterranean Conference for Environmental Integration, Italy (2023)
9. Wästlund, E., Norlander, T., Archer, T.: The effect of page layout on mental workload: a dual-task experiment. Comput. Hum. Behav. **24** (2008). https://doi.org/10.1016/j.chb.2007.05.001
10. DeStefano, D., LeFevre, J.A.: Cognitive load in hypertext reading: a review. Comput. Hum. Behav. **23** (2007). https://doi.org/10.1016/j.chb.2005.08.012
11. Baker, R.: The effects of multiple column online text on reading speed, reading comprehension, and satisfaction. Wichita State University (2002)
12. Dyson, M.C.: How physical text layout affects reading from screen (2004). https://doi.org/10.1080/01449290410001715714

13. Dyson, M.C., Haselgrove, M.: The influence of reading speed and line length on the effectiveness of reading from screen. The effects of line length on children and adults' online reading performance. Int. J. Hum.-Comput. Stud. **54**, 585–612 (2001)
14. Dyson, M.C., Kipping, G.J.: The legibility of screen formats: are three columns better than one? Comput. Graph. (Pergamon) **21** (1997). https://doi.org/10.1016/S0097-8493(97)000 48-4
15. Meyer, B.J.F.: Text coherence and readability (2003). https://doi.org/10.1097/00011363-200 307000-00007
16. De Almeida, H.M.R., Brito-Costa, S., Bem-Haja, P., Briegas, J.J.M.: Colour usage in the lettering and in background manipulation on logotypes: eyetracking evidences. Confinia Cephalalgica et Neurologica **32** (2022)
17. Abreu, C., et al.: The importance of brandy equity in natural human behavior: a study with eyetracking. Confinia Cephalalgica **30** (2020)
18. Southwell, R., Gregg, J., Bixler, R., D'Mello, S.K.: What eye movements reveal about later comprehension of long connected texts. Cogn. Sci. **44** (2020). https://doi.org/10.1111/cogs. 12905
19. Stocker, K., Hartmann, M., Martarelli, C.S., Mast, F.W.: Eye movements reveal mental looking through time. Cogn. Sci. **40** (2016). https://doi.org/10.1111/cogs.12301
20. de Almeida, H.M.R., Bem-Haja, P., Albergaria, J., Felizardo, S., Alberty, A.: Healthy but good: using eye tracking technology in context of marketing to measure the impact of the description of a healthy product on its acceptance and desirability. Espacios **38** (2017)
21. Lester, J.N., Cho, Y., Lochmiller, C.R.: Learning to do qualitative data analysis: a starting point. Hum. Resource Dev. Rev. **19** (2020). https://doi.org/10.1177/1534484320903890

Multimodal Design for Interactive Collaborative Problem-Solving Support

Hannah VanderHoeven[1]([✉])[ID], Mariah Bradford[1][ID], Changsoo Jung[1][ID],
Ibrahim Khebour[1][ID], Kenneth Lai[2][ID], James Pustejovsky[2][ID],
Nikhil Krishnaswamy[1][ID], and Nathaniel Blanchard[1][ID]

[1] Colorado State University, Fort Collins, CO 80523, USA
[2] Brandeis University, Waltham, MA 02453, USA
{hannah.vanderhoeven,nikhil.krishnaswamy,
nathaniel.blanchard}@colostate.edu

Abstract. When analyzing interactions during collaborative problem
solving (CPS) tasks, many different communication modalities are likely
to be present and interpretable. These modalities may include speech,
gesture, action, affect, pose and object position in physical space,
amongst others. As AI becomes more prominent in day-to-day use and
various learning environments, such as classrooms, there is potential for it
to support additional understanding into how small groups work together
to complete CPS tasks. Designing interactive AI to support CPS requires
creating a system that supports multiple different modalities. In this
paper we discuss the importance of multimodal features to modeling
CPS, how different modal channels must interact in a multimodal AI
agent that supports a wide range of tasks, and design considerations
that require forethought when building such a system that most effectively interacts with and aids small groups in successfully completing
CPS tasks. We also outline various tool sets that can be leveraged to
support each of the individual features and their integration, and various applications for such a system.

Keywords: Collaborative problem solving · Multimodal agents · HCI

1 Introduction

When humans engage in collaborative problem solving (CPS), the interaction
is overwhelmingly likely to involve multiple communicative modalities simultaneously. Information may be communicated by speech, gesture, pose and interacting with objects in physical space. As artificial intelligence (AI) becomes
more integrated with everyday workflows in environments such as classrooms
and workspaces, there is in increased potential for AI to support CPS in small
groups such as project teams or workgroups in classes.

In this paper, we present a vision of AI agents whose purpose is not to auto-
mate tasks or replace human workers or teachers, but rather to augment the
natural collaborative capabilities of humans and enable teams to think and reason better. That is, in a classroom context, an effective agent would not provide

the answer to a problem, but rather assist a group in discovering the answer organically, thus optimizing learning and retention. An AI agent that effectively supports CPS must be able to interpret many forms of communication to infer relevant context from a situation. However, accurate interpretations of group interaction rarely rely on any one of the above features alone (e.g., linguistic information alone may not adequately indicate which objects are the focus of attention or discussion). Therefore, many design decisions must be made in the data collection and feature extraction to make meaningful inferences about small group communication, as would be performed by an assistive AI agent in real-time. In addition, decisions need to be made about tools and common logic used for feature extraction so they can be brought together and used in a multimodal fashion. In this paper we examine design decisions made during the creation of the Weights Task Dataset—a multimodal CPS dataset that serves as our testbed, the features selected to motivate creation of a multimodal agent to support collaborative problem solving in small groups, and a vision for integration to create meaningful methods for interactive AI for a wide range of CPS tasks.

The attribution of mental states (e.g., beliefs, desires, and intentions) to interlocutors is a primary requirement of successful collaboration, but modern interactive systems, such as chatbots driven by large language models (LLMs) struggle with this capacity [46,56]. Namely they do not display fundamental characteristics of a Theory of Mind (ToM). In large part, this is due to a lack of mechanisms to interpret not just what is expressed, but *how* it is expressed, and how human interlocutors will interpret expressions in context. This requirement motivates many of the features we focus on in our proposed multimodal collaborative agent architecture. An agent endowed with the capabilities described below, both technically and theoretically, would not simply be the sum of the individual processing modules, but a gestalt system that, through the ability to process, integrate, and engage with the multitude of ways that humans may express their underlying mental states, simulates the epistemic positioning of its interlocutors toward a task *a la* [30] and thus assists them in organically achieving it.

2   Related Work

Given the interdisciplinary nature of this work, which draws on AI, human-computer interaction, linguistics, and learning sciences, among others, there is a vast background literature implicated by the various components of our research. A few key works are referenced here, and more are provided in subsequent sections.

Collaborative problem solving (CPS) is when two or more people use "their knowledge and skills to solve complex problems without predefined solutions" [50]. As such, this is a particular method of modeling interaction between users based on research in the learning sciences. Frameworks for CPS have been developed to capture relevant behaviors and different types of collaboration [1,15,49]. These frameworks are helpful in creating labeled data and provide a bridge for computer scientists to operationalize and apply knowledge from the learning sciences. Previous work has successfully detected and classified these facets and showed improvements when using multimodal models [5,48], explored technical requirements on an AI agent for tracking collaboration in small groups, such as relevant toolkits [7], and showed how adding contextual features to models improves the generalizability of the models in collaborative contexts [8]. We expand on both of these topics in this paper.

The intersection of multimodal processing (gesture, pose, and other nonverbal behavior) with interactive systems demands an increased focus on common semantic interpretations of different modal channels [42]. We draw from semantic representation schemes at various levels of abstraction (of which [3] is a seminal example), and unify them with coding schemes directed at collaborative problem solving research grounded in the learning sciences [11].

A well-designed multimodal agent is likely to leverage multiple independent communicative features to extract context from a scene to interpret the current state of a given situation. Additionally, an agent might interact with participants based on inferences drawn from the features. One such example of an interactive multimodal agent is Diana, an embodied agent that collaborates with participants as a direct participant the task itself [26,27,41]. Effective multimodal design is vital in creating a system like Diana, in order to understand and best interact with participants in real time. Diana models an interactive user, and while it does not leverage communicative features to understand and provide feedback on the current state of a task, it does leverage features, such as speech, gestures and facial expression, to meaningfully understand and interact with users as they work together to complete a task.

3   Weights Task Dataset

We ground our agent design in a dataset that represents human-human interactions that display characteristics we want such an agent to augment and amplify. The Weights Task Dataset (WTD) is a collection of audio-visual recordings where triads collaborate to identify the weights of various colored blocks, and the pattern describing block weights (an instance of the Fibonacci series) using a balance scale [23]. This dataset consists of 10 groups in which participants interact with each other and physical objects in their environment to complete this shared situated task. The interactions display reflective reasoning, consensus-building behaviors, and exposition of shared and contradictory beliefs during the course of executing actions toward the task goal. The nature of the task requires not just speech to communicate, but also gesture, action, and nonverbal behavior. Therefore, an agent in this and similar tasks would need to integrate inputs from diverse modal channels to interact effectively with the group. Figure 1 shows two example stills from the WTD, with the corresponding speech included. As a participant (Participant 2)[1] picks up and places a block on the scale, they make two statements: "By touch feels lighter" and "And that looks like it might be about even". Without the additional context provided by interpreting situated

---

[1] Participants are conventionally indexed 1–3 from left to right in the video frame.

action and the locations of objects, it is impossible to infer which block they are referring too, and whether or not their statements are correct. Detecting gestures and actions—in this case a grasp—and tracking object locations would provide the context needed to detect that the speaker is referring to the green block.

Fig. 1. Stills from the Weight Task Dataset.

The dataset has been annotated, partially or completely, with most of the individual features discussed in Sect. 5. Details on annotation procedures, including adjudication and inter-annotator agreement, are given in [23].

4   Collaborative Problem Solving

Collaborative problem solving (CPS) is a form of collaboration wherein small groups work together to solve a nonroutine task with no set plan, where the quality of the solution can be evaluated by the team members as the task proceeds, and there is a differentiation of roles but interdependence within the team [15]. Previous work has designed several frameworks for identifying characteristics of CPS. For example, Hesse et al. developed a framework to assess students for CPS skills [18] which assesses students' social and cognitive skills over the entirety of the task rather than marking specific events as occurrences of displayed skills. Andrews-Todd and Forsyth similarly broke CPS down into cognitive and social dimensions [1] but at a level that is specific to a simulated circuitboard task and therefore not easily generalizable to other settings. A general CPS support agent requires a framework that is not hyperspecific to actions only relevant to one domain, but which can also ground CPS skill indicators to specific events as the task unfolds. To this end, we use the framework developed by Sun et al. [49]. In this framework, CPS was formalized into hierarchical levels; 19 indicators that include moves such as proposing a correct solution or interrupting others, and three facets which are *Constructing shared understanding*, *Negotiation/Coordination* and *Maintaining team function*. These indicators allow us to identify specific collaborative moves; for example, in Fig. 1, the participants are discussing the results of weighing two blocks, where *discussing results* is an indicator enumerated in the Sun et al. CPS framework.

5   Features

5.1   Speech

Speech is a critical method of communication seen in group work. Participants use this modality to share their understanding, ask questions, discuss results, plan, and more. This is an explicit method of communication, making it a foundational starting point for any agent tracking group work. Previous studies demonstrated that speech is a meaningful feature for a model tracking group states [5,48]. When combined with other features, utterances can help add context to how a participant is interacting with the space around them. Existing automatic speech recognition (ASR) tools, such as Google ASR and Whisper ASR [43,59] can segment and transcribe audio into utterances of speech. Use of automatic or manual segmentation is an important design decision in integrating speech with other channels, as it affects the fidelity of downstream inference based on speech [51]. For real-time support, an agent will have to rely on an ASR system. Speech must be automatically diarized and transcribed for a system to work in real time, so these methods are a necessary component for an agent to have.

There is a high proportion of demonstrative terms and anaphors ("this", "that", "it", etc.) implicated in dialogue during situated shared tasks. Automatically interpreting them usually involves recourse to another modality such as deictic gesture. As an interpretational technique, *Dense Paraphrasing* is a linguistically-motivated textual enrichment strategy that explicitly realizes the otherwise elided compositional operations inherent in the meaning of the language. This broadly involves three kinds of interpretive processes: (i) recognizing the diverse variability in linguistic forms that can be associated with the same underlying semantic representation (paraphrases); (ii) identifying semantic factors or variables that accompany or are presupposed by the lexical semantics of the words present in the text, through dropped, hidden or shadow arguments; and (iii) interpreting or computing the dynamic changes that actions, events, and other communicative modalities impose on objects in the text.

More formally, given the pair, (S, P), where S is a source expression (e.g., a textual narrative, image caption, or a speech transcription), and P is a linguistic expression, we say P is a valid *dense paraphrase* of S if: P is a lexeme, phrase, or sentence that eliminates any contextual ambiguity that may be present in S, but that also makes explicit the underlying semantics that is not (usually) expressed in the economy of sentence structure, e.g., default or hidden arguments, dropped objects or adjuncts. P is both meaning-preserving (consistent) and ampliative (informative) with respect to S.

5.2   Acoustics

Acoustic features convey additional meaning in language. From turn-taking to posing a question, they way someone presents their statements provides additional information to others. Acoustic information allows us to understand sarcasm, perceive tone, recognize high energy, and more. For an agent, acoustics (cadence, prosody, etc.) can help classify the sentiment of statements. Prior work has shown that acoustics are useful features for a model classifying a group's state [5,48]. One system for automatically extracting acoustic features is openSMILE [13]. This allows users to retrieve the acoustic information within a detected segment. There are also existing feature sets which extract acoustic features relevant to human voice such as the GeMAPS set [12]. This is a condensed set which captures the most impactful information for sentiment in acoustics using a minimal amount of features, making it fast and lightweight— ideal for a live system. These acoustic features would be automatically extracted by an agent to more accurately process human language, including being able to distinguish questions from statements based on tone and cadence.

5.3   Gesture and Pose

Gestures and body language may also be important communicative modalities. Gesture is frequently used to disambiguate language and has complementary strengths (for instance, deictic gesture is naturally suited to indicating locations, while spoken language is more felicitous for indicating nominal qualities such as color). Pose and body language in a group context, meanwhile, can be an indicator of engagement with the team or lack thereof, focus of attention, etc. However, the interpretation of gesture and body pose may be subjective, and conditioned upon personality, background, culture, etc. [24]. Therefore, in a computational context, some form of structured representation language is required to make the continuous discrete and the intractable tractable.

The two representational schemes we build on here are **Gesture Abstract Meaning Representation** (GAMR) for gesture [6] and **Nonverbal Interactions in Collaborative-Learning Environments** (NICE) for other kinds of nonverbal behavior [10]. Annotations using these frameworks serve as output sets against which gesture and pose recognition models can be trained.

GAMR. Gesture AMR (GAMR) is a formalism intended to encode the meaning of gesture in multimodal interactions between agents. It is an extension to Abstract Meaning Representation (AMR), adopting both the annotated graph structure and the predicate-argument representation of that formalism [3]. Gesture AMR was developed to encode how gesture packages meaning both independently of and in interaction with speech; and how the meaning of gesture is temporally and contextually determined.

```
GAMR GESTURE UNIT

(g / gesture-unit
  :op1 (i / icon-GA
    :ARG0 (g2 / gesturer)
    :ARG1 (b / block)
    :ARG2 (a / addressee))
  :op2 (d / deixis-GA
    :ARG0 g2
    :ARG1 (l / location)
    :ARG2 a))
```

Gesture AMR distinguishes four general types of referential gestures: *iconic*, *deictic*, *metaphoric*, and *emblematic* [22,25,34,35]. Because our data focuses on gestures in a task-based setting, most depictions of entities and events appear to reflect their concrete properties, such as the shape of an object or the manner of an action. Similar to the interactions reported on in [6], metaphoric gestures do not appear with any frequency.

GAMR includes schemata to annotate gestures that fall into one or more of these categories, thus providing granularity when representing a variety of gestures that might be used to communicate in various CPS tasks. The inset shows the structure for a "gesture unit" including both deixis and iconic components. ARG0 denotes the gesturer, ARG1 the semantic content of the gesture and ARG2 is the addressee or intended recipient; these fields exist for each gesture subsection in the annotation.

NICE. The NICE coding scheme captures nonverbal behaviors when people are working together in groups. There is a subtle, yet important distinction between a silent individual who is nonverbally participating in their group and a silent individual who mostly works by themselves and neither verbally nor nonverbally participates. Additionally, different nonverbal cues can occur concurrently, and in clusters [63].

NICE captures multiple modalities that indicate collaborative learning and engagement, such as the direction of gaze (where are they looking?), posture (are they leaning toward or away from the activity area?), and usage of tools (including pointing at or to the tool, as well as directly manipulating it). Eye gaze could be indicative of where attention is directed [47,52], whether it is jointly on group work or on other interlocutors. Head movements (such as nodding in agreement or shaking in disagreement) are captured as an indication that the person is paying attention [38], as are leaning forwards to look at the joint activity or participating in the same [4]. The coding scheme also captures contrasting behaviors that would imply lower collaboration or attention, such as looking at or doing their own work (instead of the joint work) or outside the activity area, leaning away, "fiddling" (idly interacting with non-task-related objects or interacting with task-related objects in non-task-related ways) [16], etc. Additionally, the NICE coding scheme captures four emotions (*positive emotion*, *negative emotion*, *boredom*, and *confusion/concentration*) as they are working together, based on observational cues, which provide indications of learning [54].

NICE is designed to be calibrated to the task in that the vocabulary of objects must be pre-specified to match the perceptible object space of the common ground that evolves between participants as the task unfolds.

Gesture Recognition. There are many possible solutions to gesture recognition [14,17,36,53], but nearly all suffer from difficulties in recognizing gestures at unusual angles or that may be far from camera, and deep learning approaches come with a high training and data overhead, making them difficult to adapt to new environments and situations. This difficulty demands a more lightweight robust solution that can rapidly be deployed under novel circumstances, potentially on everyday hardware.

From the gesture semantics community comes a tradition of modeling gesture in terms of preparatory, "stroke" (including pre- and post-stroke "hold") and subsequent recovery *phases* of gestures [2,21,31]. Based on this, we previously developed a gesture recognition pipeline, with the goal to streamline the detection of complex gestures, for eventual deployment in real time [57]. This pipeline uses hand detection tools, like MediaPipe [62], to detect joint locations of individual hands in a frame (21 joints in 3D coordinates). The pipeline is made up of three major stages: a static classification model that recognizes the general static shape of a gesture in any of the "hold" phases, a movement segmentation algorithm that tracks the movement of hands over time and breaks a video stream down into segments based on changes in motion patterns, and a phase breakdown process that uses the results of the previous steps to identify segments with frames in a "hold" phase. The start and end frames of these hold segments are recorded as "key frames," or the frames that comprise the most semantic significance of any given gesture. Individual static classification models can be trained for a variety of different relevant gestures for CPS tasks, providing flexibility and granularity for a larger multimodal system. We have leveraged this pipeline to successfully detect multiple different kinds complex gesture, ranging from subtle small hand movements (*microgestures* [20,57,61]), to deictic gestures [58].

Figure 2 shows an example of our recognition method applied to pointing detection in the WTD. In the frame we can see that Participant 1 is pointing at the blocks on the scale. A pointing frustum built around the vector extended out from the participant's index finger has further narrowed down the blue block as a target of interest (see [58] for details). Through a comparison to the GAMR annotations at the same intervals, we can see that the blue block is in fact the intended target. Combining target detection using deixis with other features like speech in a multimodal system can further disambiguate the intended subjects of action during collaborative problem solving.

Pose Detection. Similar adaptability concerns inform approaches to pose detection in multimodal CPS scenarios. In this case, important features are more likely to be associated with gross body motion than fine-grained joint positions on the hand. Using the depth channel from Azure Kinect recordings, the positions and orientations of 32 joints on the body can be extracted, in a similar manner to hand detection with MediaPipe. To classify instances of non-gestural nonverbal behaviors, along the lines of those captured by the NICE coding, joint features need to be tracked over time and converted to nonverbal behavior labels.

Fig. 2. Group 1 deixis with GAMR example (reproduced from [58])

Suitable approaches to this task may include processing the concatenated raw joint positions through a sliding window of fixed size to accumulate descriptive features of the motion over time, and then training a neural classifier to fit the relationship between joint positions and NICE codes.

Because the raw joint positions are anchored to the physical location of the different participants, the individual bodies may either need to be segmented and processed individually with distinct models for each person, or transformed into a normalized space before feature processing and classification.

5.4   Actions

```
ACTION ANNOTATION

(p / put-ACT
 :ARG0 (p1 / participant-1)
 :ARG1 (gb / green-block)
 :ARG2 (o / on
          :op1 (rs / right-scale)))
```

Actions in context provide important information that situates other modalities within the environment. For instance, the subject of an action may be the antecedent of a subsequent demonstrative even if it is never explicitly labeled in dialogue. This motivates the use of a rigorously-defined interaction semantics for action tracking. Annotation of all task-specific actions engaged in by the participants, like GAMR, follows an AMR-style syntax which introduces the notion of annotating actions in the style of speech and gesture. This involves making reference to a taxonomy of action classes, adapted from relevant predicates from PropBank [39], that are interpreted as VoxML programs [40]. For example, an action of putting a green block on the right side of a scale would be assigned the annotation shown. The argument structure given for the Action AMR annotation of this event follows that of the corresponding PropBank predicate, in this case, `put-01`.

The results of actions performed over objects accommodate downstream reasoning, such that in a context or configuration $\mathcal{C}$, the execution of an action or program π results in state $\mathcal{R}$ ($\mathcal{C} \rightarrow [\pi]\mathcal{R}$ according to [41,42]) which can further indicate what a participant may be thinking or reasoning about. For instance, in Fig. 1, P2 placing the green block on the scale is also an indication of *intent* and of what P2 believes the likely results will be based on the *affordances* of the objects involved: in this example, namely, that the scale will end up balanced.

5.5 Facial Expression

Facial expression is an informative modality for an agent tracking group work, as it can indicate both level of engagement (similar to body pose) and also participants' attitudes towards individual events or even each other. Recent work has shown improvement in facial expression recognition through improvements in deep learning [32,33]. However, there is a great diversity of ways to interpret different facial expressions, often depending on context. For our purposes we care about the relations of specific expressions to collaborative problem solving. Toward identifying these affects, D'mello and Graesser defined patterns in affective states specific to learning [11]. This allows us to narrow down into expressions that will be important for an agent to track. Recent work focusing on these affective states has been able to recognize facial expressions representing these states [45]. This modality allows an agent to identify the learner's affective condition. For example, an agent may detect that a learner is confused and offer clarification. Previous work also showed eye gaze to be an informative feature for classifying group member involvement [37]. While eye gaze detection is still limited, it could be an informative channel for an agent when detecting participation.

5.6 Physical Space

Fundamentally, an agent will be unable to meaningfully interact with users and support groups in a physical context without the ability to track the movement of objects in space and make inferences regarding the relationships between them. Mechanistically, this requires common calibration settings to allow data extracted using various tools to be used together (e.g., gesture landmarks exist in the same space as the object locations). The use of 6DOF object pose estimation [9] to extract object locations admits challenges when deployed in group work scenarios, particularly those in classroom environments, where interactable objects are likely to be small, moved a lot, and subject to partial or complete occlusions. One way to address this is with a model that estimates the object mask to predict the position of an object and then crops the masked image to estimate the its rotation.

6DOF Pose. The position of an object in 3D Cartesian space can be estimated through prediction of the object's 6DOF pose (6 degrees of freedom, comprising translation and rotation in all three orthogonal dimensions [19,29,60]). By detecting the positions of objects, a system may couple that with their sizes and properties (see Sect. 5.4) to make inferences about the physical relationships between objects. Another advantage is that 6DOF pose estimation allows objects to be tracked over time, and thus allows tracking the context of an interaction with an object that may results in a change to its state or configuration. This information is typically extractable from an RGB pixel stream, but in our usages we also leverage the additional benefits of a depth channel, for instance by using Azure Kinects, for greater accuracy.

Fig. 3. 6DOF Pose Annotation Tool on CPS Data. *A* shows the current frame number, *B* shows the position and rotation information for each object of interest, and *C* (expanded in inset) shows annotated 2D and 3D bounding boxes.

The challenge of CPS tasks for 6DOF pose estimation is the difficulty of visual feature extraction. To capture a sufficient amount of the scene in which a CPS task typically unfolds, the camera must be placed further away from the relevant objects that it typically has been in other 6DOF pose estimation tasks and datasets [44,55]. This is naturally required to capture the participants and how they interact with each other using modalities such as gesture and pose (see Sect. 5.3), but also renders the relevant objects very small in the frame, making them difficult to annotate for training, and to capture at inference time. Figure 3 shows the challenge of 6DOF pose annotation in the WTD.

Figure 4 shows the convergence of pointing and object detection. When performing automated object selection using deixis, an end-to-end solution would require that the objects be automatically detected within the scene at the same time that gestures are also recognized, rather than using pre-annotated bounding boxes (as in Fig. 2). Current state of the art approaches to tasks of this kind are typically composed of multiple modules, trained over a combination of real images and 3D renderings of the objects of interest in a variety of orientations. A typical solution may start with a convolutional neural network (CNN) to extract spatial information and visual features of objects. Visual features are used to predict the poses of objects in the next module. Following this, a "refinement step" takes place, in which the module estimates object pose and those estimates are used to render images of the objects, which are then compared to the real training images. Error is backpropagated until the renderings and real images are within an appropriately small epsilon.

One or more objects may be detected within a region singled out by deixis, indicating the object or set of objects that are the likely foci of attention. This may be further disambiguated by linguistic information, such as nominal descriptors or previous discussion of objects that have been acted upon.

Fig. 4. Ground truth object bounding boxes (blue) and predicted bounding boxes (red). Deixis is used to select a spatial region containing one or more objects, which may be further disambiguated by contemporaneous speech or prior context. (Color figure online)

6   Multimodal Fusion

A key foundational challenge of signal fusion is one of aligning the different modal channels. For instance, a non-linguistic feature could align with more than one utterance. One common strategy to handle such instances is mapping non-linguistic inputs to the utterances that they share the greatest temporal overlap with. A potential problem with this strategy may arise if, for instance, a very brief gesture begins at the end of one utterance A, but lasts long enough to overlap more with the next utterance B. Another possible issue is when ASR models detect speech where none exists, causing non-linguistic inputs to end up aligned with a "hallucinated" transcription. Alternate mapping strategies could involve choosing the overlapping utterance based on length, semantic qualities, or distance metrics between feature representations, such as a GAMR annotation and an utterance's AMR.

With the level of feature diversity presented and the wide variation within each, to arrive at a representation usable by an AI system, a deep learning solution is *de rigueur*. Design choices in fusion algorithms will primarily revolve around the step at which the fusion of the different feature types takes place, of which there are 3 primary classes: *early fusion*, *late fusion*, or *hybrid fusion*.

In *early fusion*, the data is fused at the start of the learning algorithm, such as through concatenation, then processed as a single input. This may lead to imbalance in feature contribution to the final output. If the different modalities differ in format or size (e.g., input dimensions or one-hot vs. real-valued vectors), the output will be biased toward the numerically richer type of data, regardless of semantic contribution. *Late fusion* trains on each modality separately in unimodal submodules, and then merges those outputs. This method can better handle imbalance in feature input size, as the submodules' output sizes are controllable and specifiable. This may result in a larger neural network with associated potential issues, such as the vanishing gradient problem. *Hybrid fusion* mixes the previous two: some modalities are trained separately, but if two or more modalities have a certain connection (e.g., overlaps between gesture and action), or if they have the same format and sizes, they may be handled together. Fusion may be as simple as concatenating the features, depending on the stage at which it is performed, or could involve more complex methods such as learning attention weights between queries of one modality, and keys/values of another modality. Figures 5a and 5b show high-level schematic diagrams of early and late fusion, respectively. Hybrid fusion combines the two, in that the some modalities may be processed through individual submodules while others are input directly to the fusion layer.

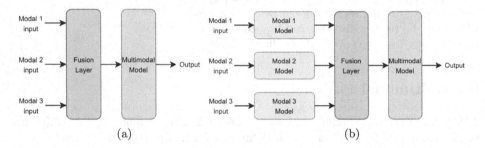

(a)   (b)

Fig. 5. (a) Early fusion schematic diagram. (b) Late fusion schematic diagram.

Finally, the joint representation is considered as a standard feature vector by the prediction head. The model may leverage linear or non-linear layers either as a discrete classification head or the joint representation may be fed into another module, such as a pre-trained language model for output generation (see below).

7 Behavior Generation

Our focus in this paper is on processing and integrating multimodal channels to enable an agent to process human task behavior. To actually act upon its inferences, however, the agent also needs to produce naturalistic output that is coherent, on-topic, supports the task goal, and scales beyond deterministic and trivial use cases. Such an agent would itself be multimodal, to symmetrically replicate the same modes of interaction as human group members. Examples of previous multimodal agents (e.g., Diana from Sect. 2) interact directly with the user using speech, gesture, and action. This contrasts with our aims here, which is to build an agent that supports group dynamics rather than performing the task itself, but shows the importance of a multimodal generation capability.

The advent of generative AI models, of which large language models (LLMs) such as ChatGPT/GPT-4 are noteworthy exemplars, provides a partial solution to such a problem, with their facility in generating language that on occasion appears indistinguishable from human writing or speech. A key challenge is that off-the-shelf generative AI systems tend to 1) generate longer outputs than the sentence fragments actually used by people during collaborative interaction and 2) display pronounced weaknesses in problems pertaining to situational and multimodal reasoning. Open-weight LLMs can be tuned on task dialogue samples to replicate more realistic dialogue structure. That is, rather than an LLM that produces fully informative, complete sentences, generated utterances should actually be more fragmented and ambiguous, and dependent on multimodal information that can then be validated against the environment.

Likewise, to generate multimodal information such as gestures and actions, the underlying model needs to be trained to insert non-linguistic "tokens" into the output. This may involve fine-tuning the autoregressive mechanism over specialized datasets that include naturalistic multimodal ensembles, for example of multimodal referring expressions (e.g., [28]). Multimodal information like gesture and action annotations can be represented as special tokens, such as unique non-human-interpretable identifiers added to the model's vocabulary, with their representations projected into the LLM's space to facilitate generation in context. Outputted special tokens, when encountered by the agent's linguistic parser, would be skipped by the agent's linguistic renderer (e.g., text-to-speech system), and routed instead to a gesture and action manager to make the agent execute behaviors that the language must then be grounded to. These behaviors could be animated gestures and actions in a simulated environment, or, with the right hardware support, deployed on a physical robot co-situated with the group.

8 Evaluation

With a new type of interactive agent comes a need to develop appropriate evaluation metrics to gauge success or failure of the agent design. Here we propose a number of quantitative and qualitative metrics that may be considered.

1. Agent-augmented team vs. non-augmented team task completion rate. Agent inferences and corresponding outputs can be correlated to group factors like task completion time/rate and time to resolve uncertainties;
2. Agent adaptation to human behavior. Adaptations to improve group collaboration can be assessed with respect to which agent moves prompt increased collaboration in the group members. This can be assessed over time to see how the adaptation of agent outputs prompts more positive CPS from humans;
3. Common ground among agent-augmented team vs. non-augmented team. A proxy for the ToM capabilities of an agent (human or artificial) is its ability to build a consensus with its interlocutors and act according to it. Given a task and a set of relevant propositions, CPS skills displayed by a group (with

or without the agent) can be correlated to beliefs or intentions the group members correctly attribute to each other;

4. Decision making quality. While this is largely a subjective metric, an agent-supported group should be more transparent, reflective, and deliberative, while drawing on the perspectives of everyone involved and the collective knowledge of the group, resulting in decisions supported by all parties and the maximum spectrum of available evidence.

9 Applications

There are many different applicative use cases for multimodal systems that interpret and return feedback based on small group communication. A well-designed AI agent would collect and interpret enough context from a situation to aid in the problem solving process. For example, it could point out information the group members may not have considered, realign priorities based on team needs, and incorporate collaborator knowledge on the fly through a representation of objectives, subgoaling, changing plans, uncertainty, etc. Using the WTD as a specific example, the collaborative AI agent could maintain a model of the Fibonacci sequence as the goal and would be able to interpret the group's general understanding as they work to discover said pattern, based on how they communicate and the CPS skills they display. The agent would aid the participants by helping them reach the correct conclusion organically, and could also learn based on participants' task behavior, further tuning its feedback to the group to support their learning in an optimal way. A similar feedback cycle could be applied to any collaborative task, thus empowering teams to think and reason better in a wide range of different tasks and circumstances.

An agent might also take a more direct interactive approach to aiding small groups. One way would be to model the shared and individual beliefs of group members. This would enable it to raise questions about unspoken or unresolved conflicts or intervene in cases of groupthink for which there is no evidence. This is an important capability to prevent groups from making critical errors. As the agent gathers data on communication style and the beliefs of individuals, it would directly intervene and steer the conversation to correct misapprehensions or encourage more productive solutions to relevant subgoals. In the WTD, this might occur when one or more individuals believe a block is the incorrect weight. The agent could step in and ask participants to try weighing a specific combination of blocks. It could then analyze both if the correct conclusion was drawn from the action, and which CPS skills were displayed during the subdialogue. This interaction style could also be applied to a variety of CPS tasks providing a more direct teaching style for team support.

Fig. 6. Still of Group 10 from the Weights Task. The group is working to discover the weight of the blue block, based on inferences about the red block. Red text over each participant shows beliefs each apparently holds at this point, based on their prior utterances and actions. (Color figure online)

Figure 6 shows a still from the WTD where a group is working to determine the weight of the blue block, based on previous inferences about the red blocks. In this scene multiple different modalities can be leveraged by an agent to determine the validity of the group's thought process, including but not limited to, what participants are saying, which blocks they are pointing at or grasping, and the location of the blocks relative to the scale. For instance, the whole group believes the blue block weighs 10g, but P2 and P3 disagree about the red block. P3 *acts* based on his belief but P2 makes an inference based on his (expressed in speech).

Both of the aforementioned agent styles would be valid ways to help the group succeed. In the Weights Task example, in a more organic approach the agent would continually collect and process dialogue moves and analyze how the group is working towards the intended goal; for example, by performing inferences over recognized gestures and actions to understand what blocks are being interacted with, object recognition of their locations on the scale, and linguistic understanding of the group's statements to each other, the agent could verify that the current thought process is generally directed toward discovering the correct pattern even if there are specific inaccuracies at the current time. Using a more direct approach, the agent could reason over the inferences of each individual up to the current point in the task and intervene with corrective measures to help drive valid inferences toward the discovery of the overall pattern.

10   Conclusion and Future Work

Small groups engaged in CPS are likely to engage in various forms of multimodal communication, often simultaneously. In this paper we presented a design for an AI agent intended to support small group learning and collaboration by interacting with or providing feedback to individuals participating in various CPS tasks, specifically in a classroom setting. Potential communicative modalities such a group could utilize include speech, gestures, pose, and interaction with objects in physical space. To create such a system, tracking and interpreting various multimodal features is vital to gather the requisite level of context about how individuals interact with each other at any given time while completing the task. This leads to a set of deliberately-chosen requirements on individual components to maintain tractability, generalizability, and robustness.

Fig. 7. Still of Group 1 from the Weights Task. Potential communicative modalities in the scene include but are not limited to, *speech*, *gesture*, *pose*, *action*, *gaze*, and *acoustics*.

Figure 7 shows an example of a single interaction in the Weights Task. In this situation, there are many inferences an AI agent could draw about the current state of the task. For instance, P1 and P3 are speaking and gesturing. P3 says "one of these," while performing what appears to be a *grasp* gesture (cf. [57]). With hand and object detection to localize the blocks in the working space, an agent could infer that the group is speaking about the red or blue blocks. This could be used further determine if the overall statement made by P3 is true, thus helping the agent understand the current progress toward successful task completion. P2 is not speaking, gesturing or interacting with the blocks, however the general direction of their gaze and forward-leaning pose indicate they remain engaged in the task. P1's statement "but I think it's still 20," combined with certain cadence or prosodic patterns could signal P1's confusion or hesitation about the group's current trajectory (cf. [5]). Leveraging the combined modalities, such an agent would be able to maintain a relatively detailed model of what is currently happening in the scene, from specific action-level occurrences to the general level of contribution of each participant.

Additional design considerations concerning the exact methods that will bring features together, in addition to how the participants will interact with the agent, remain to be determined. A complete system should integrate implementations of 6DOF object recognition, action detection, expression recognition, and pose estimation, and would open up the wide variation of AI-assisted CPS to experimentation and evaluation, both from a human factors and multimodal fusion perspective. For instance, emergent properties of group behavior with AI assistance could be correlated to CPS skills displayed and other modalities predictive thereof, to determine the chain of events from individual behaviors to dialogue moves to CPS indicators to outcomes, which could be communicated back to the participants in real time.

Acknowledgments. This work was partially supported by the National Science Foundation under subcontracts to Colorado State University and Brandeis University on award DRL 2019805. The views expressed are those of the authors and do not reflect the official policy or position of the U.S. Government. All errors and mistakes are, of course, the responsibilities of the authors.

References

1. Andrews-Todd, J., Forsyth, C.M.: Exploring social and cognitive dimensions of collaborative problem solving in an open online simulation-based task. Comput. Hum. Behav. **104**, 105759 (2020). https://doi.org/10.1016/j.chb.2018.10.025
2. Arnheim, R.: Hand and mind: what gestures reveal about thought by David McNeill. Leonardo **27**(4), 358 (1994)
3. Banarescu, L., et al.: Abstract meaning representation for sembanking. In: Proceedings of the 7th Linguistic Annotation Workshop and Interoperability with Discourse, pp. 178–186 (2013)
4. Barron, B.: When smart groups fail. J. Learn. Sci. **12**(3), 307–359 (2003)
5. Bradford, M., Khebour, I., Blanchard, N., Krishnaswamy, N.: Automatic detection of collaborative states in small groups using multimodal features. In: AIED (2023)
6. Brutti, R., Donatelli, L., Lai, K., Pustejovsky, J.: Abstract meaning representation for gesture, pp. 1576–1583, June 2022. https://aclanthology.org/2022.lrec-1.169
7. Castillon, I., Venkatesha, V., VanderHoeven, H., Bradford, M., Krishnaswamy, N., Blanchard, N.: Multimodal features for group dynamic-aware agents. In: Interdisciplinary Approaches to Getting AI Experts and Education Stakeholders Talking Workshop at AIEd. International AIEd Society (2022)
8. Chejara, P., Prieto, L.P., Rodriguez-Triana, M.J., Kasepalu, R., Ruiz-Calleja, A., Shankar, S.K.: How to build more generalizable models for collaboration quality? Lessons learned from exploring multi-context audio-log datasets using multimodal learning analytics. In: LAK2023, pp. 111–121. Association for Computing Machinery, New York, NY, USA, March 2023. https://doi.org/10.1145/3576050.3576144
9. Cunico, F., Carletti, M., Cristani, M., Masci, F., Conigliaro, D.: 6D pose estimation for industrial applications, pp. 374–384, September 2019. https://doi.org/10.1007/978-3-030-30754-7_37
10. Dey, I., et al.: The NICE framework: analyzing students' nonverbal interactions during collaborative learning. In: Pre-Conference Workshop on Collaboration Analytics at LAK 2023. SOLAR (2023)
11. D'Mello, S., Graesser, A.: Dynamics of affective states during complex learning. Learn. Instr. **22**(2), 145–157 (2012)
12. Eyben, F., et al.: The Geneva minimalistic acoustic parameter set (GeMAPS) for voice research and affective computing. IEEE Trans. Affect. Comput. **7**(2), 190–202 (2016). https://doi.org/10.1109/TAFFC.2015.2457417
13. Eyben, F., Wöllmer, M., Schuller, B.: OpenSMILE: the Munich versatile and fast open-source audio feature extractor. In: Proceedings of the 18th ACM International Conference on Multimedia, pp. 1459–1462. Association for Computing Machinery, New York, NY, USA, October 2010. https://doi.org/10.1145/1873951.1874246
14. Fan, H., et al.: Multiscale vision transformers. In: Proceedings of the IEEE/CVF International Conference on Computer Vision, pp. 6824–6835 (2021)
15. Graesser, A.C., Fiore, S.M., Greiff, S., Andrews-Todd, J., Foltz, P.W., Hesse, F.W.: Advancing the science of collaborative problem solving. Psychol. Sci. Pub. Interest **19**(2), 59–92 (2018). https://doi.org/10.1177/1529100618808244
16. de Haas, M., Vogt, P., Krahmer, E.: When preschoolers interact with an educational robot, does robot feedback influence engagement? Multimodal Technol. Interact. **5**(12), 77 (2021)
17. Hara, K., Kataoka, H., Satoh, Y.: Can spatiotemporal 3D CNNs retrace the history of 2D CNNs and ImageNet? In: Proceedings of the IEEE Conference on Computer Vision and Pattern Recognition, pp. 6546–6555 (2018)

18. Hesse, F., Care, E., Buder, J., Sassenberg, K., Griffin, P.: A framework for teachable collaborative problem solving skills. In: Griffin, P., Care, E. (eds.) Assessment and Teaching of 21st Century Skills. EAIA, pp. 37–56. Springer, Dordrecht (2015). https://doi.org/10.1007/978-94-017-9395-7_2

19. Hu, Y., Fua, P., Wang, W., Salzmann, M.: Single-stage 6D object pose estimation. In: Proceedings of the IEEE/CVF Conference on Computer Vision and Pattern Recognition (CVPR), June 2020

20. Kandoi, C., et al.: Intentional microgesture recognition for extended human-computer interaction. In: Kurosu, M., Hashizume, A. (eds.) HCII 2023. LNCS, vol. 14011, pp. 499–518. Springer, Cham (2023). https://doi.org/10.1007/978-3-031-35596-7_32

21. Kendon, A.: Gesticulation and speech: two aspects of the process of utterance. In: The Relationship of Verbal and Nonverbal Communication, vol. 25, pp. 207–227 (1980)

22. Kendon, A.: Gesture: Visible Action as Utterance. Cambridge University Press (2004)

23. Khebour, I., et al.: When text and speech are not enough: a multimodal dataset of collaboration in a situated task (2024)

24. Kita, S.: Pointing: a foundational building block of human communication. In: Pointing: Where Language, Culture, and Cognition Meet, pp. 1–8 (2003)

25. Kong, A.P.H., Law, S.P., Kwan, C.C.Y., Lai, C., Lam, V.: A coding system with independent annotations of gesture forms and functions during verbal communication: development of a database of speech and gesture (dosage). J. Nonverbal Behav. **39**, 93–111 (2015)

26. Krishnaswamy, N., et al.: Diana's world: a situated multimodal interactive agent. In: Proceedings of the AAAI Conference on Artificial Intelligence, vol. 34, pp. 13618–13619 (2020)

27. Krishnaswamy, N., et al.: Communicating and acting: understanding gesture in simulation semantics. In: IWCS 2017-12th International Conference on Computational Semantics-Short papers (2017)

28. Krishnaswamy, N., Pustejovsky, J.: Generating a novel dataset of multimodal referring expressions. In: Proceedings of the 13th International Conference on Computational Semantics-Short Papers, pp. 44–51 (2019)

29. Labbé, Y., Carpentier, J., Aubry, M., Sivic, J.: CosyPose: consistent multi-view multi-object 6D pose estimation. In: Vedaldi, A., Bischof, H., Brox, T., Frahm, J.-M. (eds.) ECCV 2020. LNCS, vol. 12362, pp. 574–591. Springer, Cham (2020). https://doi.org/10.1007/978-3-030-58520-4_34

30. Lai, K., et al.: Modeling theory of mind in multimodal HCI. In: Digital Human Modeling and Applications in Health, Safety, Ergonomics and Risk Management. Springer (2024)

31. Lascarides, A., Stone, M.: A formal semantic analysis of gesture. J. Semant. **26**(4), 393–449 (2009)

32. Li, J., Jin, K., Zhou, D., Kubota, N., Ju, Z.: Attention mechanism-based CNN for facial expression recognition. Neurocomputing **411**, 340–350 (2020). https://doi.org/10.1016/j.neucom.2020.06.014

33. Li, S., Deng, W.: Deep facial expression recognition: a survey. IEEE Trans. Affect. Comput. **13**(3), 1195–1215 (2022). https://doi.org/10.1109/TAFFC.2020.2981446

34. Mather, S.M.: Ethnographic research on the use of visually based regulators for teachers and interpreters. In: Attitudes, Innuendo, and Regulators, pp. 136–161 (2005)

35. McNeill, D.: Hand and mind. In: Advances in Visual Semiotics, vol. 351 (1992)
36. Narayana, P., Beveridge, R., Draper, B.A.: Gesture recognition: locus on the hands. In: Proceedings of the IEEE Conference on Computer Vision and Pattern Recognition, pp. 5235–5244 (2018)
37. Oertel, C., Salvi, G.: A gaze-based method for relating group involvement to individual engagement in multimodal multiparty dialogue. In: Proceedings of the 15th ACM on International Conference on Multimodal Interaction - ICMI 2013, pp. 99–106. ACM Press, Sydney, Australia (2013). https://doi.org/10.1145/2522848.2522865
38. Ogden, L.: Collaborative tasks, collaborative children: an analysis of reciprocity during peer interaction at key stage 1. Br. Edu. Res. J. **26**(2), 211–226 (2000)
39. Palmer, M., Gildea, D., Kingsbury, P.: The proposition bank: an annotated corpus of semantic roles. Comput. Linguist. **31**(1), 71–106 (2005)
40. Pustejovsky, J., Krishnaswamy, N.: VoxML: a visualization modeling language. In: Proceedings of the Tenth International Conference on Language Resources and Evaluation (LREC 2016), pp. 4606–4613. European Language Resources Association (ELRA), Portorož, Slovenia, May 2016. https://aclanthology.org/L16-1730
41. Pustejovsky, J., Krishnaswamy, N.: Embodied human computer interaction. KI-Künstliche Intelligenz **35**(3–4), 307–327 (2021)
42. Pustejovsky, J., Krishnaswamy, N.: Multimodal semantics for affordances and actions. In: Kurosu, M. (ed.) HCII 2022. LNCS, vol. 13302, pp. 137–160. Springer, Cham (2022). https://doi.org/10.1007/978-3-031-05311-5_9
43. Radford, A., Kim, J.W., Xu, T., Brockman, G., McLeavey, C., Sutskever, I.: Robust speech recognition via large-scale weak supervision (2022)
44. Rennie, C., Shome, R., Bekris, K.E., De Souza, A.F.: A dataset for improved RGBD-based object detection and pose estimation for warehouse pick-and-place. IEEE Rob. Autom. Lett. **1**(2), 1179–1185 (2016)
45. Ruan, X., Palansuriya, C., Constantin, A.: Affective dynamic based technique for facial emotion recognition (FER) to support intelligent tutors in education. In: Wang, N., Rebolledo-Mendez, G., Matsuda, N., Santos, O.C., Dimitrova, V. (eds.) AIED, vol. 13916, pp. 774–779. Springer, Cham (2023). https://doi.org/10.1007/978-3-031-36272-9_70
46. Sap, M., LeBras, R., Fried, D., Choi, Y.: Neural theory-of-mind? On the limits of social intelligence in large LMS. arXiv preprint arXiv:2210.13312 (2022)
47. Schneider, B., Pea, R.: Does seeing one another's gaze affect group dialogue? A computational approach. J. Learn. Anal. **2**(2), 107–133 (2015)
48. Stewart, A.E.B., Keirn, Z., D'Mello, S.K.: Multimodal modeling of collaborative problem-solving facets in triads. User Model. User-Adap. Inter. **31**(4), 713–751 (2021). https://doi.org/10.1007/s11257-021-09290-y
49. Sun, C., Shute, V.J., Stewart, A., Yonehiro, J., Duran, N., D'Mello, S.: Towards a generalized competency model of collaborative problem solving. Comput. Educ. **143**, 103672 (2020). https://www.sciencedirect.com/science/article/pii/S0360131519302258
50. Sun, C., et al.: The relationship between collaborative problem solving behaviors and solution outcomes in a game-based learning environment. Comput. Hum. Behav. **128**, 107120 (2022)
51. Terpstra, C., Khebour, I., Bradford, M., Wisniewski, B., Krishnaswamy, N., Blanchard, N.: How good is automatic segmentation as a multimodal discourse annotation aid? (2023)
52. Tomasello, M., et al.: Joint attention as social cognition. In: Joint Attention: Its Origins and Role in Development, vol. 103130, pp. 103–130 (1995)

53. Tong, Z., Song, Y., Wang, J., Wang, L.: VideoMAE: masked autoencoders are data-efficient learners for self-supervised video pre-training. In: Advances in Neural Information Processing Systems, vol. 35, pp. 10078–10093 (2022)
54. Törmänen, T., Järvenoja, H., Mänty, K.: Exploring groups' affective states during collaborative learning: what triggers activating affect on a group level? Educ. Tech. Res. Dev. **69**(5), 2523–2545 (2021)
55. Tyree, S., et al.: 6-DoF pose estimation of household objects for robotic manipulation: an accessible dataset and benchmark. In: IROS (2022)
56. Ullman, T.: Large language models fail on trivial alterations to theory-of-mind tasks. arXiv preprint arXiv:2302.08399 (2023)
57. VanderHoeven, H., Blanchard, N., Krishnaswamy, N.: Robust motion recognition using gesture phase annotation. In: Duffy, V.G. (ed.) HCII 2023. LNCS, vol. 14028, pp. 592–608. Springer, Cham (2023). https://doi.org/10.1007/978-3-031-35741-1_42
58. VanderHoeven, H., Blanchard, N., Krishnaswamy, N.: Point target detection for multimodal communication. In: Digital Human Modeling and Applications in Health, Safety, Ergonomics and Risk Management. Springer (2024)
59. Velikovich, L., Williams, I., Scheiner, J., Aleksic, P., Moreno, P., Riley, M.: Semantic lattice processing in contextual automatic speech recognition for google assistant, pp. 2222–2226 (2018). https://www.isca-speech.org/archive/Interspeech_2018/pdfs/2453.pdf
60. Wang, G., Manhardt, F., Tombari, F., Ji, X.: GDR-Net: geometry-guided direct regression network for monocular 6D object pose estimation. In: Proceedings of the IEEE/CVF Conference on Computer Vision and Pattern Recognition (CVPR), pp. 16611–16621, June 2021
61. Wolf, K., Naumann, A., Rohs, M., Müller, J.: A taxonomy of microinteractions: defining microgestures based on ergonomic and scenario-dependent requirements. In: Campos, P., Graham, N., Jorge, J., Nunes, N., Palanque, P., Winckler, M. (eds.) INTERACT 2011. LNCS, vol. 6946, pp. 559–575. Springer, Heidelberg (2011). https://doi.org/10.1007/978-3-642-23774-4_45
62. Zhang, F., et al.: MediaPipe hands: on-device real-time hand tracking. arXiv preprint arXiv:2006.10214 (2020)
63. Zoric, G., Smid, K., Pandzic, I.S.: Facial gestures: taxonomy and application of non-verbal, non-emotional facial displays for embodied conversational agents. In: Conversational Informatics: An Engineering Approach, pp. 161–182 (2007)

Intelligent Information Design Based on Human-Machine Collaboration in Lane Change Overtaking Scenarios

Jianmin Wang[1,2], Xinyi Cui[1], Qianwen Fu[1], Yuchen Wang[1,2], and Fang You[1,2(✉)]

[1] Car Interaction Design Lab, College of Arts and Media, Tongji University, Shanghai 201804, China
cuixinyi0905@163.com
[2] Shenzhen Research Institute, Sun Yat-Sen University, Shenzhen 518057, China

Abstract. In the realm of human-machine interaction, when vehicles possess the intelligence to autonomously perceive and make decisions, to a certain extent, they can be considered as collaborators with humans. As members of a human-machine intelligent collaboration team, team members need to attain mutual predictability. The absence of predictability may induce negative automation surprises in drivers, leading to discomfort, anxiety, or loss of trust. To facilitate collaboration in human-machine interaction, interface design should be grounded in human-machine cooperation methodologies to ensure that drivers maintain cognitive presence within the environment. In this context, we propose compensating for the lack of predictability in human-machine interaction by providing Human-Machine Interface (HMI) to enhance trust between agents. Departing from the perspective of Artificial Situational Awareness (ASA), we investigate the impact of HMI with and without perceptual decision information semantics on human-machine trust. Our findings suggest that delivering HMI with perceptual decision information can elevate the level of mutual predictability between humans and machines. Specifically, expressing perceptual information in the first phase of Situational Awareness (SA) proves to be more effective in preventing the erosion of driver trust and improving overall driver predictive capabilities.

Keywords: Human-Machine Collaboration · Predictability · Trust · Team SA

1 Introduction

In the contemporary landscape of intelligent automobiles, which have already assumed partial control of human driving tasks, achieving effective collaboration within human-machine intelligence teams hinges upon the precise comprehension of partner behaviors and the anticipation thereof. A pivotal challenge confronting intelligent agents is the intrinsic unpredictability inherent in human behavior. Cooperative human-machine interaction necessitates that team members possess a certain level of predictability regarding each other's actions. Given the divergent cognitive capabilities between humans and machines, such discrepancies may lead to asynchronous actions, potentially resulting

H. Mori and Y. Asahi (Eds.): HCII 2024, LNCS 14689, pp. 81–96, 2024.
https://doi.org/10.1007/978-3-031-60107-1_7

in a lack of understanding and predictability on the part of humans towards machine behaviors. Walch et al. [1] posited four fundamental prerequisites for the effective collaboration between humans and machines: mutual predictability, instructiveness, shared situational representation, and calibrated trust in automation. The former two requirements can be realized through interface design, thereby facilitating mutual predictability between humans and machines. Achieving mutual predictability necessitates that both human and machine counterparts within a team comprehend each other's ongoing activities and planned future actions. In support of human-machine collaboration, interface design should maintain humans within the loop, facilitating the exchange of information based on collaborative approaches. This forms the foundation for mutual predictability and team-shared situational awareness, where Human-Machine Interface (HMI) serves as the information carrier capable of displaying and conveying such information.

In the realm of autonomous vehicles, human supervision is imperative, requiring machines to timely convey transparent information to facilitate human monitoring and operation. Discrepancies between human cognition and machine cognition give rise to automation surprise when humans are unable to accurately predict machine behavior, consequently diminishing trust in machines and impeding effective human-machine collaboration. Existing research often leans towards machine safety algorithm models without due consideration for human sentiments. Thus, this paper proposes a psychological model-based HMI information design approach to bridge the cognitive gap in the prediction and judgment phase of human-machine interaction. Drawing upon a psychological model of machine cognition in the context of autonomous driving, this study devises an intelligent information push design. It evaluates and compares interface solutions derived from Augmented Reality Heads-Up Display (AR-HUD), culminating in the identification of superior predictive human-vehicle interface design strategies and guidelines. The findings affirm the capacity to enhance mutual predictability among team members from the machine's perspective.

The specific research questions addressed in this paper are as follows:

1. Cognitive mismatches between humans and machines can breed distrust; this can be mitigated by providing information through HMI.
2. Machine presentation of intentions, operational rationale, and predictive outcomes positively impacts human-machine collaboration.

2 Related Work

In addressing research questions 1 and 2, we undertook a comprehensive review of existing human-machine collaboration studies and observed a current scarcity in research efforts originating from the machine side to enhance mutual predictability. Finally, leveraging group situational awareness, we propose the provision of specific information to bridge the gap formed by the distrust resulting from cognitive mismatches.

2.1 Human-Vehicle Collaboration

The concept of human-machine collaboration, as initially defined by Flemisch et al. [2], extends to a scenario where vehicles primarily engage in cooperative use with humans.

In such a context, human-machine collaboration manifests as a synergistic interaction, wherein both entities form a collective intent based on shared perception. Walch [3] posits that collaborative interaction enables real-time communication and maneuver planning between two agents, aiming to enhance shared situational awareness and mutual comprehension of intentions and actions. Previously, Wang et al. proposed a comprehensive human-vehicle collaboration framework that guides the specific implementation of collaborative Human-Machine Interface (HMI) [4, 5]. This framework delineates interaction between humans and Automated Driving (AD) systems across four hierarchical levels: perception, prediction, planning, and control.

Given that cooperative behaviors in current Level 3 autonomous driving scenarios, such as lane changing, rely on a voluntary basis, the design and implementation of interactive concepts during the driving process to coordinate and enhance cooperation become pivotal research questions at Level 3. To ensure safe driving, drivers must trust intelligent systems, while machines need to provide drivers with all relevant information pertaining to the state and behavior of intelligent agents. Various studies on human-machine collaboration have indicated that the manner in which information is shared is integral for each agent to understand the actions of others. When collaboration integrates multiple levels, encompassing perception, analysis, decision-making, and action, the system becomes more cooperative. Thus, human-machine collaboration not only involves the coordination of actions but is also contingent upon the fusion of perceptual information, conflicts in the analysis of the current environment and state, and the coherence of various decision-making processes.

2.2 Trust

John D. Lee et al. [6] identified two fundamental components of human-machine collaboration: trust and transparency. They defined trust in automated systems as the "attitude of the agent in assisting human interaction goals in situations of uncertainty." Trust forms the basis for effective teamwork [7], and Hancock et al. [8] developed a robot trust model in which machine factors play a predominant role in shaping trust in human-machine systems. In the context of human interaction with intelligent machines, trust is considered a key element and a "fundamental enabling factor" [9] for human interaction with autonomous systems.

In the context of autonomous driving vehicle systems, trust can be extended to denote a driver's inclination to establish trust when the system promptly provides useful suggestions to reduce driver uncertainty. Ekman et al. proposed that trust formation is a dynamic process and introduced a guiding framework for implementing trust-related factors into HMI interfaces, encompassing usage phases, intelligent driving tasks, influencing factors, and task-level interpretation [10]. Trust has been explicitly identified as a crucial concept in Human-Machine Interaction (HMI): on one hand, users should trust artificial systems; on the other hand, devices must be capable of estimating the extent to which other agents trust them and the trustworthiness of other agents. Various solutions have been proposed in human-machine interaction scenarios [11, 12] to build robots capable of assessing the trust placed in them by human interactants. A comprehensive literature review indicates that trustworthiness in automation can be described based on features such as "purpose," "process," and "performance." However, these deep features of automation cannot be directly experienced, and for AI, the human-machine interface can be used to reveal these deep features of automation, making them apparent to humans, sometimes referred to as "transparent" or "observable" automation. The "purpose," "process," and "performance" features of automation determine the information requirements of the human-machine interface. In our study, the vehicle must convey information related to "purpose," "process," and "performance" through the interface throughout the entire lane-changing process.

2.3 Team Situation Awareness

In the pursuit of decision-making and execution towards shared goals within a human-machine team, the foundation lies in shared team cognition. Team cognition encompasses team perception, shared mental models, and situational awareness [13]. Among these concepts, the idea of shared mental models is one of the most frequently employed in team cognition [14]. Shared mental models aim to assess whether team members are "on the same page" as they share a common understanding of tasks, roles, interdependencies, and strategies [15]. Particularly, with the transition from manual to automated driving and the advent of Level 3 autonomous driving as an intermediate state, individuals may not engage in manual task execution, but they are required to participate in decision-making tasks and occasionally resume driving control. This necessitates that humans remain at the core of the human-machine environment, requiring drivers to comprehend both the external and internal vehicle conditions for accurate situational awareness [16].

To support human-machine collaboration, communication between humans and machines is crucial for shared situational awareness and achieving common goals [17]. Simultaneously, drivers may appreciate intelligent systems more when they are aware of the vehicle's perception, potentially enhancing trust in the system [18]. System actions should be fully observable, understandable, and reliable, and the human-machine interface should assist drivers in prediction. Therefore, developing a comprehensive strategy for collaborative human-machine interfaces is essential [19]. These interfaces should be designed to facilitate real-time communication between human drivers and automation, enabling the allocation of tasks between agents in a beneficial and safe manner. Collaborative interactions can facilitate real-time communication and maneuver planning between two agents, aimed at enhancing mutual understanding of intentions and actions. Through the Head-Up Display (HUD), we aim to convey essential visual information to drivers, elucidating the vehicle's perception content and how to integrate it to guide driving decisions [20].

There is currently a lack of extensive research on promoting mutual predictability from the machine's perspective. Therefore, we initiate research from the machine's viewpoint, integrating team situational awareness, shared situational awareness, and human-machine mental models. The objective is to explore entry points for machine-level predictive collaboration and the types of information that HMI should present. This approach seeks to enhance trust and situational awareness in human-machine collaboration.

3   Concept and System Design

This section initially elucidates the causes of cognitive differences in human-machine teams and the phenomenon of automation surprises, which may adversely impact team situational awareness, team trust, and system usability. Subsequently, starting from cognitive differences, and in conjunction with specific scenarios, it sequentially introduces the phenomenon of automation surprises and the situational awareness in human-machine teams. This then leads to the exploration of potential Human-Machine Interface (HMI) composite element designs that could mitigate the effects of these surprises.

3.1   Automation Surprise

Automation surprise refers to instances where the observed actions of a machine, as perceived by the driver, deviate from the driver's expectations. Such disparities result in a diminished level of trust in the human-machine collaborative system. In the context of autonomous driving, the occurrence of lane-changing maneuvers by the machine exhibits a certain degree of discrepancy from human predictions. During such intervals, intelligent information push through Augmented Reality Heads-Up Display (AR-HUD) should dynamically and promptly relay the machine's intentions to mitigate automation surprise, thereby enhancing predictability of machine behavior and trust in the machine.

Automation surprise phenomena can be categorized into two types: the absence of anticipated actions and the existence of unexpected actions. In scenarios involving lane changes, if the system autonomously changes lanes and leaves responsibility for blind spot detection to the driver, it results in a lack of comprehension on the part of the driver. Even if the driver agrees to the lane change, the system should verify the safety of such an action. Higher-level autonomous driving necessitates predictability, displaying forthcoming events such as lane changes or other maneuvering actions. The AR-HUD interface exhibits information about machine behavior, intentions, and strategies, aligning machine changes with human expectations and reducing inaccuracies in human predictions of machine behavior (uncertainty). As illustrated in Fig. 1. Human-computer bias, under Level 3 autonomous driving, where machine actions predominate, drivers anticipate the machine's action points, leading to deviations between human-predicted points and actual machine action points. In such situations, effective design leveraging HMI serves to convey the machine's mental model to the human user.

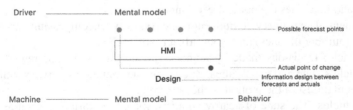

Fig. 1. Human-computer bias

3.2 Human-Machine Team Situation Awareness

The Team SA framework [4] comprises five essential components: the psychological models of humans and systems, various levels of Situation Awareness (SA), and environmental considerations involving the ego vehicle and other vehicles. Each component encompasses variables directly relevant to interaction design. For the purposes of this study, theoretical models integrating SA, Artificial SA (ASA), and environmental elements have been constructed, as illustrated in Fig. 2.

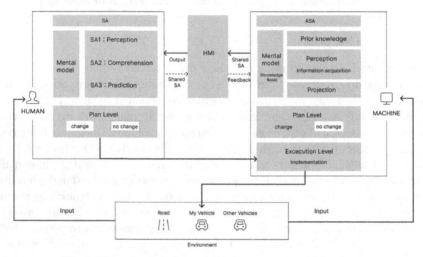

Fig. 2. Team SA Relations within the Human-Machine System

Figure 2 encompasses the following constituent elements:

1. Mental Models: Within Team Situational Awareness (SA), human and machine possess respective psychological models, grounded in knowledge-based repositories. Variables manifest during the information processing stages.
2. SA Hierarchy: For human agents, SA can be delineated into three stages: perception, comprehension, and prediction. In the case of machine agents, the capacity to predict future actions based on prior knowledge, perception, and prediction is termed Artificial Situation Awareness (ASA). Variables signify that the SA stages between humans and machines are not entirely congruent.
3. Environment: The primary component is the roadway, encompassing variables such as width (number of lanes) and type (urban roads/highways).
4. Host Vehicle: Decisions made by humans and machines are contingent upon the host vehicle's state and capabilities. The negotiated outcomes between humans and machines manifest in the motion of the host vehicle.
5. Other Vehicles: The state of nearby vehicles, including variables such as position, velocity, acceleration, and signals.

The figure illustrates the content of situational awareness, psychological models, HMI information transmission, and guidance planning and execution layers in Level

3 autonomous driving under human-machine collaboration. The role of HMI here is to receive the machine's shared SA. It outputs this information to the human before planning, intervening at the perception level to avoid potential safety issues arising from divergent/asynchronous human-machine planning.

3.3 HMI Portfolio Element Analysis

Building upon the deviations in situational awareness among human-machine team members, the previously outlined process is further detailed into points of conflict and the requisite supplementary Human-Machine Interface (HMI) information among team members, as shown in Table 1.Given that lane-changing scenarios represent a prototypical context for human-machine collaboration under Level 3 automation, this study opts to scrutinize the driving task processes and types of information pertinent to lane-changing scenarios. Subsequent experiments are then conducted based on this scenario.

Table 1. Potential Discrepancies between Human and Vehicle Situation Awareness

Agents	Perception	Comprehension	Projection
Driver	Sensory deficit	Misunderstand	Physical limitations Psychological limitations, such as mood swings affecting predictions Driving style effects
Vehicle	Loss of detection	Information transparency Mismatch between prior knowledge and skills	Insufficient a priori experience leads to errors in prediction calculations Difficulty in predicting the intentions of other vehicles

Figure 3 delineates the potential discrepancies between the anticipated lane-change points by humans and the actual lane-change points executed by the machine within a lane-changing scenario. Additionally, it highlights the types of information that the machine is required to provide, with all such information types emanating from the machine's Artificial Situation Awareness (ASA).

The design of information content and layout is predicated upon the knowledge state display requirements identified through the analysis of the Decision Ladder Model. Modeling diagnostic and decision tasks using the hierarchical structure defined by Rasmussen [17], the study explores the situational awareness and control tasks of humans and machines at various stages within the human-machine system activity flow, particularly in the context of the vehicle lane-changing scenario, as illustrated in Fig. 4.

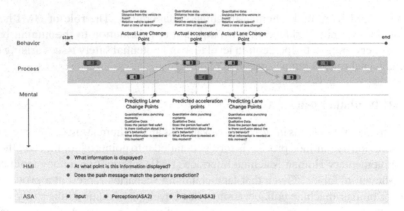

Fig. 3. Lane Change Scenario Analysis

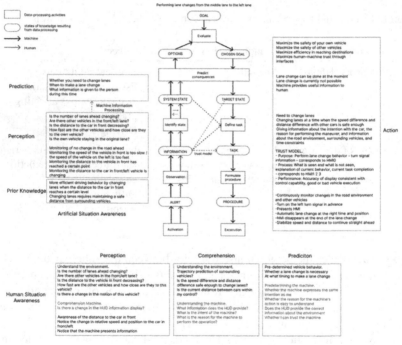

Fig. 4. Decision Ladder

4 Experiment

4.1 Experiment Design

Utilizing the driving simulator provided by the Automotive Interaction Lab, a scenario program was developed using Unity3D and C# to simulate lane-changing maneuvers on urban roads. Leveraging pre-experimental measurements of prediction times, a Heads-Up Display (HUD) interface prototype was crafted using video editing tools and integrated into the scene for temporal synchronization, as shown in Fig. 5 and Fig. 6. Informed by pre-experimental analysis, specific scenarios were defined as follows:

1. Impact of Front Vehicle on Lane Change:The machine's prediction for lane change lags behind that of the human.The vehicle ahead is traveling at 50 km/h, while the rear-left vehicle is moving at a speed below 60 km/h and maintains a substantial distance from the host vehicle. The host vehicle's speed is set at 60 km/h.
2. Impact of Left Vehicle on Lane Change:The machine's prediction for lane change precedes that of the human.Conditions: Both the front vehicle and the host vehicle are moving at 60 km/h. The rear-left vehicle is traveling at a speed of 70 km/h. The host vehicle follows the front vehicle until the left vehicle passes, and then initiates the lane change.

Fig. 5. Initial vehicle trajectory setup and adjustments in Unity3D

Employing the AH analysis method, a secondary refinement was conducted on the functional scenarios and information presentation formats, as depicted in Fig. 7. In conjunction with the experimental scenarios, it was determined that the pertinent information to be displayed includes turn signal status, relative distances to surrounding vehicles, and the level of hazard associated with the lane change.

In conjunction with information content and presentation methods, as well as the intelligent situational awareness levels represented by each type of information, Table 1 is formulated to elucidate the visualization, meaning, associated hierarchy, occurrence timing, and 3D type of each information category. Subsequently, a single-factor controlled experiment was conducted, with the independent variable being different combinations

Fig. 6. Simulated experimental scenario with predefined vehicle behaviors and overlay of 3D visual interface

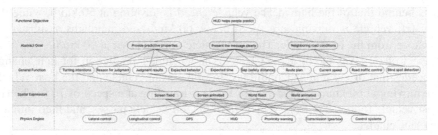

Fig. 7. AH Analysis – HUD Assisting Prediction

of HMI elements (HMI1; HMI2; HMI3). The dependent variables encompass trust, situational awareness, and system usability. A blank control labeled as HMI0 was set as a baseline, with specific details for HMI0 through HMI3 outlined in Table 3.

We posit the following hypotheses:

- H1: Cognitive mismatches between humans and machines engender a sense of distrust.
- H2: Predictive collaboration in autonomous driving is considered beneficial, and the provision of information through HMI enhances human predictability of machine behavior.
- H3: The presentation of machine intentions, operational rationale, and predictive outcomes to humans by the machine positively influences human-machine collaboration (Table 2).

The specific tasks were as follows: Participants initially engaged in simulated manual marking of lane-changing points to ascertain their predictive timing. Video overlays were created based on their predicted points, and participants watched the concatenated eight videos. Each participant experienced all four HMIs (HMI0-HMI3) in a complete manner, with the video sequence arranged according to Latin square allocation to minimize the impact of learning effects. After each viewing session, participants completed relevant questionnaires, details of which are outlined in Table 4 regarding content and metric roles. Subsequent to completing all experiments, participants underwent semi-structured interviews.

Table 2. HMI Information Element Types

	Icon	Explanation	ASA Hierarchy	Time of Occurrence	3D Type
(1)		Turning information	Input	Appears as soon as the car in front/left appears and disappears at the end of the lane change	Screen fixed
(2)		Relative distance to vehicle in front	Perception(ASA2)	Appears as soon as the car in front appears, disappears 2s before changing lanes	World animated
(3)		Relative distance to the rear vehicle on the left	Perception(ASA2)	Appears before this vehicle changes lanes and disappears when the left vehicle comes into view ahead	World animated
(4)		Lane Change Guidance	Projection(ASA3)	Appears before lane change, disappears after successful lane change	World animated

Table 3. HMI combinations and experimental group design

Group	(1)	(2)/(3)	(4)	Combined approach (front vehicle affecting lane change scenarios)	Combined approach (left rear vehicle impact lane change scenario)	Note
HMI0	√	/	/	(1)	(1)	Default display of steering intent
HMI1	√	√	/	(1) + (2)	(1) + (3)	
HMI2	√	/	√	(1) + (4)	(1) + (4)	
HMI3	√	√	√	(1) + (2) + (4)	(1) + (3) + (4)	

4.2 Experiment Results

Subjective assessment data collected using scales (Trust, SART, SUS) are depicted in Fig. 8, Fig. 9 and Fig. 10 In the independent variable rows, "HMI1-HMI3" refers to different combinations of HMI elements, while "frontcar/leftcar" indicates the impact of the front vehicle and the left rear vehicle on lane-changing, respectively.

During the interviews, the majority of participants expressed a tendency to change lanes when the current vehicle speed is perceived as excessively slow, dedicating time to assess the safety of the environment. All respondents acknowledged the importance of

Table 4. Measurement Metrics

Evaluation Dimension	Evaluation Indicators	Role of indicators
Subjective Scale	Trust	Measuring subjects' trust in the effective implementation of automation
	SUS	Measures subjects' assessment of the usability of the system, including effectiveness, efficiency, and satisfaction
	SART	A simple post-test subjective evaluation (self-evaluation) technique that triggers a subjective opinion of one's level of awareness during task performance
Semi-open interviews	/	Investigating subjects' primary focus during lane changes

monitoring relative distances and speeds with surrounding vehicles, with a higher priority placed on the conditions of vehicles in the target lane to inform lane-changing decisions. Most participants emphasized the significance of relative distance as a primary factor, and currently, they retain greater trust in their own manual lane-changing, casting doubt on the safety of automated lane changes. Some participants suggested that semantic understanding could be further optimized, but the prevailing sentiment was that the provision of information yielded a more favorable experience compared to control groups without information. Among the crucial aspects highlighted was the communication of perceptual information about other vehicles. Additionally, some participants suggested the incorporation of feedback channels such as sound or tactile sensations to enhance the overall user experience.

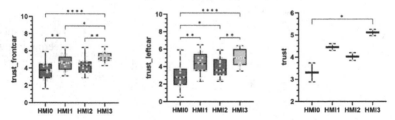

Fig. 8. Trust grades. From left to right, they represent the front car influencing scenario, left car influencing scenario, and their combination

4.3   Results Discussion

Trust. Regarding HMI0 and HMI1–3, the comparative variable involves the presence or absence of HMI for information supplementation, aiming to explore the impact of information supplementation on human perception. Under the condition of no supplementary information (HMI0), trust levels in both scenarios remained at a relatively

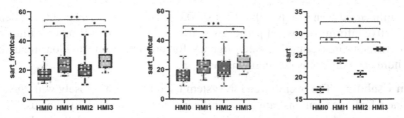

Fig. 9. SART grades. From left to right, they represent the front car influencing scenario, left car influencing scenario, and their combination

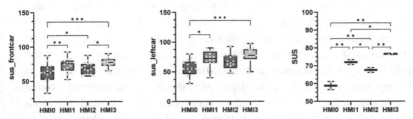

Fig. 10. SUS grades. From left to right, they represent the front car influencing scenario, left car influencing scenario, and their combination

low level (3.5/7), corroborating our hypothesis H1 that cognitive mismatches between humans and machines elicit distrust. In comparison to HMI0, HMI1–3 demonstrated varying degrees of improvement, with HMI1 and HMI3 exhibiting more significant enhancement. This outcome supports hypothesis H2, suggesting that predictive collaboration in autonomous driving is considered beneficial, and providing information through HMI enhances human predictability of machine behavior. The responses to these two hypotheses also validate Research Question 1: Cognitive mismatches between humans and machines engender distrust, which can be mitigated through information provision via HMI. Simultaneously, the inter-group comparisons address Research Question 2.

Team Situation Awareness. The quantity and types of information displayed on the Head-Up Display (HUD) have varying impacts on participants' situational awareness. Using no HUD information (HMI0) as a blank control, providing HMI1 and HMI3 led to a significant enhancement in participants' situational awareness scores. This conclusion supports hypothesis H2, suggesting that improvements in team situational awareness have a positive impact on human-machine collaboration. However, for HMI2, we observed only marginal improvement when presenting solely machine prediction information, and in some instances, it could even reduce participants' situational awareness. In comparison to HMI1, HMI3, as a composite information category, exhibited a significant increase in scores, and post-experiment interviews revealed a general preference among participants for composite information.

In scenarios influenced by the front and left vehicles, the differences in situational awareness were minimal, confirming a certain degree of transferability. Notably, regarding situational awareness performance, the provision of HMI information in the left vehicle-influenced scenario led to a more significant improvement compared to the front vehicle-influenced scenario ($p = 0.0017 < 0.0037$). This suggests a heightened demand for predictive information when participants are unable to perceive other traffic conditions, potentially indicating a greater urgency for predictive information in situations where human autonomous perception is lacking.

System Usability. The overall trend in system usability aligns closely with the aforementioned findings, demonstrating a significant improvement in system usability ($p < 0.0001$), particularly when information supplementation, especially in the form of combined predictive information, is applied. Additionally, we observed a correlation between user satisfaction with the system and the transparency of information presentation, extending from hypothesis H3, emphasizing the necessity of appropriate interface transparency design. Participants expressed a desire to understand the system's current recognition, prediction, and planning, as well as the machine's current processes. Participants evaluated the system's capabilities and trustworthiness based on the current driving behavior of the machine and the information provided, contrasting with their own driving style and habits. This aligns with the human situational awareness process, emphasizing that individuals need to comprehend the information provided by the machine to make more accurate predictions. The closer the machine's perception and behavior align with the mental model of the human, the more likely it is to be used and accepted.

5 Conclusion

In this study, we extended a framework that combines human-machine collaboration, situational awareness, and the internal information processing mechanisms of the machine. Through a comprehensive analysis of prior research, we identified, implemented, and evaluated the entry points for predictive-level supplementation. Specifically, presenting composite information transparently to humans from the machine's Artificial Situation Awareness (ASA) can effectively address human predictive biases at opportune moments. The information provided includes the machine's perception, predictive information, and the basis for the machine's information processing. Our practical implementation demonstrated that delivering machine situational awareness information through an Augmented Reality Head-Up Display (AR-HUD) enhances the predictability of the machine and significantly improves trust between humans and machines, thereby enhancing human situational awareness. Throughout the experimental process, various recommendations were identified to enhance the usability and user experience of predictive-level collaboration. For instance, only specific information or combinations of information prove effective for supplementation, and visual or auditory cues are essential for transitioning between these pieces of information to improve system usability and acceptance. It is worth noting that the manual adjustment of the human-machine gap by experimenters in the experiments may not entirely replicate real-world human-machine discrepancies. Additionally, the use of a static driving simulator may impact the comfort and perception levels of participants. In future research, we plan to deepen this concept by enhancing information transparency and evaluating the impact of different information presentation timings on the predictability of human-machine collaboration.

References

1. Walch, M., Woide, M., Mühl, K., Baumann, M., Weber, M.: Cooperative overtaking: overcoming automated vehicles' obstructed sensor range via driver help (2019). https://doi.org/10.1145/3342197.3344531

2. Flemisch, F.O., Bengler, K., Bubb, H., Winner, H., Bruder, R.: Towards cooperative guidance and control of highly automated vehicles: h-mode and conduct-by-wire. Ergonomics 57, 343–360 (2014). https://doi.org/10.1080/00140139.2013.869355

3. Walch, M., Mühl, K., Kraus, J., Stoll, T., Baumann, M., Weber, M.: From car-driver-handovers to cooperative interfaces: visions for driver – vehicle interaction in automated driving (2017). https://doi.org/10.1007/978-3-319-49448-7_10

4. Wang, C.: A framework of the non-critical spontaneous intervention in highly automated driving scenarios (2019). https://doi.org/10.1145/3349263.3351326

5. Wang, C., Krüger, M., Wiebel-Herboth, C.B.: "Watch out!": prediction-level intervention for automated driving (2020). https://doi.org/10.1145/3409120.3410652

6. Lee, J.D., See, K.A.: Trust in automation: designing for appropriate reliance. Hum. Factors 46, 50–80 (2004). https://doi.org/10.1518/hfes.46.1.50_30392

7. Hou, M., Ho, G., Dunwoody, D.: Impacts: a trust model for human-autonomy teaming. Human-Intell. Syst. Integrat. (Online) 3, 79–97 (2021). https://doi.org/10.1007/s42454-020-00023-x

8. Hancock, P.A., Billings, D.R., Oleson, K.E., Chen, J.Y., De Visser, E., Parasuraman,R,: A meta-analysis of factors influencing the development of human-robot trust (2021)

9. Baber, C.: Intelligent adaptive systems: an interaction-centred design perspective. Ergonomics 60, 1458–1459 (2017). https://doi.org/10.1080/00140139.2017.1330498

10. Ekman, F., Johansson, M., Sochor, J.: Creating appropriate trust in automated vehicle systems: a framework for hmi design. Ieee T. Hum. -Mach. Syst. 48, 95–101 (2018). https://doi.org/10.1109/THMS.2017.2776209

11. Sapienza, A., Cantucci, F., Falcone, R.: Modeling interaction in human–machine systems: a trust and trustworthiness approach. Automation 3, 242–257 (2022). https://doi.org/10.3390/automation3020012

12. Hu, W., Akash, K., Reid, T., Jain, N.: Computational modeling of the dynamics of human trust during human–machine interactions. Ieee T. Hum. -Mach. Syst. 49, 485–497 (2019). https://doi.org/10.1109/THMS.2018.2874188

13. Cooke, N.J., Salas, E., Cannon-Bowers, J.A., Stout, R.J.: Measuring team knowledge. Human Fact. 42(1), 151–173 (2000)

14. Schelble, B.G., Flathmann, C., Mcneese, N.J., Freeman, G., Mallick, R.: Let's think together! assessing shared mental models, performance, and trust in human-agent teams. Proc. ACM Hum.-Comput. Interact. 6, 1–29 (2022). https://doi.org/10.1145/3492832

15. Mohammed, S., Ferzandi, L., Hamilton, K.: Metaphor no more: a 15-year review of the team mental model construct. J. Manag. 36(4), 876–910 (2010). https://doi.org/10.1177/0149206309356804

16. Endsley, M.R.: Toward a theory of situation awareness in dynamic systems. Hum. Fact. J. Hum. Fact. Ergon. Soc. 37, 32–64 (1995). https://doi.org/10.1518/001872095779049543

17. Debernard, S., Chauvin, C., Pokam, R., Langlois, S.: Designing human-machine interface for autonomous vehicles. IFAC-PapersOnLine 49(19), 609–614 (2016). https://doi.org/10.1016/j.ifacol.2016.10.629

18. Lindemann, P., Lee, T., Rigoll, G.: Catch my drift: elevating situation awareness for highly automated driving with an explanatory windshield display user interface. Multimodal Technol. Interact. 2, 71 (2018). https://doi.org/10.3390/mti2040071

19. Pacaux-Lemoine, M., Flemisch, F.: Layers of shared and cooperative control, assistance and automation. IFAC-PapersOnLine **49**, 159–164 (2016). https://doi.org/10.1016/j.ifacol.2016.10.479
20. Wintersberger, P., Riener, A.: Trust in technology as a safety aspect in highly automated driving. I-Com **15**, 297–310 (2016). https://doi.org/10.1515/icom-2016-0034

Information and Service Design

Dynamic Labeling: A Control System for Labeling Styles in Image Annotation Tasks

Chia-Ming Chang[1]($\boxtimes$), Yi He[2], Xusheng Du[2], Xi Yang[3], and Haoran Xie[2]

[1] The University of Tokyo, Tokyo, Japan
info@chiamingchang.com
[2] Japan Advanced Institute of Science and Technology, Ishikawa, Japan
[3] Jilin University, Jilin, China

Abstract. Labeling style affects labeling efficiency and quality in image annotation tasks. For example, a "label quickly" style can increase labeling efficiency when the data are easy, and a "label carefully" style can increase label quality when the data are difficult. However, the selection of an appropriate labeling style is difficult as different annotators have different experiences and domain knowledge, affecting their subjective feelings of data difficulties (for example, User 1 feels Data A to be easy, while User 2 feels it difficult). In this paper, we propose "Dynamic Labeling" as a control system for labeling styles used in image-labeling tasks. Our control system analyzes the labeling behaviors of annotators (i.e., label selection time) and dynamically assigns an appropriate labeling style (label quickly or label carefully). We conducted a user study to compare a conventional "non-dynamic" and the proposed "dynamic" labeling approaches for an image-labeling task. The results suggest that Dynamic Labeling increased the label quality and labeling efficiency.

Keywords: Data Annotation · Labeling Styles · Annotator Behaviors · Crowdsourcing · Dynamic Control System

1 Introduction

Data annotation is a labor-intensive process that often relies on crowdsourcing platforms, such as Amazon's Mechanical Turk, where task requesters can recruit workers to assist with their annotation tasks [61]. Although crowdsourcing is a typical solution for annotation tasks of large datasets, data quality is often an issue in such situations [17, 24, 28, 29, 33]. Several studies have proposed annotation interfaces [7, 13, 51, 60, 66], and workflows [4, 14, 16, 23, 47, 68] to address this quality issue. A previous study [15] investigated the effect of label styles used by annotators in an image labeling task with different data difficulties. It showed that a "label quickly" style could increase labeling efficiency (i.e., less time cost) when the data were easy, and a "label carefully" style could increase label quality (i.e., success in selecting an appropriate label) when the data were difficult; but, the labeling styles were "fixed" during the entire labeling process. This may not be efficient because a labeling task may contain both easy and difficult data. Hence, it becomes difficult to select an appropriate labeling style as different annotators have different experiences and domain knowledge that may affect their subjective feelings of data difficulties (e.g., User 1 feels Data A to be easy, while User 2 feels it difficult).

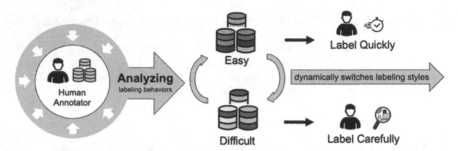

Fig. 1. Concept of Dynamic Labeling.

In this study, we propose a process called Dynamic Labeling, a control system for labeling styles used in image labeling tasks which can dynamically control the labeling styles during the labeling process. Figure 1 illustrates the concept of Dynamic Labeling. First, the system observes and analyzes the labeling behavior of the annotator (i.e., the label selection time) during the labeling process. Second, the system classifies the data (images) into easy and difficult groups based on the analysis. Third, when the data are defined as "easy," the system assigns a "label quickly" style to the annotator and when the data are defined as "difficult," a "label carefully" style is assigned. During the labeling process, the system dynamically switches the two labeling styles based on data difficulties. Our hypothesis is that the proposed "dynamic" labeling approach can increase the label quality and labeling efficiency in an image-labeling task by providing customized labeling styles for each individual annotator.

We conducted a user study (n = 40) to compare the proposed "dynamic" labeling approach with the conventional "non-dynamic" labeling approach in an image-labeling task. The results showed that the proposed "dynamic" labeling approach increased label quality (7% higher) and labeling efficiency (15% faster). Additionally, there was a temporal effect in the annotation accuracy when using the "dynamic" labeling approach, and the labeling process got faster in this approach. The three main contributions of this study are as follows.

- Dynamic Labeling, a control system for dynamically switching between "label quickly" and "label carefully" styles in a manual image-labeling task.
- A user study comparing the proposed "dynamic" labeling approach with the conventional "non-dynamic" labeling approach in an image-labeling task, demonstrating the benefits of the "dynamic" labeling approach.
- Discussion of temporal effects on annotation accuracy and task completion time in Dynamic Labeling.

2 Related Work

2.1 Crowdsourcing Data Annotation

Manual data annotation is one of the most important parts of machine learning [35, 43, 48]. Using a large amount of data is one way to improve the performance of machine learning [15]. For example, ImageNet [18], AudioSet [26], and YouTube-8M [1] are three popular and large datasets manually annotated by humans. Manual data annotation is a labor-intensive process that often relies on crowdsourcing platforms, such as Amazon's Mechanical Turk [30, 49], as expert annotators are not always available [36, 46]. However, label quality is a critical issue when crowdsourcing an annotation task [17, 24, 28, 29, 33, 41].

Many studies have proposed various annotation tools to address the challenge of manual data annotation, such as selecting and training competent crowd workers [19, 20, 31, 67], conducting dynamic task assignments [10, 57], and motivating crowd workers by designing payment structures [27, 44, 50]. Nguyen et al. [45] proposed a joint aggregation and clustering model to explicitly explain worker mistakes, demonstrating that users could better predict the instances in which workers might make mistakes, given the cluster output from their model. Russell et al. [51, 56] proposed a web-based image annotation tool, LabelMe, which allowed annotators to "share" annotation results instantly with other annotators. Von Ahn et al. [58] proposed an image annotation tool called ESP that was integrated with computer games and allowed annotators to complete annotation tasks while playing games. Bianco et al. [8] proposed iVAT, a video annotation tool that supported manual, semiautomatic, and automatic annotations. Tang et al. [70] introduced "PDFChatAnnotator", a semiautomatic human-LLM tool for document annotation. Zhou et al. [69] proposed "RelRoll", a relative labeling interface highlighting emotion-changing sentences and an approach to estimating absolute labels from relative labels. OneLabeler [59] supports the configuration and composition of common software modules through visual programming to build diverse data labeling tools. Spatial Labeling [13] proposes a complementary solution, based on the concept of "self-improvement," to support annotators to work alone and improve label quality by themselves.

Most of these studies focused on improving label quality by designing efficient annotation tools and interfaces. Chang et al. [15] focused on the cognitive psychology of data annotation and explored the effects of labeling styles used in a manual image annotation task. The results indicated that both quick and careful labeling styles had advantages and disadvantages in terms of annotation efficiency, label quality, and machine learning performance. In this study, we explore the same concept and investigate the use of different labeling styles based on the behaviors of the annotators.

2.2 Annotation Workflow and Annotator Behaviors

In addition to annotation tools, annotation workflows are alternative solutions for improving annotation quality. Chang et al. [14] introduced a hierarchical task assignment approach to reduce the workload by decomposing a labeling task into multiple steps and assigning them to multiple annotators. Otani et al. [47] introduced a label aggregation method for hierarchical classification tasks to classify annotations based on the annotator tagging data in a hierarchical structure. Interactive concept learning can guide users in assigning labels [2, 3, 25] and interactive methods using data visualization can assist experts in label verification [42]. Additionally, many studies have proposed solutions to improve the quality of non-expert annotations by exploiting the collaborative character of crowdsourcing. Revolt [16] is a crowdsourcing collaborative annotation approach based on an expert annotation workflow (label–check–revise) to improve the quality of data annotation of non-experts. Baba et al. [4] introduced two types of labeling workflows to improve annotation quality by allowing multiple annotators to participate in the same annotation task in different ways. Sunahase et al. [55] proposed Pairwise HITS, which allowed annotators to compare pairs of data labels and select the best for annotation quality assessment. Fang et al. [23] introduced a two-round workflow. In the first round, the annotator selected a label for the target image. In the second round, the best label for the image was decided by referring to multiple labels from the first round. Schilling et al. [54] presented an evolved concept of label inspection and post-processing, implemented, and directed within the annotation process to increase label quality.

Annotator behavior may affect label quality and efficiency [52]. Real-time crowd-sourcing technologies have been widely explored to understand annotator behaviors [12, 21, 32, 53]. Lasecki et al. [39] introduced the idea of involving synchronous crowds in continuous real-time tasks by using the crowd to collectively control an existing user interface as if they were one person. The Retainer model [6, 22] analyzes crowdsourcing from a mathematical perspective, considering the trade-off between the cost of hiring workers to respond immediately when asked to perform a task and the expected waiting time for a new task. Safran et al. [53] proposed two real-time recommendation algorithms for crowdsourcing systems, TOP-K-T (calculating the most suitable task for a worker) and TOP-K-W (calculating the most suitable worker for the requested task), which were useful for real-time performance. CRITICAl [9] combined crowdsourcing with task assignment techniques to determine the most suitable group of human workers for distributing a set of tasks. In addition, many studies minimized the response time of crowdsourcing user interfaces [5, 8, 11, 37, 40] or increased the speed of data collection [34, 38] to meet the requirements of real-time crowdsourcing tasks.

In this study, we investigated a similar concept and developed a "real-time" technique to observe and analyze the behaviors of annotators (i.e., label selection time) and dynamically control the labeling styles used during an annotation task. We believe that this can benefit crowdsourcing of data annotation tasks by improving label quality and labeling efficiency.

3   Dynamic Labeling

We propose "Dynamic Labeling," a dynamic control system of labeling styles during an image-labeling task. The system dynamically assigns an appropriate labeling style (label quickly or carefully) to the annotator during the labeling process based on the labeling behavior of the annotator (i.e., label selection time). If the system detects that the annotator spent a shorter time selecting a label (i.e., is more confident in the label selection), it assigns a "label quickly" style the next time the annotator selects this label.

If the system detects that the annotator spent a longer time selecting a label (i.e., is less confident in the label selection), the system assigns a "label carefully" style to the annotator the next time the label is selected. The basic hypothesis is that a "label quickly" style can increase labeling efficiency when the target images are easy for the annotator, and a "label carefully" style can increase label quality when the target images are difficult for the annotator.

3.1 Dynamic Control Algorithm

Our Dynamic Labeling system (algorithm) automatically measures the time that the annotator spends on each image-labeling task (i.e., selecting an appropriate label for an image). The timer starts when an image is displayed and stops when the image is given a label (i.e., the "Next Image" button is pressed). The recorded time belongs to the category of the selected label, regardless of whether the label selection is correct (i.e., there is no ground truth in a realistic task). The system calculates the overall average time of label selection in all label categories and the average time of label selection in each label category. Below is the Algorithm used to calculate the average labeling time for Dynamic Labeling.

> For all n images,   for image $i(i \in [1, n])$
>
> the time spend is $t_i^j > 0$ seconds, here, i means the i-th image, j
>
> means the selected label is j-th label in label set $\{L_1, ..., L_m\}$, and
>
> totally we have m types of labels.
>
>
> so,
>
> the overall time average $T_{avg} = (\sum_{i=0}^{i=n} t_i^j)/n$ for any j.
>
> for j-th label, the average time of Label L_j is $T_{avg}^j = (\sum t_i^{k=j})/$
>
> n_j , where n_j is the number of j-th label in all annotation.

The overall average time and the label average time dynamically changed throughout the entire process based on the time spent by the annotator on each image-labeling task. The overall average time is used as the baseline to define the "difficult" and "easy" label categories. A label is classified as "difficult" if the label average time is longer than the overall average time and "easy" if the label average time is shorter than the overall average time. The system then dynamically assigns an appropriate labeling style to the annotator, as shown in Fig. 2.

Table 1 presents an example of how to calculate the overall average time and the label average time. The overall average time is 4.8 s $((8 + 3 + 5 + 2 + 6)/5 = 4.8)$. The average time of Label A is 7 s $((8 + 6)/2 = 7)$, the average time of Label B is 3.5 s $((5 + 2)/2 = 3.5)$, and Label C is 3 s.

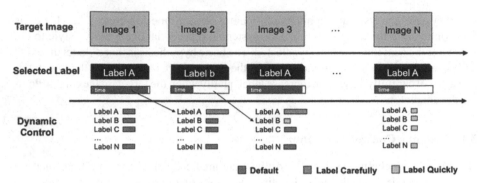

Fig. 2. Workflow of Dynamic Labeling.

Table 1. Example of the overall average time and the average time of each label category.

Target Image	Selected Label	Time Spend
Image 1	Label A	8 s
Image 2	Label C	3 s
Image 3	Label B	5 s
Image 4	Label B	2 s
Image 5	Label A	1 s

3.2 Label Quickly and Label Carefully Styles

The two labeling styles (label quickly and label carefully) used in this study refer to a study [15] that investigated the effect of quick and careful labeling styles in image-labeling tasks. This study showed that "label quickly" was advantageous (i.e., required less time) when the data were easy, while "label carefully" was advantageous (i.e., obtained higher data quality) when the data were difficult. We adopted the same concept with some modifications to match our research scope. The previous study designed a time limit of 5 s for "label quickly" style and no time limit for "label carefully" in their user study. In this study, we designed a specific workflow to define "label quickly" and "label carefully".

Figure 3 shows a screenshot of the baseline image-labeling system designed for our user study. The left side of the interface lists the labels (12 cat breeds). The right side of the interface presents the target image that must be labeled. The user must select an appropriate label for the target image from the list of labels which this is displayed under the target image. The user then clicks "Next Image" to label the next image. The user can also change the selected label before moving to the next image. However, they are not allowed to return to previous images.

Figure 4 shows a screenshot of the "label quickly" system. The interface is almost identical to that of the baseline labeling system (Fig. 3). The only difference is that the interface of "label quickly" style does not contain a "Next Image" button. After selecting

Fig. 3. Screenshot of the annotation tool/system (baseline).

a label for a target image, it automatically moves to the next target image. This can reduce the operating time. However, the users are not allowed to change the selected labels. We define this as the "label quickly" style and believe that this "small but specific" design can increase labeling efficiency without reducing the label quality when the data are easy.

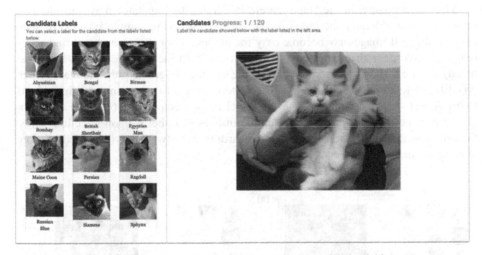

Fig. 4. Screenshot of the annotation tool/system (label quickly).

Figure 5 shows a screenshot of the "label carefully" system. The interface is similar to that of the baseline labeling system (Fig. 3) but additional sample images are provided by the interface for the selected label. After selecting a label for the target image, the interface shows five sample images of the selected label (i.e., provided additional information and cues of the cat breed). This allowed the user to think carefully by observing the sample images before moving on to the next image. The user can switch between similar labels (confusing labels) and compare them before making the final decision. We define this as the "label carefully" style and believe that this style can increase the label quality when the data are difficult.

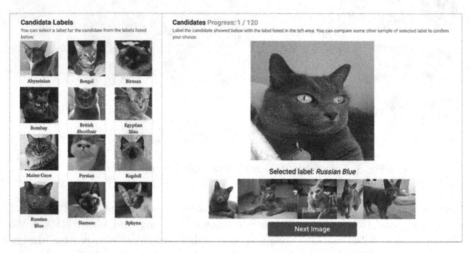

Fig. 5. Screenshot of the annotation tool/system (label carefully).

More importantly, in the "label carefully" style, the annotator may gain domain knowledge (i.e., identify the breed of the cat) by observing sample images. In such cases, a difficult image may become easy for the annotator if the annotator finds cues (e.g., eye color, ear shape, or body style) that can help identify the correct label (cat breed). Figure 6 shows an example of how the sample images help the annotator when it is difficult to identify the target image. As seen in Fig. 6(a), the annotator first selects Label A and sees five sample images of Label A. As seen in Fig. 6(b), the annotator also considers Label B and sees five sample images of Label B upon selection. Thus, the annotator can obtain more information regarding these two labels (cat breeds) before making the final decision.

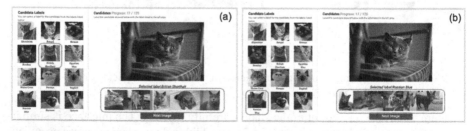

Fig. 6. Example of observing sample images between two confusing cat breeds.

4   User Study

A user study was conducted to compare the conventional "non-dynamic" and the proposed "dynamic" labeling approaches in an image-labeling task (i.e., to select an appropriate cat breed label for a cat image). Our hypothesis is that the proposed "dynamic" labeling approach can increase label quality without reducing labeling efficiency (i.e., spending longer time completing the task).

4.1   Participants

We recruited forty participants (20 men and 20 women, aged 18–49 years) using Amazon Mechanical Turk (MTurk) [62]. All participants were MTurk Master Workers with a 98% HIT approval rate [62]. None of the participants had professional knowledge about cat breeds or have (or had) cats as pets. We paid $10 to each participant to participate in the user evaluation (task of approximately 15–30 min).

4.2   Image Dataset

The Oxford IIIT Pet dataset was used for image-labeling tasks [60]. This image dataset contained 37 different breeds of cats and dogs with a total of 7,349 images. To satisfy our research requirements, we used cat images containing 12 cat breeds (labels). A total of 120 images were used as the dataset in the user study with 10 randomly-selected images of each cat breed (label). The order of the 120 images was randomly presented in the labeling task. Table 2 lists the 12 cat breeds (labels).

Table 2. Image dataset of the 12 cat breeds (labels).

Abyssinian	Bengal	Birman	Bombay
British Shorthair	Egyptian Mau	Maine Coon	Persian
Ragdoll	Russian Blue	Siamese	Sphynx

Manual image labeling is time consuming. To evaluate the proposed approach, we designed a small-scale labeling task to maintain a reasonable evaluation duration. The labeling task involved labeling 120 cat images by selecting an appropriate cat breed label (from the list of 12 cat breeds/12 labels). It took less than one hour to complete the entire user study. A "between-subjects" method was used, where half of the participants were asked to complete the given labeling task via a conventional "non-dynamic" labeling approach and the other half were asked to use the proposed "dynamic" labeling approach. The interface of the "non-dynamic" labeling approach was same as the baseline image labeling system described above (Fig. 2). The interface of the "dynamic" labeling approach was the "label quickly" (Fig. 3) and "label carefully" (Fig. 4) image-labeling systems.

4.3 Procedure

The user study consisted of three parts: (1) instructions and trial (5–10 min), (2) image-labeling tasks (10–15 min), and (3) questionnaire survey (3–5 min). We completed the entire evaluation process in approximately 15–30 min. Initially, we gave the participants instructions which explained the details of the user evaluation process, labeling tasks, and labeling interfaces. This included a step-by-step demonstration of how to use the labeling interfaces to complete the given image-labeling tasks. After the instructions, the participants were allowed to practice a small labeling task (to label 10 images). Participants were encouraged to select a label as appropriately as possible (they were informed that there was no time restriction in the user evaluation process). Participants were asked to concentrate on the tasks until they completed them. After completing the labeling task, they were asked to complete a questionnaire about the labeling tasks.

4.4 Measurement

Task Performance. In the user study, the labeling system automatically recorded and measured the time taken and the accuracy (i.e., success in selecting an appropriate label for an image) of the labeling task completed by the participants. The timer started when the participants pressed on the "Start" button on the task page and stopped when they selected a label for the last image.

Questionnaire. Following the evaluation of the labeling task, participants were asked to answer a questionnaire regarding the labeling approach used in the image-labeling task. The questions asked to the participants who used the "dynamic" labeling approach were:

Q1 Do you agree that the "label quickly" style was assigned to the tasks that you felt were easy?

Q2 Do you agree that the "label carefully" style was assigned to the tasks that you felt were difficult?

Q3 Do you agree that the "label quickly" style is efficient when the images are easy? Why?

Q4 Do you agree that the "label carefully" style is helpful when the images are difficult? Why?

Q5 Do you agree that you learned something (some cues) from the sample images? Please provide a specific example.

5 Results

5.1 Annotation Accuracy

Figure 7 shows the accuracy (i.e., success in selecting an appropriate cat breed label for a cat image) of the labeling tasks (label 120 images) completed by the participants using the "non-dynamic" and "dynamic" labeling approaches. The results indicate that the accuracies of the "non-dynamic" and "dynamic" labeling approaches were 67.12% and 74.51%, respectively. Accuracy analysis using a paired t-test indicated a significant difference ($p < 0.01$) between the two labeling approaches. This shows that the proposed "dynamic" labeling approach can increase label quality. More specifically, the accuracy was 83.6% for the "label quickly" style and 65.42% for the "label carefully" style in the dynamic labeling task.

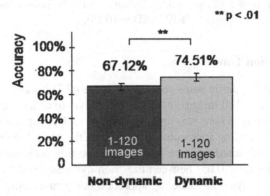

Fig. 7. Annotation accuracy (Non-dynamic: mean = 67.12%; SD = 8.21; Dynamic: mean = 74.51%; SD = 8.96).

Figure 8 shows the accuracy of the image labeling process in the first half (1–60 images) and the second half (61–120 images) using the "non-dynamic" and "dynamic" labeling approaches. The results indicate that the accuracies were 67.4% and 68.6% in the first and second halves of the labeling task using the "non-dynamic" labeling approach, and 71.02% and 78.03% in the first and second halves of the labeling task using the "dynamic" labeling approach. The accuracy analysis using a paired t-test indicated a significant difference ($p < 0.05$) between the first and second halves of the labeling task in the "dynamic" labeling approach, but, there was no significant difference ($p > 0.05$) between the first and second halves of the labeling task in the "non-dynamic" labeling approach. This indicated that there was a temporal effect in the annotation accuracy when the "dynamic" labeling approach was used.

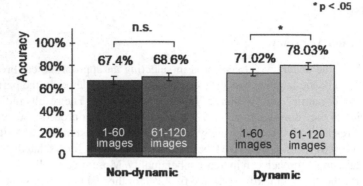

Fig. 8. Annotation accuracy of the first-60 and second-60 images using the non-dynamic and dynamic labeling approaches (Non-dynamic: for 1–60 images: mean = 67.40%, SD = 8.44; for 61–120 images: mean = 68.60%, SD = 9.60; Dynamic: for 1–60 images: mean = 71.02%, SD = 9.06; for 61– 120 images: mean = 78.03%, SD = 10.15).

5.2 Task Completion Time

Figure 9 shows that the participants spent an average of 712 s and 619 s to complete the labeling tasks (label 120 images) using the "non-dynamic" and "dynamic" labeling approaches, respectively. There was an approximate 15% reduction in the time taken using the "dynamic" labeling approach compared with the "non-dynamic" labeling approach. The analysis of paired t-test on task completion time indicated that there was a significant difference (p < 0.05) between the "non-dynamic" and "dynamic" labeling approaches, with the "dynamic" labeling approach being more efficient (i.e., requires less time to complete the task) than the "non-dynamic" labeling approach. More specifically, the participants spent an average of 3 s to select a label in the "label quickly" style and 7 s in the "label carefully" style in the dynamic labeling task.

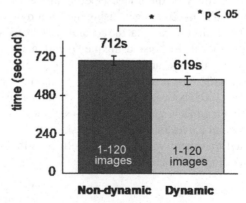

Fig. 9. Task completion time (Non-dynamic: mean = 712.30 s; SD = 151.20; Dynamic: mean = 619.32 s; SD = 135.34).

Figure 10 shows the average time taken for the image labeling process for the first half (1–60 images) and the second half (61–120 images) using the "non-dynamic" and "dynamic" labeling approaches. The results indicate that the participants spent an average of 364 s and 347 s to complete the first and second halves of the labeling task using the "non-dynamic" labeling approach, and an average of 346 s and 272 s to complete the first and second halves of the labeling task using the "dynamic" labeling approach. The analysis of paired t-test on task completion time indicated a significant difference ($p < 0.05$) between the first and second halves of the labeling task in the "dynamic" labeling approach and no significant difference ($p > 0.05$) between the first and second halves of the labeling task in the "non-dynamic" labeling approach. This shows that the proposed "dynamic" labeling approach keeps on getting faster compared to a conventional labeling technique.

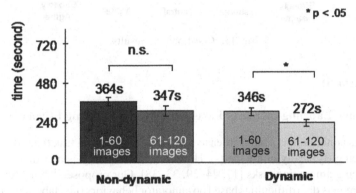

Fig. 10. Average time of the first-60 and second-60 images using the non-dynamic and dynamic labeling approaches (Non-dynamic: for 1–60 images: mean = 364.77 s, SD = 117.45; for 61–120 images: mean = 347.51 s, SD = 163.37; Dynamic: for 1–60 images: mean = 346.78 s, SD = 104.57; for 61–120 images: mean = 272.52 s, SD = 81.03).

5.3 Questionnaire

Figure 11 shows the questionnaire results from the 20 participants who used the "dynamic" labeling approach. The results for Q1 indicate that 90% (n = 18) of the participants agreed (or strongly agreed) that the "label quickly" style was assigned correctly to the tasks when the images were easy. For Q2, 60% (n = 12) of the participants agreed (or strongly agreed) that the "label carefully" style was assigned correctly to the tasks when the images were difficult. The results for Q3 show that 95% (n = 19) of the participants agreed (or strongly agreed) that the "label quickly" style was efficient when the images were easy. For Q4, 90% (n = 18) of the participants agreed (or strongly agreed) that the "label carefully" style was helpful when the images were difficult. The results for Q5 show that 90% (n = 18) of the participants agreed (or strongly agreed) that they learned something (some cues) from the sample images. Further details are presented in the following section.

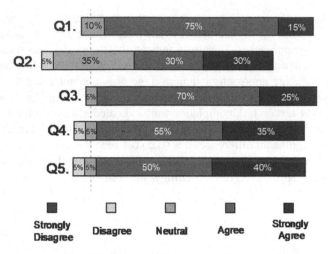

Fig. 11. Questionnaire results.

6 Discussion

6.1 Dynamic Labeling Increases Label Quality and Labeling Efficiency

Manual data annotation is a labor-intensive and time-consuming task that often relies on crowdsourcing (typically non-experts). However, label quality is a critical issue when crowdsourcing annotation tasks [17, 24, 29, 33, 38]. Our proposed "dynamic" labeling approach predicts data difficulties based on annotator behaviors (i.e., label selection time) and dynamically assigns appropriate labeling styles to annotators during the labeling. The results indicate that the "dynamic" labeling approach significantly increases the label quality (7% higher) and labeling efficiency (15% faster) of a manual image-labeling task. Participants felt that the "label carefully" style was helpful when the images were difficult. For example, one participant stated, *"when I was considering possible cat breeds, the sample images helped me in confidently making the label decision."* Another participant stated, *"it was difficult to select an appropriate label from the two labels which were very similar; in such cases, the five sample images were helpful."* In addition, participants felt that the "label quickly" style was efficient when the images were easy. In the words of a participant, *"some images were very easy and clear; I could select a label instantly without thinking. I do agree that the 'label quickly' style is efficient. It is unnecessary to have to press a button to move to the next image."* We believe that improvements in the label quality and labeling efficiency have brought significant benefits to crowdsourcing image labeling tasks.

6.2 Temporal Effect in the Dynamic Labeling

Temporal effects describe how people change their behavior over time. This approach is used to analyze the efficiency of activities or studies [63–65]. It has also been used to analyze the performance of image-labeling tasks [15]. The results showed that there were significant temporal effects on the annotation accuracy and task completion time between the first-half (1–60 images) and second-half (61–120 images) of the image-labeling task when using the proposed "dynamic" labeling approach. However, there were no temporal effects in the conventional "non-dynamic" labeling approach. This indicated that the labeling efficiency as well as the annotation accuracy was gradually increasing during the labeling process in the "dynamic" labeling approach. The main reason for this was that the participants acquired domain knowledge by observing five additional sample images (i.e., 'label carefully' style). For example, one participant stated, *"I am not a cat expert, but I found some cues that could help me distinguish cat breeds."* Another participant said, *"In the beginning, I was confused about 'Russian Blue' and 'British Shorthair.' After seeing the sample images of the two cat-labels several times, I felt like I knew the difference between the two cats and gave a label more confidently."* This is a significant indicator of the learning effect in the crowdsourced image-labeling process.

6.3 Limitations of the Dynamic Labeling

A limitation of this study is that the "label carefully" style may not work properly if the annotator learns "wrong" cues from the sample images as the sample images were shown without any description. This may result in additional errors. A participant who disagreed that the "label carefully" style was helpful stated *"Although the sample images provided more information of cat breeds, it confused me sometimes, especially when some images were too similar between two labels. It was still difficult to choose a label."* Another participant said, *"I got some cues from the sample images and made a label decision. But, I could not know if my selected label was right or wrong. I am worried if the cues guided me to a wrong selection."* Another limitation is that the annotation accuracy was not very high (77%) when the images were difficult. However, we believe that the proposed "dynamic" labeling approach has already made a significant contribution to manual image-labeling tasks. In future, we would like to investigate the possibility of highlighting personal cues in sample images. For example, a system automatically compares the similarities and differences between sample images. This can be useful for non-expert users in observing and identifying cues more correctly; further improving the annotation accuracy when the images are difficult. Moreover, we plan to explore other ways to observe annotator behavior, such as eye-tracking, during the labeling process.

7   Conclusion

In this study, we proposed a process called Dynamic Labeling, a labeling system (algorithm) that analyzes labeling behaviors (i.e., label selection time) of annotators during the labeling process and dynamically assigns an appropriate labeling style in an image-labeling task. We conducted a user study (n = 40) to compare the proposed "dynamic" labeling approach with a conventional "non-dynamic" labeling approach in an image-labeling task. The results showed that the proposed "dynamic" labeling approach could increase label quality (7% higher) and labeling efficiency (10% faster). Additionally, the results showed the proposed "dynamic" labeling approach getting more accurate and faster during the labeling process. The findings of this study indicate that a customized labeling workflow (style) can significantly improve the label quality and labeling efficiency in a crowdsourced annotation task. This finding demonstrates the importance of considering human behavior in the development of data annotation tools. We believe that this study provides valuable insights for the future development of relevant tools for manual annotation tasks.

Acknowledgments. This work was supported by JST ACT-X Grant Number JP-MJAX21AG, Japan.

References

1. Abu-El-Haija, S., et al.: Youtube-8m: a large-scale video classification benchmark. arXiv preprint arXiv:1609.08675 (2016)
2. Amershi, S., Fogarty, J., Kapoor, A., Tan, D.: Overview based example selection in end user interactive concept learning. In: Proceedings of the 22nd Annual ACM Symposium on User Interface Software and Technology, pp. 247–256 (2009)
3. Amershi, S., Fogarty, J., Kapoor, A., Tan, D.: Examining multiple potential models in end-user interactive concept learning. In: Proceedings of the SIGCHI Conference on Human Factors in Computing Systems, pp. 1357–1360 (2010)
4. Baba, Y.: Statistical quality control for human computation and crowdsourcing. In: IJCAI, pp. 5667–5671 (2018)
5. Bernstein, M. S., Brandt, J., Miller, R.C., Karger, D.R.: Crowds in two seconds: enabling realtime crowd-powered interfaces. In: Proceedings of the 24th Annual ACM Symposium on User Interface Software and Technology, UIST 2011, pp. 33–42 (2011)
6. Bernstein, M.S., Karger, D.R., Miller, R.C., Brandt, J.: Analytic methods for optimizing realtime crowdsourcing. arXiv preprint arXiv:1204.2995 (2012)
7. Bianco, S., Ciocca, G., Napoletano, P., Schettini, R.: An interactive tool for manual, semi-automatic and automatic video annotation. Comput. Vis. Image Underst. **131**, 88–99 (2015)
8. Bigham, J.P., et al.: VizWiz: nearly real-time answers to visual questions. In: Proceedings of the 23nd Annual ACM Symposium on User Interface Software and Technology, UIST 2010, pp. 333–342 (2010)
9. Boutsis, I., Kalogeraki, V.: On task assignment for real-time reliable crowdsourcing. In: 2014 IEEE 34th International Conference on Distributed Computing Systems, pp. 1–10 (2014)
10. Bragg, J., Weld, D.: Crowdsourcing multi-label classification for taxonomy creation. In: Proceedings of the AAAI Conference on Human Computation and Crowdsourcing, vol. 1, pp. 25–33 (2013)
11. Burton, M.A., Brady, E., Brewer, R., Neylan, C., Bigham, J.P., Hurst, A.: Crowdsourcing subjective fashion advice using VizWiz: challenges and opportunities. In: Proceedings of the 14th International ACM SIGACCESS Conference on Computers and Accessibility, ASSETS 2012, pp. 135–142 (2012)
12. Chan, J., Dang, S., Dow, S.P.: Improving crowd innovation with expert facilitation. In: Proceedings of the 19th ACM Conference on Computer-Supported Cooperative Work & Social Computing, pp. 1223–1235 (2016)
13. Chang, C.M., Lee, C.H., Igarashi, T.: Spatial labeling: leveraging spatial layout for improving label quality in non-expert image annotation. In: Proceedings of the 2021 CHI Conference on Human Factors in Computing Systems, pp. 1–12 (2021)

14. Chang, C.M., Mishra, S.D., Igarashi, T.: A hierarchical task assignment for manual image labeling. In: 2019 IEEE Symposium on Visual Languages and Human-Centric Computing (VL/HCC), pp. 139–143. IEEE (2019)

15. Chang, C. M., Yang, X., Igarashi, T.: An empirical study on the effect of quick and careful labeling styles in image annotation. In: Graphics Interface (2022)

16. Chang, J.C., Amershi, S., Kamar, E.: Revolt: collaborative crowdsourcing for labeling machine learning datasets. In: Proceedings of the 2017 CHI Conference on Human Factors in Computing Systems, pp. 2334–2346 (2017)

17. Dekel, O., Shamir, O.: Vox Populi: collecting high-quality labels from a crowd. In: COLT (2009)

18. Deng, J., Dong, W., Socher, R., Li, L.J., Li, K., Fei-Fei, L.: ImageNet: a large-scale hierarchical image database. In: 2009 IEEE Conference on Computer Vision and Pattern Recognition, pp. 248–255. IEEE (2009)

19. Difallah, D.E., Demartini, G., Cudré-Mauroux, P.: Pick-a-crowd: tell me what you like, and I'll tell you what to do. In: Proceedings of the 22nd International Conference on World Wide Web, pp. 367–374 (2013)

20. Doroudi, S., Kamar, E., Brunskill, E., Horvitz, E.: Toward a learning science for complex crowdsourcing tasks. In: Proceedings of the 2016 CHI Conference on Human Factors in Computing Systems, pp. 2623–2634 (2016)

21. Dow, S., Kulkarni, A., Klemmer, S., Hartmann, B.: Shepherding the crowd yields better work. In Proceedings of the ACM 2012 Conference on Computer Supported Cooperative Work, pp. 1013–1022 (2012)

22. Ellero, A., Ferretti, P., Furlanetto, G.: Realtime crowdsourcing with payment of idle workers in the retainer model. Procedia Econ. Finan. **32**, 20–26 (2015)

23. Fang, Y.L., Sun, H.L., Chen, P.P., Deng, T.: Improving the quality of crowdsourced image labeling via label similarity. J. Comput. Sci. Technol. **32**, 877–889 (2017)

24. Feng, D., Besana, S., Zajac, R.: Acquiring high quality non-expert knowledge from on-demand workforce. In: Proceedings of the 2009 Workshop on The People's Web Meets NLP: Collaboratively Constructed Semantic Resources (People's Web), pp. 51–56 (2009)

25. Fogarty, J., Tan, D., Kapoor, A., Winder, S.: CueFlik: interactive concept learning in image search. In: Proceedings of the SIGCHI Conference on Human Factors in Computing Systems, pp. 29–38 (2008)

26. Gemmeke, J.F., et al.: Audio set: an ontology and human-labeled dataset for audio events. In: 2017 IEEE International Conference on Acoustics, Speech and Signal Processing (ICASSP), pp. 776–780. IEEE (2017)

27. Hansen, D.L., Schone, P.J., Corey, D., Reid, M., Gehring, J.: Quality control mechanisms for crowdsourcing: peer review, arbitration, & expertise at family search indexing. In: Proceedings of the 2013 Conference on Computer Supported Cooperative Work, pp. 649–660 (2013)

28. He, J., van Ossenbruggen, J., de Vries, A.P.: Do you need experts in the crowd? A case study in image annotation for marine biology. In: Proceedings of the 10th Conference on Open Research Areas in Information Retrieval, pp. 57–60 (2013)

29. Hsueh, P.Y., Melville, P., Sindhwani, V.: Data quality from crowdsourcing: a study of annotation selection criteria. In: Proceedings of the NAACL HLT 2009 Workshop on Active Learning for Natural Language Processing, pp. 27–35 (2009)

30. Ipeirotis, P.G., Provost, F., Wang, J.: Quality management on amazon mechanical turk. In: Proceedings of the ACM SIGKDD Workshop on Human Computation, pp. 64–67 (2010)

31. Kamar, E., Hacker, S., Horvitz, E.: Combining human and machine intelligence in large-scale crowdsourcing. In: AAMAS, vol. 12, pp. 467–474 (2012)

32. Kim, J., Cheng, J., Bernstein, M.S.: Ensemble: exploring complementary strengths of leaders and crowds in creative collaboration. In Proceedings of the 17th ACM Conference on Computer Supported Cooperative Work & Social Computing, pp. 745–755 (2014)

33. Kittur, A., Smus, B., Khamkar, S., Kraut, R.E.: CrowdForge: crowdsourcing complex work. In: Proceedings of the 24th Annual ACM Symposium on User Interface Software and Technology, pp. 43–52 (2011)

34. Krishna, R.A., et al.: Embracing error to enable rapid crowdsourcing. In: Proceedings of the 2016 CHI Conference on Human Factors in Computing Systems, CHI 2016, pp. 3167–3179 (2016)

35. Kulesza, T., Amershi, S., Caruana, R., Fisher, D., Charles, D.: Structured labeling for facilitating concept evolution in machine learning. In: Proceedings of the SIGCHI Conference on Human Factors in Computing Systems, pp. 3075–3084 (2014)

36. Kwitt, R., Hegenbart, S., Rasiwasia, N., Vécsei, A., Uhl, A.: Do we need annotation experts? A case study in celiac disease classification. In: Golland, P., Hata, N., Barillot, C., Hornegger, J., Howe, R. (eds.) MICCAI 2014. LNCS, vol. 8674, pp. 454–461. Springer, Cham (2014). https://doi.org/10.1007/978-3-319-10470-6_57

37. Laput, G., Lasecki, W.S., Wiese, J., Xiao, R., Bigham, J.P., Harrison, C.: Zensors: adaptive, rapidly deployable, human-intelligent sensor feeds. In: Proceedings of the 33rd Annual ACM Conference on Human Factors in Computing Systems, CHI 2015, pp. 1935–1944 (2015)

38. Lasecki, W.S., Gordon, M., Koutra, D., Jung, M.F., Dow, S.P., Bigham, J.P.: Glance: rapidly coding behavioral video with the crowd. In: Proceedings of the 27th Annual ACM Symposium on User Interface Software and Technology. UIST 2014, pp. 551–562 (2014)

39. Lasecki, W.S., Murray, K.I., White, S., Miller, R.C., Bigham, J.P.: Real-time crowd control of existing interfaces. In: Proceedings of the 24th Annual ACM Symposium on User Interface Software and Technology, UIST 2011, pp. 23–32 (2011)

40. Lasecki, W.S., Wesley, R., Nichols, J., Kulkarni, A., Allen, J.F., Bigham, J.P.: Chorus: a crowd-powered conversational assistant. In: Proceedings of the 26th Annual ACM Symposium on User Interface Software and Technology, UIST 2013, pp. 151–162 (2013)

41. Li, J., Baba, Y., Kashima, H.: Incorporating worker similarity for label aggregation in crowd-sourcing. In: Kůrková, V., Manolopoulos, Y., Hammer, B., Iliadis, L., Maglogiannis, I. (eds.) ICANN 2018. LNCS, vol. 11140, pp. 596–606. Springer, Cham (2018). https://doi.org/10.1007/978-3-030-01421-6_57

42. Liu, S., Chen, C., Lu, Y., Ouyang, F., Wang, B.: An interactive method to improve crowdsourced annotations. IEEE Trans. Vis. Comput. Graph. 25(1), 235–245 (2018)

43. Marcus, M., Santorini, B., Marcinkiewicz, M.A.: Building a large annotated corpus of English: The Penn Treebank (1993)

44. Mitra, T., Hutto, C.J., Gilbert, E.: Comparing person-and process-centric strategies for obtaining quality data on amazon mechanical turk. In: Proceedings of the 33rd Annual ACM Conference on Human Factors in Computing Systems, pp. 1345–1354 (2015)

45. Nguyen, A.T., Lease, M., Wallace, B.C.: Explainable modeling of annotations in crowdsourcing. In: Proceedings of the 24th International Conference on Intelligent User Interfaces, IUI 2019, pp. 575–579 (2019)

46. Nowak, S., Rüger, S.: How reliable are annotations via crowdsourcing: a study about inter-annotator agreement for multi-label image annotation. In: Proceedings of the International Conference on Multimedia Information Retrieval, pp. 557–566 (2010)

47. Otani, N., Baba, Y., Kashima, H.: Quality control for crowdsourced hierarchical classification. In: 2015 IEEE International Conference on Data Mining, pp. 937–942. IEEE (2015)

48. Post, M., Callison-Burch, C., Osborne, M.: Constructing parallel corpora for six Indian languages via crowdsourcing. In: Proceedings of the Seventh Workshop on Statistical Machine Translation, pp. 401–409 (2012)

49. Rashtchian, C., Young, P., Hodosh, M., Hockenmaier, J.: Collecting image annotations using amazon's mechanical turk. In: Proceedings of the NAACL HLT 2010 Workshop on Creating Speech and Language Data with Amazon's Mechanical Turk, pp. 139–147 (2010)

50. Rogstadius, J., Kostakos, V., Kittur, A., Smus, B., Laredo, J., Vukovic, M.: An assessment of intrinsic and extrinsic motivation on task performance in crowdsourcing markets. In: Proceedings of the International AAAI Conference on Web and Social Media, vol. 5, pp. 321–328 (2011)
51. Russell, B.C., Torralba, A., Murphy, K.P., Freeman, W.T.: LabelMe: a database and web-based tool for image annotation. Int. J. Comput. Vis. **77**(1), 157–173 (2008)
52. Rzeszotarski, J., Kittur, A.: CrowdScape: interactively visualizing user behavior and output. In: Proceedings of the 25th Annual ACM Symposium on User Interface Software and Technology, pp. 55–62 (2012)
53. Safran, M., Che, D.: Real-time recommendation algorithms for crowdsourcing systems. Appl. Comput. Inf. **13**(1), 47–56 (2017)
54. Schilling, M.P., et al.: Label assistant: a workflow for assisted data annotation in image segmentation tasks. In: Proceedings of the 31st Workshop Computational Intelligence, pp. 211–234 (2021)
55. Sunahase, T., Baba, Y., Kashima, H.: Pairwise hits: quality estimation from pairwise comparisons in creator- evaluator crowdsourcing process. In: Proceedings of the AAAI Conference on Artificial Intelligence, vol. 31 (2017)
56. Torralba, A., Russell, B.C., Yuen, J.: Labelme: Online image annotation and applications. Proc. IEEE **98**(8), 1467–1484 (2010)
57. Tran-Thanh, L., Huynh, T.D., Rosenfeld, A., Ramchurn, S. Jennings, N.R.: BudgetFix: budget limited crowdsourcing for interdependent task allocation with quality guarantees. In: Proceedings of the 2014 International Conference on Autonomous Agents and Multi-Agent Systems, AAMAS 2014, pp. 477–484 (2014)
58. Von Ahn, L., Dabbish, L.: Labeling images with a computer game. In: Proceedings of the SIGCHI Conference on Human Factors in Computing Systems, pp. 319–326 (2004)
59. Zhang, Y., Wang, Y., Zhang, H., Zhu, B., Chen, S., Zhang, D.: OneLabeler: a flexible system for building data labeling tools. In: Proceedings of the 2022 CHI Conference on Human Factors in Computing Systems, CHI 2022, pp. 1–22 (2022)
60. Parkhi, O.M., Vedaldi, A., Zisserman, A., Jawahar, C.V.: Cats and dogs. In: 2012 IEEE Conference on Computer Vision and Pattern Recognition, pp. 3498–3505 (2012)
61. Buhrmester, M., Kwang, T., Gosling, S.D.: Amazon's mechanical Turk: a new source of inexpensive, yet high-quality, data? Perspect. Psychol. Sci. **6**(1), 3–5 (2011)
62. Peer, E., Vosgerau, J., Acquisti, A.: Reputation as a sufficient condition for data quality on Amazon Mechanical Turk. Behav. Res. Meth. **46**(4), 1023–1031 (2014)
63. Mosheiov, G.: Parallel machine scheduling with a learning effect. J. Oper. Res. Soc. **52**(10), 1165–1169 (2001)
64. Sun, K.T., Lin, Y.C., Yu, C.J.: A study on learning effect among different learning styles in a Web-based lab of science for elementary school students. Comput. Educ. **50**(4), 1411–1422 (2008)
65. Kammerer, Y., Nairn, R., Pirolli, P., Chi, E.H.: Signpost from the masses: learning effects in an exploratory social tag search browser. In: Proceedings of the SIGCHI Conference on Human Factors in Computing Systems, pp. 625–634 (2009)
66. Chang, C.M., He, Y., Yang, X., Xie, H., Igarashi, T.: DualLabel: secondary Labels for Challenging Image Annotation. In: Graphics Interface 2022 (2022)
67. Miyata, S., Chang, C.M., Igarashi, T.: Trafne: a training framework for non-expert annotators with auto validation and expert feedback. In: Degen, H., Ntoa, S. (eds.) International Conference on Human-Computer Interaction, pp. 475–494. Springer, Cham (2022). https://doi.org/10.1007/978-3-031-05643-7_31

68. Lu, Y., Chang, C.M., Igarashi, T.: ConfLabeling: assisting image labeling with user and system confidence. In: Chen, J.Y.C., Fragomeni, G., Degen, H., Ntoa, S. (eds.) International Conference on Human-Computer Interaction, pp. 475–494. Springer, Cham (2022). https://doi.org/10.1007/978-3-031-21707-4_26

69. Zhou, Y., Lu, J., Xiang, C., Chang, C.M., Igarashi, T.: RelRoll: a relative elicitation mechanism for scoring annotation with a case study on speech emotion. In: Graphics Interface 2023 (2023)

70. Tang, Y., Chang, C.M., Yang, X.: PDFChatAnnotator: a human-LLM collaborative multimodal data collection tool for PDF-format catalogs. In: Proceedings of the 29th International Conference on Intelligent User Interfaces, IUI 2024 (2024)

Research on Evacuation Care System for People with Low Vision

Zitao Cheng[1](✉), Keiko Kasamatsu[1], and Takeo Ainoya[2]

[1] Tokyo Metropolitan University, 6-6 Asahigaoka, Hino, Tokyo, Japan
chengzitao_tao@163.com
[2] Tokyo University of Technology, 5-23-22 Nishikamata, Ota City, Tokyo, Japan

Abstract. According to statistics, by 2020, the number of people with low vision worldwide had exceeded 1 billion, and this number is still rising. This shows that people with low vision have become an important group that cannot be ignored in today's society. On the other hand, as Japan is located in the Pacific Ring of Fire, it experiences a higher frequency of natural disasters compared to other countries. Although the Japanese government has implemented many disaster prevention strategies to minimize civilian casualties during disasters, there are currently no special care measures for people with low vision, who are a vulnerable group.

Therefore, this study believes it's necessary to develop an evacuation care system to further ensure the safety of people with low vision during disasters.

Keywords: people with low vision · disaster · evacuation care system

1 Introduction

1.1 Current Situation of People with Low Vision

As of 2020, there are 1.1 billion people with low vision in the world. Among them, about 43 million are completely blind, and this number is still increasing. According to predictions by the IAPB [1], by 2050, the number of visually impaired people will rise to 1.7 billion (Fig. 1). Therefore, people with low vision have become a group that cannot be ignored in today's society. In an effort to reduce the difficulties faced by visually impaired people in their daily lives, the Japanese government enacted the 'Law for Promoting the Smooth Movement of the Elderly and Persons with Disabilities' in December 2006. By promoting a number of excellent barrier-free designs, they have improved the convenience of life for visually impaired people, thus reducing the difficulty of their participation in society and minimizing the gap between them and people without disabilities.

Data from VLEG/GBD 2020 model, accessed via the IAPB Vision Atlas.

1.2 Natural State of Japan

Because Japan is located in the Pacific Ring of Fire, earthquakes occur more frequently there compared to other regions. Additionally, due to its geographical, topographical,

H. Mori and Y. Asahi (Eds.): HCII 2024, LNCS 14689, pp. 119–130, 2024.
https://doi.org/10.1007/978-3-031-60107-1_9

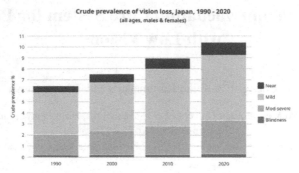

Fig. 1. People With Lowvision in japan

and meteorological conditions, Japan is prone to natural disasters such as typhoons, heavy rains, and heavy snowfalls. [2] Although the Japanese government has formulated relevant disaster prevention policies to protect the lives of citizens as much as possible during disasters, most of these measures are essentially designed to protect the majority of the population. As a minority, people with low vision will suffer from various situations and even life-threatening situations due to lack of care during disasters. Therefore, in the current disaster prevention strategies of the Japanese government, there are still inadequacies for people with low vision.

1.3 People with Lowvision in Disasters

According to statistics, during the 1995 Great Hanshin Earthquake, the mortality rate of people with disabilities far exceeded that of the general population. [3] According to statistics from Miyagi Prefecture during the 2011 Great East Japan Earthquake, the mortality rate of people with physical and mental disabilities was 1.92 times higher than that of the general population [4].

Furthermore, at the 3rd United Nations World Conference on Disaster Risk Reduction held in Sendai, Japan, in 2015, it was pointed out that people with low vision are at a higher risk in some natural disasters because they may not be able to accurately perceive changes in their surroundings, making them more vulnerable than other people with physical disabilities [5].

It can be seen that people with low vision often face greater life threats in natural disasters than ordinary people or other physically handicapped people.

Therefore, it is necessary to provide an additional evacuation care system for people with low vision.

2 Research of the Evacuation Care System

2.1 The Role of the Evacuation Care System

The evacuation care system is composed of multiple components. When a disaster occurs, through the operation of each component, the evacuation care system can maximize the protection of the user's life, extend their survival time as much as possible, and ensure their daily living needs are met while waiting for rescue to arrive.

2.2 Examples of Evacuation Care Systems

In Japan, some house makers add evacuation care systems to the homes they design to increase the residents' sense of peace of mind and the safety of the home. For example, the "Misawa Life Continality Performance" (Misawa-LCP) [6] developed by the house maker "Misawa homes", this system aims to use three designs: Prepare design, Protect design, and Support design to address pre-disaster and disaster situations respectively. Provide corresponding assistance at the three stages of disaster and after it occurs, and solve problems that may arise in these three stages, thereby achieving the goal of protecting residents and extending their survival time. Among them, the main purpose of Prepare design is to ensure that residents can more easily obtain disaster prevention resources when a disaster occurs by placing disaster prevention supplies in multiple storage spaces in the house. Protect design is to minimize the damage to the house due to disasters by adding earthquake-resistant structures or waterproofing boards to the structural design of the house. Support design ensures that residents will still have backup energy to use in the event of power and water outages due to natural disasters by adding solar power panels and water storage systems.

2.3 Application Scenarios of the Evacuation Care System

The evacuation care system can be applied to two situations: at home and outdoors. The evacuation care systems currently developed by Japanese house makers are all for home use. In this case, residents are accustomed to the environment and have made sufficient preparations in advance, which gives them a high sense of security and makes it easier to implement an evacuation care system. Since being outside is unknown to the residents, the residents' sense of security decreases. At the same time, resource allocation is also a major issue. Therefore, in this case, the intervention of the evacuation care system is more necessary. Therefore, in the following research, this study will focus on the development and design of a evacuation care system for scenarios outside of the home.

3 Types of Disasters for Which Care Should Be Provided

3.1 Two Types of Disasters

This research considers that evacuation care is necessary for the following two natural disasters.

First, Frequent natural disasters may require frequent emergency evacuations, which makes evacuation care that focuses on evacuation and ensuring safety even more important.

The second type is natural disasters, which are dangerous and have great destructive power. Although these types of natural disasters are relatively infrequent, a single occurrence can cause large numbers of personnel to be injured. Evacuation care is critical to maximizing injury reduction.

3.2 Major Disasters in Japan

Japan's Cabinet Office Reiwa's three-year Disaster Prevention White Book [7] lists the major natural disasters in Japan since Showa 20. Data show that as of July 2018, the most frequent natural disasters were: 23 typhoons, 21 earthquakes, 11 heavy rains, 9 volcanoes, and 9 snow disasters. In addition, this data also reveals the number of dead and missing people caused by natural disasters (Fig. 2). The disasters that caused the largest number of casualties in a single disaster are: earthquake - 22,303 people, typhoon - 5098 people, heavy rain - 1,124 people, snow disaster - 231 people, volcano - 63 people. Through this set of data, we can find that earthquakes, typhoons, and heavy rains are both frequent and destructive.

Therefore, this study believes that in the subsequent design process, developers should deliberately consider reasonable care provision methods for the three major disasters of typhoons, heavy rains, and earthquakes, so as to maximize the role of the system and protect lives.

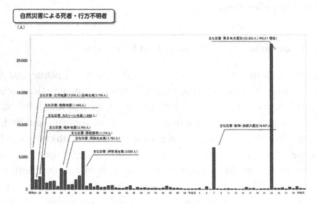

Fig. 2. Number of dead and missing persons caused by natural disasters [7]

3.3 Secondary Disasters

In fact, when the above three disasters occur, they are often accompanied by other secondary disasters. For example, when a typhoon occurs, it often causes heavy rain. With the occurrence of heavy rain, it may eventually develop into floods. In addition, when large-scale earthquakes occur in coastal areas, huge tsunamis can sometimes occur. Take the Great East Japan Earthquake in 2011 as an example. In this disaster, 14,308 people drowned due to tsunami, accounting for 90.64% of the total victims. However, there were only 667 buried victims due to earthquakes, accounting for 4.23% of the total victims [8]. It can be seen that the harm of secondary disasters is not only no less than that of primary disasters, but may even cause greater casualties. Therefore, in the subsequent research process, it is also necessary to include secondary disasters in the scope of care.

4 Disaster Timeline

4.1 Disaster Interviewing for People with Low Vision

To better provide evacuation care for low-vision people, we first need to understand the difficulties and problems that this group has during disaster evacuation.

In order to explore this issue, this study extracted the descriptions of low-vision people's experiences and difficulties in different disaster stages from several interviews with low-vision people about their disaster experiences, and further organized and simplified them. Finally, summarize its description into simple and clear text and rearrange it according to the chronological order of the disaster.

According to the content, this study divides the description into environmental description, action description, psychological description and difficulty description, and presents them in the form of a timeline. In this way, we can more clearly and intuitively observe and understand the experiences of low-vision people in natural disasters.

4.2 Timeline of Earthquakes and Tsunamis

The first thing to introduce is the timeline of earthquakes and tsunamis (Fig. 3). The content of this timeline is compiled from five interviews with people with low vision during earthquakes and tsunamis. The specific content is shown in Table 1.

This timeline is mainly divided into the awareness stage before the disaster, the disaster stage and the evacuation stage after the disaster. In the cognitive stage, people with low vision will first hear the sound and then feel the violent shaking of the earthquake. At the same time, many people with low vision reported that when earthquakes occur, they are often accompanied by loud noises. And because the surrounding noise was too loud, they were unable to hear much useful information during the earthquake.

In addition, strong vibrations from earthquakes can also affect the mobility of people with low vision. A person with low vision said: Even though he knew clearly where to hide at the moment, the earthquake made it difficult for him to move his body.

After the earthquake stops, most people with low vision will choose to turn on the radio and try to broadcast through the radio to learn as much as possible about the surrounding disaster conditions and determine whether further evacuation is needed.

4.3 Difficulties Faced by People with Low Vision During Tsunami and Earthquake Evacuation

An evacuation timeline provides insight into the difficulties faced by people with low vision during different stages of a disaster.

For example, during the awareness stage, many people with low vision are unable to react in time because the time between hearing sound and the occurrence of an earthquake is too short. In addition, research by [12] shows that many low-vision people are poorly prepared for disasters. Therefore, when a disaster occurs, low-vision people have neither time to react nor effective means of self-protection. This will put people with low vision at greater risk during disasters.

Table 1. Interviews with people with low vision on their experiences during earthquakes and tsunamis

source	original text
[9]	■ "…said he thought he felt that the earth would suck him in…" ■ "…and then the iron at the bus shed started jerking too…"
[10]	■ "震災の日。地鳴りが聞こえ、激しい揺れに身構えた。" ■ "3メートル程度の津波予想を知らせる防災行政無線が響いていたが途,,絶えた。" ■ "物がぶつかり合う音がし、浸水して鳴り続ける車のクラクション…""
[11]	■ "…I heard the noise and the noise was horrific and I had no idea what it was and I thought, "What in the world was that?"… [B]y that time [guide dog] was up and he wanted to run out into the living room area and it started to shake…" ■ "… I couldn't walk anywhere because it kept knocking me over….I just couldn't move and… I could hear crockery falling and breaking in the living room and in the kitchen and I thought, "I don't know what to do."" ■ "…. I've been told many, many times during an earthquake go and stand under a door jamb but I couldn't even get there." ■ "Like most people, the first thing you do… When it did stop shaking, I went to flick on my stereo in my bedroom just to turn on the radio to see if I could find out what was happening around Christchurch, how bad it really was, and of course realized the power was out. Flicked the lights, no, that's not working, so I fished out a transistor radio." ■ "In preparation for emergencies, it can be crucial for people with impaired vision to acquire and keep transistor radios in working order and with a good supply of batteries" ■ "…noted that accessible information that helped rather than frightened was hard to come by in the aftermaths of the earthquakes. Getting information proved to be especially complex for those who are deafblind…" ■ "Familiar landmarks disappeared in the aftermath of the large earthquakes" , "however, when terrain was dramatically changed and roadways and footpaths were damaged or blocked by debris and liquefaction." ■ "Those with minimal established social supports reported feeling isolated and panic-stricken, and would have valued the opportunity to share their stories with someone who would listen." , "I just want to sit in a chair in a house with somebody else in it…. I just need to be where there's someone for the night…." ■ "but what do they do for people who are visually impaired? Have they got somebody sort of assigned to that particular aspect?…"
[12]	■ "The analysis revealed that the level of preparedness of the emergency response plan, the majority of visually disabled people has a low level of preparedness to plan an emergency response (63%), especially the total blindness group (46.3%)."
[13]	■ "Some research participants, especially those with visual impairments, expressed that adapting to and utilising temporary shelter facilities could be challenging." ■ "…visually impaired individuals being unable to use written and visual information sources…" , "a visually impaired participant expressed concerns about being unable to see assistance."

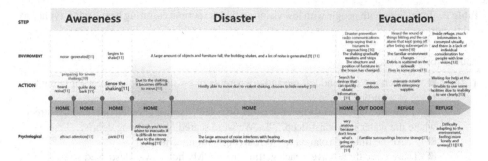

Fig. 3. Timeline of earthquakes and tsunamis

During the disaster stage, many people with low vision have emphasized that it is difficult to move during an earthquake. Moreover, with the shaking of the earthquake, many furniture in the home may overturn or change positions, which will cause people with low vision to be unable to accurately judge their own position, and thus disorientation. The loud noise during earthquakes will directly interfere with the hearing of people with low vision, making them unable to pay attention to some potential dangers.

In addition, many people with low vision described how important it was to them to obtain accurate information after the earthquake. Complex, repetitive or inaccurate information may make people with low vision feel anxious and uneasy, and this anxiety will be more intense during the evacuation process.

When people with low vision successfully leave the building and go outdoors, they will face more serious problems. Earthquakes or tsunamis will change the environment into a look that is unfamiliar to people with low vision. Because it is difficult to see the surroundings clearly, compared with ordinary people, People with low vision have a higher chance of wandering into dangerous places.

Even if people with low vision reach the refuge safely, existing shelters have not been individually adjusted for people with low vision in many details. For example, a lot of information is only conveyed through visual means, and the facility design is not convenient for people with low vision. There is a lack of guidance for people with low vision.

4.4 Timeline of Heavy Rains, Typhoons and Floods

Next is a timeline of typhoons, heavy rains, and floods (Fig. 4). As before, this study collated relevant literature and organized it in the form of a timeline. See Table 2 for details.

Unlike earthquakes and tsunamis, because typhoons, heavy rains, and floods are relatively easy to predict, people with low vision also have longer time to prepare and evacuate. However, due to the different importance they attach to disasters, people with low vision adopt different strategies when evacuating. For example, some people with low vision believe that this is a small disaster that can be quelled quickly, so they choose to stay at home. Some people may only seek refuge in the homes of relatives and friends who are relatively safe, but some people choose to seek refuge in shelters.

Table 2. Interviews with people with low vision on their experiences during heavy rains, typhoons and floods

source	original text
[14]	■ "…when my husband left me and my parents threw us out in the street for being too much of a burden…" ■ "…but after a few hours the roof came off…", "…so we crawled out onto the street, where the water was waist-deep.", "…We were scared of the flying debris…" ■ "… At the time of Yolanda we were living with my friend…" ■ "There were three waves, each getting bigger. My house was destroyed straight away, and I was floating in the storm surge, clinging onto a water container." ■ " One young lady with a visual impairment had survived the storm by hiding under a table with her mother and father." ■ "It is hard to lie in a house that is not yours, especially as a blind person." ■ "One resident with low vision reported that he had injured himself on several occasions when accidentally wandering off the narrow concrete path that connected the bunkhouses" ■ "which she refers to as 'the monster'"
[15]	■ "Additionally, for people with visual impairments, safe city travel for pedestrians was compromised after Hurricane Maria—traffic lights were unusable, street poles and electric cables littered the sidewalks, and public transportation was no longer available.", "the low-hanging electrical cables, the impassable sidewalks broken from uprooted trees, and a walkway completely blocked by a large fallen advertising sign, among other things." ■ "Finding safe alternative routes proved more difficult for many people with visual impairments due to not knowing the locations of dangerous and broken infrastructure." ■ "The lack of light at night meant that many people with low vision were unable to travel at night with much confidence at all." ■ "Even the familiarity of the home temporarily altered a sense of independence as furniture was moved around to avoid roof leaks." ■ "multiple people with visual impairments had lost their long canes.", "Lost canes meant that until people could replace these tools for travel, which for some were relatively expensive, they would lose an important option enabling them to travel independently." ■ "She had the unfortunate experience that her home was flooded, and there was debris and fallen trees around her home. She had to throw away a lot of things from inside the house since it got wet" ■ "I don't remember anybody telling that they have a training for blind people on a shelter situation. How to get there… And how to deal in the situation."

(continued)

Table 2. (*continued*)

source	original text
[15]	■ "Many interviewees said that over their lifetime prior to 2017, hurricanes predicted to reach Puerto Rico either missed the island or did not cause as much damage as was anticipated. This created a sense of apathy in them regarding preparing for Hurricane Maria." ■ "all the noise, all the wind, it was horrible, it was very, very, scary,", "the winds were very strong and loud,", "A lot of blind people just does not open any kind of window or are very scared." ■ "stay in a room and do nothing." ■ " and they sleep on the floor. So now, OK, you have to go to the bathroom, but there are people on the floor. Will you hit them with the cane in the head?", "Luis was specifically concerned about navigating the shelter with many people laying on cots on the ground while he tried to find" ■ "it was difficult because I have a hard time watching TV, I can hear it, but I cannot see it clearly" ■ "Additionally, the representative of MAVI stated that effective communication throughout the disaster cycle, such as audio descriptions of visual images, is a common problem when organizations try to serve people with visual impairments." ■ "Paternalism was seen in the present study as negatively impacting the experience of people with visual impairment and their experience of the disaster cycle. Paternalism ultimately minimizes independent living skills (ILS), which makes the experience of the disaster cycle even more difficult for people with visual impairments and is disempowering."
[16]	■ "Hurricane Irma hit the northern coast of the island as a category-five hurricane on September 6, causing flooding and electrical power outages that affected more than one million people in Puerto Rico"
[17]	■ "such as damage to the clean water system, which was one of the major problems in Puerto Rico post-Hurricane Maria "
[18]	■ "A person with a visual impairment traveling independently with a long cane may not find this obstacle since the long cane is not able to detect obstacles that only protrude at the upper-body level"
[19]	■ "Shelters were challenging for [people with visual impairments] as well because cots were moved, everything was moved around, so they didn't have the structure to navigate across the different scenarios they had." The MAVI representative described one of the challenges for a person with a visual impairment in a shelter, where the floor plan can change because of people moving their sleeping cots as well as their belongings that might be spread into a walkway. Although many people will make way for a person with a visual impairment when they are walking with a long cane, making way in a shelter may not always be possible"

If the disaster is not destructive, people who do not seek refuge in designated shelters may not be in danger. However, once severe typhoons and heavy rains occur, these people may face greater risks.

According to people with low vision, when a typhoon or heavy rain occurs, the roof of a house may be blown off by strong winds, and the house may leak or be damaged by flooding. When a house is flooded, many of the equipment of the evacuees will not work. In this case, it will also be difficult for people with low vision to evacuate a second time.

After a disaster, the surrounding environment will be severely damaged, for example: roads will be flooded, debris will fly, power lines will be scattered, etc. These factors threaten the life safety of people with low vision. Moreover, as the disaster destroys power and street lights, this will further reduce visibility for people with low vision during nighttime activities.

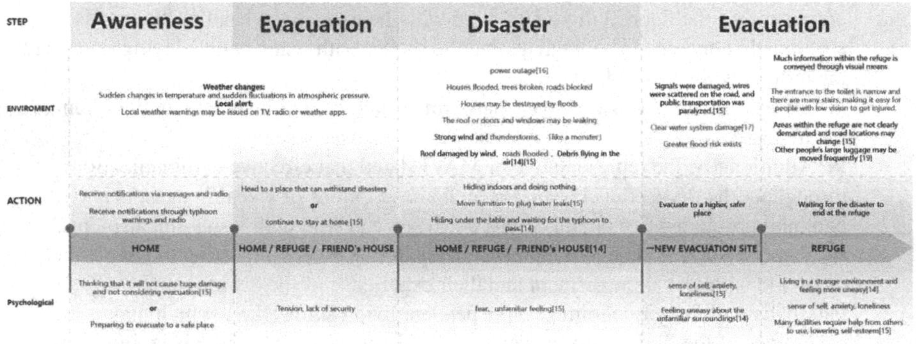

Fig. 4. Timeline of heavy rains, typhoons and floods

4.5 Difficulties Faced by People with Low Vision During Heavy Rains, Typhoons and Floods

During the evacuation stage, many hazard warnings are communicated visually, so some people with low vision may miss hazard warnings. And by the time they realized a disaster was happening, it was too late to evacuate. In addition, some people with low vision may misjudge the severity of a disaster and therefore lose the opportunity to take refuge.

In addition, some people with low vision pointed out that when going to a designated refuge to evacuate, because the place may be a place that the person with low vision has never been before, even if they know the address, it will take a lot of time to get there. Additionally, due to the physical impairments of people with low vision, they may be viewed as a burden by their peers and left behind when taking refuge.

In addition, when a disaster occurs, the loud sound of wind and rain makes it difficult for people with low vision to judge the current situation.

Likewise, there are many problems in refuge design. For example: Since the configuration of items in the refuge often changes, even if a floor plan is provided, a person with low vision cannot fully understand the current situation of the refuge. In addition, according to the interview of [18], people with low vision may also be injured because they cannot detect raised obstacles on some walls using a blind stick.

5 Conclusion and Future Works

Through the timeline, we can find some commonalities and differences in how people with low vision evacuate from earthquakes, typhoons, and heavy rains. On the one hand, the three disasters are accompanied by huge destructive power and noise, and will also cause major changes to the environment, thereby affecting the judgment of people with low vision. On the other hand, the evacuation strategies for different disasters are different, which will also lead to changes in the evacuation process. The commonalities and differences between the three disasters will be further discussed in future research.

In addition, from the aforementioned data in this study, it can be known that: on the one hand, the existing evacuation care system designs are mainly set up in the user's home, and are not individually adjusted for the situation of low-vision people. On the other hand, when people with low vision are forced to leave their homes and seek refuge in unfamiliar places, this group is not only more physically and mentally disadvantaged than the general population, but also faces greater life risks. Therefore, this study believes that it is necessary to develop an evacuation care system for low-vision people who leave their homes in the future.

Disclosure of Interests. The authors have no competing interests to declare that are relevant to the content of this article.

References

1. International agency for the prevention of blindness (2022). Magnitude and Projections. Vision Atlas. https://www.iapb.org/zh/learn/vision-atlas/magnitude-and-projections/
2. Cabinet Office, Government of Japan. Disaster Management in Japan
3. Osaki, Y., Minowa, M.: Factors associated with earthquake deaths in the great hanshin-awaji earthquake. Am. J. Epidemiol. **153**(2), 153–156 (2001). https://doi.org/10.1093/aje/153.2.153
4. Tatsuki, S.: Old age, disability, and the Tohoku-Oki earthquake. Earthq. Spectra **29**, S403–S432 (2013). https://doi.org/10.1193/1.4000126
5. UNESCAP. ncheon strategy to "make the right real" for persons with disabilities in AsiaandthePacific (2012). https://www.unescap.org/resources/incheon-strategy-%E2%80%9Cmake-right-real%E2%80%9D-persons-disabilities-asia-and-pacific. Accessed 24 July 2018
6. Misawa Home. MISAWA-LCP防災住宅はミサワホーム ｜防災・減災住宅 ｜住まいの災害対策 [MISAWA-LCP|Disaster prevention housing is Misawa Home|Disaster prevention and mitigation housing|Disaster prevention measures for living]. Accessed 8 Jan 2024
7. Cabinet Office. Disaster Prevention White Paper, Reiwa 3rd Edition. Cabinet Office of Japan (2023). Cabinet Office of Japan website
8. National Police Agency. Keibi Keisatsu 50 Nen (2014). Accessed 12 Apr 2014. Internet Archive Wayback Machine
9. Blind man, others recall frightening earthquake experience. Jamaica Observer (2023)
10. 高尾具成.(2023).犬が西向きゃ: 視覚障害者の震災体験. 毎日新聞, 東京夕刊.
11. Good, G.A., Phibbs, S., Williamson, K.: Disoriented and immobile: the experiences of people with visual impairments during and after the christchurch, new zealand, 2010 and 2011 earthquakes. J. Visual Impairment Blindn. **110**(6), 425–435 (2016). https://doi.org/10.1177/0145482x1611000605

12. Fatin, M., Sofia, S., Oktari, R.S.: Earthquake and tsunami emergency preparedness of visually disabled people. Int. J. Disaster Manag. **3**(1), 1–10 (2020). https://doi.org/10.24815/ijdm.v3i1.15787

13. Aslan, R., Şahinöz, S.: The experiences of people with disabilities in the 2020 Izmir earthquake: a phenomenological research. Int. J. Disaster Risk Reduct. **95**, 103868 (2023). https://doi.org/10.1016/j.ijdrr.2023.103868

14. Cobley, D.: Typhoon Haiyan one year on: disability, poverty and participation in the Philippines. Disabil. Global South **2**(3), 686–707 (2015). https://disabilityglobalsouth.files.wordpress.com/2012/06/dgs-02-03-01.pdf

15. McCormack, K.D.: Effects of visual impairment on the preparation, response, and recovery from the 2017 Hurricane Season in Puerto Rico. Graduate Doctoral Dissertations, 524 (2019). https://scholarworks.umb.edu/doctoral_dissertations/524

16. Cangialosi, J.P., Latto, A.S., Berg, R.: National Hurricane Center tropical cyclone report: Hurricane Irma (Report No. AL112017) (2018). https://www.nhc.noaa.gov/data/tcr/AL112017_Irma.pdf

17. Government of Puerto Rico. Build back better Puerto Rico: Request for federal assistance for disaster recovery (2017). https://www.documentcloud.org/documents/4198852-BuildBackBetterPuertoRico.html#document/p1

18. Americans with Disabilities Act. ADA checklist for emergency shelters (2010). https://www.ada.gov/pcatoolkit/chap7shelterchk.htm

19. Welsh, R.L.: Psychosocial dimensions of orientation and mobility. In: Wiener, R.W., Welsh, R.L. (eds.) Foundations of Orientation and Mobility: Volume I, History and Theory, 3rd edn. Kindle Paperwhite version (2010). https://amazon.com/

Analysis of Interest and Satisfaction of Accommodation Users

Naoki Hemmi(✉) and Yumi Asahi

Graduate School of Management, Tokyo University of Science, 1-11-2, Fujimi, Chiyoda-Ku 102-0071, Tokyo, Japan
8623515@ed.tus.ac.jp, asahi@rs.tus.ac.jp

Abstract. The purpose of this study is to clarify the relationship between the interest and satisfaction of accommodation users in terms of usage situations such as travel purposes and companions. Using the topic model, we analyzed review data from an online travel reservation site and found that the following factors were most frequently mentioned: "room reservation and change of reservation," "customer service by employees," "hot spring facilities," "location of lodging facilities," "food," "travel purpose," and "travel companion. And food", "location of lodging facilities", "facilities of accommodations", "facilities in the room", and "check-in and check-out". These topics were then assigned to each review data, aggregated by facility use situation, and subjected to a chi-square test, which revealed that the topics of interest varied by use situation. In addition, a two-way ANOVA was conducted to determine whether the topics and usage situations to which reviews were assigned were related to satisfaction with the accommodations. The results revealed that both the assigned topic and usage situation were significant and that an interaction effect also existed.

Keywords: Customer experience · Consumer satisfaction · Accommodation satisfaction

1 Introduction

As the world economy grows and globalization progresses, the number of tourists worldwide continues to increase. Tourism is an important industry, both culturally and economically, as it allows for interaction with people from outside the region and for generating revenue from outside the region. The importance of tourism is becoming increasingly recognized in Japan, and the Japanese government is vigorously pursuing activities such as visa relaxation and airport expansion to increase the number of foreign visitors to Japan and the amount of tourism spending. The number of foreign visitors to Japan and tourists in Japan is on the rise [1]. However, within the Japanese tourism industry, the management of lodging facilities faces a variety of problems, including a lack of successors, a chronic shortage of labor, and low profitability [2]. Since lodging facilities are in the service industry, hospitality is important in gaining customer loyalty, but excessive service may worsen profitability in the end. Therefore, it is an important issue in the management of lodging facilities to understand customer satisfaction factors toward lodging facilities and then provide appropriate services. Previous studies on traveler satisfaction evaluation include satisfaction with tourism resources and facilities [3], satisfaction with accommodation facilities and facility employees [4–11], and satisfaction with guides who support travel [12, 13]. This study focuses on the satisfaction factors of accommodations among these travel experiences. There are two reasons for analyzing the satisfaction factors of accommodations. The first is that spending on accommodations accounts for a large portion of travelers' expenditures. The second is that, as mentioned earlier, the problems faced by lodging facilities are serious within the Japanese tourism industry. For these two reasons, this study analyzes customer satisfaction factors in Japanese lodging facilities.

In service research, word-of-mouth has been widely used. This is because word of mouth influences consumers' purchase decisions and brand choices [14], in addition to reflecting the value of the customer experience and satisfaction. Methods for analyzing word-of-mouth and customer review text include text mining, which counts the number of occurrences of words and analyzes the strength of their connections to other words; topic modeling, which statistically analyzes topics that are latent in the text; and natural language modeling using deep learning. Since natural language models have problems such as the black box nature of the model itself and low interpretability, we decided to conduct our analysis with topic models using LDA [15] in this study.

The structure of this paper is as follows. Section 2 reviews previous studies and explains the research hypothesis; Sect. 3 describes the data used in the analysis and preprocessing; Sect. 4 presents the specific analysis method; and Sect. 5 presents the results and discussion. Finally, Sect. 6 concludes the paper with a summary of the study, its contributions, limitations, and future research agenda.

2   Previous Studies and Hypotheses

As for studies on accommodations in general, there is one that revealed that reviews on "bath" and "meals" appeared more frequently in accommodations with high satisfaction [9], and another that showed the importance of "employees," "breakfast," "dinner," "bath and lodging," and "room" [7].

There are also many studies analyzing differences by accommodation type. [10] Analyzed customer reviews by text mining for three Japanese lodging hotel chains. He found that the words that appeared in each chain and the evaluations differed, suggesting that "food," "room," and "location or station" were important for customer satisfaction. [5] also used text mining to analyze the number of occurrences of words and the strength of connections between words for each type of lodging, and found that "hot springs," "meals," and "rooms" were frequently mentioned in all types of lodging. On the other hand, some studies suggest that satisfaction and dissatisfaction factors differ for each type of lodging [4]. A study that analyzed satisfaction factors of luxury hotels [6] suggests that "room quality" or "communication with employees" are satisfaction factors for users of lodging facilities. Similarly, a study that analyzed the satisfaction factors of luxury hotels suggests that the relationship between service quality and price is important.

Most of these studies have focused on the accommodation side, the service provider, rather than the users, and few studies have focused on the situations of use. Therefore, in this study, the following hypotheses are formulated with a focus on usage situations.

H1: Interest in accommodations differs depending on the situation in which the facility is used.

Furthermore, to analyze not only the difference in interest by usage situation but also the satisfaction and dissatisfaction factors with accommodations, the following hypotheses were set up for this study.

H2: Satisfaction and dissatisfaction factors with accommodations differ by the situation of facility use.

3 Data

3.1 Data

Online review data from Rakuten Travel, a travel reservation site operated by Rakuten, Inc. Was used as the hotel review data. Rakuten Travel is the second most used travel reservation site in Japan. Reviews were submitted from January 1, 2019, to December 19, 2019. In addition to user reviews, this data includes information such as "facility ID," "purpose of the trip," and "companions," as well as satisfaction with the "location," "room," "bath," "service," and "facilities" of the accommodation and overall satisfaction. In addition to user reviews, "purpose of trip" and "companions" are used in this study because the analysis focuses on usage situations. In addition, "overall satisfaction" will be used in analyzing the satisfaction factors. Therefore, rows with deficiencies in "purpose of trip," "companions," "overall satisfaction," or "user reviews" were deleted.

In this study, the situation of using accommodations was defined as a combination of "purpose of trip" and "companion. There were three types of trip purposes: "business," "leisure," and "other." Review data with "other" trip purposes were excluded from the analysis, and data with "business" or "leisure" trip purposes were used. There were five types of companions: "alone," "friend," "family," "colleague(s)," and "lover. In other words, there are 10 possible usage situations (2 x 5), i.e., combinations of travel purpose and companion.

Table 1 shows the number of people in each situation. As Table 1 shows, the number of people who stay with friends or lovers for business purposes is extremely small, so it was excluded from the analysis in this study. In other words, the use situations were "Business/ Alone," "Business/ Colleague(s)," "Business/ Family," "Leisure/ Alone," "Leisure/ Colleague(s)," "Leisure/ Friend(s)," "Leisure/ Family," "Leisure/ Family", and "Leisure/ Lover".

Table 1. Crosstabulation table of travel purpose and companion.

Objective \Companion	Alone	Colleague(s)	Family	Friend(s)	Lover
Business	130776	12533	361	2591	325
Leasure	114244	2618	24539	183713	22133

3.2 Preprocessing

In analyzing the user review data, morphological analysis was performed to remove stop words. For morphological analysis, MeCab, a morphological analyzer for Japanese, was used. Stop words are words that should be excluded from the analysis because they appear frequently in the text or have no meaning as characters. In this study, special characters such as symbols, numbers, URLs, and pictograms were removed as stop words. In addition, although the user reviews were basically in Japanese, some of the review data also contained English words, and therefore, common words such as 'a', 'the', 'of ', and other common English stop-words were also removed. Words other than nouns and adjectives were also removed because adjectives and nouns were the parts of speech for analysis in this study. Morphological analysis was performed, and since the removal of stop-words caused some review data to be missing, the missing lines were also removed. After the missing lines were removed, the data were tabulated by situation, and the smallest situation left 2567 data. Therefore, a total of 20536 data, 2567 randomly sampled from eight situations, were included in the analysis in this study.

4 Method

4.1 Extraction of User Interests

To analyze the customer experience of overnight travelers, a topic model with LDA was used. In dealing with the topic model, it is necessary to determine the number of topics. There are several methods for determining the number of topics, including the use of indices and the method in which the analyst determines the number of topics in consideration of interpretability. Perplexity is widely used as an indicator to determine the number of topics.

However, problems may arise when the index is used, such as the optimal number of topics being too large or the number of topics lacking interpretability. Therefore, in this study, models were created with a number of topics ranging from 2 to 10, and the number of topics with the highest interpretability was used for the analysis. The gensim library in Python was used to create the LDA models.

4.2 Differences in Interest by Usage Situation

Using the topic model created the probability of attributing each user review to each topic can be determined. In this study, we cross-tabulated the lodging situations and attribution topics by assigning the topic with the highest attribution probability to each user review data. A chi-square test with a significance level of 5% was then conducted to determine if a difference in user interest in lodging exists by situation (H1). After conducting the chi-square test, we analyzed which situations each topic was more likely to appear in.

4.3 Difference in Satisfaction Factors by Scene of Use

To analyze whether the combination of usage situation and attribution topic affects overall satisfaction with the accommodation, a two-way ANOVA was conducted with usage situation and attribution topic as factors (H2). The significance level was set at 5%. After conducting a two-way ANOVA, we analyzed whether each topic was a satisfaction or dissatisfaction factor for each situation.

5 Results

5.1 Occurrence Words and Topic Meanings for Each Topic

After topic analysis by LDA, the number of topics was determined to be seven in terms of interpretability. The top 20 words with the highest probability of occurrence for each topic are shown in Table 2. Topic 1 was determined to be "room reservation and change of reservation" based on the top occurrence of words such as "reservation," "room," "plan," "smoking," "change," and "phone." Topic 2 was judged to be "customer service by employees" because the words "staff," "support," and "customer service" appeared at the top of the list. Topic 3 was judged to be "hot spring facilities and food" because the words "bath," "delicious," "cuisine," "meal," and "hot spring" appeared at the top of the list. Topic 4 was judged to be "location of lodging facilities" because words such as "use," "station," "close by," "location," "convenience," "parking," and "convenience store" appeared at the top of the list. Topic 5 was judged to be "facilities of accommodations" because words such as "old," "use," "facility," "building," and "hot spring" appeared at the top of the list. Topic 6 was judged to be "facilities in the room" because words such as "room," "toilet," "towel," "small," "bath," "shower," "bed," and "air conditioner" appeared at the top of the list. Topic 7 was determined to be "check-in and check-out" based on the top occurrence of words such as "check," "in," "check-out," "time," "luggage," and "front. "

While in the previous study, factors such as "food," "bath," "customer service," "location," and "room" were cited as concerns, this study is unique in that topics related to reservation of facilities and, among customer service, topics related to check-in and check-out appeared.

Table 2. Top 20 words with the highest probability of occurrence for each topic.

Topic 1	Topic 2	Topic 3	Topic 4	Topic 5	Topic 6	Topic 7
予約 reservation	方 person	風呂 bath	利用 use	方 person	無い not available	チェック check
部屋 room	スタッフ staff	美味しい delicious	駅 station	宿 inn	部屋 room	イン in
ルーム room	対応 support	露店 open-air	良い good	良い good	トイレ toilet	時 occasion
無い not available	良い good	料理 cuisine	ホテル hotel	古い old	タオル towel	時間 time
プラン plan	素晴らしい great	食事 meal	近く close by	宿泊 accommodation	狭い small	無い not available
喫煙 smoking	事 thing	温泉 hot spring	立地 location	利用 use	風呂 bath	事 thing
事 thing	利用 use	良い good	部屋 room	施設 facility	シャワー shower	ホテル hotel
為 reason for	従業 employee	夕食 dinner	便利 convenience	事 thing	ベッド bed	チェックアウト check-out
変更 change	ホテル hotel	満足 satisfaction	朝食 breakfast	部屋 room	欲しい want	客 guest
時 occasion	接客 customer service	部屋 room	近い close by	建物 building	良い good	部屋 room
駐車 parking	度 degree	最高 best	駐車 parking	スタッフ staff	エアコン air conditioner	前 front
得 benefit	宿泊 accommodation	景色 view	満足 satisfaction	風呂 bath	コンディショナー conditioner	荷物 luggage
電話 phone	思い出 memory	子供 child	コンビニ convenience store	温泉 hot spring	洗面 bathroom	機 machinery
チェック check	本当 real	御飯 meal	宿泊 accommodation	刺し身 sashimi	点 point	フロント front

5.2 User Interest by Usage Scenario

From the model created, each review data was assigned a topic to which it was attributed, and a crosstabulation table of usage situations and attributed topics is presented in Table 3. Overall, it was found that topic 4 regarding location, and topic 3 regarding bath and meal were more likely to appear, while topic 1 regarding reservation, and topic 7 regarding check-in and check-out were less likely to appear.

A chi-square test based on the data in Table 3 yielded significant results ($\chi^2 = 864.526$, $p = 4.167e\text{-}154$, $df = 42$), indicating that there is an association between usage situations and topics.

Table 3 also shows in which situations individual topics are likely to be of interest. Topic 1, "Room Reservations and Reservation Changes," is more likely to appear for business purposes than for leisure purposes and is also more likely to appear when traveling for leisure purposes and accompanied by colleague(s). Therefore, it is desirable to promote accommodation plans that are sufficient to meet the diverse needs of business hotel customers and the ability to flexibly support changes in reservations. Topic 2, "Customer service by employees," is more likely to appear when traveling with family or friends and is relatively less likely to appear when traveling for business purposes or when traveling alone. Therefore, it is important to improve the quality of customer service when targeting groups of travelers for leisure purposes. Topic 3, "Onsen facilities and meals," is also a topic that is more likely to appear in Topic 2, except for solo travelers, and is especially likely to appear in leisure travel with family members. When targeting leisure group travelers, it is important to improve the quality of hot spring facilities and meals offered as well as customer service. Topic 4, "Location of accommodations," is more likely to appear in business travel. Since it is not easy to change the location, it is advisable to keep this in mind when opening a new business hotel. Topic 5, "Facilities of Accommodations," is less likely to appear when respondents are staying with colleague(s) or family members for business purposes. Topic 6, "In-Room Facilities," was found to be more likely to appear when traveling for leisure purposes and less likely to appear when traveling for business purposes. Topic 7, "Check-in and check-out," was found to be more likely to appear in the case of business trips with family members and leisure trips with lovers.

Table 3. Crosstabulation table of topics and situations of use of accommodations.

Situation/ Topic	Topic 1	Topic 2	Topic 3	Topic 4	Topic 5	Topic 6	Topic 7	All
Business Alone	235	284	297	931	297	311	212	2567
Business Colleague(s)	252	294	359	931	206	303	222	2567
Business Family	209	334	347	789	215	395	278	2567

(continued)

Table 3. (*continued*)

Situation/ Topic	Topic 1	Topic 2	Topic 3	Topic 4	Topic 5	Topic 6	Topic 7	All
Leisure Alone	221	288	427	739	267	399	226	2567
Leisure Colleague(s)	204	282	637	667	273	305	199	2567
Leisure Family	134	302	819	478	272	364	198	2567
Leisure Friend(s)	186	364	615	593	260	322	227	2567
Leisure Lover	167	315	595	598	270	360	262	2567
All	1608	2463	4096	5726	2060	2759	1824	20536

5.3 User Satisfaction Factors by Usage Situation

A two-way ANOVA was conducted to analyze whether the combination of usage situations and attributional topics differed in terms of satisfaction with the accommodations. The eight usage situations were Business/ Alone, Business/ Colleague(s), Business/ Family, Leasure/ Alone, Leasure/ Colleague(s), Leasure/ Family, Leasure/ Friend(s), and Leasure/ Lover. There are seven levels of attribution topics from Topic 1 to Topic 7. The significance level was set at 5%. Table 4 shows the results of the two-way ANOVA. As Table 4 shows, there were significant differences in both usage situation and topic, and an interaction effect was also observed.

Table 4. Results of two-way ANOVA.

	sum_sq	df	F	PR(>F)
Topic	497.5101657	6	100.7789086	1.72E-125
Situation	115.6605895	7	20.08196951	4.82E-27
Topic: Situation	65.88678323	42	1.906636735	0.000368243
Residual	16850.43087	20480		

Figure 1 shows the average overall satisfaction for each lodging situation and topic. From Fig. 1, the reviews assigned to Topic 6 and Topic 7 have low satisfaction in both lodging situations. This suggests that "facilities in the room" and "support at the front desk" may be unsatisfactory factors. After Topic 6 and Topic 7, the next topic with the lowest average satisfaction was Topic 1. Topic 2 was found to be the most satisfying factor for family trips for business purposes and leisure trips with colleague(s). Topic 3 was found to be the most satisfying factor for solo business travel and leisure travel with friends or loved ones. Topic 4 was found to be the most satisfying factor for leisure travel with family. Topic 5 is a satisfaction factor when staying with colleague(s) for business purposes. These results indicate that the dissatisfaction factors of accommodations do not differ significantly by situation, while the satisfaction factors vary by situation.

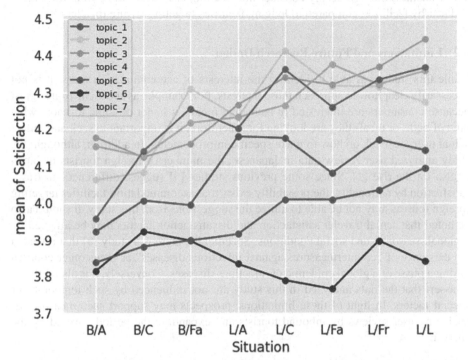

Fig. 1. Mean overall satisfaction with accommodations by usage situation and topic. The first half of / is the purpose of the trip (B: Business, L: Leisure) and the second half is the companion (A: Alone, C: Colleague(s), Fa: Family, Fr: Friend(s), L: Lover)

6   Discussion and Conclusion

6.1   Managerial Implications

After identifying the interests of accommodation users, this study clarified the interests that are likely to appear in each usage scenario. Furthermore, the relationship between lodging facility users' interests and their satisfaction was analyzed. This allows lodging facility managers to understand the points of interest that are likely to be expressed in each situation of customer use and to understand whether these points are likely to influence customer satisfaction or dissatisfaction. Understanding the relationship between customer interest and satisfaction can help determine which points to focus on for improvement to increase satisfaction based on the accommodation facility's target audience. For example, when targeting business travelers, having a variety of rooms and accommodation plans available and being able to support room changes is important in achieving customer satisfaction.

Furthermore, the results of this study will also help facility managers who are considering the development of new lodging facilities to design the optimal facility concept for their intended target. For example, it is important for managers considering opening a new business hotel to deeply consider the location, such as distance from the station and nearby facilities, compared to lodging facilities targeting leisure travelers.

6.2 Limitations and Future Research Design

While this study was able to identify the interests of accommodation users, it is not necessarily clear how to approach those interests. For example, as shown in Topic 3, just because consumers are interested in baths and meals, it is not possible to know what kind of baths or meals they are looking for. Therefore, it is important to seek and reflect actual user feedback on how to make specific improvements. In addition, although this study analyzed user review data in Japanese, the number of foreign tourists in Japan is also on the rise [1]. Since some previous studies [3] suggest differences in travel satisfaction by nationality, the possibility exists that accommodation facilities targeting foreign tourists may not be able to utilize the suggestions from this study. It should also be noted that actual traveler satisfaction and dissatisfaction factors may be affected by regional, seasonal, and social conditions. Specifically, there is a study [8] that revealed the existence of "countermeasures against infectious diseases" as a customer concern during a phase of a global epidemic of infectious diseases. Conversely, it is also difficult to assert that the data analyzed in this study are not influenced by such temporary or special factors. In light of these limitations, prospects may support such measures as analyzing user reviews by inbound tourists and expanding the period covered by the analysis.

Acknowledgments. We would like to express our appreciation to Rakuten, Inc. For providing us with the data to conduct this study.

References

1. Dai, S., Tetsuro, H.: A study on characteristics of overnight tourist demand by overnight travel statistics survey in Japan. J. Japan Soc. Civil Eng. Ser. D3 (Infrastruct. Planning Manag.) **77**(5), I_279-I_290 (2022). https://doi.org/10.2208/jscejipm.77.5_I_279
2. Wada, T., Kohara, A.: The current situation and issues of ryokan management in Japan. Res. Educ. Econ. **1**, 26–35 (2022). [in Japanese]
3. Kozak, M.: Comparative assessment of tourist satisfaction with destinations across two nationalities. Tour. Manage. **22**, 391–401 (2001)
4. Xun, X., Li, Y.: The antecedents of customer satisfaction and dissatisfaction toward various types of hotels: a text mining approach. Int. J. Hosp. Manag. **55**, 57–69 (2016). https://doi.org/10.1016/j.ijhm.2016.03.003
5. Sawada, A.: An analytical method proposal for tourist motivation using online hotel reviews. Memoirs Hokuriku Gakuin Univ., Hokuriku Gakuin Junior Coll. **6**, 277–283 (2014). [in Japanese]
6. Padma, P., Ahn, J.: Guest satisfaction and dissatisfaction in luxury hotels: an application of big data. Int. J. Hosp. Manag. **84**, 1–8 (2020)

7. Morishita, S.: An analysis of relationships between factors of hospitality and customer satisfaction in the Japanese inns utilizing online customer reviews. J. Japan Manag. Diagn. Assoc. **18**, 115–120 (2018). [in Japanese]

8. Araki, S., Komura, A., Hirai, H.: Relationship between ranking and word-of-mouth on Japanese travel information websites. J. Japan Ind. Manag. Assoc. **73**, 15–26 (2022). [in Japanese]

9. Tanabe, W., Goto, M.: A study on user review analysis to support accommodation strategy development. J. Center Inf. Stud. **4**(9), 91–101 (2008) [in Japanese]

10. Kubota, T.: Text mining of review's data of hotel in internet travel advisory service. Tama Univ. J. Manag. Inf. Sci. **20**, 149–156 (2016). [in Japanese]

11. Lu, C., Berchoux, C., Marek, M.W., Chen, B.: Service quality and customer satisfaction: qualitative research implications for luxury hotels. Int. J. Cult., Tourism, Hosp. Res. **9**(2), 168–182 (2015)

12. Endo, Y., Wakabayashi, Y., Masuda, H.: Study on factors that satisfy luxury travelers: from a perspective of the business suppliers serving Japan travels to luxury travelers from Europe and the United States. Japan Tourism Manag. Rev. **1**, 10–15 (2021). [in Japanese]

13. Huang, S., Hsu, C.H., Chan, A.: Tour guide performance and tourist satisfaction: a study of the package tours in Shanghai. J. Hosp. Tourism Res. **34**(1), 3–33 (2010)

14. Bigne, E., Ruiz, C., Curras, R.: Destination appeal thorough digitalized comments. J. Bus. Res. **101**, 447–453 (2019)

15. Blei, D.M., Ng, A.Y., Jordan, M.I.: Latent dirichlet allocation. J. Mach. Learn. Res. **3**, 993–1022 (2003)

A Generative Bottle Design System Based on Users' Touch Feelings

Yinghsiu Huang(✉) 📵

Department of Industrial Design, National Kaohsiung Normal University, Taiwan. No.62,
Shenjhong Road, Yanchao District, Kaohsiung City 82446, Taiwan
yinghsiu@mail.nknu.edu.tw

Abstract. Designers or consumers cannot easily identify their preferred designs from such a large searching space of designs. Thus, the problem of this research is how designers or consumers generate designs based on their touch-feeling Kansei vocabularies. This research features a Kansei vocabulary experiment in which critical form-related parameters of bottles are imported into the Grasshopper platform for the creation of experimental samples that respond to user touch-feelings in product forms. The generative design system outcomes reflect consumers' tactile perceptual needs, and the associated Kansei vocabulary can be deployed as vectors for executing bottle modifications. Thus, designers and users can benefit from a faster, more straightforward, and more intuitive process to create product designs tailored to consumers' touch-feeling preferences.

Keywords: Generative Design System · Kansei Engineering · Conceptual Design · Tactile Perceptual · Parametric Design

1 Introduction

From the 19th century, trends and styles in modern design are grounded in the theory of Louis Sullivan (1856–1924), the shape of a product changes with its function. The concept of "form follows function" later shifts to "form follows fun." For users today, the form of a product should be engaging and feature an emotional component, which can be characterized as "form follows emotion" [1]. The renowned Savoy Vase by Finnish designer Alvar Aalto, for example, was inspired by Finland's winding coastline. The designer studied natural forms and applied those visual principles to the design, rendering the product emotively charged. Thus, users experience an additional visual-emotive dimension when using the product. Furthermore, it is imperative to acknowledge that emotional responses can be incited not only through visual stimuli but also through tactile or acoustic sensations.

Computers assume a pivotal role across diverse design phases, primarily serving to aid designers in crafting products aligned with user demands. From Computer-Aided Industrial Design (CAID), Computer-Aided Evaluation (CAE), to more modern Computer-Aided Conceptual Design (CACD), following the development of Generative

Design System (GDS), the application of computer software during the concept development phase helps designers identify quick, multifarious, and systemic solutions for solving design problems [2]. By doing so, GDSs also increase design productivity by helping designers to consolidate the numerous and disordered drawing routines, freeing designers to devote more energy to creative thinking. Moreover, generative design method (GDM) proposed by Krish [2], is a system grounded in parametric CADs, in which parameters cover a specific range from the maximum to minimum values that comprise the program's query scope. While GDSs have the capacity to expeditiously generate hundreds and thousands of designs, the challenge lies in the subsequent selection of a preferred form from this vast pool, be it by designers or consumers.

Contemporary parametric generative designs employ parameters for the refinement of product design, where each adjustment pertains to a singular value, and each value exhibits a low correlation with the inherent features of product forms. While certain systems permit consumers to directly manipulate parameters, the resultant alterations in form may not manifest as conspicuously significant. In the design of eyeglasses, for example, consumers' preferences relate to the perception of "smartness" or "stylishness" when wearing the eyeglasses instead of struggling with parametric components such as the upper tilt angle of the frame, frame thickness, or lead angles of the frame.

In a groundbreaking contribution, Huang [3] introduced a generative design system predicated on consumers' visual and emotional preferences. This innovative approach involves establishing a nexus between visual image vocabularies and parameters, contingent upon relative weights. Through this linkage, the configuration of vases can be dynamically adjusted by leveraging Kansei vocabulary. Through the correlation between each numerical value on the shape characteristics, a gradual shape can be formed according to level-1 to 5 of the visual Kansei vocabulary. Therefore, designers not only can generate the shape of products based on the parameters by using the generative design systems; but also develop product forms due to visual preferences from consumers' visual and perceptual needs for the product.

Moreover, consumers purchase products not only depending on visual preferences, but also based on tactile preferences, such as a gear shift, bicycle handles, kettle handle, or bottle-forms etc. Thus, the problem of this study is how to convert the user's tactile preference into parameters of a generative shape-design system? By doing so, users can adjust tactile preferences to meet their touch feelings of a bottle shape.

In this study, bottle shapes with aesthetically pleasing forms are used to create eight samples within the GDS Grasshopper, by selecting six key form-related parameters. The bottles then serve as test objects for a 5-paired touch-feelings experiment. The aim is to analyze the correlation between the six key parameters and 5-paired touch-feelings vocabularies. The results are then applied in generative design to produce bottle shapes that correspond to consumer demands. Subsequently, touch-feelings vocabulary can be deployed by the users as design modification vectors to produce touch-feeling preferred bottle shapes in a rapid, simple, and intuitive manner.

2 Related Works

Initially, this investigation presents an exploration of Kansei impressions and tactile linguistic expressions associated with product configurations. Subsequently, Kansei vocabularies signifying antithetical tactile sensations is discerned. Parametric designs, theories in generative design research, and relevant software, along with their design-centric applications, are comprehensively scrutinized.

2.1 Kansei Image and Cognition

Humans perceive environments and forms according to intuitive experience acquired through their senses when observing their everyday surroundings. When they purchase products, their choices will be based on certain affective impressions, of sturdiness, luxuriousness, and brightness, for example. In order to understand this phenomenon, Nagamachi proposed the Kansei engineering concept, with Kansei derived from a Japanese expression for psychological perceptions and impressions of a product. Nagamachi [4] regarded product semantics as users' intuitive associations based on their sensory perception of products' forms, among which image associations is most prominent; Kansei engineering is a technique that translates consumers' perceptual image into new products [4].

The semantic differential (SD) method is the most prevalent type of research methodology in Kansei engineering. The concept of SD originated from the synesthesia research proposed by Osgood et al. [5] in 1942. Their approach uses a bipolar adjective scale to measure participants' responses to an object or concept. The approach establishes the connotation of a concept or object; that is, the sensory or psychological opinions or significance that a person attributes to concepts and objects. The synesthetic approach can detect nuances in the participants' positive and negative impressions, feelings, and preferences in relation to test samples. Furthermore, the SD evaluation method is fixed and objective, whereby interviewees may provide a series of score evaluations, producing a rich data set for statistical analysis. The scales used can also be designed according to actual needs to generate abundant reference data.

The SD approach has been widely studied in the field of design. For example, Zhai et al. [6] used the SD approach to convert complex affective factors into quantifiable design rules to increase user satisfaction for specific products. The SD approach can be used to evaluate and analyze affective image for a product, aiming to identify the relationship between design elements and emotions for cellphone designs [7].

From 1987, in the field of cognitive psychology, Lederman and Klatzky proposed that human beings with high intelligence can use their hands to touch the properties and attributes of objects systematically [8]. At the same time, through the process of exploration, they can also determine the shape, material, texture and other physical characteristics of objects in terms of tactile identification. Nowadays, tactile researches of Kansei image and cognition could be divided into three major categories: tactile imagery of "product shape"; tactile imagery of "materials"; and tactile imagery of "textures" [9]. In this study, only tactile Kansei vocabularies of the "product shape" will be discussed, while the "materials" and "textures" of bottle designs will be the same formulations, and will not be discussed.

2.2 Parametric and Generative Design

The term "parametric" in parametric design refers to the types of measures that define the specific characteristics of systems and functions. Parametric design enables CAD systems to execute interactive graphics as well as automated graphic mapping. Parametric design can substantially accelerate model generation and modification; thus, it has higher value for application in product design and development. Such design is not bound by time and exhibits reversibility and linked-motion properties. Specifically, designers can revisit previous operation steps to modify a model. The changes made are then automatically applied to subsequent design phases. In CAD, parametric modeling has become a mainstream method to increase design flexibility. Parametric modeling can also reduce the challenges caused by design modifications, and it is conventionally described as a parametric design [10].

In computing design application, the research of Oxman [11] is generally regarded as the first published study to set the baseline definitions and operation modes for generative design to assert its theoretical existence. In generative design, designers operate and modify preset generative systems to create the first mutation, which then serves as the basis for system modifications. Modification methods include the adjustment of parameters, which involves the determination of interactive judgment between illustration commands and data transfer effects so that the outcomes produced for the new generation more closely resemble the designer's intentions. This dynamic design concept greatly contrasts with the linear thinking that underlies conventional design concepts. Moreover, designers use diverse system-generated products as the basis or the scope for selection. In conventional design, the designer relies on brainpower to generate a limited number of design projects. By contrast, CAD achieves selection optimization or, at the minimum, the exposure of design flaws.

Krish [2] also proposed the GDM, a generative system based on parametric CAD environments. The system parameters are bounded by a limit, defined by maximum and minimum values, which define the program's search area. For each parameter, the search area forms a complete design space and also limits the area in which the computer conducts search functions. The GDS randomly generates new designs based on these parameter values, which resemble the genes of a design. Performance filters, based on design demands and conditions, are set to filter meaningful concepts. A separate proximity filter eliminates concepts with high similarity to ensure the generation of unique concepts. Then, these data are stored and primed for further modifications.

Grasshopper has experienced rapid development and popularization in digital architecture, with widespread and multifarious applications. In particular, freeform surface and digital architecture have emerged as realistic concepts because of the availability of such a parametric modeling apparatus. Uniform yet robust computing power has tremendously benefited digital architecture in which the computation involves large components with few variations. The use of rapid computing to present changes in real-time is another advantage that enables designers to repeatedly use dynamic nonlinear design techniques for locating optimal forms and structural performance.

3   The Structure and Process of Experiment

The initial step of this research was the establishment of the bottle design using parameters. Thus, eight bottle samples were then generated for the perception experiment by users. In the second step, a team of design experts were enrolled to compile touch-feeling vocabularies describing the bottle shapes. In the third step, a perception experiment was conducted to determine the users' touch-feeling preferences. Specifically, users' perceptions of the eight bottle samples were measured using the compiled touch-feeling vocabularies. Finally, the results were then used for statistical analysis, such as the regression analysis. The contribution of regression analysis will be used to the Kansei shape design system, which created design concepts based on users' touch-feeling vocabularies.

3.1   Building Bottle Samples

Krish [2] proposed a generative system based on a parametric computer-aided design system. Maximum and minimum values limit the parametric system within an area that is also defined the searching space of the parametric program. These parameters can be regarded as the DNA for design. Thus, the design within maximum and minimum parametric values represents all possibilities for the entire design. This research attempted to use Grasshopper to generate various bottles by six parameters: the angle of bottle mouth, the up-section dimension, mid-section dimension, low-section dimension, height ratio, and mid-to-low section ratio. Eight bottle designs were constructed (Fig. 1) by six parameters. All parametric values of 8 bottle designs are recorded in Table 1.

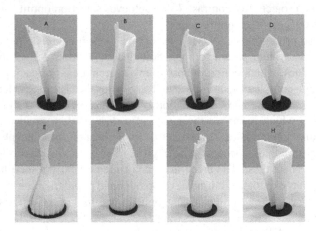

Fig. 1. Eight bottle designs of this research.

3.2   Selection of Touch-Feeling Vocabularies

In this research, touch-feeling vocabularies associated with product form were collected from related researches. Valuable resources included Huang [12], who focused on element design systems regarding the form image of mobile audio-visual products, and Lin

Table 1. All parametric values of 8 bottle designs.

	the angle of bottle mouth	low-section dimension	height ratios	mid-to-low section ratio	mid-section dimension	up-section dimension
sample A	0.75	2.44	9.83	5.39	5.6	9.52
sample B	0.7	8.45	12	3.42	6.05	6.15
sample C	0.53	1.82	9.82	5.31	8.36	7.7
sample D	0.44	2.5	22.49	3.88	6.96	2.21
sample E	0.36	7.63	11.65	2.86	1.97	3.02
sample F	0.58	4.03	9	3.27	5.09	1.17
sample G	0.65	3.07	13.16	1.46	1.81	4.21
sample H	0.58	2.44	9.83	5.04	7.15	9.38

(2004), who investigated the correlations between product form images and features. And Chou's research [13], "Creating Product Forms with Preferred Kansei via Formal Features", also referred for collecting Kansei vocabulary.

After collecting Kansei vocabularies from previous references, five experts with design backgrounds and relevant work experiences were then invited to form a focus group to discuss whether the selected Touch-Feeling vocabulary appropriately described form features of 8 generated bottles. Thus, 5 Touch-Feeling Kansei vocabularies were selected, and their antonyms were also identified following a discussion (Table 2). Therefore, 5-paired Touch-Feeling Kansei vocabularies selected by experts were used in the experiment, and participants have to evaluate 8 bottle samples, produced by the generative form system.

Table 2. 5-paired Touch-Feeling Kansei vocabularies.

5-paired Touch-Feeling vocabularies
Geometric - Organic
Vivid - Dull
Rough - Delicate
Soft - Hard
Rational - Emotional

3.3 Experiment Process

The focus of this research is bottle design, and no specific user was targeted. During the experiment, participants first received an explanation on the experiment's goals and procedures. The eight bottle samples were named from A to H (Fig. 1). An assistant then retrieved a bottle sample by random from a box and put it into another box; Moreover, the participant could use both hands touching the bottle sample, and there is no time limitation.

After touching one bottle, the named bottle was recorded by participant on the questionnaire, and the questionnaire was presented to the participant for an evaluation according to 5 touch-feeling Kansei vocabularies (Fig. 2). The methodology of this experiment was employed the "Semantic Differential Method, SD" [5]. Specifically, touch-feeling vocabularies were placed on one side of the questionnaire with their respective antonyms being placed on the other side. Between the opposite vocabularies, there is a 5-point scale (1 to 5 from left to right). The number 1 signifies strong responses in favor of the vocabularies on the left, and 5 denotes the same in favor of the vocabularies on the right. The median value is 3, indicating no preference for neither left side nor right side of touch-feeling vocabulary. The experiment enrolled 49 participants in total.

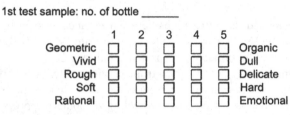

Fig. 2. The example of the questionnaire.

3.4 Single Sample *t* Test for Bottle Forms

In this research, each bottle sample will be evaluated by 5 antonymous touch-feeling vocabularies with which users could describe their perceptions after touching each computer-generated bottle design. After collecting data, rating of 1 represents stronger agreement to the vocabulary on the left side, whereas that of 5 denotes stronger agreement to the vocabulary on the right side (Fig. 2). In this experiment, participants described the eight samples using 5-paired touch-feeling Kansei vocabularies; thus, an Single samples t test was performed to distinguish users' preferences between antonymous touch-feeling vocabulary and whether significance was achieved. By doing so, a statistical software, such as SPSS, was used to conduct the Single samples t test on the eight experiment samples.

Single Ssample t-Test Analysis: Sample A. The generated bottle sample A produced with the method described in Sect. 3.1 was analyzed by using SPSS, focusing on 5 paired of touch-feeling Kansei vocabulary for the Single samples t test. Outcomes with test value 3 are presented in Table 3.

Among the 5 sets of touch-feeling Kansei vocabularies, only one set of t values achieved 0.05 significance, which is Vivid - Dull (t = −2.248*, * means p < .05). For the antonymous Kansei vocabulary, a negative t value indicates greater preference for the Kansei vocabulary on left side, whereas a positive t value denotes preference for the vocabulary on the right.

Table 3. Single sample *t* test for sample A.

			test value = 3			
					95% confidence interval of the Difference	
	t	DF	Sig.(2-tailed)	Std. Error Difference	Lower	Upper
Geometric - Organic	.474	48	.637	.082	-.26	.43
Vivid - Dull	-2.248	48	.029*	-.286	-.54	-.03
Rough - Delicate	.139	48	.890	.020	-.28	.32
Soft - Hard	.540	48	.591	.082	-.22	.39
Rational - Emotional	.961	48	.341	.143	-.16	.44

Single Sample t-Test Analysis: Sample B. Outcomes of single sample t test of sample B presented in Table 4 with test value 3. Among 5 sets of Kansei vocabularies, none set of t values achieved significance.

Table 4. Single sample *t* test for sample B.

			test value = 3			
					95% confidence interval of the Difference	
	t	DF	Sig.(2-tailed)	Std. Error Difference	Lower	Upper
Geometric - Organic	1.296	48	.201	.224	-.12	.57
Vivid - Dull	-.136	48	.892	-.020	-.32	.28
Rough - Delicate	-.148	48	.883	-.020	-.30	.26
Soft - Hard	.000	48	1.000	.000	-.23	.23
Rational - Emotional	-.139	48	.890	-.020	-.32	.28

Single Samples t-Test Analysis: Sample C. Outcomes of single sample *t* test of sample C presented in Table 5 with test value 3. Among 5 sets of *Kansei* vocabularies, only one set of *t* values achieved 0.01 significance, which is Vivid - Dull (t = −4.219**, ** means p < .01). For the remaining, significance was not achieved.

Single Samples t-Test Analysis: Sample D. The result of single sample *t* test of sample D presented in Table 6 with test value 3. Among 5 sets of *Kansei* vocabularies, 4

Table 5. Single sample *t* test for sample C.

	t	DF	Sig.(2-tailed)	Std. Error Difference	95% confidence interval of the Difference	
					Lower	Upper
Geometric - Organic	1.968	48	.055	.347	-.01	.70
Vivid - Dull	-4.219	48	.001**	-.551	-.81	-.29
Rough - Delicate	-.141	48	.888	-.020	-.31	.27
Soft - Hard	.636	48	.528	.102	-.22	.42
Rational - Emotional	1.268	48	.211	.184	-.11	.47

sets of *t* values achieved 0.01 significance, and 1 set of *t* values achieved 0.05 significance. According to their *t* values representing intensity in descending order, 5 sets of *Kansei* vocabularies are Soft, Vivid, Delicate, Organic, and Emotional (t $= -5.888**$, $-4.431**$, 4.215**, 3.997**and 2.367*, respectively, ** means $p < .01$, and * means $p < .05$).

Table 6. Single sample *t* test for sample D.

	t	DF	Sig.(2-tailed)	Std. Error Difference	95% confidence interval of the Difference	
					Lower	Upper
Geometric - Organic	3.997	48	.001**	.673	.33	1.01
Vivid - Dull	-4.431	48	.001**	-.653	-.95	-.36
Rough - Delicate	4.215	48	.001**	.612	.32	.90
Soft - Hard	-5.888	48	.001**	-.673	-.90	-.44
Rational - Emotional	2.367	48	.022*	.327	.05	.60

Single Samples t Test Analysis: Sample E.   The result of single sample *t* test of sample E presented in Table 7 with test value 3. All 5 sets of touch-feeling *Kansei* vocabularies of *t* values achieved 0.01 significance. According to their *t* values representing intensity in descending order, they are Organic, Vivid, Emotional, Soft, and Delicate (t $= 7.292**$, $-6.319**$, 4.215**, $-3.112**$and 3.071**, respectively, ** means $p < .01$).

Single Samples t Test Analysis: Sample F.   Outcomes of single sample *t* test of sample F presented in Table 8 with test value 3. Among 5 sets of *Kansei* vocabularies, only one set of *t* values achieved 0.01 significance, which is Organic (t $= 3.167**$, ** means p $< .01$). For the remaining, significance was not achieved.

Single Samples t Test Analysis: Sample G.   The result of single sample *t* test of sample G presented in Table 9 with test value 3. Among 5 sets of *Kansei* vocabularies,

Table 7. Single sample *t* test for sample E.

	t	DF	Sig.(2-tailed)	Std. Error Difference	Lower	Upper
			test value = 3		95% confidence interval of the Difference	
Geometric - Organic	7.292	48	.001**	1.041	.75	1.33
Vivid - Dull	-6.319	48	.001**	-.918	-1.21	-.63
Rough - Delicate	3.071	48	.004**	.531	.18	.88
Soft - Hard	-3.112	48	.003**	-.490	-.81	-.17
Rational - Emotional	4.215	48	.001**	.612	.32	.90

Table 8. Single sample *t* test for sample F.

	t	DF	Sig.(2-tailed)	Std. Error Difference	Lower	Upper
			test value = 3		95% confidence interval of the Difference	
Geometric - Organic	3.167	48	.003**	.490	.18	.80
Vivid - Dull	-.256	48	.799	-.041	-.36	.28
Rough - Delicate	-.785	48	.436	-.122	-.44	.19
Soft - Hard	.144	48	.886	.020	-.26	.30
Rational - Emotional	.417	48	.679	.061	-.23	.36

all 5 sets of *t* values achieved 0.01 significance. According to their *t* values representing intensity in descending order, they are Soft, Organic, Vivid, Emotional, and Delicate (t = -7.325**, 6.000**, -5.386**, 5.000**, and 4.495**, respectively, ** means $p < .01$). Only Traditional – Innovative was not achieved significance.

Table 9. Single sample *t* test for sample G.

	t	DF	Sig.(2-tailed)	Std. Error Difference	Lower	Upper
			test value = 3		95% confidence interval of the Difference	
Geometric - Organic	6.000	48	.001**	.857	.57	1.14
Vivid - Dull	-5.386	48	.001**	-.673	-.92	-.42
Rough - Delicate	4.495	48	.001**	.612	.34	.89
Soft - Hard	-7.325	48	.001**	-.837	-1.07	-.61
Rational - Emotional	5.000	48	.001**	.714	.43	1.00

Single Samples t Test Analysis: Sample H. The result of single sample t test of sample H presented in Table 10 with test value 3. Among 5 sets of *Kansei* vocabularies, two sets of t values achieved 0.01 and 0.05 significance. According to their t values representing intensity in descending order, two sets of Kansei vocabularies are Hard and Rough ($t = 2.705**$ and $-2.521*$, respectively, ** means $p < .01$ and * means $p < .05$). Others was not achieved significance.

Table 10. Single sample t test for sample H.

			test value = 3		95% confidence interval of the Difference	
	t	DF	Sig.(2-tailed)	Std. Error Difference	Lower	Upper
Geometric - Organic	1.278	48	.207	.224	-.13	.58
Vivid - Dull	.417	48	.679	.061	-.23	.36
Rough - Delicate	-2.521	48	.015*	-.388	-.70	-.08
Soft - Hard	2.705	48	.009**	.367	.09	.64
Rational - Emotional	-.670	48	.506	-.102	-.41	.20

According to the independent samples t test results on the eight experiment samples obtained in previous section, users' responses (indicating their perceptions) to various generative form samples were significantly different regarding the touch-feeling Kansei adjectives they selected. In the following discussion, the six Kansei vocabulary sets serve as a basis for identifying the unique traits of touch-feeling vocabulary used for formal description (Table 11).

Table 11. Comparison among 5 paired touch-feeling Kansei vocabularies.

	A	B	C	D	E	F	G	H
Geometric - Organic		Organic (t= 1.296)	Organic (t= 1.968)	Organic (t= 3.997**)	Organic (t= 7.292**)	Organic (t= 3.167**)	Organic (t= 6.000**)	Organic (t= 1.278)
Vivid - Dull	Vivid (t= -2.248*)		Vivid (t= -4.219**)	Vivid (t= -4.431**)	Vivid (t= -6.319**)		Vivid (t= -5.386**)	
Rough - Delicate				Delicate (t= 4.215**)	Delicate (t= 3.071**)		Delicate (t= 4.495**)	Rough (t= -2.521*)
Soft - Hard				Soft (t= -5.888**)	Soft (t= -3.112**)		Soft (t= -7.325**)	Hard (t= 2.705**)
Rational - Emotional			Emotional (t= 1.268)	Emotional (t= 2.367*)	Emotional (t= 4.215**)		Emotional (t= 5.000**)	
Traditional - Innovative	Innovative (t= 1.000)	Traditional (t= -2.138*)	Innovative (t= 1.184)		Innovative (t= 4.963**)		Innovative (t= 1.474)	Traditional (t= -1.268)

** means $p < .01$ and * means $p < .05$

In Table 11, the adjectives in the gray background cells indicate that they reach significant level (** $p < 0.01$ or *$p < 0.05$). The t-value of right-side adjective is positive, while t-value of left-side is negative. The larger the positive value or the smaller the negative value, the stronger the t values. For example, in Rough-Delicate adjective, the right-side adjective is "Delicate", which t-values are positive, shown in samples D, E, and G, and t-values reach the significance within the gray background cell (**$p < 0.01$). On contrary, the left-side adjective is "Rough", which t-value is negative, shown in samples H, and t-value also reaches the slight significance in gray background cell (*$p < 0.05$). Moreover, adjectives without gray background means that t-values are greater than 1 or less than -1 without significant.

Through the SD analysis of Kansei vocabularies, only the features of individual touch-feeling adjectives could be identified. However, as described in Sect. 3.1, the impression of each sample was formed from six parametric combinations, that means each touch-feeling Kansei vocabularies of participants' preference was a combination of six parameter variations. The previous outcomes permit only preliminary analysis on the features of touch-feeling vocabularies when being used to describe bottle samples; however, they cannot be used to observe how touch-feeling vocabularies influence generated forms. Therefore, in Sect. 4, this research uses regression analysis to examine the correlation between touch-feeling Kansei vocabularies and six parameters used to describe the generated samples in Sect. 3.1. Finally, how to use touch-feeling vocabularies to generate new bottle designs, according to users' preferences, is also presented.

4 Touch-Feeling Vocabulary with Regression Analysis

In terms of cognitive behavior, users perceived a product form, which is associated to experiences in their brain. But, the results of preferences for touch-feeling vocabularies will be divergent. Moreover, parameters affecting such differentials among forms are not only limited to a single line, dimension, ratio, or other changes. Instead, these changes may exhibit different degrees of correlations of all form-related parameters.

In parametric design systems, parameters can be used to create series of forms, in which all parameters from maximum to minimum ranges constructed the searching space of designs [2]. As shown in Fig. 3, the bottle samples of this study were constructed by 6 form-related parameters. However, in the perception experiment, participants only perceived differences in terms of touch-feeling vocabularies among 8 samples. In this process, participants were unable to make connections from touch-feeling vocabularies to form-related parameters. Thus, the most important concern for users is how to utilize touch-feeling Kansei vocabularies to control form-related parameters for producing vase designs that correspond to the users' expectations (the red arrow in Fig. 3).

Regression analysis is a data analytics tool for determining whether two or more variables are correlated, how they are correlated, and the correlation intensity, enabling mathematical models to be constructed to observe specific variables and predict changes in variables of interest. Specifically, regression analysis helps clarify the extent of change in a dependent variable when only one Single sample variable exists. In this study, multiple regression analysis was used for confirming the correlations between each pair of touch-feeling vocabulary (regarded as dependent variables) and multiple form-related parameters (Single sample variables).

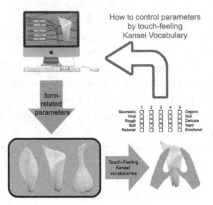

Fig. 3. Utilizing touch-feeling *Kansei* vocabularies to control form-related parameters.

4.1 Geometric - Organic

In the regression analysis results for Geometric-Organic (Table 12), the *t* value indicated that the intensities of the formal parameters are as follows: the angle of botte mouth ($t = -2.466^*$), low-section dimension ($t = -.702$), height ratio ($t = .311$), mid-to-low section ratio ($t = -.942$), mid-section dimension ($t = -1.000$), up-section dimension($t = .201$) ($^* p < .05$). Only the angle of botte mouth reaches the slight significance.

Table 12. Regression analysis results for Geometric-Organic.

Model	Unstandardized Coefficients		Standardized Coefficients	-t	+t	Sig.
	B	Std. error	Beta			
1 (constant)	5.101	.605			8.425	<.001
the angle of botte mouth	-1.599	.648	-.165	-2.466		.014
low-section dimension	-.020	.028	-.040	-.702		.483
height ratio	.006	.018	.019		.311	.756
mid-to-low section ratio	-.113	.120	-.123	-.942		.347
mid-section dimension	-.053	.053	-.101	-1.000		.318
up-section dimension	.007	.036	.019		.201	.841

a. Dependent variable: Geometric - Organic

The participants expressed their touch-feeling perception of Geometric-Organic paired vocabulary from 1 to 5 in the experiment; on the other hand, the six form-related parameters used to construct the bottle samples were also continuous sequences (Table 1). Therefore, in this research, the proportional values for t-value intensities were used to generate a new set of form-related parameters. When participants selected values between 1 and 5 in terms of Geometric-Organic paired vocabulary, the six form-related parameters will follow the proportion of t-values for responding to the changes. By doing so, the form constructed by new set of form-related parameters may be acceptable and preferable from the statistical results of users.

In the regression analysis, 1 of the 6 form-related parameters' t values achieved slight significance (p < .05), which is the angle of botte mouth (t = − 2.466*). Although, only one form-related parameter reaches slight significance, other parameters still influence the bottle shapes. Therefore, when users adjust value for Geometric-Organic, the angle of botte mouth has change apparently. Although the mid-section dimension (t = 1.000) didn't reach significance, it still changed the bottles from Geometric (1) to Organic (5) (Fig. 4).

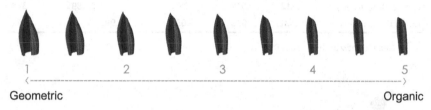

Geometric   Organic

Fig. 4. The generative samples in terms of Geometric-Organic paired vocabulary.

On the far right, Organic (5), which represents Organic forms, the angle of bottle mouth is flatten, and mid-section dimension is also small. On contrary, on the far left, Geometric (1), the angle of bottle mouth is upright, and mid-section dimension is also large. Compared with the measurements in Table 11, the "Organic" from 7 bottle samples are greater than 1, even sample D, E, F, and G reach the significance; however, there is no "Geometric" touch-feeling, but in the results of generative system, the Geometric side may exhibit that the bottle of Geometric is similar to the form of cone.

4.2 Vivid–Dull

In the regression analysis results for Vivid–Dull (Table 13), the t value indicated that the intensities of the formal parameters are as follows: the angle of botte mouth (t = 2.795*), low-section dimension (t = 1.115), height ratio (t = -1.990), mid-to-low section ratio (t = − .249), mid-section dimension (t = 2.389), up-section dimension(t = −.993) (* p < .05). Only the angle of botte mouth reaches the slight significance.

In the regression analysis, 1 of the 6 form-related parameters' t values achieved slight significance (p < .05), which is the angle of botte mouth (t = 2.795*). Although, only one form-related parameter reaches slight significance, other parameters still influence the bottle shapes. Therefore, when users adjust value for Vivid–Dull, the angle of botte mouth has change apparently. Although the height ratio (t = - 1.990) and the low-section dimension (t = 1.115) didn't reach significance, they still influence the bottles from Vivid (1) to Dull (5) (Fig. 5).

On the far right, Dull (5), which represents Dull forms, the angle of bottle mouth is upright, the height ratio is short, and the low-section dimension is also large. On contrary, on the far left, Vivid (1), the angle of bottle mouth is flatten, the height ratio is heigh, and the low-section dimension is also small. Compared with the measurements in Table 11,

Table 13. Regression analysis results for Vivid–Dull.

Model	Unstandardized Coefficients		Standardized Coefficients	-t	+t	Sig.
	B	Std. error	Beta			
1 (constant)	1.659	.534			3.109	<.001
the angle of botte mouth	1.598	.572	.187		2.795	.014
low-section dimension	.027	.025	.063		1.115	.483
height ratio	-.032	.016	-.124	-1.990		.756
mid-to-low section ratio	-.031	.106	-.038	-.294		.347
mid-section dimension	.112	.047	.240		2.389	.318
up-section dimension	-.032	.032	-.092	-.993		.841

a. Dependent variable: Vivid–Dull

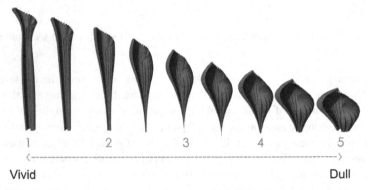

1   2   3   4   5

<--->

Vivid   Dull

Fig. 5. The generative samples in terms of Vivid-Dull paired vocabulary.

the "Vivid" from 5 bottle samples, sample A, C, D, E, and G, reach the significance; however, there is no "Dull" touch-feeling from the results of t-value, but in the results of generative system, the Dull side may show that the bottle of Dull is a fat and short form.

4.3 Rough - Delicate

In the regression analysis results for Rough-Delicate (Table 14), the t value indicated that the intensities of the formal parameters are as follows: the angle of botte mouth ($t = -.653$), low-section dimension ($t = -.533$), height ratio ($t = 3.589$**), mid-to-low section ratio ($t = .049$), mid-section dimension ($t = -2.264$*), up-section dimension($t = .222$) (** $p < .01$ and * $p < .05$). The height ratio reaches the significance and mid-section dimension reaches the slight significance.

In the regression analysis, 2 of the 6 form-related parameters' t values achieved significance (** $p < .01$), and slight significance (* $p < .05$), respectively. They are height ratio (t = 3.589**), and mid-section dimension (t = -2.264*), which dominate major changes of bottle forms from Rough (1) to Delicate (5); other parameters still

Table 14. Regression analysis results for Rough-Delicate.

	Unstandardized Coefficients		Standardized Coefficients			
Model	B	Std. error	Beta	-t	+t	Sig.
1 (constant)	3.243	.557			5.822	<.001
the angle of botte mouth	-.389	.597	-.043	-.653		.514
low-section dimension	-.014	.026	-.030	-.533		.594
height ratio	.059	.017	.222		3.589	<.001
mid-to-low section ratio	.005	.111	.006		.049	.961
mid-section dimension	-.111	.049	-.225	-2.264		.024
up-section dimension	.007	.033	.020		.222	.824

a. Dependent variable: Rough - Delicate

influence the bottle shapes. Therefore, when users adjust value for Rough-Delicate, the height ratio has positive change apparently, and the mid-section dimension has negative change, simultaneously (Fig. 6).

Rough   Delicate

Fig. 6. The generative samples in terms of Rough-Delicate paired vocabulary.

On the far right, Delicate (5), which represents Rough forms, the height ratio is large, and mid-section dimension is relatively small. On contrary, on the far left, Rough (1), the height ratio is small, and mid-section dimension is relatively big. Compared with the measurements in Table 11, the "Delicate" among 3 bottle samples, sample D, E, and G, reaches the significance; on the other hand, the "Rough" of 1 bottle, sample H, also reaches the slight significance. Thus, from the results of generative system, the "Delicate" has high and slim touch-feelings, which "Rough" has short and rocky touch-feelings, maybe similar to sample H.

4.4 Soft–Hard

In the regression analysis results for Soft–Hard (Table 15), the t value indicated that the intensities of the formal parameters are as follows: the angle of botte mouth ($t = .500$), low-section dimension ($t = 1.342$), height ratio ($t = -3.831^{**}$), mid-to-low section ratio

Table 15. Regression analysis results for Soft–Hard.

Model	Unstandardized Coefficients		Standardized Coefficients	-t	+t	Sig.
	B	Std. error	Beta			
1 (constant)	2.406	.511			4.707	<.001
the angle of botte mouth	.274	.547	.032		.500	.618
low-section dimension	.032	.024	.073		1.342	.180
height ratio	-.058	.015	-.230	-3.831		<.001
mid-to-low section ratio	.109	.101	.135		1.073	.284
mid-section dimension	.087	.045	.187		1.929	.055
up-section dimension	-.008	.030	-.023	-.262		.794

a. Dependent variable: Soft - Hard

($t = 1.073$), mid-section dimension ($t = 1.929$), up-section dimension($t = -.262$) (** $p < .01$). Only height ratio reaches the significance.

In the regression analysis, 1 of the 6 form-related parameters' t values achieved significance (p < .01), which is the height ratio (t = −3.831**). Although, only one form-related parameter reaches significance, other parameters still influence the bottle shapes. Therefore, when users adjust value for Soft–Hard, the height ratio has change apparently. Moreover, there are 3 of the 6 form-related parameters' t values, low-section dimension (t = 1.342), mid-to-low section ratio (t = 1.073), and mid-section dimension (t = 1.929), are larger than 1.000 without significance, which also influence the bottle forms from Soft (1) to Hard (5), simultaneously (Fig. 7).

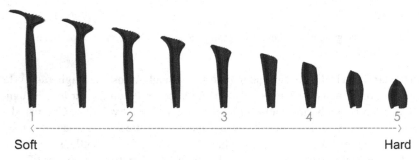

Soft   Hard

Fig. 7. The generative samples in terms of Soft–Hard paired vocabulary.

On the far right, Hard (5), which represents Hard forms, the height ratio is small, and other 3 no significant t values, low-section dimension, mid-to-low section ratio, and mid-section dimension, are relatively wide; On contrary, on the far left, Soft (1), the height ratio is large; the low-section dimension, the mid-to-low section ratio, and the mid-section dimension are relatively narrow. Compared with the measurements in Table 11, the "Soft" among 3 bottle samples, sample D, E, and G, reaches the significance; on the other hand, the "Hard" of 1 bottle, sample H, also reaches the slight significance. Thus, from the results of generative system, the 3.5 and 4 values of "Hard" touch-feeling of bottle are similar to sample H. On contrary, from 3 to 1 value of "Soft", the top of bottles seems the same as Sample D, E, and G.

4.5 Rational - Emotional

In the regression analysis results for Rational-Emotional (Table 16), the t value indicated that the intensities of the formal parameters are as follows: the angle of botte mouth ($t = -1.357$), low-section dimension ($t = -1.380$), height ratio ($t = 1.125$), mid-to-low section ratio ($t = -.534$), mid-section dimension ($t = -2.008*$), up-section dimension($t = .801$) (* $p < .05$). Only mid-section dimension reaches the slight significance.

Table 16. Regression analysis results for Rational-Emotional.

Model	Unstandardized Coefficients		Standardized Coefficients	-t	+t	Sig.
	B	Std. error	Beta			
1 (constant)	4.205	.542			7.763	<.001
the angle of botte mouth	-.787	.580	-.092	-1.357		.176
low-section dimension	-.034	.025	-.079	-1.380		.168
height ratio	.018	.016	.071		1.125	.261
mid-to-low section ratio	-.057	.107	-.070	-.534		.594
mid-section dimension	-.096	.048	-.204	-2.008		.045
up-section dimension	.026	.032	.075		.801	.423

a. Dependent variable: Rational - Emotional

In the regression analysis, 1 of the 6 form-related parameters' t values achieved slight significance (p < .05), which is the mid-section dimension (t = −2.008*). Although, only one form-related parameter reaches slight significance, other parameters still influence the bottle shapes. Therefore, when users adjust value for Rational-Emotional, the mid-section dimension has change apparently. Moreover, there are 3 of the 6 form-related parameters' t values, the angle of botte mouth (t = −1.357), low-section dimension (t = −1.380), height ratio (t = 1.125), are larger than 1.000 or smaller than -1.000 without significance, which also influence the bottle forms from Rational (1) to Emotional (5), simultaneously (Fig. 8).

On the far right, Emotional (5), which represents Emotional forms, the mid-section dimension is small; other 2 no significant t values, the angle of botte mouth, and low-section dimension, are relatively small; but height ratio is relatively big. On contrary, on the far left, Rational (1), the mid-section dimension is big; other 2 no significant t values, the angle of botte mouth, and low-section dimension, are relatively big; but the height ratio is relatively small. Compared with the measurements in Table 11, the "Emotional" among 2 bottle samples, sample E and G, reaches the significance; moreover, sample D, also reaches the slight significance. Thus, from the results of generative system, value

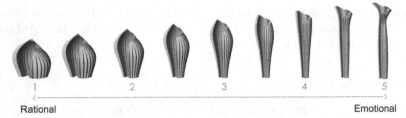

Fig. 8. The generative samples in terms of Rational-Emotional paired vocabulary

4 to 5 of "Emotional" touch-feeling of bottle are similar to top part of sample E and G; while value 2 to 3 of "Emotional" touch-feeling of bottle are similar to sample D.

5 Conclusions and Suggestions

In this study, the Grasshopper platform was used for the creation of eight bottles by using six form-related parameters. These bottles were employed as experiment samples for touch-feeling Kansei vocabularies experiment to determine participants' preferences for bottle forms. Regression analysis was used to analyze and determine the correlations between form-related parameters and Kansei vocabulary. Moreover, the analysis results were then applied to parametric generative design, enabling users to regard Kansei vocabulary as a reference for bottle modification. The method assists designers and users in their pursuit of faster, simpler, and more intuitive designs that accommodate consumers' needs in relation to Kansei in bottle design.

A computer-aided GDS can generate hundreds and thousands of forms in a short time [2]; however, for designers or consumers, to select preferred shapes from such large pools of generated bottles is challenging. This research converted participants' preferences into parameters of a generative form system, enabling users to simply indicate their touch-feelings for Kansei vocabularies to modify bottle design according to their demands. Therefore, consumers can not only select their preferred products from market, but also could use generative-aided systems to identify their needs in terms of Kansei image; thereby generated forms could represent their touch-feeling preferences.

In addition, most research using statistical methods for analysis tends to use numbers to map possible trends. The outcomes of this research, however, are not only presented through statistical data, but also combine statistical values with a generative system. Therefore, users or designers can adopt touch-feeling Kansei vocabularies to create design concepts that accommodates users' preferences in the generative system; moreover, artificial intelligence may also be incorporated in such systems in near further.

References

1. Norman, D.: Emotional Design: Why We Love (or Hate) Everyday Things, Basic Books (2005)
2. Krish, S.: A practical generative design method. Comput. Aided Des. **43**(1), 88–100 (2011)

3. Huang, Y.: A generative vase design system based on users' visual emotional vocabulary. In: Mori, H., Asahi, Y. (eds.) Human Interface and the Management of Information, HCII 2023. LNCS, vol. 14015. Springer, Cham (2023). https://doi.org/10.1007/978-3-031-35132-7_37

4. Nagamachi, M., Imada, A.S.: Kansei Engineering: an ergonomic technology for product development. Int. J. Ind. Ergon. **15**(1), 1 (1995). https://doi.org/10.1016/0169-8141(95)900 25-X

5. Osgood, C.E., Karwoski, T.F., Odbert, H.S.: Studies in synesthetic thinking: II. The roles of form in visual responses to music. J. Soc. Psychol. **28**, 199–222 (1942)

6. Zhai, L.Y., Khoo, L.P., Zhong, Z.W.: A rough set based decision support approach to improving consumer affective satisfaction in product design. Int. J. Ind. Ergon. **39**(2), 295–302 (2009)

7. Desmet, P.M.A., Overbeeke, C.J., Tax, S.J.E.T.: Designing products with added emotional value: develop application of an approach for research through design. Des. J. **4**(1), 32–46 (2001)

8. Lederman, S.J., Klatzky, R.L.: Hand movements: a window into haptic object recognition. Cogn. Psychol. **19**(3), 342–368 (1987). https://doi.org/10.1016/0010-0285(87)90008-9

9. Hsieh, K.W., Huang, Y.: A tactile emotional and sensory study on generative textures of product design. In: IASDR 2013 Consilience Innovation Design, Tokyo, Japan (2013)

10. Hernandez, C.R.B.: Thinking parametric design: introducing parametric Gaudi. Des. Stud. **27**(3), 309–324 (2005)

11. Oxman, R.: Theory and design in the first digital age. Des. Stud. **27**(3), 229–265 (2006). https://doi.org/10.1016/j.destud.2005.11.002

12. Huang, T.-S.: The form element system design for portable multimedia digital products. J. Des. **12**(4), 59–77 (2007)

13. Chou, C.-J., Chen, K.-H.: Creating product forms with preferred Kansei via formal features. J. Des. **8**(2), 77–88 (2003)

Exploring Requirements
for Neurosurgical Augmented Reality
Design and Evaluation of an Infrared-Based Inside-Out
Tracking Approach on HoloLens 2

Thore Keser[1]([⊠]) [ID], Florian Niebling[2] [ID], Rahel Schmied-Kowarzik[1] [ID],
Rebecca Rodeck[1] [ID], and Gerko Wende[1]

[1] German Aerospace Center (DLR), Hamburg, Germany
thore.keser@dlr.de
[2] Technische Hochschule Köln, Cologne, Germany

Abstract. Medical professionals require in-situ visualization of X-ray imaging in 3D to assist with surgical navigation and planning. Research on surgical Augmented Reality (AR) focuses on improving the tracking quality of devices and tools but disregards human requirements. Our user study evaluates application areas and potentials for AR in neurosurgery, as well as feedback for HoloLens 2 based inside-out tracking systems. The main findings include a reported simplification in perception and lowered mental workload. Additionally, we propose a simplified implementation for an infrared-based inside-out rigid body pose estimation system on HoloLens 2 to redirect feedback away from the tracking problem and gain access to human requirements for such systems. Decent patient and exemplary instrument tracking are reached.

Keywords: Mixed Reality · Extended Reality · Human-Computer Interaction · Research Mode · Sensors · Contextual Design · User Study

1 Introduction

Surgical treatment relies on the physician's fine motor skills and the utilized technology. Medical technology is relevant for identifying areas of concern and conducting specific treatments. Identification of tissue and bone structures is done with the help of Computed Tomography (CT) and Magnetic Resonance Imaging (MRI) scans.

In a meeting with staff from the University Clinic Würzburg, neurosurgeons expressed a high mental workload in the interaction with CT images. Images are presented on several flat displays during surgery. Each screen shows the object as a cross-sectional slice image from a different perspective. Additionally, the displays are located aside from the patient, creating an additional rotation offset between the images and the situs. Physicians can use a wheel to scroll through the depth of the images by traversing through individual image slices. This way, medical professionals are forced to put a lot of cognitive effort into understanding the 2D pictures, mapping them back into 3D objects, and mentally aligning them with the patient. Even though CT images are beneficial before and during surgery, they allocate mental resources that could be freed for surgical procedures. Hence, surgeons suggest a digital representation and virtual positioning of CT images to reduce the workload.

Augmented Reality (AR) is a technology that renders digital information with respect to its environment. The technology can create interactive and spatially aligned virtual content. In surgery, AR is able to assist by creating an in-place visualization and thus compensating for relocation and mapping difficulties. Studies show that AR usage can reduce mental load [9] and improve situational awareness in medical (and other) contexts [21].

Aside from tablets and smartphones, a commonly used AR device is Microsoft's HoloLens 2 Mixed Reality Head Mounted Display (HMD). The HMD could apply to hygiene restrictions in surgeries [4,6], as it is hands-free. HMDs can place virtual content closer to or inside the patient, whereas conventional instruments, tablets, smartphones, or documentation would keep a distance to prevent infections. The overlapping of real and virtual content can be used for guidance and visualization with limited accuracy.

To create convincing visual effects and alignment with the patient, AR needs to understand the patient's position and orientation (pose). To date, research focuses on improving the alignment by enhancing the tracking quality [3,6,19]. Challenges lie in the compensation of the low-quality HoloLens sensors and in the reduction of drift and offset, which are introduced through outside-in tracking systems that are combined with the HoloLens inside-out self-localization system [12,19]. While tracking precision is important for the technical development of future systems, there is little information about human requirements [4], which provide specific information on the most needed features from the users' side of view. An investigation of relevant factors besides tracking quality is necessary.

A user study on AR for neurosurgery requires a functioning tracking system to implement domain-specific features. Moreover, qualitative study results could draw attention to the potentially poor tracking system. Hence, we aim for a simplified tracking approach with decent quality to unlock qualitative feedback on domain-specific aspects and pull the attention away from the tracking quality. A qualitative user study helps exploring neurosurgery's deep insights and needs.

This paper describes both the implementation of a simplified tracking approach for neurosurgical AR (see Fig. 1) and the qualitative user study to gain expert domain knowledge.

2   Related Work

The literature regarding the use of AR in the neurosurgical domain describes most problems within technical areas, such as tracking of tools, its accuracy, precision and refresh rate [5]. To achieve good performance with the used technology, literature quickly dives into a deeper analysis of the inbuilt components of used devices and tracking approaches.

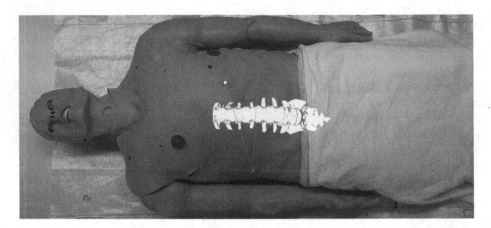

Fig. 1. Infrared target tracking and patient pose estimation for neurosurgical navigation. The green lines visualize the selected anchor points to align the pose of the virtual spine segment with the patient. (Color figure online)

Schmalstieg and Hollerer [15] split tracking approaches into two major categories. Outside-in systems use sensors mounted around a tracked object and are strong in detecting position changes whereas the observation of rotation is less precise. Inside-out systems use sensors at the object and observe its surrounding to calculate pose changes of the tracked object. These systems provide improved rotation detection, but are less precise in positioning the object [15].

The HoloLens 2 HMD is an inside-out device, which calculates its own pose using a Simultaneous Localization and Tracking (SLAM) algorithm [20]. When combining the device with external outside-in tracking systems, drift and offset are introduced [3,12,17,19], which is found to originate from the Inertial Measurement Unit (IMU) [12,19]. Coupling HoloLens to an outside-in system would also limit the developed application to specifically equipped rooms and is thus not preferred. When working in neurosurgical environments, drift and offset need to be minimized. Hence, it is helpful to create a system that tries to overpower device limitations to estimate a more stable pose.

Commonly used tracking approaches rely on fiducial markers, which are fixated at objects to identify them using a camera. For HoloLens, markers with larger diameters are required[1], which might cover relevant working areas in surgery. Furthermore, fiducial markers are rather difficult to detect if the angle to the camera is shallow.

Previous work shows the possibility to access the infrared sensor of the HoloLens 2 HMD. Infrared is already used in current equipment for surgical navigation [13] and is thus unlikely to interfere with medical procedures. Infrared approaches promise better tracking performance and require smaller marker spheres.

---

[1] Physical Properties of Image Targets:
   https://library.vuforia.com/objects/physical-properties-image-based-targets.

Kunz et al. [11] utilize the HoloLens Research Mode to access the four visual light cameras and the infrared (IR) sensor. They compare two methods of reflective marker tracking, a) using two of four environmental cameras as a stereo camera setup and b) combining the depth and Active Brightness (AB) stream of the IR sensor. The authors describe relevant steps of the IR tracking implementation. After binarization of the raw image and using a not further specified blob detection algorithm, they apply a HoloLens function, which provides a mapping from frame pixels to world coordinates and vice versa. Position estimation is reached by connecting opposing markers with lines and placing the target center at the cross in the middle. There are no further references on the use of a rigid body pose estimation algorithm or whether a rotation is applied to the target. The authors test the approach by placing the markers on a robotic arm and fixating the HoloLens to a known position. Measuring the actual and virtual movements allows for position comparison between the robot and HoloLens coordinate system. Even though accuracy for the IR setup is slightly lower, they recommend this approach due to the need for an additional light source for the dual camera approach [11].

Another research project [6] also accesses the HoloLens 2 Research Mode to track IR reflective marker spheres. A stereo camera setup with visual light cameras was implemented and the precision optimized by running a custom calibration sequence. When tracking was not available, rigid body movement was predicted using a custom algorithm. The authors tested their approach by comparing the tracked coordinates with a ground truth measurement, which was obtained by an outside-in OptiTrack system. The accuracy correlates with the distance of the target to the device. Without the prediction and thus optimization, they reach refresh rates of 37 Hz (Hz) [6].

Within most technical approaches, the users' point of view is not evaluated. There is very little information on human interaction that investigates domain insights and user needs. Some research addresses these questions, for example a project [4] that supports surgeons by visualizing the correct screw angle in surgery. Authors highlight the tool as intuitive in use and radiation-free. Limitations are high costs and long setup time, as well as the need to train surgeons before using the headset [4].

A literature review [14] shows that AR can reduce sight deviation and increase the comfort level of team members. Moreover it provides additional information to surgeons, which improves decision making and situational awareness. However, surgeons demand manual activation of functionalities to prevent cluttering and show guidance only if it is required [14]. In general, AR benefits the medical context, especially in surgical workflow improvement and ease of use [1]. Besides clear interfaces and lightweight devices, an unobtrusive patient tracking to increase tolerance against tracking errors is required [1].

The above research describes solutions and psychological factors that are able to benefit the surgical domain. User feedback, which ensures the relevance and priority of solutions and factors for surgeons are missing. Moreover, thresholds are not defined, hence hindering requirement based implementations.

3   Method

We introduce a simplified tracking approach for tool and patient pose estimation as a vehicle to gain access to deeper neurosurgical requirements. As depicted in Table 1, we experimented with different fiducial libraries on HoloLens 2 but rejected many for low performance, such as slow detection or low refresh rate. Some libraries were no longer compilable on current development platforms.

Table 1. Rejected libraries for fiducial tracking using Unity3D.

Library	low performance	not compileable
MRTK QR-Code	×	
Vuforia	×	
ARToolkit	×	
OpenCVForUnity	×	
AprilTag		×
ArUco		×

The introduced approach utilizes the Unity IL2CPP build pipeline to provide a plugin to the Unity3D game engine. The plugin is built into the final HoloLens app. It is derived from a public repository[2] and written in C++ to access relevant sensors through the HoloLens Research Mode API [20]. This project uses the IR sensor in Articulated Hand Tracking (AHAT) mode to gain fast-updating information about the user's close environment. The IR sensor yields two types of raw data: the Active Brightness (AB) image, which is a grayscale image representing the reflectivity of objects, and the depth buffer, which shows the distance of objects to the camera.

Reflective spheres, initially designed for the OptiTrack[3] system, are used to mark real objects. The spheres are brightly visible in the AB images of the IR sensor and are easier to detect in the IR spectrum than with RGB cameras (see Fig. 2). The AB image is probed in a grid pattern to find bright marker blobs. Blob detection is performed on the object reflectivity in the AB image and on depth information to separate blobs that appear behind each other. Blobs are outlined using a contour tracing algorithm [16], which shows to be fast and robust for the occasionally fringed and incomplete images produced by the sensor. The blob centers are retrieved from valid blob contours by calculating the mean coordinates from their contour pixels.

The HoloLens Research Mode API provides functions to map image pixels to 3D points from pixel coordinates, depth values, and timestamps. We use this function to transform blob center points to world space coordinates and

---

[2] HoloLens2-ResearchMode-Unity on Github:
https://github.com/petergu684/HoloLens2-ResearchMode-Unity.

[3] OptiTrack Motion Capture Systems: https://www.optitrack.com.

provide them to Unity in app coordinate space. With Unity, compounds of targets, called multi-targets, are defined and calibrated. Multi-targets represent a group of markers that belong to the same rigid body. The implemented system repeatedly aligns the calibrated multi-target with the reflective marker spheres detected in the surroundings of HoloLens.

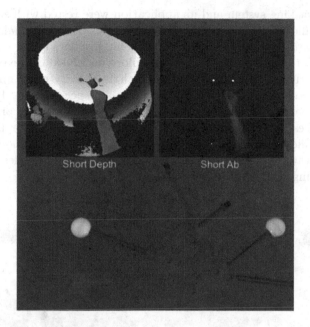

Fig. 2. Depth and AB image from HoloLens 2 sensors.

To align multi-targets with their reflective marker spheres, the system must identify each marker. As markers are equal in size and shape, the only differentiating factor is the set of distances to other markers. To minimize errors, we followed the approach of Gsaxner et al. [6] and determined that every distance within a multi-target must be unique [18]. A marker can be identified by measuring the distances between markers and reconstructing each relative position.

The assignment of a target structure in Unity to a corresponding reflective marker point is calculated using the Hungarian Method [10]. The method is a mathematical approach to solving the assignment problem, which applies to this case. The three best assignments per multi-target are selected by minimum weight [6] and used for the pose calculation of the tracked rigid body.

The pose calculation is performed following Horn's approach [8], where three points define a coordinate space. The pose is expressed as a relative rotational and translational difference, which is applied to the virtual object to align it with its real counterpart.

The introduced approach reduces resource usage for low latency and high performance. Even though the assignment calculation is fast for small point clouds, it still overflows the performance capabilities of HoloLens. Hence, a between-frames assignment, based on close-by pixel movement, is executed to reduce the computational footprint further.

3.1 Study Design

The created tracking system and its application were tested with staff from the University Clinic Würzburg. In a cost-benefit consideration, qualitative interviews are expected to provide the most comprehensive data range with negligible costs. A qualitative evaluation is able to explore undefined contexts. Hence, we chose a semi-structured interview coupled with an activity phase and the Think Aloud [2] method to collect unfiltered and domain-specific data. The collected data was evaluated utilizing methods from the User-Centered or Contextual Design [7] process. The process includes guidelines for qualitative data preparation and consolidation using the Affinity Diagram [7]. The method is qualified for user observations and interviews and is intended to derive design ideas for agile prototyping and software development.

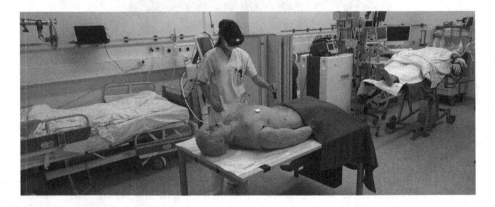

Fig. 3. Participant testing the prototype in the simulator room.

In preparation for the evaluation, key areas of interest were identified. These include the practicability of the system and its ability to integrate into the surgical domain. Moreover, the system's usability is chosen to evaluate the simplicity and value of support for surgeons. Also, measures of quality are intended to answer questions about accuracy, precision, and perceived fidelity. Our interview aims to extract requirements for neurosurgical Augmented Reality.

The interview was scheduled for five working days in a medical simulation room (see Fig. 3) and conducted with the knowledge and cooperation of supervisors and responsible medical directors. Interested staff could drop in and participate to prevent disturbance in medical acute care. Individual sessions took about 30 min and were carried out in German language.

Each session consisted of three parts. First, several questions about the participants' demographic data, experience, and enthusiasm regarding new technologies were asked. Participants were briefly introduced to the HoloLens device to ensure proper fit during testing. With an introduction and reminder about the Think Aloud procedure, they were exposed to the demo application. During the second phase, participants were given small tasks to try out the application and improve the user's awareness and perception of all virtual elements in the scene. Tasks included implicit requirements for position and view direction changes, patient movement, and clipping tool interactions (see Fig. 4). Users were instructed to take their time to test all imaginable prototype features before requesting new tasks incentives from the study supervisor. After completing all tasks, participants stopped the testing and proceeded to the interview (third phase).

The interview was recorded and transcribed. Written sentences were shortened, and information that didn't contain relevant aspects to the study was excluded. Participant data was anonymized with the change from audio to text format. We extracted and interpreted key information from the transcribed interview answers according to the Contextual Design method by Holtzblatt, Wendell, and Wood [7]. The captured data was written onto Affinity notes and consolidated into an Affinity Diagram to provide insights into the user's context [7]. Key information was rearranged to represent the main factors of experience, quality, practicability, and usability.

4   Results

The created application incorporated a sample spine segment aligned with the patient's pose using the introduced tracking system (see Fig. 1). The system is able to track the patient's pose and a hand-held clipping tool (see Fig. 4) while maintaining a low computational footprint. Compared to previous work, which reached five and 55 to 60 frames per second (FPS), respectively [11,12], the system updates the pose with 45 FPS, originating from the infrared sensor refresh rate. We additionally achieved Unity3D integration with an app performance of 59 to 60 FPS on the HoloLens 2 HMD. The tracking quality is decent and drift-free through direct coupling with the HoloLens built-in environment tracking.

The system acts as an enabler for staff imagination and requirement generation. The semi-structured interview provides rich feedback and shows insights into challenges and procedures within the neurosurgical domain.

A total of five participants (U1 - U5) attended the interviews. Four identified as male and one as female. The age of the participants ranged from 25 to 37 (M=31.2 SD=4.0). Two subjects were students without chosen specialization. Three were specialized orthopedics and/or trauma surgeons with experience in neurosurgery. The students reported being in 8th and 13th semesters, while the professionals reported a work experience between four and nine years (M=5.7 SD=2.4). One of five participants reported a light debility of sight, which wasn't corrected by wearing glasses or contact lenses while using the AR HMD. Also, one participant was affected by red-green blindness.

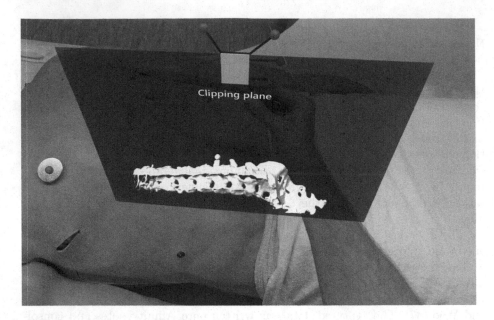

Fig. 4. Sample application using the implemented tracking approach to track a mannequin patient and sample tool to clip the virtual spine segment.

4.1   Qualitative Feedback

In this section, we summarize the gathered user feedback. The qualitative data has been rearranged and interpreted to compress the information and identify relevant factors. In total, 23 data groups were created, which fit into five major categories. Please note that user quotes have been translated into English and do not contain literal speech.

Augmented Reality in Neurosurgery. Interview participants see great advantages to the use of AR technology in neurosurgery. *It reduces distractions by blending out irrelevant objects and other people. It emphasizes on the shown content* (U3).

Perspective-aligned renderings are currently uncommon for the domain. *The spine is visualized in perspective* (U2) expresses the perception of patient-aligned content that follows real-world perspective cues. *I think this helps with understanding the situation* (U1).

Users are also amazed about the interaction methods that have become possible with the technology. When reporting ideas of separating holographic content and zooming into detailed areas, medical professionals often showed gestures with their hands to explain the intended interaction technique. *I could divide the hologram and look at each part separately* (U2). When separating the hologram, users could take it out of the aligned pose to drag it closer or above the patient. Users expect that dragging the hologram back into the patient will snap it back into place, where it is correctly aligned and reacts to tracking changes.

It is an obligation to keep the surgical area (situs) clear of objects to prevent infections. However, *with HoloLens I could place X-ray images onto the patient* (U1) because virtual images are sterile by default. With an open situs, the surgeon's hands are used to feel the way for navigation and planning. *For the interaction with HoloLens, I do not need to touch anything* (U1). Thus, the device would remain uncontaminated.

It could have been more apparent to some users that the tracking system solely relies on HoloLens' inbuilt sensors. Line-of-sight errors were anticipated as current navigation systems are based on fixture-mounted sensors. *Where is the sensor?* (U3) was asked to prevent tracking issues. The independence of other devices is positively mentioned.

Some feedback attributed to the HoloLens 2 device itself is collected. *A larger visor and visualization area would be beneficial* (U3). The device's weight is reported to be acceptable, and the overall comfort is good. For tall people, more than the one-meter AHAT tracking distance is required. *I need to take the head down. In this position, I would not operate on patients.* (U3). In general, the requirements for the maximum tracking distance of the system are expressed to be within one arm's distance. *Usually, I stand with my thighs against the operating table when conducting surgery* (U1). Larger distances can be useful in multi-user environments where assistants or students observe.

Tracking Approaches. Feedback was also given concerning the currently used surgical navigation system. It is able to combine information from medical imaging devices with the position of tracked instruments and patient. The system consists of a sensor arm, which tracks infrared markers. Results are visualized on screens aside from the patient. As the system provides only 2D visualizations, different viewing angles are presented aside from each other in a split screen layout. Users described the system as helpful but rather challenging to handle. *The positioning of the camera is error-prone* (U3) and *the system faults when markers are moved.* (U1). *It takes a lot of time until the system is set up and ready to use* (U1).

The data shows a difference between tracking of the clipping tool and the patient for the implemented tracking approach, even though the implementation for both features is the same. Differences originate from different smoothing settings that allow a faster but less smooth position change for the clipping tool but slower and smoother spine alignment.

For patient tracking, users noticed that they had to stay in a specific range. *From further away, the tracking was less sophisticated* (U4). Also, small movements did not take effect. The latter appears if movements are tiny so that adjustments are not seen or not even recognized by the system. Moreover, strong smoothing created a perceived delay in position updates. *The spine could move faster, so I don't have to wait for it to adjust* (U4). *For surgery, the delay is too long. When I move the patient, the visualization has to act faster.* (U1).

The tracked area of the clipping tool was not limited (U2). As the tool stays in the surgeon's hands, the range of the AHAT sensor is sufficient for this task. However, *The tool must be oriented with a specific angle to the camera* (U3). This issue could be fixed by adding another marker to the tool. *For placing corrective screws during surgery, the tool is not precise enough* (U5). Regarding delay, the clipping tool is perceived more positively than patient tracking. Most users rate the current delay as not noticeable, reasonable, or adequate for the sample task. *There is too much delay for surgery, but it would be okay for diagnostics* (U2).

Requirements proposed by participants can be grouped into translational and rotational precision. More precise tools are expected to improve patient outcomes in surgery. *In surgery, every millimeter is crucial* (U1). Demands also vary based on experience level. More experienced surgeons require higher precision, while students estimate lower values. Moreover, *the tolerance for deviation during surgery is higher at the lower spine and reduces with the size of the vertebral bodies* (U3). The requirements for translational precision and accuracy are stated by multiple participants to be below one millimeter and one degree for rotational deviations.

System Quality. The overall visualization quality and level of detail of the spine model are delicate enough for medical professionals to name various areas of the spine. However, surgeons state that they *would need a more detailed hologram to work with it in surgery* (U2). Some users rate the image resolution sufficient, while others demand higher resolutions for detailed inspection. Regarding hologram size and proportions, surgeons trust the application to show a correct scale.

The colors of the selected spine structure are almost well selected. Even if nobody reported difficulties with the selected color, medical professionals know the shades of different structures from educational books and personal experience. They stated to prefer applications to respect these color schemes.

The HMD's brightness is disturbing when trying to see details in the hologram from shades. *I believe that the visualization could dazzle in surgery* (U1). As HoloLens has a physical button for brightness settings, this would not be an issue as long as gestures are available to manipulate the setting during surgery. However, contrast is lost when the HMD adds less light to the scene, and a more substantial transparency effect might occur.

All experiences were positively denoted. Differences are in affective emotions that show surprise and fascination, as well as retrospective reflections summarizing the experience as helpful. Many positive emotions can be attributed to the first contact with AR, which makes the experience exciting and new.

Additional feedback can be grouped into Usability measures defined by DIN EN ISO 9241–11, which consist of effectiveness, efficiency, and satisfaction. For effectiveness, users stated that the tool helps them reach their goals, e.g., *I was able to take a look into the spinal canal* (U5). With efficiency, users report that interactions happen fast, and the scene changes according to their position in the room. *The clipping of the spine happens in real-time. I really like it* (U2).

Users were also satisfied with the provided interaction techniques, audio and visual feedback, and User Interface (UI) elements.

With the introduced application, visualizations are in 3D, which was attributed to being helpful for the understanding process. *With X-Ray images, the visualization is rather confined* (U2) and *X-Ray images are more precise, but this system is simpler because it is in three dimensions* (U5). Users reported the application to be *very easy* (U1) to use with no requirement for additional guidelines. All visualizations appear real and correct, as one *would expect from the real world* (U4). This corresponds to the user's reality perception and lowers the mental load.

Application Areas. This section summarizes application areas for the system and technology within the medical domain. A central area of work is surgery, in which medical professionals wish more support for navigation and confirmation of correct placement. *By showing an angle or an axis, the system could improve screw and plate placement in surgery* (U2). With the hypothetical possibility of connecting HoloLens with a patient data platform, it is possible to quickly view and exchange data without requiring an office space. *With access to my desk, I could view relevant reports, documents, and X-ray images during surgery and in the ward* (U1). Moreover, users anticipate the technology to be beneficial in orthopedics, vascular surgery, or other medical areas, such as psychology.

For complex disease patterns, collaboration is required. As virtual content on HoloLens is only visible to one user, professional communication and exchange are hindered. Hence, the need to share the view and visual content and the ability to interact with a virtual scene in a multi-user scenario is required. *After primary treatment, we could discuss a complex trauma in our team* (U2). With the help of AR, viewing content is not restricted to a single device, but every user could see their image and communicate with others. This would also fix the rotational offset problem, which has been a central goal for this work.

Students who attend the surgery for educational purposes examine the situs and all relevant information. *Currently, all students must gather around one display* (U1), which limits class sizes and requires students to switch places for better views. Augmented Reality in educational contexts increases the ability to understand and reconstruct three-dimensional shapes. Students are equipped with many images but need to combine them to understand the visualized content. *Using a book, I will need at least five images to understand a situation. With this technology, it would be much simpler* (U5).

In anatomy classes, the utilization of donated bodies is common. These are limited resources, as every cut irreversibly changes the sample. Also, preserving the bodies is costly. *With this system, we could repeat certain scenarios* (U2) and reduce resource consumption. With the ability to virtually create content and artificially track movements, it is possible to create training applications that allow the simulation of surgical procedures without costly resources. *We could simulate surgeries and train our cutting techniques* (U1).

System Potential. Participants stated that *the technology has high potential* (U1) within the medical domain. *The technology can improve and speed up our processes* (U4). *With the currently existing staff shortage, technology and digitalization can help to utilize the resources with the existing staff more efficiently* (U1). This would also result in a less stressful workplace and better care.

The patient outcome, which describes the treatment quality, speed, and success of therapy, remains the primary goal for medical professionals. This is the main reason for rejecting technological advances if they are more complex than helpful or do not speed up the process. *New technology must be worthwhile to become helpful* (U2). Current systems are trustworthy and create an appreciated assistance within the surgical domain. Medical devices are trusted to create little to no errors by maintaining high standards.

When referring to the implemented system and application, users are willing to use it in real scenarios. *If patient and setting allow it, one could try the system with a rather simple diagnosis. However, I would not trust it yet* (U3). The reason for the experimental initiative is the hope that the technology and application will solve long-term goals with further development and research. *In the long run, I believe this project will be very beneficial for us* (U3).

At the same time, there are great concerns about the system's usefulness. *I do not believe that we can resign from the current imaging system* (U4). *With the current situation, I would rely on existing systems* (U1). As the current tools are well proven, a transition period to the new system would require parallel coverage with traditional systems for a long time.

Radiation imagery such as CT or X-ray is a helpful and often used tool in preparation and surgery. As radiation potentially harms human bodies, its use is carefully balanced between patient benefits and disadvantages. *Daily, we face the risks of radiation* (U3), as it also affects staff in the operating room. Every additional image adds to that risk, and consecutive images must be taken to confirm the current position or placement of tools. If systems align virtual content with the patient, react to position changes, and are interactable, they increase the potential to reduce radiation in surgery.

5 Discussion

An infrared-based tracking approach for neurosurgical AR was achieved and comprises several factors. These include patient tracking, which is required for augmentation in object (patient) coordinate space, instrument tracking for guidance visualizations, infrared light technology for more straightforward marker detection, and efficient marker assignment. Those components provide a simplified solution and implementation for the complex idea of neurosurgical task related AR.

The IR sensor is the fastest but not the most accurate sensor. Marker detection is simpler to implement, as binarization quickly yields the marker positions in camera image coordinates. With the depth stream of the IR sensor and HoloLens internal functions, these coordinates can be joined with depth information and projected into 3D space. As HoloLens is aware of its environment, the calculated world coordinates align with the refined SLAM-based world and app coordinate systems. Our solution is drift-free and performant on HoloLens.

The qualitative evaluation is able to provide rich feedback and shows excellent insights into challenges and work within the neurosurgical domain. It remains arguable if more participants would show more aspects of the surgical domain regarding the implemented system. More extended opportunities to attend the interview sessions might not yield more participants due to their high workload and sudden medical events. More participants are not expected to enlarge the picture significantly but rather strengthen the results by emphasizing individual factors.

Within the evaluation, novice and experienced medical professionals showed different results, because novices might not have experience in surgery or knowledge about specific procedures and tools. Thus, the given feedback sometimes shows the gap in experience through the ability to answer specific questions, as well as differing impressions about the system and stated requirements.

Using the qualitative approach, we extracted requirements for neurosurgical Augmented Reality, which applications should fulfill to be of value for the domain. Applications must:

- fulfill usability measures in effectivity, efficiency, and satisfaction.
- be self-descriptive with its UI elements and interactions.
- solve a specific problem that is relevant to the domain.
- respect expectations and experiences from the surgeon's real world.
- provide a transition period and fallback technology on system introduction.
- minimize the time required to set up and launch the system.
- render virtual content in perspective with respect to the patient's pose.
- remain sterile in interaction and device usage.
- be able to place virtual content close or into the situs.
- be self-contained and independent from external sensors.
- provide trackable space in arm-length distance.
- be able to track objects outside of the optimal range (with less precision).
- reach 0.5 to 1 mm translational precision.
- reach below 1° rotational precision.
- reach firm real-time updates of the tracked position (at least 45 FPS).
- provide a resolution that can show X-ray grade details.
- show detailed 3D visualizations.

6   Conclusion

We introduced a simplified tracking approach on HoloLens 2 to unlock domain-specific insights from qualitative interviews. An infrared-based inside-out rigid body pose estimation system has been implemented. The system utilizes the HoloLens Research Mode to access the IR sensor and provided API methods for reflective marker sphere tracking and coordinate system transformation. By running a fast contour tracing algorithm, the marker sphere centers are extracted and assigned to tracking targets using the Hungarian Method. A pose for the tracked patient and tool is calculated from the three best assignments.

The system addresses problems that originate form technical limitations. For example, in surgery space around the patient is occupied and hinders conventional approaches in establishing a line of sight to the tracked object. Using the inside-out approach, the system is able to provide a drift-free augmentation in close range using markers that do not impede the small augmentation area. As processing power on the HoloLens 2 device is limited, the system remains a low computational footprint reach an experience with reduced latency.

Surgeons reported lower mental workload, which was contributed by the 3D reconstruction of the medical image and simultaneous patient-aligned positioning of the reconstruction. Medical professionals focus on central tasks and discard distractions, which they attribute to the illumination effect of the visualization. Moreover, hands-free interaction and sterility are rated to be beneficial.

The feedback concerning the future use of the system was very positive. With the knowledge of close-by critical tissues or blood vessels, delicate tool positioning and path planning are possible. Visual guidance in tool positioning in relation to the situs would also reduce the need for radiation during surgery. Additionally, multi-user visualization can improve training, where the space around the patient is limited. At the same time, team collaboration during surgery can be improved.

Our system acts as an enabler for staff imagination and requirement generation. The Affinity Diagram provides rich feedback and opens great insights into challenges and procedures within the neurosurgical domain. Medical professionals hope the system revolutionizes their work in simplicity, flexibility, surgical planning, and navigation.

References

1. Burström, G., Persson, O., Edström, E., Elmi-Terander, A.: Augmented reality navigation in spine surgery: a systematic review. Acta Neurochir. **163**, 843–852 (2021). https://doi.org/10.1007/s00701-021-04708-3
2. Charters, E.: The use of think-aloud methods in qualitative research an introduction to think-aloud methods. Brock Educ. J. **12**(2) (2003). https://doi.org/10.26522/brocked.v12i2.38
3. Doughty, M., Ghugre, N.R., Wright, G.A.: Augmenting performance: a systematic review of optical see-through head-mounted displays in surgery. J. Imag. **8**(7), 203 (2022)
4. Farshad, M., Fürnstahl, P., Spirig, J.M.: First in man in-situ augmented reality pedicle screw navigation. North American Spine Society J. (NASSJ) **6**, 100065 (2021). https://doi.org/10.1016/j.xnsj.2021.100065
5. Fida, B., Cutolo, F., di Franco, G., Ferrari, M., Ferrari, V.: Augmented reality in open surgery. Updat. Surg. **70**(3), 389–400 (2018). https://doi.org/10.1007/s13304-018-0567-8
6. Gsaxner, C., Li, J., Pepe, A., Schmalstieg, D., Egger, J.: Inside-out instrument tracking for surgical navigation in augmented reality. In: Proceedings of the 27th ACM Symposium on Virtual Reality Software and Technology, pp. 1–11 (2021). https://doi.org/10.1145/3489849.3489863

7. Holtzblatt, K., Wendell, J.B., Wood, S.: Rapid contextual design: a how-to guide to key techniques for user-centered design. Elsevier (2004)
8. Horn, B.K.: Closed-form solution of absolute orientation using unit quaternions. Josa a **4**(4), 629–642 (1987). https://doi.org/10.1364/JOSAA.4.000629
9. Jeffri, N.F.S., Rambli, D.R.A.: A review of augmented reality systems and their effects on mental workload and task performance. Heliyon **7**(3) (2021). https://doi.org/10.1016/j.heliyon.2021.e06277
10. Kuhn, H.W.: The Hungarian method for the assignment problem. Naval Res. Logist. Quart. **2**(1–2), 83–97 (1955). https://doi.org/10.1002/nav.3800020109
11. Kunz, C., et al.: Infrared marker tracking with the hololens for neurosurgical interventions. Curr. Directions Biomed. Eng. **6**(1), 20200027 (2020). https://doi.org/10.1515/cdbme-2020-0027
12. Lee, S., Jung, H., Lee, E., Jung, Y., Kim, S.T.: A preliminary work: mixed reality-integrated computer-aided surgical navigation system for paranasal sinus surgery using Microsoft HoloLens 2. In: Magnenat-Thalmann, N., Interrante, V., Thalmann, D., Papagiannakis, G., Sheng, B., Kim, J., Gavrilova, M. (eds.) CGI 2021. LNCS, vol. 13002, pp. 633–641. Springer, Cham (2021). https://doi.org/10.1007/978-3-030-89029-2_47
13. Mezger, U., Jendrewski, C., Bartels, M.: Navigation in surgery. Langenbecks Arch. Surg. **398**(4), 501–514 (2013). https://doi.org/10.1007/s00423-013-1059-4
14. Qian, L., Wu, J.Y., DiMaio, S.P., Navab, N., Kazanzides, P.: A review of augmented reality in robotic-assisted surgery. IEEE Trans. Med. Robot. Bionics **2**(1), 1–16 (2019). https://doi.org/10.1109/TMRB.2019.2957061
15. Schmalstieg, D., Hollerer, T.: Augmented reality: principles and practice. Addison-Wesley Professional (2016)
16. Seo, J., Chae, S., Shim, J., Kim, D., Cheong, C., Han, T.D.: Fast contour-tracing algorithm based on a pixel-following method for image sensors. Sensors **16**(3), 353 (2016). https://doi.org/10.3390/s16030353
17. Sitole, S.P., LaPre, A.K., Sup, F.C.: Application and evaluation of lighthouse technology for precision motion capture. IEEE Sens. J. **20**(15), 8576–8585 (2020). https://doi.org/10.1109/JSEN.2020.2983933
18. Steinicke, F., Jansen, C.P., Hinrichs, K.H., Vahrenhold, J., Schwald, B.: Generating optimized marker-based rigid bodies for optical tracking systems. In: VISAPP (2), pp. 387–395 (2007)
19. Tu, P., Gao, Y., Lungu, A.J., Li, D., Wang, H., Chen, X.: Augmented reality based navigation for distal interlocking of intramedullary nails utilizing Microsoft Hololens 2. Comput. Biol. Med. **133**, 104402 (2021). https://doi.org/10.1016/j.compbiomed.2021.104402
20. Ungureanu, D., et al.: Hololens 2 research mode as a tool for computer vision research. arXiv preprint arXiv:2008.11239 (2020). https://doi.org/10.48550/arXiv.2008.11239
21. Woodward, J., Ruiz, J.: Analytic review of using augmented reality for situational awareness. IEEE Trans. Visual Comput. Graphics **29**(4), 2166–2183 (2022). https://doi.org/10.1109/TVCG.2022.3141585

Exploring User Preferences in AI-Generated Car Wheel Frame Designs: A Preliminary Study of Users with Varied Design Experience

Yu-Hsu Lee[(⊠)] [iD] and Hsin-Wei Huang [iD]

National Yunlin University of Science and Technology, Yunlin 64002, Taiwan R.O.C.
jameslee@yuntech.edu.tw, yanwei5148@gmail.com

Abstract. This study explores the application of AI in a specific product design field and investigates the differences between individuals with professional and non-professional backgrounds. Using wheel rim design as an example, the study illustrates the preferences and perceptual differences of participants with vary-ing backgrounds and experiences towards elements like style, color, layout, and design, as presented by AI image generation tools (such as Midjourney). The choices are categorized into two aspects: creativity and feasibility. In this exper-iment, participants were divided into wheel rim experts and non-experts (with non-experts further categorized into those with and without design experience). Non-expert participants were first asked to create designs using AI, followed by both experts and non-experts selecting proposals for creative and feasible sporty and luxurious style car wheel rims. The study found that individuals without design experience tended to show more creativity in their ideas when using AI tools, but their targeted selections lacked consistency. In contrast, participants with a design background were more consistent in their choices, particularly in the assessment of feasibility. There is a noticeable difference between experts and non-experts in defining style, with experts making more informed choices when targeting spe-cific selections. In summary, both experts and non-experts are capable of creating designs with creativity and feasibility using AI tools. However, experts, compared to those with design experience, have a clearer personal opinion on styling, while those without design experience show the least effective outcomes.

Keywords: AI image generation Differences in design experience · car wheel frame design · text to image

1 Introduction

1.1 Research Background

New a day artificial intelligence technology, especially Generative Adversarial Networks (GANs), can create extremely realistic images in the field of image design. By learning from a vast amount of image data to identify visual patterns, it is capable to generate a variety of images, ranging from artworks to practical product designs. With the advance-ment of technology, AI has become more efficient in understanding and applying styles,

H. Mori and Y. Asahi (Eds.): HCII 2024, LNCS 14689, pp. 178–193, 2024.
https://doi.org/10.1007/978-3-031-60107-1_13

colors, and layouts, and can generate specific visual content based on user instructions. This not only speeds up the creative process but also provides designers with new creative tools to explore unprecedented design concepts. Despite this, AI-generated images still require fine-tuning and creative guidance from human artists or designers and currently cannot fully replace designers. The rapid development of AI has garnered attention from experts in the field of visual creation, with some even expressing concern about the potential of being replaced by technology in the future, leading to lively discussions in the design community.

Car wheels customization is a way to demonstrate personality and taste for many car owners. The variety of styles and shapes provide endless options for personalization, allowing their vehicles to stand out among numerous modified cars. Car owners can express themselves through unique wheel designs, gaining recognition and respect from fellow enthusiasts. This allure and incentive is not just about aesthetics, but also involves performance, social interaction, and economic benefits. Therefore, the specialized project of wheel customization is widely popular among car modification enthusiasts. This study aims to use AI technology to verify whether there are differences in cognition and insight between experts and non-experts in utilizing AI-generated design proposals for wheel designs. It explores whether professionals in the field can produce distinct outcomes compared to non-professionals when considering design proposals provided by AI.

1.2 Research Purposes

This study aims to explore the differences in perspectives between non-experts and experts in the use of AI-generated wheel designs, especially in terms of performance under targeted selection. The experimental process is divided into three stages: firstly, the differences in instructions and choices of generated images among users with different experience backgrounds was compared; secondly, the differences in understanding and thinking about wheel design concepts among participants was explored; and finally, the differences between non-experts and experts in selecting feasible and creative wheel designs was analyzed. These experiments were perfomed to examine the capability of AI in the field of wheel design and compare it with professional designers' choices to see if the outcomes can fulfill experts expect. Based on the experimental results, this study proposes recommendations for both ordinary users and experts in using AI, to enhance its application value and precision in the field of professional design. Through this research, a better understanding of AI's potential in professional design can be gained, providing guidance for future development directions in the integration of AI and design. This research aims as below.

1. To explore the differences in purposeful text interpretation among individuals with vary experiences and backgrounds.
2. To explore the differences that arise from purposeful choices among individuals with diverse experiences and backgrounds, illustrating if that those with design experience tend to have more logical thinking.
3. To explore the rationale behind experts' choices, comparing them with those of non-experts. Through observation and interviews, gain a deeper understanding of these differences and discuss their implications.

4. To synthesize all the results of this experiment and the content obtained from interviews for a more detailed analysis, leading to comprehensive conclusions.

2 Literature Review

2.1 Research on Artificial Intelligence and Image Generation Software

Verganti et al. (2020) stated in their research that AI automates decision-making and learning processes, which are at the core of innovation. The study indicated that AI, being user-centric, can offer better outcomes in terms of creativity and the speed of innovation. Hanafy (2023) stated that Midjourney allows various users to generate diverse visual effects based on their written descriptions, offering designers and artists a novel method to quickly sketch out ideas and thoughts. It is also particularly helpful for those who want to explore creative ideas but lack a foundation in traditional artistic methods.Jaruga (2022) The study notes that image generation software similar to Midjourney includes DALL-E, NightCafe, Wombo Dream, and Latent Majesty Diffusion. These are AI generation softwares based on the same foundations, capable of producing digital images with high aesthetic value. Compared to other software in research studies Midjourney was rated as the most user-friendly software by participants after use. The literature explains that AI generation serves as a creative source of inspiration. It also elucidates that Midjourney, in the realm of AI image generation technology, is currently more advanced and user-friendly compared to other AI software. This study takes Midjourney's advantage of practical and mature usage as the experimental tool.

2.2 Car Wheel Frame Shape Design

Current research on car wheel rims primarily explores materials or mechanics, as indicated by sources such as Hirsch (2011), Huminic & Huminic (2008). In terms of wheel rim design, Luo et al. (2012) conducted a study identifying consumer emotional evaluations of car and wheel rim design styles through Kansei attributes. The research results indicated that for the Coupé car's wheel rim design contains character with lower number of spokes, between 5 to 7, with medium thickness and featuring rotational decorations. The other characteristic involves a higher number of spokes, more than 10, which are thin and radial with less decoration. These characteristics convey a sense of sporty style, agility, and high speed, aligning with the streamlined design style of the Coupe. Another result indicates that full-size executive or luxury cars have specific design requirements. The first characteristic is a complex and refined structure, mainly featuring 5–7 spokes, medium thickness, geometric shapes, and rich decorations, emphasizing ornamental aspects. The second characteristic involves thicker spokes, adopting radial or geometric shapes, with less decoration, multiple spokes, and thick/medium structural thickness. The study suggests that wheel rim designers can base their designs on a solid, sturdy, and simple wheel rim design, reflecting the luxury, elegance, safety, and reliability of sedans. Through the research proposed by Luo et al. (2012), the elements characteristic of both sporty and luxurious styles was identified. This research aims to use popular AI technology in wheel rim design as its main focus, while also exploring the cognitive differences between experts, non-experts, and individuals with varying experiences when designing wheel rims using AI technology.

2.3 The Impact of Text Input and Output

Duan & Zhang (2022) indicated that to truly aid in creative ideation, it is necessary to deeply understand the design and thinging process of designers, address challenges encountered during the design process, and identify the optimal application points for artificial intelligence in this process. Artificial intelligence can enhance the quality of design stimuli more effectively, thereby supporting the creative thinking of designers. Vermillion (2022) suggested that although designers and illustrators are fully capable of creating graphics to design and communicate ideas independently, AI generation offers two unique values: one is faster speed, and the other is the ability of AI to interpret in diverse ways, thereby producing unexpected results. This is particularly helpful for designers in the conceptualization and early stages of creativity. The aim of the research is to test the accuracy of AI-generated results using a lexicon co-created with design experts as a reference. Yildirim. (2022) The article mentions that artificial intelligence has played a significant role in the field of architecture, assisting architects in tasks such as architectural design, simulating building strength, and layout planning. With the maturation of generative AI technology, AI can provide even more assistance to architects.

2.4 The Difference Between Experts and Non-experts "Design Experience"

Lyu et al. (2022) conducted one-on-one interviews to explore the differences in interaction processes among people with different backgrounds. The results showed that individuals with an artistic background spent an average of 22 min on creative tasks, significantly more than the 14 min spent by those without an artistic background. Artists also exceeded non-artistic participants in the number of times they modified prompts and regenerated images. This indicates significant behavioral differences between creators of different backgrounds in the co-creation process with AI. Wong et al. (2016) pointed out that experienced designers are capable of considering and evaluating a wider range of issues, often referencing similar past design experiences. These designers typically conduct preliminary evaluations after generating new concepts, before starting implementation (Ahmed et al., 2003). Lawson (2004) and Goldschmidt (1998) also indicated that, in contrast, novice designers tend to proceed directly to implementation after concept generation with less evaluation. While novice designers encounter problems, they usually need to return to the concept generation stage, a process akin to trial and error, leads to delay progress and reduce efficiency. Alsagour (2020) explored the differences in design thinking processes between expert and novice designers. Qualitative interviews were conducted with fifteen experts and fifteen novice designers. The results revealed significant differences between experts and novices during the inspiration phase of design thinking. Experts used more resources and tools than novices to define problems and collect data, leading to a deeper understanding of the issues. Expert designers were more active in cognitive activities than novices, possessing more experience and skills in understanding and addressing design problems. Gero & Wells (2019) pointed out that there is a significant cognitive difference between high school students who have received engineering design education and those who have not, in terms of design thinking and creativity. Using an enhanced Function-Behavior-Structure (FBS) coding scheme, the study found that students who received engineering design education generate new ideas faster in the creative design process, highlighting the important role of engineering design education in fostering design creativity.

The synthesis of the aforementioned literature indicates that, whether in the field of engineering design, artistic creation, or design thinking, there are multifaceted differences between experts and novices. These differences manifest in both cognitive aspects of design and in design thinking processes. However, it is necessary to revalidate this issue. Moreover, by examining the differences between novices and experts, we aim to explore how the integration of AI in wheel rim design can create varying perspectives and insights between experts and non-experts. This will help us to preliminarily understand whether the outcomes of those with professional knowledge using AI are superior.

3   Research Methods and Experimental Design

3.1   Experimental Process and Methods

The study primarily employs a mixed-method approach to explore the performance and preferences of individuals with varying experiences and backgrounds in wheel rim design using AI image generation tools. Participants are categorized into two main groups: wheel rim design experts and non-experts, with the latter further subdivided into those with and without design experience. In the first phase of the experiment, participants are required to use the Midjourney AI tool to create wheel rim designs, focusing on both sporty and luxurious styles. Observation methods are used to understand the text command inputs of different experience levels, and interviews are conducted to understand their choices, preliminarily verifying the cognitive and selection differences among individuals with diverse backgrounds and experiences. In phase one, part two, the AI-generated wheel rim design proposals from four participants are compiled for subsequent experimental testing and use. In the second phase, non-experts are asked to select feasible and creative wheel rims in both sporty and luxurious styles, with comparisons made through semi-structured interviews. In the third phase, experts are asked to do the same, with comparisons and discussions conducted through semi-structured interviews. Overall, this experimental approach, which includes experimental design, text and image selection analysis, and a mixed method of semi-structured interviews, aims to deeply understand how different participants utilize AI tools and to reveal the cognitive and behavioral differences between experts and non-experts in the design process.

3.2   Experimental Software and Operating Instructions

This study utilizes the AI image generation software Midjourney for experimentation, aimed at generating images of various wheel rim designs. Midjourney can produce four similar images at once, offering a U key function to generate a more detailed version of a selected image, and a V key function to generate four slightly different images. Due to its ease of use and maturity, Midjourney is chosen as the primary experimental tool. This research consulted with experts familiar with AI and wheel rim domains to develop a design glossary including styles, shapes, and materials before the experiment.

Four participants were asked select terms from this glossary for text generation, creating wheel rim designs in both sporty and luxurious styles, with each style generating 20 images, totaling 160 images for comparison. To maintain consistency and accuracy in the experiment, all participants will make their image selections on screens ranging from 15 to 16 inches, ensuring standardized viewing quality.

3.3 Background Information for Non-experts and Experts

In this experiment, four participants with different backgrounds are invited to represent non-wheel rim experts, including students from National Yunlin University of Science and Technology to represent diverse experience backgrounds. Among them, two non-design field participants have limited knowledge of design theory and technique, but possess fresh perspectives and innovative thinking. The other two design background participants have deeper understanding of design theory and conceptualization. Detailed information is available in Table 1.

Table 1. Background description of the four subjects in experimental phases one and two

non-experts	Age and gender as well as experience and background
A	21 years old, electronic science student, no design experience
B	22 years old, finance and banking student, novice with less than one year of design experience
C	23 years old, design student graduated less than a year, 7 years design training
D	23 years old, design student graduated less than a year, 7 years design training. Intern in automotive design

There are three-wheel rim experts participated the experiment, all of them have extensive experience in automotive design and profound knowledge in the automotive field. These experts are coded as Expert E, Expert F, and Expert G, and they will represent wheel rim experts in this experiment. Detailed information can be found in Table 2.

Table 2. Background description of the three rim experts in Phase 3

Expert	Age and gender as well as experience and background
E	25 years old, male, expert in automotive related fields and wheel frames
F	28 years old, male, expert in automotive related fields and wheel frames
G	50 years old, male, expert in automotive related fields and wheel frames

3.4   Experimental Steps

Stage 1: Differences and Discussion of Text Command Input by Non-experts.   The experiment is divided into three phases: First, the four non-wheel rim experts A, B, C, D are introduced to the purpose, procedure, and the AI software Midjourney's usage in the experiment. The adjective glossary (Table 3) co-developed by AI operators and wheel rim designers was provided. Then, the participants are guided to use the words from the glossary to conceptualize wheel rim designs in sporty and luxurious styles. They are informed to focus on wheel rim design instead of car exterior style elements. Participants can insert their design concepts into a preset sentence structure (Table 4). Finally, this research will analyze the textual differences used by the four participants and conduct preliminary discussions on the differences.

Table 3.   Glossary of car wheel frame shapes.

Styling elements				
Classic Lines	Retro Styling	Traditional Craftsmanship	Time-Honored Aesthetics	Classic Forging
Elegant Curves	Durable Materials	Hand finished	Classic Chrome Plating	Traditional Spokes
Traditionally Sturdy	Eternal Design	Old-School Style	Pure Craftsmanship	Intricate Detailing
Antique Reproduction	Refined Polishing	Historical Style	Traditionally Luxurious	Classically Beautiful
Innovative aesthetics	Innovative aesthetics	Intelligent interactive design	Minimalist Futurism	Dynamic Fluidity
Multi-Functional Integration	Avant-Garde Technology	High-Tensile Styling	Lightweight design	Digitally Carved Textures
Aerodynamic Design	Innovative Structures design	Sustainable Material Use	Adjustable Dynamic Balance	Precision craftsmanship
Innovative avant-garde design	Streamline	Modular Concept	Geometric cuts	Visionary
Dynamic Appearance				

Shape				
Spokes	Chrome Plating	Engraved Details	Center Cap	Solid Design
Vintage Logo	Oval Spokes	Metallic Finish	Screw Details	Classic Width
Line Engravings	Inner Rim Engraving	Old structure	Double Layered Spokes	
Asymmetrical Spokes	Floating Spokes	Interlaced Design	Compound shape	Dynamic Contours
Wavy Spokes	Geometric type	Twisted Shapes	Variable Geometry	Extended Spokes
Multi-Layered Structure	Spiral Design	Composite Structure	Flexible Construction	Streamline
Hidden Spokes	Translucent Effects			

Material application				
Steel	Aluminum	Magnesium Alloy	Chrome Plated	Stainless Steel
Zinc	Copper	Nickel	Polycarbonate	Polyester
Carbon Fiber	Titanium Alloy	High-Performance Plastics	Aluminum-Magnesium Alloy	High-Strength Steel
Fiber-Reinforced Plastics	Thermoplastic Polymers	Glass Fiber	Aluminum-Lithium Alloy	Ceramic Materials
Synthetic Fibers				

Table 4.   The sentence's structure

Image of car wheel, front view, sports / luxury,_____ styling elements, __(structure & shape)__ shape, material application is _____.

Stage 1–2 Convert Four-Digit Text Instructions into Images and Compile them into Charts. Step One: AI Image Generation. Using commands input by the four participants with different backgrounds. The sentence by each participant was regenerated five times to receive 20-wheel rim images for each style. The image generation process is kept confidential to ensure the accuracy of subsequent experimental selection results. Step Two: the image generation results from four participants were divided into sporty and luxurious styles. Each style contains four parts and was labeled according to participant's code as participant and style which were AS, BS, CS, DS for sports style and AL, BL, CL, DL for luxurious style.

Stage 2, Four Non-experts with Different Backgrounds were Asked to Select Appropriate Images and to Explain the Reason. Step One: The AI generated wheel rim images from Stage 1–2 were organized as picture 1 and 2 then presented to four participants in blind. Participants were asked to choose 16 feasible images and 16 creative images form 80 AI images in picture 1 and 2. After the image selection phase, independent semi-structured interviews were conducted to discuss their reasons of choosing and the criteria used in their judgment.

Stage 3: The Images Selection Difference and Analysis by Experts. Step One: There are three wheel rim experts, participants E, F, and G, invited to evaluate AI generated wheel rim images. After experimental purpose introduction, the three experts were asked to select 16 suitable wheel rim images for each feasible and creative style through the two pictures from Stage 1–2. Step Two: Conduct independent semi-structured interviews with experts E, F, and G. Interview them about their reasons for selecting the images and the criteria used in their judgment. Finally, consolidate the results chosen by the three experts, providing a basis for a comprehensive discussion of differences in subsequent research.

The interviews focus on participants' views and thought processes when choosing sporty and luxurious styles. The goal is to summarize whether there are differences in the thinking of novices versus experts. The affecting factors of AI-generated design proposals are also explored. Moreover, to discuss whether AI could potentially replace design experts. The following is the content of the semi-structured interview:

- What are the reasons or rationales for choosing feasible sports wheel rim designs? What elements, characteristics, or design aspects influenced your selection of these 16 designs? Did the AI-generated images provide shape ideas that match the sporty style you were looking for?
- What are the reasons or rationale for choosing creatively sports wheel rim designs? What elements, characteristics, or design decisions influenced your selection of these 16 designs? Did the AI-generated images provide shape ideas that align with the sporty style you were aiming for?
- What were your reasons or rationale for choosing feasible luxurious wheel rim designs? What elements, characteristics, or design decisions influenced your selection of these 16 designs? Did the AI-generated images provide shape ideas that align with the luxurious style you were aiming for?

- What were your reasons or rationale for choosing creatively luxurious wheel rims? What elements, characteristics, or design decisions influenced your selection of these 16 designs? Did the AI-generated images provide shape ideas that align with the luxurious style you were aiming for?

4   Experimental Results and Analysis

4.1   Experimental Stage 1: Results and Discussion of Text Instructions for Non-wheel Rim Experts

The discussion of text input differences in sport styles by four non-experts:

This study preliminarily observed that the participant without design experience (Participant A) chose text terms that were more unconventional and creative compared to the others. It was also noted that all four participants shared some common ideas in their text commands for the sporty style, the terms such as streamline, aerodynamic design, and carbon fiber are mentioned. The participant with one year of design experience (Participant B) and the one with over seven years of experience in car design (Participant D) chose terms for shape representation and materials that were more practical and reasonable in their textual instructions. Specifically, the participant without a design background (Participant A) additionally chose fiberglass as a second material option, showing some creativity. In contrast, the material choices of the participant with one year of design experience (Participant B) were common materials used in currently marketed sporty car models.

The discussion of text input differences in luxurious style by four non-experts:

The four participants' textual input results are also individuals with significant variations for luxurious style wheel rim. However, both the participant with no design experience (Participant A and B) frequently mentioned adjectives related to sculpting and even complex details in their selection of terms fitting the luxurious style. The textual records showed that the participant with over seven years of design (Participant C) and automotive (Participant D) had more reserved approach in defining luxurious style terms, mentioning traditional luxury, chrome plating, pure craftsmanship, classic, and timeless. All four participants shared some common ideas in their text choices for luxurious style, mentioning terms such as Refined Polishing and Multi-Layered Structure. Lastly, it's important to note that Participant C (7 years automotive design) differed from the others in material selection, using Stainless Steel, a material commonly found in luxurious wheel rims of currently marketed luxury cars.

4.2   Experimental Stage 1–2: Four-Bit Image Aggregation Results

The first chart is for sport style (Fig. 1), containing a total of 80 car wheel images, divided into AS, BS, CS, DS sections. The second chart is for luxurious style (Fig. 2), also with 80 car wheel images, divided into AL, BL, CL, DL sections. These charts will be used for image selection and comparison in phases two and three of the experiment.

The AI-generated images of sporty and luxurious style wheel rims by the four participants are compiled into the following two charts Table 5:

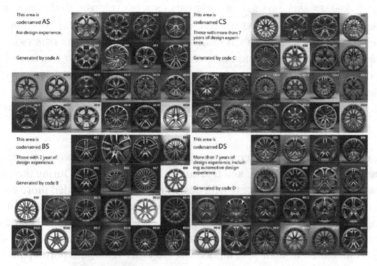

Fig. 1. 80 photos of sports style rims

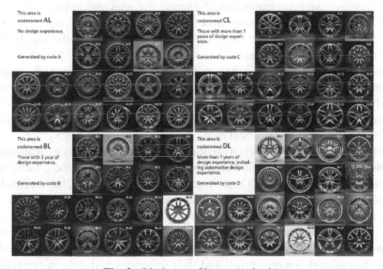

Fig. 2. 80 photos of luxury style rims

4.3 Experimental Stage 2: Comparism of Design/non Design Participants' (4 Non-experts) Opinions for Sports and Luxury Style Images

The semi-structured interview and results of selecttion differences between non-experts for feasibilitysport style wheel rim:

Table 5. Chart 1. The selection of feasibility and creative images for sports styles by non-experts

A	feasibility	AS1.AS6.AS7.AS14.AS15.AS17.BS.1.BS15.CS2.CS7.CS9.DS2.DS8.DS1111.DS12.DS17
	creativity	AS6. AS9. AS12. AS13. AS17. BS2. CS2. CS15. CS18. DS4. DS8. DS10. DS14. DS16. DS17. DS20
B	feasibility	AS5. AS9. AS15. AS19. BS5. BS6. BS8. BS10. BS12. BS20. CS9. CS13. CS17. DS1. DS9. DS15
	creativity	AS5. AS9. AS19. BS9. CS4. CS5. CS8. CS11. CS15. CS17. DS4. DS6. DS13. DS16. DS17. DS20
C	feasibility	AS1. BS1. BS2. BS3. BS5. BS6. BS7. BS8. BS11. BS12. BS15. BS16. BS17. DS2. DS8. DS15
	creativity	AS2.AS3.AS6.AS7.AS11.AS12.AS13.AS14.AS17.CS2.CS7.DS4.DS7.DS10.DS16
D	feasibility	AS9.BS2.BS4.BS9.BS10.BS14.BS15.BS.16.BS18.DS2.DS.3.DS5.DS8.DS9.DS12.DS19
	creativity	AS3.AS4.AS6.AS7.AS13.AS19.CS1.CS7.CS11.CS12.CS15.DS4.DS9.DS12.DS12.DS13.DS16

The data results and comprehensive interviews reveal that the two participants with design background (Participants C and D) choice similarly overlap. During the interview phase, it was also found that students with design background provided more consistent explanations in their design rationale, including structural elements for feasibility, shape characteristics, material application, and concepts of weight reduction. Their explanations included professional terminology and their selection criteria matched the personal design focus indicated in their text inputs. On the other hand, the participant without design background (Participant A) and the novice with one year of design experience (Participant B) made more diverse choices with almost no overlap. The interviews also revealed that these two participants lacked a strong personal philosophy in their design choices. Their selection criteria seemed to be influenced by the images, and when explaining their choices, they did not use specific design terminology or indicative feasibility. Instead, they used more basic, ambiguous terms like "feels light," "looks beautiful," "seems sportier," etc. However, it is noteworthy that although Participant B lacked concrete ideas during image selection, his text input and the resulting images both conveyed a distinctly sporty appearance for othrt participants.

The semi-structured interview and results of selecttion differences between non-experts for creative sport styles wheel rim:

In the selection of creative sports style designs, the two participants with design background displayed similar criteria and conceptual thinking regarding the creative aspects of sports style wheel rim designs. Their choices, shown in the chart 2, had a considerable amount of overlap. Through interviews, it was understood that these participants found the designs generated by the participant without design background (AS section) to be innovative, complex, and creatively aesthetic. On the other hand, the participant without design background (Participant A) and the design novice (Participant B) showed more dispersed choices with lower overlap, and their selections had little in common with Participants C and D. Although they did not specify which elements influenced their creative choices during the interviews, both participants had broad perspectives. They did not focus on specific elements, but their thinking processes were more global and diverse, received inspiration from the images. Finally, this research observed that non-experts' wheel rim images tended to deviate from the focus, often overly concentrating on creativity, which blurred the primary theme of the sports style Table 6.

Table 6. Chart 2. The feasibility and creative image selection for luxury style by non-expert:

A	feasibility	AL4.BL5.BL18.CL1.CL3.CL5.CL9.CL10.CL13.CL17.CL19.DL3.DL7.DL9.DL15.DL20
	creativity	AL4.AL5.AL7.AL16.AL17.AL19.BL1.BL8.BL10.BL11.CL1.CL10.CL14.DL1.DL7.DL9
B	feasibility	AL11.AL16.BL1.BL2.BL9.BL10.BL11.CL5.CL12.CL14.CL16.DL1.DL5.DL8.DL16.DL20
	creativity	AL1.ALAL2.AL7.AL8.AL10.AL12.AL14.AL15.AL17.BL3.BL9.CL1.CL10.DL5
C	feasibility	BL4.BL10.BL14.BL15.BL16.CL6.CL9.CL12.CL15.DL2.DL4.DL6.DL12.DL14.DL17.DL19
	creativity	AL2.AL5.AL7.AL14.AL15.AL17.AL19.BL2.BL5.BL8.BL17.CL9.CL10.DL9.DL13
D	feasibility	BL2.CL2.CL6.CL9.CL10.CL15.CL16.DL2.DL3.DL4.DL12.DL14.DL16.DL17.DL19.DL20
	creativity	AL1.AL2.AL5.AL6.AL7.AL9.AL12.AL14.AL15.BL5.BL8.CL1.CL10.DL13

The differences in selection of feasible luxury style wheel rim images by non-experts and the results of semi-structured interviews:

Regarding the selection of feasible luxury style wheel rims, the judgment criteria and perspectives of the participants with a design background, participant C and D, were similarly aligned. Their choices were primarily concentrated in the DL section (Fig. 2), followed by the CL section. The DL and CL areas were generated by them, but they were unaware of this in the blind test, and there was a significant overlap in their selections. The interview records of both participants indicated that they chose several images with a lot of chrome plating, glossy surfaces, polishing, or pure craftsmanship. The blind test result further corroborates that the images generated from their text input were quite accurate and met their expectations. In contrast, the participant without design background (Participant A) and the design novice (Participant B) displayed more scattered selections in their choices, with almost no overlap or consistency.

The differences in selection of **creative** luxury style wheel rim images by non-experts and the results of semi-structured interviews:

In the selection of creative luxury style wheel rims, all four participants unusually focused their choices in the AL area (Fig. 2). The AL area consisted of wheel rim images generated by the participant with no design experience. This aligns with the textual input differences discussed in Experiment One, where Participant A's input was characterized by its uniqueness and emphasis on complex sculpted lines, leading to these distinctive and creative wheel rim designs. However, the participants with a design background, C and D, had more aligned choices and perspectives in this instance, with significant overlap observed. Their similar viewpoints on luxury and creativity were revealed in interviews. Notably, the participant without design experience, A, predominantly chose designs from the AL area, which were generated by himself. During the interview, participants expressed that their definition of luxury involved elaborate, detailed carving, reflecting a direct correlation with their textual input for the experiment. This suggests that AI met their expectations and highlights that individual without design experience may incorporate higher levels of creativity in their thinking Table 7.

Table 7. Chart 3. The selection of feasibility and creative images for **sports styles** by experts:

E	feasibility	AS9.BS2.BS3.BS8.BS11.BS14.BS15.BS16.BS17.BS20.DS1.DS3.DS5.DS8.DS9.DS16
	creativity	AS5.AS9.AS17.BS18.BS20.CS6.CS8.CS15.CS16.CS18.DS9.DS13.DS14.DS16.DS20
F	feasibility	AS9.AS10.AS14.BS1.BS.5.BS11.BS15.BS17.BS20.DS2.DS3.DS7.DS8.DS9.DS15.DS16
	creativity	AS4.AS8.AS10.AS14.AS15.AS17.CS2.CS6.CS7.CS8.DS4.DS11.DS12.DS13.DS16.DS20
G	feasibility	AS1.AS9.AS17.BS1.BS4.BS11.BS13.BS15.BS16.BS17.BS20.CS4.CS6.DS7.DS12.DS15
	creativity	AS2.AS6.AS17.AS20.BS2.CS3.CS11.CS12.CS13.CS14.CS15.CS19.DS4.DS10.DS16.DS18

4.4 Experimental Stage 3: The Discussion of the Results and Interview Results of Experts' Selection for Sports and Luxury Style Images

The differences in selection of feasible sports style wheel rim images by experts and the results of semi-structured interviews:

The experiment revealed that the three-wheel rim experts, E, F, and G, showed a high degree of overlap in their selections for feasible sporty style designs, primarily focusing on the BS and DS areas (Fig. 1). The combined interview results of E, F, and G also clarified that factors such as the structure of the wheel rim, lightweight design, a clean five-spoke structure, and simple yet subtly varied designs, influenced their choices. The wheel rim design experts achieved a high level of consensus in their design perspectives and decision-making criteria. Furthermore, the choices of experts in feasible sporty style wheel rims were quite close to those of the non-expert participants, with a significant level of overlap, indicating a consensus in views between experts and non-experts under this condition.

The differences in selection of creative sports style wheel rim images by experts and the results of semi-structured interviews:

For the selection of creative designs, the experts predominantly chose from the CS area (Fig. 1), but their selections were not unified and were rather dispersed. The interviews revealed several reasons for this dispersion: Experts E, F, and G each had their own strong opinions on defining creativity, each carrying a distinct personal design style, which led to varying choices. In this round of creative decision-making, their selections differed from those of the non-expert wheel rim designers, who mainly preferred the AS area. However, the three experts, E, F, and G, collectively noted that while the AS area was creative, its overly rigid lines lacked the strong characteristics of a sports style, leading them to prefer the CL area. This illustrates a clear difference in selection criteria and perspectives between the experts and non-experts. The non-expert wheel rim designers mostly focused on creativity, thereby blurring the primary theme of sporty style Table 8.

Table 8. Chart 4. The selection of feasibility and creative images for **luxury style** by experts:

E	feasibility	AL4.BL1.BL3.BL12.BL13.BL16.BL19.CL2.CL9.CL12.CL13.DL10.DL15.DL18.DL20
	creativity	AL3.AL7.AL12.AL15.AL17.BL3.BL5.BL8.BL11.BL17.CL1.CL2.CL7.CL8.CL13.CL20
F	feasibility	AL4.AL8.AL11.AL17.AL20.BL2.BL5.BL9.BL11.CL5.CL7.CL14.DL5.DL8.DL12.DL16
	creativity	AL4.AL7.AL8.AL11.AL12.AL13.AL17.AL20.BL2.BL9.CL14.CL15.DL8.DL9.DL10.DL16
G	feasibility	AL4.AL8.AL9.AL19.BL3.BL5.BL9.BL10.BL20.CL6.CL8.CL10.CL13.DL15.DL16.DL18.DL20
	creativity	AL4.AL8.AL11.BL8.BL9.BL18.BL20.CL8.CL9.CL10.CL13.DL5.DL7.DL10.DL16.DL20

Comprehensive results of experts' selection differences and semi-structural interviews on feasible luxury-style wheel frame designs:

Regarding the selection of feasible luxurious styles, the experts' choices showed significant differences. From the compiled results of the interviews focusing on their selection criteria, it was found that the three-wheel rim experts, E, F, and G, each had their own strong personal opinions and subjective perceptions of luxury style. Participant E favored complex designs and simple but progressively stretched forms. Participant F preferred shiny surfaces, intricate lines, and sharp spokes as aligning more with their understanding. Participant G believed that dense, intricate, blocky structures with fine details and stainless-steel shiny elements better matched their perception. These individual subjective viewpoints influenced their different selection outcomes. Compared to non-experts, experts had more in-depth and focused arguments to support their ideas and explanations.

The differences in selection of creative luxury style wheel rim images by Experts and the results of semi-structured interviews:

The selection criterion were more similarly dispersed than those of the non-experts. However, both experts and non-experts generally focused on the AL area. Consolidated interviews with experts and non-experts revealed a common view that the AL area was both luxurious and creative. They generally agreed that Participant A's textual commands included more sculpted details, intricate craftsmanship, and an interwoven, repetitive structure, leading to unexpected and uncommon results, perceived as highly creative.

5 Conclusion

5.1 Using AI to Provide Effects for Non-rim Experts

This research gathered from experiments and interviews with four non-expert participants demonstrates their high appreciation for AI's capabilities in design. The study identified significant cognitive differences between participants with and without design backgrounds, particularly in evaluating feasibility or creativity. Notably, those lacking design experience chose more unique and varied vocabulary in their text instructions, resulting in images of greater distinctiveness. However, when these participants were tasked with making purposeful choices, their thought processes tended to be more scattered. Interviews further revealed a relatively vague understanding of stylistic concepts and design thinking among them, lacking a clear personal ideology. Faced with a multitude of selectable images, they struggled to focus on their design theme. Based on these findings, we recommend further study of basic design concepts and knowledge, as such foundational skills can significantly enhance the benefits of using AI in design assistance.

5.2 Differences in Cognition and Judgment Standards Between Wheel Rim Experts and Non-experts

In the process of selecting design images, experts in wheel frame design tend to prioritize practicality, technical feasibility, and traditional design aesthetics. Their evaluation criteria include the suitability of materials, structural stability, and the harmony between overall and detailed designs. This indicates that, even with AI-assisted design, experts rely on their extensive design experience and profound professional knowledge, incorporating these elements into a comprehensive consideration for decision-making, thus leading to more logical choices. In contrast, non-experts prefer innovations in appearance and uniqueness when selecting design proposals. Their choices are more often based on personal preference and visual appeal rather than practicality or technical details, although this does not represent all individuals. Overall, non-experts may focus more on exploration and creative expression when using AI, rather than being constrained by the norms and limitations of traditional design.

5.3 Does AI Image Generation Have Expert-Level Design Capabilities? !

Although AI can create innovative and eye-catching designs, the involvement of experts is crucial to ensure the practical applicability and technical accuracy of these designs. Experts can conduct in-depth analysis on AI-generated designs to assess their suitability for actual production and market demands. For non-experts, AI serves as a powerful tool that allows them to break through the boundaries of traditional design and stimulate creative thinking. However, the designs created by these users may not reach the maturity in technical feasibility and market adaptability as those designed by experts. This demonstrates that while AI can enhance creativity and visual innovation, it cannot fully replace the need for professional knowledge and experience in the field of professional design, making the guidance of experts indispensable. Overall, this study highlights the differences in cognition and selection between experts and non-experts in AI-assisted design: experts evaluate AI designs based on their profound professional knowledge, whereas non-experts use AI to explore more innovative and personalized design directions. This research finds that AI's application in the design field shows broad possibilities, but to maximize its effects, the support of professional knowledge is still needed to achieve design solutions that are both innovative and practical.

5.4 Future Recommendations

The market adaptability of AI-generated creative designs constitutes an important area of research. Future studies should investigate how to ensure that products designed by AI are not only aesthetically innovative but also meet the practical demands of production and market needs. This involves transforming AI-generated designs from conceptual stages into products that are feasible for production and aligned with market trends. However, this research has limitations, especially when exploring the differences between experts and non-experts in creativity and feasibility assessments of AI-generated designs, which may vary due to the personal characteristics and thoughts of the researchers. Future research could delve deeper into the differences in thoughts and evaluation criteria between experts and non-experts in AI-assisted design, and explore what kind of professional knowledge can enable AI to create superior design proposals, thereby satisfying and validating the application and potential of AI in professional fields.

References

1. Alsagour, M.: Comparing Novice and Expert Designers' Approaches to Design Thinking and Decision Making. Western Michigan University. (2020)
2. Ahmed, S., Wallace, K. M., Blessing, L. T.: Understanding the differences between how novice and experienced designers approach design tasks. Research in engineering design, 14, 1–11. https://doi.org/10.1007/s00163-002-0023-z (2003)
3. Duan, Y., Zhang, J.: A novel AI-based visual stimuli generation Ap-proach for environment concept design. Comput. Intell Neuro-Sci. (2022). https://doi.org/10.1155/2022/8015492
4. Goldschmidt, G.: Creative architectural design: reference versus precedence. J. Architectural Plan. Res. 258–270. (1998)
5. Gero, J., Yu, R., Wells, J.: The effect of design education on creative design cognition of high school students. Int J. Des. Creativity Innov. 7(4), 196–212 (2019). https://doi.org/10.1080/21650349.2019.1628664
6. Hanafy, N.O.: Artificial intelligence's effects on design process creativity:" a study on used AI Text-to-Image in architecture. J Build. Eng. 80, 107999. (2023).https://doi.org/10.1016/j.jobe.2023.107999
7. Hirsch, J.: Aluminium in innovative light-weight car design. Mater. Trans. 52(5), 818–824. (2011). https://doi.org/10.2320/matertrans.L-MZ201132
8. Huminic, A., Huminic, G.: On the aerodynamics of the racing cars (No. 2008–01–0099). SAE Tech. Pap. (2008). https://doi.org/10.4271/2008-01-0099
9. Jaruga-Rozdolska, A.: Artificial intelligence as part of future practices in the architect's work: Mid Journey generative tool as part of a process of creating an architectural form. Architectus, 3 (71). (2022)
10. Lawson, B.: What designers know. Routledge (2012)
11. Luo, S.J., Fu, Y.T., Zhou, Y.X.: Perceptual matching of shape design style between wheel hub and car type. Int. J. Ind. Ergon. 42(1), 90–102 (2012). https://doi.org/10.1016/j.ergon.2011.10.001
12. Lyu, Y., Wang, X., Lin, R., Wu, J.: Communication in human–AI co-creation: perceptual analysis of paintings generated by text-to-image system. Appl. Sci. 12(22), 11312 (2022). https://doi.org/10.3390/app122211312
13. Verganti, R., Vendraminelli, L., Iansiti, M.: Innovation and design in the age of artificial intelligence. J. Prod. Innov. Manag. 37(3), 212–227 (2020). https://doi.org/10.1111/jpim.12523
14. Vermillion, J.: Iterating the design process using AI diffusion models. (2022)
15. Wong, J.J., Chen, P.Y., Chen, C.D.: The metamorphosis of industrial designers from novices to experts. Int. J. Art Des Educ. 35(1), 140–153 (2016). https://doi.org/10.1111/jade.12044
16. Yildirim, E.: Text-to-image generation AI in architecture. Art and Architecture.: Theory, Pract. Experience, 97. (2022)

Current Research and Application Status of Mental Models in the Field of Design in China: A Literature-Based Approach

Shixiang Li[✉]

School of Art and Design, Wuhan University of Technology, Wuhan, China
1342102663@qq.com

Abstract. Objective: This study comprehensively analyzes the current status and overall characteristics of the application of mental models in the field of Chinese design literature.

Methods: Design-related literature incorporating mental model applications, indexed by CNKI, served as the data source. Scientific literature visualization tools, VOSviewer and CiteSpace, were employed. A scientific knowledge map was constructed, visualizing aspects such as the distribution of literature by year, research institutions, authors, and keyword clusters to reveal the research trends.

Conclusion: Research findings indicate an overall increasing trend in literature within the scope of this study. Leading institutions in engineering and management dominate the application of mental models in the field of Chinese design. Research focuses primarily on user satisfaction, needs, analytic hierarchy process (AHP), user experience, service design, and product design. Highly cited papers form the primary knowledge base, linking a significant portion of the research. Future development trends include cultural and creative design, CMF design, as well as the analysis of personalized and differentiated user demands. However, current research faces limitations such as a lack of apparent methodological innovation, limited research collaboration, and a scarcity of highly productive authors.

Keywords: Mental model · Design research · CiteSpace · VOSviewer · Visualization · Graph analysis

1 Introduction

Mental Models theory, originating from cognitive psychology, was first proposed in 1943 by Scottish psychologist Kenneth Craik. It represents the brain's reconstruction of the external world based on internal cognitive representations. Renowned designer Donald Norman, in his 1998 work "The Design of Everyday Things," conceptualized mental models as tools to study subjective user behavior, motivations, thought processes, emotions, and philosophical perspectives. He introduced the designer model, user model, and system image within the design process. In essence, mental models, shaped by past cognitive experiences, influence how people perceive and decide on actions in the world, aiding in the assessment of design effectiveness by comparing external situations with expected states.

H. Mori and Y. Asahi (Eds.): HCII 2024, LNCS 14689, pp. 194–206, 2024.
https://doi.org/10.1007/978-3-031-60107-1_14

In the design of product attributes, interaction design pioneer Alan Cooper introduced three models in "About Face": user mental model, reflecting user expectations based on cognitive knowledge; representation model, established by designers through visual representations and interaction pathways; and implementation model, detailing the product's operational principles. Cooper emphasized that good product design aligns the representation model closely with the user's mental model.

In today's rapidly evolving internet era, the diversification and personalization of user needs present ample opportunities for the design discipline. In the face of intensifying market competition, timely design and development of innovative products and services are crucial for company growth. The mental model, as an effective method for exploring user cognitive feedback and design evaluation, has been widely applied in optimizing design solutions and feasibility studies, generating a substantial body of literature.

Simultaneously, the rapid rise in the development of mental model theory in recent years has positioned it as a key component in interdisciplinary research across various fields. In disciplines like interaction design, product design, and design art within the realm of design studies, the theory holds significant research application value. Given the absence of comprehensive literature reviews on the application of mental models in the Chinese design field, it is essential to further summarize and analyze relevant research, especially the current status in China. Utilizing scientific literature metrics for quantitative analysis of various literature types can aid in systematically uncovering potential patterns and information within the vast dataset.

2 Data Sources and Study Methods

Please note that the first paragraph of a section or subsection is not indented. The first paragraph in this paper, the most comprehensive CNKI (abbr. China national knowledge infrastructure) database in China is selected to search and obtain relevant literature data. In order to ensure the comprehensiveness and accuracy of the data, the Chinese literature is limited. The search date is August 23, 2023, and the publication time is all literature before December 31, 2022. Search TS = ("Mental Model" and "Design") is set in the CNKI Advanced search interface. The search obtained 654 valid documents, including the topics but not about the application of mental model in the field of design, such as Model Mechanism and Practice Enlightenment of Library Cross-language Auxiliary Reading Service, etc.; conference news; books and materials; review papers, etc. Finally, 507 valid documents were obtained and then TXT plain text was exported in Refworks format for further quantitative analysis.

In order to obtain more rigorous and comprehensive data indicators, VOSviewer and CiteSpace measurement visualization software are used in the research. VOSviewer Developed in 2009 by vanEck and Waltman of the Science and Technology Research Center of Leiden University in the Netherlands, it has a powerful user graphical interface and mapping visualization function. CiteSpace Is a scientific metrology visualization software developed by Professor Chen Chaomei team of Drexel University based on Java platform. Both can carry out bibliometric analysis of the literature in a specific field, and can intuitively and profoundly reflect the development context and law of a certain discipline in the form of visual knowledge graph, which has been widely used in bibliometric analysis in recent years. This paper will use the above two visual tools, with mental model in the field of Chinese design research and application as the breakthrough point, using biblientation, content analysis, empirical research, such as the literature post time distribution, research institutions and high author distribution, literature sources, keywords and highly cited literature analysis, summarize MM-CDR related literature research hotspot, the overall research status and the development trend in the future.s that follows a table, figure, equation etc. does not have an indent, either.

3   Statistical Analysis of the MM-CDR Study

3.1   Time Distribution Analysis of Publication Volume

The time distribution of the amount of publications is the embodiment of the sustainability and attention of research. The output changes of the development of academic literature over time can effectively evaluate the research dynamics in this field. Since 1998–2022, the annual number of published articles increased from 1 in 1998 to 54 in 2022, and the MM-CDR literature overall showed a fluctuating trend over time. The literature was analyzed by visualization, and the time distribution trend is shown in Fig. 1. From the time distribution of retrieval, the research of mental model in the field of design in China can be divided into the following three development stages.

Phase 1. Development and Exploration period (1998–2008). During this period, the number of publications was small and in the initial stage, with the average annual publication volume of 1.8. Early mental model research is more used in cognitive education

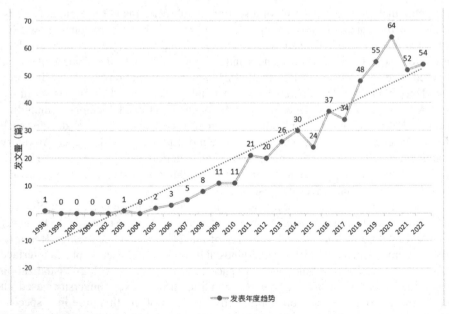

Fig. 1. A figure caption is always placed below the illustration. Short captions are centered, while long ones are justified. The macro button chooses the correct format automatically.

and consumer behavior, in 1998 Wang Qiong classification about human-computer interface design method for test method, prediction model method, anthropomorphic method and cognitive method, introduced the use of GOMS model prediction user model method [1], the model in 1983 by Card[1], Moran & Newall[2] In The Psychology of Human Computer Interaction, a method for evaluating the quality of human-computer interaction interface, based on the theory of cognitive psychology, brings the theory of cognitive psychology into the field of design scholars. After further study of the literature, it can be seen that although the scholars were in the exploratory stage in this period, they created a new perspective of cognitive psychology theory and mental model application in the field of design, which laid a good foundation for the subsequent research.

Phase 2. Fluctuation development period (2009–2015). During this period, the development trend of the number of articles increased, the overall growth, the annual average number of articles was 20.4. During this period of time, the research of mental model tends to be diversified. Under the research needs of complex situations, it expands the practice of user mental model, shared mental model and other contents, and focuses on interaction design, user experience, mobile Internet and other fields as the main research objects for in-depth application research. After further analysis found that mainly about the early research on mental model in the field of design has preliminary results, and with the development of the Internet into 3.0 era, technology innovation form is gradually changing, interface design as a window of information product design, from the pursuit to meet the needs of the user's function and aesthetic demand, gradually focus on more human and more likely to accept the user experience [2]. It promotes scholars to improve user experience and build a user-centered experience design and service design system research.

Phase 3. Rapid growth period (2016- -present). Compared with the previous two stages, the number of published articles in this period had an explosive increase, with the average annual publication volume increased to 49.1 articles. After 2016, domestic scholars became increasingly enthusiastic about the design of mental models. In 2020, the number of articles reached the highest in three stages, with a total of 64 articles. On the one hand, the reason for the rapid growth is the Opinions of The State Council on Promoting the Integrated Development of Cultural Creativity and Design Services and Related Industries promulgated by The State Council in 2014[3], the support of the state and the guidance of policies have played a certain role in boosting. On the other hand, a large number of excellent design achievements appeared after 2016. The in-depth exploration of user experience design, the design perspective has also expanded to "emotional design", "multi-modal interaction" [3], "virtual reality" [4], "artificial intelligence" [5] and other aspects.

---

[1] Stuart K.Card American researcher, xerox company palo alto research center senior researcher, is one of the pioneers of human-computer interaction.

[2] Thomas P. Moran is a distinguished engineer at the IBM Almaden Research Center in San Jose, California.

[3] https://www.cnipa.gov.cn/art/2014/7/15/art_381_138230.html.

Cultural creativity and design services have run through various fields and industries in the economy and society, showing a trend of multi-direction interaction and integration. It is expected that after 2022, the research of mental models in the field of design will continue to heat up, bringing more and more excellent academic results.

3.2 Distribution of Literature Sources

According to the distribution of literature sources, among 507 valid documents, 346 dissertations (37 doctoral, 309 masters), 157 journal papers and 4 conference papers. Among the journal papers, Packaging Engineering contains 25 articles, which is the most published journal in the research field and has the highest total citations among various journals. It is the core journal in the MM-CDR research field. Post TOP10 literature source are jiangnan university (29), the packaging engineering (25), Zhejiang university (17), southeast university (15), Nanjing university of science and technology (12), "design" (11), southwest jiaotong university (11), Hunan university (11), "art and design (theory)" (10), east China normal university (9). From the distribution of literature sources, the thesis is the main carrier of MM-CDR research, accounting for 68.24% of the total publications (Fig. 2).

Frequency/times	Intermediation centrality	Key words
175	0.47	Mental model
10	0.29	Availability
17	0.2	Product design
27	0.19	Interface design
56	0.18	User experience
68	0.13	Interaction design
5	0.11	Experience Design

Fig. 2. Mediation centrality of high-frequency keywords in MM-CDR literature

3.3 Research Hotspot Analysis

The key words of the literature are the author's high refining of his research results, which usually includes the research object, research perspective and research methods, etc. The high-frequency co-occurrence keywords reflect the long-term research hotspot of MM-CDR.507 articles within the scope of search contained 1342 keywords. Running VOSviewer, keyword co-occurrence frequency was set to 4. After screening and merging synonyms, 57 keywords obtained keyword co-occurrence cluster, see Fig. 3. The keywords with the same color in the figure are the same cluster, forming four main clusters (Clusters), namely # 1 (red) user mental model and product design, # 2 (green)

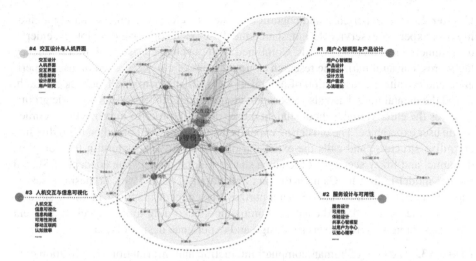

Fig. 3. Cluster plot of keyword co-occurrence in MM-CDR literature

user experience and cognition, # 3 (blue) human-computer interaction and information visualization, # 4 (yellow) interaction design and human-computer interface.

CiteSpace Mediation centrality is the importance of keyword nodes in keyword collinear an index, centrality is greater than 0.1 nodes for the core nodes in the field, combined with the analysis results, mental model application in the field of design in China mainly distributed in "product design" "interface design" and the "user experience" class research topic, it is consistent with the core function of the mental model. When using mental models, they are often used in conjunction with hierarchical analysis (AHP), Saltman metaphor lure technology (ZMET) and cognitive theory. As shown in Fig. 3, the application of MM-CDR mainly focuses on virtual reality, user research, artificial intelligence, smart TV, augmented reality and other directions, while the design objects are more diversified, covering the traditional product design, interaction design, emerging service design, experience design, etc. Based on each cluster subnetwork:

Cluster 1. User mental model and product design include 19 members, mainly including user mental model, interface design, product design, user needs, heart flow theory, metaphor extraction technology, design methods, etc. The clustering reflects the core function of the mental model around the product design content, which is applied to the optimization of the product design solutions. In the specific research, the rest of the cluster also reflect the use of design methods such as metaphor extraction technology and design consistency principle, and determine the relationship between the performance model and the user's mental model, so that the product is more in line with user expectations. The method is also applied to the teaching design, such as wang lei based on the development of mental model advanced teaching——teaching "centripetal force" concept, for example, [6], on the basis of combining with students 'mental model development, will learn advanced theory applied to the concept of "centripetal force" teaching, improve students' thinking ability, in order to realize from the mental model to the advanced scientific model.

Cluster 2. User experience and cognition include 15 cluster members, mainly including user experience, service design, shared mental model, cognitive psychology, elderly, user-centered and other keywords. Combined with the characteristics of high frequency keywords, can summarize the research characteristics of cluster 2 based on user experience and cognitive construction of mental model measurement and feedback research, found the mental model can also be used to identify and mining special, specific groups (such as the elderly, high school students) user needs in order to improve the accuracy of the user experience. The clustering expands the mental model based on the individual cognitive structure, and calls the extension of the cognitive structure in the complex, dynamic, and fuzzy scenarios of teams a shared mental model. The concept of Shared mental model is first by Cannon-Bowers and Sarah [7] and 1990, domestic research started late, 2004 white new [8] summarizes the concept mapping method, similarity assessment method, card classification method, according to user types in different scenarios, more systematic service design and experience design output.

Cluster 3. The field of human-computer interaction and information visualization contains 12 cluster members, mainly including human-computer interaction, information visualization, information construction, usability testing, mobile Internet, augmented reality, virtual reality, gesture interaction, etc. The mental model in the design of human-computer interaction interface refers to the user's understanding of the system. This cluster reflects how to transform data into matching information conducive to users' understanding in mobile Internet, augmented reality, virtual reality and other carriers, as well as gesture interaction and multi-contact interaction, so as to achieve the usability goal [9].

Cluster 4. Interaction design and man-machine interface, mainly including 11 main members, including interaction design, man-machine interface, interaction interface, design principles, emotional design, hierarchical analysis method, smart home, etc. Combined with the characteristics of high frequency keywords, can cluster 4 research hotspot as, follow the premise of design principle, using systematic, hierarchical and combining qualitative and quantitative methods, statistical elements of product function weight value, to establish the evaluation matrix, provide scientific basis for design scheme, realize the goal of human-computer interaction user experience [10].

3.4 Evolution of the Research Hotspots

In order to further study the frontier themes and development trends of MM-CDR and ensure the accuracy of the data indicators, the average occurrence time of the keywords was analyzed and superimposed in the original cluster map to obtain the cluster superposition map of the time keywords (see Fig. 4). The keyword co-present area map (Timezone View) (see Fig. 5) directly reflects the theme evolution of MM-CDR and the development trend of keywords in each time period within the search range. As shown in Fig. 6, the keywords of the emergent intensity Top15 are listed, in which the dark part represents the year when the reference frequency of the paper keywords is relatively prominent, reflecting the changing trend of the study. By ranking Top15 sudden keywords by time, the research hotspots are divided into three obvious intervals. Time keyword

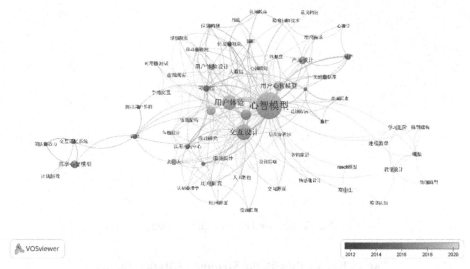

Fig. 4. Overlay diagram of time keywords clustering

clustering superposition map, keyword co-occurrence map and high-density occurrence of keywords are all analysis indicators of keyword introduction of time dimension, and more objective and accurate results can be obtained by mutual evidence and reference.

Combined with the evolution trend of Burst keywords and the cluster superposition of time keywords, it can be seen that the distribution of keywords of Kano model in the applied research of design science in China shows the characteristics of cycle, which is also consistent with the results of time zone map. From 2008 to 2018, the high-frequency keywords were the most intensive, reflecting this golden period for the application of mental models in the field of design. In the specific application research, scholars have combined the mental model with user research, heart flow theory, service design and hierarchical analysis (AHP) to improve, improve and innovate the mental model. There were 225 documents related to MM-CDR from 2019 to 2022 (including 55 in 2019,64 in 2020,52 in 2021, and 54 in 12.31,2022), reflecting the recent application of mental models in the field of design in China.

Among them, the more high-frequency keywords are hierarchical analysis method, heart flow theory, artificial intelligence, user research, big data, virtual reality, design research, service design, design strategy, teaching design and so on. High frequency keywords and 2009–2018 interval keywords overlap degree is reduced over time, it reflects the recent mental model application in the field of design, is from conventional interaction design, product design, service design function application to virtual reality, design strategy, artificial intelligence, cognitive model, big data, intelligent home construction and application, the innovation in the theory and method is not obvious, and application field mainly concentrated in virtual reality, artificial intelligence, model construction, meaning, etc., visible in the application field and scene change and innovation is more obvious.

Combined with time keywords clustering superposition diagram (see Fig. 4) and Burst high density appear (see Fig. 5), time zone chart (see Fig. 6) in high frequency

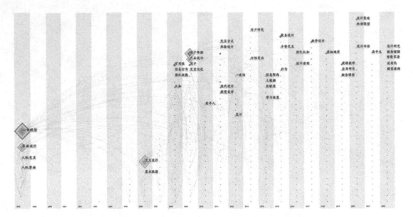

Fig. 5. Keyword co-present area map

Top 15 Keywords with the Strongest Citation Bursts

Keywords	Year	Strength	Begin	End	1998 - 2022
可用性	2006	2.49	2006	2011	
界面	2006	1.33	2006	2008	
交互方式	2011	2.03	2011	2015	
情感	2011	1.42	2011	2014	
中间用户	2011	1.2	2011	2012	
一致性	2012	1.25	2012	2017	
智能手机	2012	1.19	2012	2013	
用户体验	2009	1.82	2015	2016	
设计原则	2015	1.67	2015	2016	
用户需求	2015	1.67	2015	2016	
人工智能	2017	1.74	2017	2020	
智能电视	2017	1.35	2017	2019	
服务设计	2015	1.94	2018	2019	
虚拟现实	2015	1.41	2018	2020	
设计策略	2020	1.64	2020	2022	

Fig. 6. Key words high density

keyword distribution trend, can predict the future design mental model application will focus on artificial intelligence, multimodal interaction, virtual reality technology, design strategy research, and combining mental model with other tools for accurate acquisition and analysis user personalized, differentiation, emotional needs in order to improve the user experience.

3.5   Analysis of the High-Influence Literature

The MM-CDR related documents within the search range were ranked according to the total amount of citation, and 16 classical documents with more than 40 citation volume were extracted, as shown in Table. Among these highly cited documents, 5 are from the core journal Packaging Design Engineering, and 8 are from graduate papers. The research paradigm of highly cited literature in the table can be roughly divided into two categories. One is the combination of mental model with other design theoretical models and methods to expand and improve the traditional design scheme; the other is the improvement of mental model in design practice (Fig. 7).

序号	题目	作者	来源	发表时间
1	大数据时代背景下的数据可视化概念研究	曾悠	浙江大学	2014/1/16
2	用户体验中基于心智模型的手持移动设备界面设计研究	黄蓉蓉	浙江大学	2010/1/1
3	基于用户心智模型的手持移动设备界面设计	杨颖; 雷田; 张艳河	浙江大学学报(工学版)	2008/5/15
4	移动互联网终端界面设计研究	宋尹淋	山东大学	2009/5/15
5	基于心智模型的虚拟现实与增强现实混合式移动导览系统的用户体验设计	林一; 陈靖; 刘越; 王涌天	计算机学报	2014/10/14
6	心智模型在以用户为中心设计中的应用研究	赵辰羽	清华大学	2013/4/1
7	信息可视化中交互设计方法探议	覃京燕; 朱丹未; 李丹碧林	装饰	2007/3/1
8	老年人科技生活环境设计研究	宫晓东	北京理工大学	2014/6/1
9	基于多点触摸技术的人机交互研究	季红艳	华东师范大学	2011/5/1
10	乔纳森建构主义学习环境研究	李研	华东师范大学	2007/4/1
11	基于用户心智模型的产品设计	黄群; 朱超	包装工程	2009/12/15
12	基于情境感知多维数据可视化的产品服务系统创新设计研究	窦金花; 覃京燕	包装工程	2017/1/20
13	具身认知视角下的无意识设计	何灿群; 吕晨晨	包装工程	2020/4/20
14	人工智能对交互设计的影响研究	覃京燕	包装工程	2017/10/20
15	隔空手势交互的设计要素与原则	孙效华; 周博; 李彤	包装工程	2015/4/20
16	以用户行为为导向的智能电视交互设计研究	邱信权	江南大学	2017/5/1

Fig. 7. High cited literature

Among them, numbers 1, 6, 7, 8, 13, 14, 15 and 16 are the improvement studies of theoretical methods of mental models. No. 7 discusses that the goal of information visualization is to establish a good mental model interface to realize "thinking with vision" [9]. The important conditions for realization include the visual presentation form in line with the user's mental model, the correct representation of information elements, the design of reasonable operation tools and operation methods and so on, etc.

Numbers 2, 3 and 4 are the research results of mental models in the field of interface design. No.4, Song Yin Lin contacted the interface design of mobile network terminal with various disciplines, and finally chose to analyze the mental model of smartphone users from the perspective of users, and conducted typical function analysis on the design content of mobile terminal. On the basis of this, in the design of the smart phone operation interface, the layout of the interface, icon design and the establishment of the interface level, in the design of the small screen interface, the existing problems of the design objectives and principles are discussed, focusing on the design of its constituent elements. This system design method will give full play to the advantages of operators, manufacturers and third-party software suppliers, and can better design a mobile Internet user interface [22] that truly meets the needs of consumers.

No. 5, 9, 11, 12 for the mental model in the field of human-computer interaction and product design application research, number 11 reported the purpose of the product design is to meet the user demand, in the "user-centered design" under the concept, through the study of the user mental model to understand the product, design more suitable for the user use of the product, the user mental model formation and characteristics, analyzes the users and designers, the differences between the mental model, summarizes the mental model applied in product design theory and method [16].

4 Epilogue

MM-CDR research showed an upward trend in the literature output, and a steady growth trend in the past 5 years. The dominant institutions of engineering and management are the main application institutions of applied mental models in the field of design in China. Han Zhengbiao, Qin Jingyan, Wu Peng, Gong Xiaodong, Hu Weifeng and other authors are the main application team of MM-CDR.

Through keyword clustering, it can be seen that the research content of MM-CDR is comprehensive and diversified, and the application is mainly distributed on the problem of "user cognitive feedback". The research hotspots can be divided into four categories, namely, # 1 user mental model and product design, # 2 user experience and cognition, # 3 human-computer interaction and information visualization, and # 4 interaction design and human-computer interface. Keyword co-occurrence clustering covers four major fields, including user mental model and product design, user experience and cognition, human-computer interaction and information visualization, interaction design and human-computer interface. This shows that mental models mainly focus on the optimization of product design scheme, user experience and cognitive construction, human-computer interaction interface design, and the evaluation and optimization of interaction interface. Specific research shows the wide application of mental models in the field of design science, including product design, service design, virtual reality, user research, artificial intelligence and other directions.

In the field of design science in China, a number of influential MM-CDR highly cited literature has been produced. In the highly cited MM-CDR literature, 16 articles were cited more than 40 times, which are divided into two categories: the research of deeply combining mental models with other design theories, and the improvement of mental models in design practice. Among them, "Packaging design engineering" and master and erudite paper as the main contribution units. The research topics cover the areas of information visualization, interface design, human-computer interaction and product design. These literature emphasize the design conditions in line with user mental model, explore the application of mental model in mobile Internet and product design, and provide theoretical and method support for the realization of user-centered design concept.

In terms of the disciplinary background, design science, as an interdisciplinary field, integrates the disciplinary knowledge of science, engineering, liberal arts and art. In the field of Chinese design, the application of mental model has gradually emerged, providing a new perspective for design research. The highly cited literature reveals the profound application of mental models in interface design, product design, and user experience. In recent years, the theoretical method of mental model has not only been widely integrated into the research of master and doctoral papers, but also occupies a significant position in the core journals such as Packaging Design Engineering. This shows that mental models are gradually recognized and valued in the research of Chinese design, and are expected to play a role in a wider field of design, especially under the integration of emerging technologies such as virtual reality, human-computer interaction and artificial intelligence. Through deeper research, we can explore how mental models can lead design innovation to meet the evolving needs of users and promote the development of design science in China to a higher level.

References

1. Wang, Q.: Four design methods for the human-machine interface. Comput. Sci. **04**, 37–41 (1998)
2. Gong, R.: Research on the interface design of handheld mobile device based on mental model in user experience. Zhejiang University (2011)
3. Lin, Y., Chen, J., Liu, Y., et al.: User experience design of virtual reality and augmented reality hybrid mobile navigation system based on mental model. J. Comput. Sci. **38**(02), 408–422 (2015)
4. Willow, Y., Tang, S.: Research on the design method of exercise health management APP based on mental model. Packag. Eng. **38**(22), 20–24 (2017). https://doi.org/10.19554/j.cnki. 1001-3563.2017.22.007
5. Qin, J.: Study on the influence of AI on interaction design. Packag. Eng. **38**(20), 27–31 (2017). https://doi.org/10.19554/j.cnki.1001-3563.2017.20.008
6. Wang, L., Zhou, L.: Advanced teaching based on the development of mental models——take the concept of "centripetal force" teaching as an example. Middle School Teach. Ref. **14**, 41–44 (2022)
7. Canno-Bover, J.A., Salas, E.: Coonitive psychooay and team training. Shared menta models in compexsvstems Paper presented at the annua meetino of the society for Industrial and Organizational Psychology. Miami. FL (1990)
8. Bai, X., Wang, E.: Current status of shared mental model research. Adv. Psychol. Sci. (05), 791–799 (2004)
9. Qin, J., Zhu, X., Li, D.B.: Interaction design methods in information visualization. Decor, (03), 22–23 (2007). https://doi.org/10.16272/j.cnki.cn11-1392/j.2007.03.009
10. Wang, M., Hu, Y.: Study on attachment product design for children with autism based on the AHP-TOPSIS method. Packag. Eng. **42**(18), 220–226 (2021). https://doi.org/10.19554/j. cnki.1001-3563.2021.18.025
11. Zeng, Y.: The concept study of data visualization in the era of big data. Zhejiang University (2014)
12. Sun, X., Zhou, B., Li, T.: Design elements and principles of space-free gesture interaction. Packag. Eng. **36**(08), 10–13 (2015). https://doi.org/10.19554/j.cnki.1001-3563.2015.08.004
13. Ji, H.: Research on human-computer interaction based on multi-touch technology. East China Normal University (2011)
14. Dou, J., Qing, J.: Research on the innovative design of product and service system based on context-aware multi-dimensional data visualization. Packag. Eng. **38**(02), 87–91 (2017). https://doi.org/10.19554/j.cnki.1001-3563.2017.02.022
15. Lin, Y., Chen, J., Liu, Y., et al.: User experience design of virtual reality and augmented reality hybrid mobile guide system based on mental model. J. Comput. Sci. **38**(02), 408–422 (2015)
16. Huang, Q., Zhu, C.: Product design based on the user's mental model. Packag. Eng. **30**(12), 133–135+153 (2009). https://doi.org/10.19554/j.cnki.1001-3563.2009.12.045
17. Yang, Y., Lei, T., Zhang, Y.: Interface design of a handheld mobile device based on a user mental model. J. Zhejiang Univ. (Eng. Ed.) (05), 800–804 + 844 (2008)

18. He, C., Lu, C.: Unconscious design from an embodied cognitive perspective. Packag. Eng. **41**(08), 80–86 (2020). https://doi.org/10.19554/j.cnki.1001-3563.2020.08.010
19. Gong, X.: Study on the scientific and technological living environment for the elderly. Beijing Institute of Technology (2014)
20. Li, Y.: Jonathan Constructivism. East China Normal University (2007)
21. Zhao, C.: Application of mental models in user-centered design. Tsinghua University (2013)
22. Song, Y.L.: Mobile Internet terminal interface design research. Shandong University (2009)
23. Qiu, Z.: User behavior-oriented smart TV interaction design study. Jiangnan University (2017)
24. Gong, R.: Research on the interface design of handheld mobile devices based on the mental model in user experience. Zhejiang University (2010)

VR System for Hazard Prediction of Unsafe Behaviors in Outbound Training

Toshiki Muguruma[1]([✉]), Kaito Minohara[1], Yusuke Kometani[1], Naka Gotoda[1], Saerom Lee[1], Ryo Kanda[1], Shotaro Irie[2], and Toru Harai[2]

[1] Kagawa University, 2217-20 Hayashi-Cho, Takamatsu-shi, Kagawa, Japan
s23g366@kagawa-u.ac.jp
[2] Shinnihonkenko Co., Ltd., 6-15 Hayashi-Cho, Takamatsu-shi, Kagawa, Japan

Abstract. The construction industry has the most fatal industrial accidents in Japan, and many accidents are due to unsafe worker behavior. On-site hazard prediction training is effective in preventing unsafe behavior, but the need for completing construction projects within limited working hours and construction periods decreases the time available for such training. Therefore, it is important to conduct hazard prediction training against unsafe behavior before construction starts. Current pre-service training methods are limited to verbal or written reminders of safety and health management knowledge by safety managers, and it is difficult to provide workers with opportunities to predict hazards due to their own actions. In this study, we aim to enable safety managers to provide accurate hazard prediction training according to the hazard prediction ability of workers during outbound training, where time can more easily be secured. To that end, we develop a virtual reality system that enables risk prediction training for unsafe behavior in outbound training. We confirm that the system enables safety managers to provide appropriate guidance while grasping the comprehension level of construction site workers and improves the training's sense of realism and understanding.

Keywords: Occupational Accidents · Work Training · Outbound Training · Unsafe Behaviors · BIM · VR

1 Introduction

Among Japanese industries, the construction sector has the highest number of fatalities due to work-related accidents, with many attributed to unsafe worker behaviors [1]. Here, "unsafe behaviors" refers to actions where workers, either by neglecting established safe-work practices and safety rules or due to conditions such as ill health or momentary lapses in attention, engage in activities that compromise safety [2]. On-site hazard prediction training effectively prevents unsafe behaviors. However, the application of the so-called "36 Agreement" to the construction industry in April 2024 will create demands for completing projects within more limited labor hours and stricter deadlines [3], reducing the time available for on-site safety education. Therefore, it is crucial to conduct hazard prediction training to address unsafe behaviors before construction commences.

H. Mori and Y. Asahi (Eds.): HCII 2024, LNCS 14689, pp. 207–222, 2024.
https://doi.org/10.1007/978-3-031-60107-1_15

Japan's Occupational Safety and Health Law mandates the provision of safety and health education to workers at the start of their employment or when entering a new site. This education aims to prevent work-related accidents by imparting safety and health knowledge related to the tasks workers will engage in [4]. Prior to newcomer orientation training conducted by the main contractor, subcontractors provide their workers with "outbound training" for safety and health education [5]. While outbound training can be conducted before construction starts, challenges such as the difficulty for safety managers and workers to grasp actual conditions and work environments at the construction site make site-specific hazards hard to recognize. Furthermore, preventing unsafe behaviors requires safety managers to point out errors in workers' hazard predictions so that workers can recognize judgmental errors. However, existing outbound training methods primarily focus on safety managers reminding workers of safety and health management knowledge through verbal or written instructions, making it difficult to provide opportunities for workers to conduct hazard predictions related to their own actions.

In this study, we aimed to enable precise hazard prediction training by safety managers, tailored to workers' hazard prediction capabilities and within the timeframe of outbound training. To that end, we developed a virtual reality (VR) system that facilitates hazard prediction training for unsafe behaviors during outbound training. Our objective is to demonstrate the proposed system's effectiveness in addressing challenges associated with outbound training by clarifying the following points:

1. Safety managers can point out errors in workers' incorrect hazard predictions regarding their own work activities.
2. Safety managers' instructions affect workers' activities.

Safety science focuses on scientific methods and theories to prevent accidents and disasters and to manage risk. This field studies how interactions between human behavior, organizational operations, and technical systems affect safety. Recent trends in safety science for the construction industry include the following areas [6]:

1. Adaptable safety climate and culture models incorporating different sites, project complexity levels, or national contexts.
2. Expanding established prototypes for broader application of information technology in the construction community through more testing and case studies.
3. Continued research on subgroup factors related to workers' safety awareness and behavioral cognition models.
4. Integrating artificial intelligence and smart properties into safety program management.
5. Developing and applying information technology to enhance communication and coordination regarding safety between management and workers.
6. Assessing user acceptance and industry readiness for applying various information technologies in construction safety management.

This study aims to foster safety climates and cultures within construction industry organizations (Area 1), improve workers' safety awareness and behaviors (Area 3), and develop and apply VR technologies that facilitate safety communication between managers and workers (Area 5).

2   Related Works

2.1   Research on Hazard Classification

Considering all possible hazards, Mihic et al. [7] proposed three categories for hazard classification to realize a more accurate hazard identification process. The first category, "self-induced hazards," is the most easily recognizable danger type in this study, as it results from the workers' activities and affects the workers themselves. The second category, "peer-induced hazards," arises not from the construction workers themselves but from peers working on the same or different building elements. Other workers may pose risks not only to themselves but to all other workers present in a hazardous activity area. The final category, "global hazards," is a special type of hazard with a very large impact range, making it impractical to identify the extent of impact. Instead, the entire construction site is considered a hazard zone. These hazards affect all construction workers and other personnel on the construction site at the time of occurrence. They are typically characterized by their high severity but low occurrence probability.

According to Khosravi et al. [8], the causes of unsafe behavior and accidents at construction sites are multifaceted and commonly related to social, organizational, project management, supervision, contractor, site condition, workgroup, or individual characteristics. They emphasize the importance of distal factors such as society, the organization, and project management, which can reduce the likelihood of hazardous behaviors and accidents more than proximal factors such as site conditions and individual characteristics.

In this study, we aim to support active training by enabling construction site workers to tag their training actions with potential hazards for comparison with safety managers' feedback on hazard predictions for each hazard identified using the unsafe behavior tagging feature.

2.2   Advantages of Using VR in Construction Safety Training

Man et al. [9] noted that while VR is gaining attention in construction safety training, there has been no concrete evidence of its effectiveness. A meta-analysis of VR application research in computer science and technology education over the past decade showed its superiority over traditional construction training. As they mention, the benefits of using VR include the engaging nature of VR training, which, unlike textbook learning, simulates being on an actual site. VR training can increase employees' safety motivation, improve construction techniques, and increase work speed. Through immersion and presence, VR allows trainees to experience more realistic training.

According to Babalola et al. [10], VR-based safety education provides diverse benefits. VR allows visualizations of construction site conditions, making it easier to identify hazards in advance, and simulating actual construction sites can enhance workers' hazard identification capabilities. They also propose methods for using augmented reality (AR) systems to visually identify on-site hazards. These digital tools simulate actual site conditions more faithfully than 2D drawings and are effective in hazard management. Combining mobile-device-based VR and AR for safety education is also effective and favored by students and construction professionals.

Regarding considerations of new information technologies such as VR and mixed reality (MR) for improving safety management education and training, Yang et al. [11] focused on the lack of pedagogical guidelines for designing and developing learning content, aiming to address that issue by leveraging the Authentic Learning framework. Although VR and MR simulations could enhance participants' motivation to learn, they did not improve knowledge or teaching effectiveness, likely due to the framework's complexity. They suggest using 2D and 3D media in conjunction with systems that facilitate communication for more efficient learning.

Wolf et al. [12] suggested that while approaches such as verbal explanations, documentation, and testing exist for safety education and training in construction, they insufficiently promote learning. Moreover, modern learners prefer personalized feedback, necessitating the maximization of data provided during training. Learning environments utilizing VR can create safe education settings without risk of physical harm, providing both objective data for improvement and feedback on hazard recognition. Doing so motivates trainers and enhances learning by developing a wide range of training content, from hazard awareness to hazard recognition training.

From these insights, we aimed to develop a practical and experiential VR education support system that can realize precise hazard prediction training by safety managers, tailored to the hazard prediction capabilities of workers and able to be completed within outbound training timeframes.

3   System Design

3.1   Training Process

We propose a training process that combines construction task training with hazard prediction training. Table 1 outlines the training process. Workers initially perform construction tasks based on their own judgment without relying on prior instructions from safety managers. They then reflect on their actions and make hazard predictions regarding their behavior. By comparing their own judgment with that of safety managers, workers can recognize errors in their decision-making. When mistakes are identified, workers think about what they should be cautious of and verbalize these points.

Table 1. Training process by workers and safety managers

Step		Details
1	Confirmation of construction procedures and worker execution of construction tasks	• Workers confirm construction procedures by considering task examples • Workers perform construction tasks

(continued)

Table 1. (*continued*)

Step		Details
2	Review of construction tasks and hazard prediction by workers and safety managers	• Workers reflect on their own construction tasks • Workers evaluate risk of unsafe behaviors in their own actions • Safety managers evaluate risk of workers' unsafe behaviors in construction tasks
3	Awareness of errors in hazard prediction by workers and safety mangers	• Workers and safety managers compare differences between their assessments, so that workers notice errors
4	Guidance on errors by safety managers	• Workers and safety managers discuss how to correct errors • Workers verbalize precautions in their own words

3.2 System Design

Figure 1 illustrates the system configuration. In the "Model Registration" process, safety managers register the construction site model, unsafe behavior tags related to the construction site, and a digital twin as a model for the task. Unsafe behavior tags indicate the risk of unsafe behavior, assessed and assigned by safety managers or the workers themselves in relation to actual actions. Section 4 presents specific examples of unsafe behavior tags. In the "Model Confirmation" process, workers review the construction site model and the digital twin that models the task. During the "Task Rehearsal" process, workers mimic the work procedures verified in the "Model Confirmation" process within a virtual space and record tasks as a digital twin. In the "Tagging" process, both safety managers and workers register unsafe behavior tags for the worker's digital twin. The "Review" process involves comparing unsafe behavior tags attached to the worker's digital twin between the workers and safety managers, helping to identify commonalities and differences and complementing perspectives on evaluating unsafe behaviors. Figure 2 shows the sequence diagram. The "Model Registration," "Model Confirmation," "Work Rehearsal," "Tagging," and "Review" processes are executed as sequential steps.

Figure 3 shows a use case diagram. The system comprises "Construction Site Model Registration and Viewing," "Worker Digital Twin Registration and Viewing," and "Unsafe Behavior Tag Registration and Viewing" functions. The "Construction Site Model Registration and Viewing" function is used in all processes. The "Worker Digital Twin Registration and Viewing" function is employed during the "Model Registration" process to register a model that records the worker's tasks during the "Work Rehearsal" process and to reflect on tasks during the "Tagging" and "Perspective Sharing" processes. The "Unsafe Behavior Tag Registration and Viewing" function is used during the "Tagging" and "Perspective Sharing" processes.

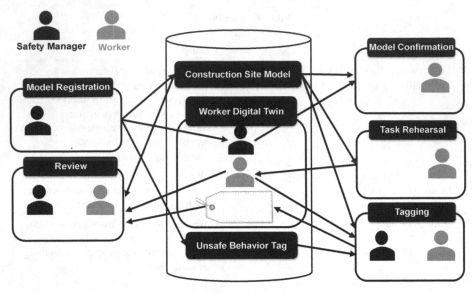

Fig. 1. System configuration.

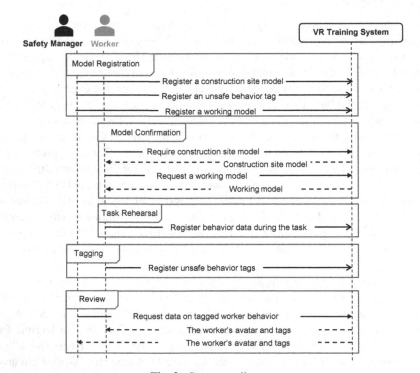

Fig. 2. Sequence diagram.

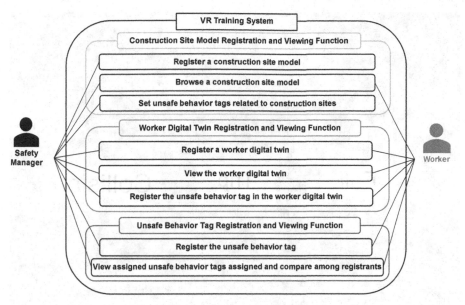

Fig. 3. Use case diagram.

4   System Implementation

4.1   Function Screens

Based on the outlined system design, we used the Unity game engine to develop a VR system that facilitates the training process within outbound training, employing virtual environments that simulate construction sites to enable hazard prediction training for unsafe behaviors while considering specific site hazards. The implementation details for each system function (Fig. 3) are as follows:

1. Construction Site Model Registration and Viewing function

Building information modeling (BIM) recreates 3D models of actual buildings, improving construction practices and serving as a standard model for construction drawings [13]. By allowing BIM of construction sites to be registered as VR objects, the system enables training within a virtual space that mimics real-world sites. We registered models imported into Autodesk Revit [14] and converted to FBX format as inputs. Figure 4 shows the unsafe behavior tags defined in this research, namely "Fall," "Trip," and "Crash", which are among the top factors in construction industry occupational accidents. Unsafe behavior tags can be added or deleted, allowing safety managers to introduce new tags while considering construction site characteristics.

3. Worker Digital Twin Registration and Viewing function

This function records tasks within the virtual space as time-series data. Tasks can later be visualized as avatar actions to review the work performed. This function is utilized when workers review construction procedures preregistered by safety managers and when

Fig. 4. Unsafe behavior tags (blue: safety manager; red: worker).

workers and safety managers assess the risks associated with a worker's actions. Figure 5 displays the worker digital twin registration function, where pressing the "Rehearsal Start" button begins task recording, and pressing the "Rehearsal Finish" button stops it. Figure 6 shows the Worker Digital Twin Viewing function, where worker digital twins are recorded as CSV files, allowing for the reproduction of specific digital twins. After loading a digital twin, pressing the play button replays the worker's behavior as an avatar in the virtual space (Fig. 7).

4. Unsafe Behavior Tag Registration and Viewing function

Tags indicating the risk of unsafe behavior can be assigned to avatars replicating workers' construction actions at times and locations deemed risky. The unsafe behavior tags illustrated in Fig. 4 can be registered. Workers and safety managers use the Worker Digital Twin Viewing function to review actions and assign unsafe behavior tags at relevant locations and times. Figure 8 shows the process of using the registration function to register unsafe behavior tags.

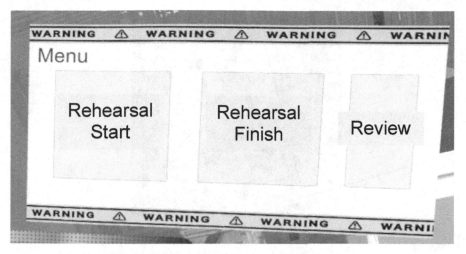

Fig. 5. Worker Digital Twin Registration function.

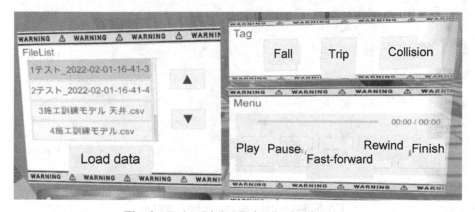

Fig. 6. Worker Digital Twin Viewing function.

Figure 9 shows how workers and safety managers use the Unsafe Behavior Tag Viewing function to compare the unsafe behavior tags they registered. This comparison aims to help workers recognize their own judgment errors in hazard prediction and serves as an opportunity for safety managers to identify new unsafe behaviors from the worker's perspective.

4.2 Hardware

The proposed system utilizes the HTC VIVE Pro Eye [15] as the VR device. To capture more detailed hand and finger movements, we combine the VR base station with a Hi5 VR Glove [16] (Fig. 10).

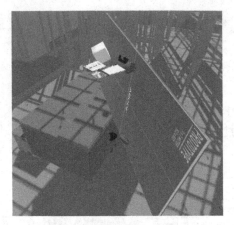

Fig. 7. Worker avatar.

Fig. 8. Registering an unsafe behavior tag.

5   Field Experiments

5.1   Objective

We conducted a field experiment with the objective of realizing a practical application to ascertain whether VR enables workers and safety managers to remotely recognize site-specific hazards and whether sharing perspectives through training could lead to more accurate safety instructions tailored to the understanding level of construction site workers.

5.2   Method

We implemented the system with the cooperation of a construction company based in Kagawa Prefecture, Japan. A training stage for a building planned for construction was

Fig. 9. Comparing unsafe behavior tags.

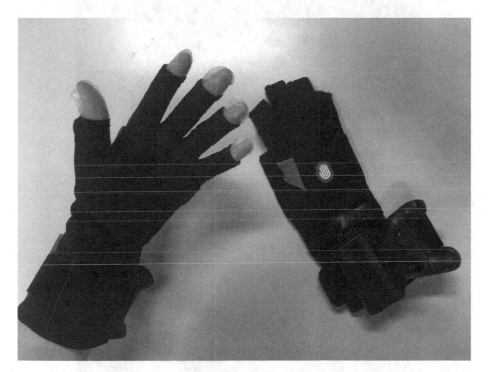

Fig. 10. Data glove.

prepared for one worker affiliated with the construction company, and actual outbound training was conducted twice. Two individuals from the safety and sales departments also used the system, and we conducted interviews regarding the system's advantages, areas for improvement, ease of instruction, and changes in worker behavior.

5.3 Procedure

The targeted work processes were side and ceiling paneling tasks for interior finishing work. Figure 11 shows the side paneling, and Fig. 12 shows the ceiling paneling. The worker's task was to transport boards from a storage area and align them at designated positions. For the ceiling paneling task, the system showed "Get On" and "Get Off" buttons when the worker approached a portable work platform, allowing the worker to move between the platform and the ground by pressing these buttons.

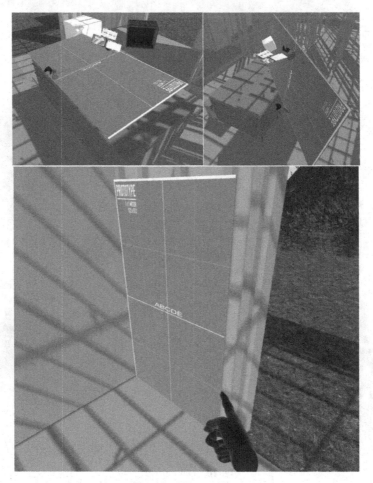

Fig. 11. Side paneling.

The sequence of the practical application is as follows:

1. Preparation

We used the Construction Site Model Registration function to recreate the construction site in the virtual space. Safety managers generally use the Worker Digital Twin Creation

Fig. 12. Ceiling paneling.

function to register work examples as data, but in this study, the authors operated both functions.

2. Work procedure confirmation

Workers immerse themselves in the virtual space and view the work examples pre-registered using the Worker Digital Twin Viewing function.

3. Task practice

Workers perform task practice based on the examples. During this time, the Worker Digital Twin Registration function records their actions. Figure 13 shows a worker engaged in task practice.

4. Hazard prediction training

Using the Worker Digital Twin Viewing and Unsafe Behavior Tag Registration functions, both safety managers and workers perform hazard prediction for the worker's construction tasks and assign unsafe behavior tags accordingly.

5. Confirmation of correctness and errors

Using the Unsafe Behavior Tag Viewing function, workers compare the tags assigned by safety managers and those assigned by themselves to identify commonalities and differences.

Fig. 13. Worker engaged in task practice.

5.4   Results and Discussion

In the first training session, interviews with the safety manager revealed that the building structure and operations were close to reality. The manager particularly praised the practical training enabled by the Construction Site Model Registration and Viewing Function, stating that it allowed easier instructions than verbal explanations. However, feedback also highlighted difficulties in grabbing virtual objects like boards and issues with wall contact, indicating a need for improved operability. In the second training session, the manager positively noted that the worker could perform risk-checking actions like pointing, which were not possible in the first session, and that the Unsafe Behavior Tagging Function facilitated discussions.

This study aimed to demonstrate the effectiveness of this system in outbound training by clarifying the following points:

1. Safety managers can point out errors in workers' incorrect hazard predictions regarding their own work activities.
2. Safety managers' instructions affect workers' activities.

From the safety manager's perspective, visualizing workers' reflections and remarks regarding unsafe behaviors enhanced their understanding of workers' comprehension level. However, they noted a need for improvements in system operability, realism, UI enhancements, and addressing language barriers, particularly noting the complexity of safety manager operations. These points highlight the need for further system development and evaluations.

6 Summary

We developed a VR system to support training processes that integrate construction practice and safety training, aiming to enable safety managers to provide appropriate guidance while understanding workers' comprehension levels. The Unsafe Behavior Tag Registration and Viewing function allowed safety managers to grasp worker understanding of hazard prediction for unsafe behaviors, facilitating instruction. We also confirmed changes in worker activities. The Construction Site Model Registration and Viewing function improved the ease of safety instruction. However, there were opinions regarding the need for interface improvements, such as unnatural object handling. The proposed system targeted training for a series of work tasks from carrying boards for siding and ceiling work to aligning them at the installation position, but it did not replicate actions such as climbing on and off portable work platforms or board weights. Climbing actions and board weights are strongly related to risks such as falls, trips, and collisions, and incorporating these factors into the training process is an outstanding issue. One solution could be an MR approach to allow the use of actual boards and portable work platforms during training. However, outbound training situations pose constraints such as limited space and tool availability, so training content may require a hybrid training process that seamlessly switches between VR and MR. In the future, we will focus on these points, advancing the development and implementation of the proposed system and aiming to establish effective safety education methods.

Acknowledgments. This work was supported by Grants-in-Aid for Scientific Research Grant Number 20K14084.

References

1. Ministry of Health, Labour and Welfare: 1. Description of Labour Standards Law. https://jsite.mhlw.go.jp/osaka-roudoukyoku/library/osaka-roudoukyoku/H23/foriginer/230715-2.pdf. Accessed 02 Feb 2024

2. Ministry of Health, Labour and Welfare: Workplace Safety Site: Analysis of Causal Factors of Occupational Accidents (2011). https://anzeninfo.mhlw.go.jp/use696-3-19.html. (in Japanese). Accessed 02 Feb 2024
3. Ministry of Health, Labour and Welfare: Regulations on Upper Limits in the Construction Industry. https://jsite.mhlw.go.jp/nara-roudoukyoku/content/contents/001474177.pd. (in Japanese). Accessed 02 Feb 2024
4. Ministry of Health, Labour and Welfare: Workplace Safety Site: Health and Safety Education. https://anzeninfo.mhlw.go.jp/yougo/yougo68_1.html. (in Japanese). Accessed 02 Feb 2024
5. Association for Special Education for Small and Medium-Sized Construction Industry "Outbound Training". https://www.tokubetu.or.jp/text_shokuan/part4/text_shokuan4-3.html. (in Japanese). Accessed 02 Feb 2024
6. Jin, R., et al.: A science mapping approach-based review of construction safety research. Saf. Sci. **113**, 285–297 (2019)
7. Mihić, M.: Classification of construction hazards for a universal hazard identification methodology. J. Civ. Eng. Manag. **26**(2), 147–159 (2020)
8. Khosravi, Y., Asilian-Mahabadi, H., Hajizadeh, E., Hassanzadeh-Rangi, N., Bastani, H., Behzadan, A.H.: Factors influencing unsafe behaviors and accidents on construction sites: a review. Int. J. Occup. Saf. Ergon. **20**(1), 111–125 (2014)
9. Man, S. S., Wen, H., So, B.C.L.: Are virtual reality applications effective for construction safety training and education? A systematic review and meta-analysis. J. Safety Res. (2023)
10. Babalola, A., Manu, P., Cheung, C., Yunusa-Kaltungo, A., Bartolo, P.: A systematic review of the application of immersive technologies for safety and health management in the construction sector. J. Safety Res. (2023)
11. Yang, F., Goh, Y.M.: VR and MR technology for safety management education: an authentic learning approach. Saf. Sci. **148**, 105645 (2022)
12. Wolf, M., Teizer, J., Wolf, B., Bükrü, S., Solberg, A.: Investigating hazard recognition in augmented virtuality for personalized feedback in construction safety education and training. Adv. Eng. Inform. **51**, 101469 (2022)
13. Autodesk. What is BIM | BIM Design for Architecture. https://bim-design.com/bim-dx/bim/01-about-bim/. (in Japanese). Accessed 02 Feb 2024
14. Autodesk. Revit 2024 Authorized Pricing and Purchase. https://www.autodesk.co.jp/products/revit/. (in Japanese). Accessed 02 Feb 2024
15. VIVE Japan. VIVE Pro Eye Overview. https://www.vive.com/jp/product/vive-pro-eye/overview/. (in Japanese). Accessed 02 Feb 2024
16. Hi5. Home | Hi5 VR Glove. https://www.hi5vrglove.com/. Accessed 02 Feb 2024

Service Providers' Logics and Behaviors in Value Co-Creation

Akira Oyabu[1]([✉]), Jing Zhang[2], and Junichi Muramatsu[3]

[1] Okayama University of Science, 1-1 Ridai-cho, Kita-ku, Okayama 700-0005, Japan
ohyabu@ous.ac.jp
[2] Kanazawa University, Kakuma-machi, Kanazawa 920-1192, Japan
[3] Gifu Shotoku Gakuen University, 1-38 Nakauzura, Gifu 500-8288, Japan

Abstract. Marketing researchers have investigated how value is co-created through direct interactions between service providers and customers. Previous studies have focused on service provider behaviors that facilitate customer value creation. It is essential to focus on both the value co-creation behaviors of service providers and the factors that influence them. However, there is currently an insufficient understanding of the factors that influence the value co-creation behavior of service providers. Previous research has focused on the institutions, norms, and practices shared by the actors involved in value co-creation. Furthermore, there has been limited discussion on specific factors based on empirical research. The impact of service providers' logic, which is assumed to drive their behavior, on value co-creation has not yet been discussed. Owing to the foregoing, this study explores how service providers' logic and behavior contribute to value co-creation. We identified four logics in this regard (i.e., frontline service employees, customers, departments, and firms), four service behaviors (i.e., performing, supporting, collaborating, and coordinating), and specific value outcomes for each actor.

Keywords: Value co-creation · Service provider's behavior · Logics · Value outcomes · Frontline service employee

1 Introduction

Recent developments in marketing and service research have focused on understanding the value co-creation process between firms and customers. Value creation, purchase, usage, and marketing are closely related (Grönroos, 2011). From a customer-centric perspective, the goal of marketing is to engage the firm in customer value creation processes, convince customers that using the company's products and services will help them achieve their goals (Crosby et al., 2002), and support customer value creation in a mutually beneficial way (Grönroos, 2011). Firms aim to achieve co-creating positive value for customers through direct interaction with customers. However, this interaction can also lead to the co-creation of negative value (Corsaro, 2019; Echeverri & Skalen, 2011). Therefore, it has been argued that frontline service employees (FSEs) who directly interact with customers play a crucial role.

H. Mori and Y. Asahi (Eds.): HCII 2024, LNCS 14689, pp. 223–236, 2024.
https://doi.org/10.1007/978-3-031-60107-1_16

Researchers have investigated how value is co-created through direct interaction between service providers and customers. Previous studies have focused on service providers' behaviors that facilitate customers' value creation (e.g., Echeverri & Skalen, 2011; Mikelsson et al., 2022). Jaakkola and Alexander (2014) identified four types of value co-creation behavior in public transport service systems. In recent years, several studies have aimed to understand the value co-creation ecosystems that contribute to customers' value creation from a customer-centric perspective. These studies discuss the networks of actors and their value-creation functions. It has been noted that the context surrounding service providers and customers influences value co-creation (Vargo & Lusch, 2017). Therefore, it is essential to focus on both the value co-creation behaviors of service providers and the factors that influence them.

However, there is currently an insufficient understanding of the factors that influence the value co-creation behavior of service providers (Echeverri, 2021). Previous research has focused on the institutions, norms, and practices shared by the actors involved in value co-creation. However, there has been limited discussion on specific factors based on empirical research. Furthermore, the impact of service providers' logic, which is assumed to drive their behavior, on value co-creation has not yet been discussed. This study addresses this issue and explores how service providers' logic and behaviors contribute to value co-creation. We view logic as the pattern of beliefs and rules of individuals and organizations. To achieve this goal, we address the following research questions:

- RQ1 What logic drives the behaviors of service providers?
- RQ2 What behaviors do service providers perform?
- RQ3 What value outcomes are emerged through service behaviors?

This empirical study focuses on interactions between frontline employees in the after-sales service department of a Japanese industrial machinery manufacturing firm and its customers. This study is based on a service logic approach (Grönroos, 2008), which considers the customer as a value creator and emphasizes that the firm, as a service provider, facilitates interaction processes with its customers to support value creation in the customer's life world. Introducing this perspective will enable a deeper understanding of how focal service providers perceive and perform their services. It, in turn, allows for a better understanding of the service provider's role in value co-creation. We identified four logics (of frontline service employee, customer, department, and firms) that influence the behaviors of service providers, four service behaviors (performing, supporting, collaborating, and coordinating), and specific value outcomes for each actor.

This study makes several contributions to the existing marketing and service literature. First, it advances existing research on value co-creation and service logic by identifying service providers' value co-creation behaviors and the factors that drive them. We extend research focusing only on service provider behaviors and demonstrate the need to focus on the different provider logics influencing these behaviors. Second, this study extends earlier work on institutional logic research by providing a framework for value co-creation between service providers and customers, including the multiple logics of frontline employees perceive. The finding that the logic of customers as perceived by service providers drives their behavior suggests the importance of introducing a customer perspective into institutional logic research.

The paper is structured as follows. The next section briefly reviews the literature on service provider behavior in value co-creation and the factors driving such behavior. Next, we outline our methodological approach. Next, using qualitative data collected from service providers engaged in value co-creation with their customers, we describe the findings on service provider service behavior, the logic driving that behavior, and value outcomes. Finally, theoretical and managerial implications and directions for future research are discussed.

2 Theoretical Background

2.1 The Typology of Value Co-Creation Behavior

Value co-creation is a process in which two or more actors work jointly to create value for customers through direct interactions (Grönroos and Gummerus, 2014). Research on value co-creation in the marketing and service fields focuses on the direct interaction between service providers and customers (Grönroos, 2008; Grönroos and Gummerus, 2014; Grönroos and Voima, 2013; Yi and Gong, 2013). Many researchers have emphasized that value co-creation consists of diverse behaviors by categorizing marketing and customer behaviors that lead to value co-creation through direct interactions. Jaakkola and Alexander (2014) and Alexander and Jaakkola (2016) analyzed value co-creation between customers, railway companies, and other stakeholders and identified four types of customer behavior: codeveloping, influencing, augmenting, and mobilizing. This study demonstrates that customers act not only for their own benefit but also for the benefit of other companies, that different forms of customer behavior can occur, and that these behaviors are voluntary. Additionally, factors influencing customer perceived value, such as service provider attitude, speed of delivery, flexibility, and support are discussed (Medberg and Gronroos, 2020), and the firm's behaviors, such as team management, partnering, and passive compliance, have been identified (McColl-Kenedy et al. 2012).

Direct interaction can lead to form both positive and negative value (Echeverri, 2021; Echeverri and Skalen, 2011). Echeverri and Skalen (2011) identified four value-forming behaviors (informing, greeting, delivering, charging, and helping) in direct interactions between providers and customers. They empirically demonstrated that incorrect value-forming behavior by service providers can result in co-creating negative value.

2.2 Drivers of Service Providers' Behavior in Co-Creation

Some studies have examined the underlying factors that influence the behaviors of service providers and customers. Studies have found that customer behavior is influenced by psychological factors such as trust, customer satisfaction, and brand commitment (Brodie et al. 2011; Van Doorn et al. 2010). Additionally, research has focused on the networks between service providers and customers (e.g., Lipkin and Heinonen, 2022; Vargo and Lusch, 2008, 2017; Echeverri 2021). These studies have shown that the networks surrounding service providers and customers can influence their behavior (Lipkin and Heinonen, 2022; Vargo and Lusch, 2008, 2017; Echeverri, 2021). Mikelsson et al.

(2022) analyzed the ecosystem of healthcare providers and customers and found that customers have a complex user-defined ecosystem that combines a wide range of services. Therefore, service providers should not only support focal customers but also contribute to a user-defined ecosystem consisting of their families and other providers.

Other studies suggest that institutions, norms, and practices influence service provider behavior (Becker and Jaakkola, 2020; Dehling et al., 2022; Echeverri and Skalen, 2011; Flaherty and Schroeder, 2022; Hartmann et al., 2018; Vargo and Lusch, 2017). Cova et al. (2019) identified three types of service provider behaviors toward customers and suggested that these behaviors are driven by the market institutional logic of business ethics and the corporate institutional logic of rationalization.

When discussing value co-creation, identifying the factors driving service providers to co-create customer value is crucial. However, there is still a lack of understanding of these drivers (Echeverri, 2021). As mentioned, the current literature focuses on psychological factors, networks, norms and institutions, and institutional logics, but there is limited discussion on the relationship between these logics and service provider behavior. Therefore, this paper defines *logics* as the firm-wide, socially, or individually constructed pattern of assumptions, beliefs, and rules that condition firms' behaviors (Friedland and Alford, 1991; Thornton and Ocasio, 1999; Thornton et al.), and conducts empirical studies on the relationship between logics and service providers' behaviors.

3 Methodology

This case study examines how service providers' logic and behavior contribute to value co-creation with customers. This study focuses on the direct interaction between employees of the after-sales service department of Company Z, a Japanese industrial machinery manufacturer, and its customers and their related behaviors. Client companies have operated these machines for 25–50 years. To ensure a continuous and stable operation, it is crucial to conduct periodic inspections and maintain each machine. In addition, it is important to provide technical guidance to those who regularly operate machines in client companies. Company Z, which is divided into several groups based on the machine type, provides various services to client companies, including design for production equipment, manufacturing, installation, maintenance, and technical guidance. Supervisors (SVs) assigned to each group spend several weeks or months at the client company's factory or plant. They install and maintain machinery and provide technical guidance to onsite workers for operating and maintaining machines. During this process, the SVs interact directly with the client company's site managers, site workers, and Company Z's staff.

3.1 Data Collection

Data were collected through in-depth interviews to gain a deeper understanding of the service-providing behavior of SVs. Leaders in the manufacturing and service departments of the Industrial Machinery Division were asked to recruit 21 highly valued service providers (see Table 1; all names have been changed for anonymity). All the informants were male and had 7–28 years of SV experience. To ensure diversity in the interview content, we attempted to avoid bias in the groups to which the participants belonged.

Semi-structured interviews were conducted with all the 21 SVs using an interview guide. The interviews took place face-to-face between September 11 and 22, 2023, in a conference room at the Industrial Machinery Division office. Each interview lasted between 60 and 80 min and was digitally recorded with permission. A total of 500 pages of textual data were transcribed and analyzed. During the interviews, the informants were asked about the specific duties of the SVs, their attitudes and approaches towards their duties, and to share their experiences with satisfied and dissatisfied customers. We sought to gain insight into the specific service behaviors of SVs and their underlying factors.

Table 1. List of informants

No	Name	Gender	Age	Years of SV work experience	Affiliated group
1	Sato	Male	40s	23	A
2	Suzuki	Male	50s	28	A
3	Takahashi	Male	30s	17	B
4	Tanaka	Male	30s	over 20	C
5	Watanabe	Male	40s	22	D
6	Ito	Male	30s	16	D
7	Nakamura	Male	30s	15	E
8	Kobayashi	Male	30s	over 15	C
9	Yamamoto	Male	30s	9	E
10	Kato	Male	30s	12	B
11	Yoshida	Male	30s	7	E
12	Yamada	Male	30s	over 15	C
13	Sasaki	Male	20s	over 5	C
14	Yamaguchi	Male	30s	16	D
15	Matsumoto	Male	40s	over 20	C
16	Saito	Male	30s	16	D
17	Inoue	Male	40s	over 20	C
18	Kimura	Male	30s	11	B
19	Hayashi	Male	50s	24	D
20	Shimizu	Male	40s	over 15	C
21	Yamazaki	Male	40s	25	A

3.2 Data Analysis

An abductive approach to data analysis is followed, which broadens the understanding of both theoretical and empirical phenomena (Dubois and Gadde, 2002) and allows us to better interpret the logic behind SVs and the service behaviors they perform. To ensure the reliability and validity of the analysis, coding was performed as described by Saldana (2016). We used QSR NVivo12 to analyze the data efficiently and effectively.

The specific analysis process is as follows. First, the two authors repeatedly read the transcribed text data and examined each SV's narrative through open coding according to three themes: the logic that SVs perceive, service behaviors that SVs perform, and value outcomes that SVs create for different actors. Next, selective coding was conducted by one of the authors on the thematically categorized data to derive new concepts and categories and identify their relationships. The categories were then refined through repeated reviews of the data to confirm the validity of the concepts and categories.

4 Findings

4.1 Multiple Logic of Service Providers

Our analysis identified four logics that drive service providers' behavior in value co-creation with customers. We found that the various logics perceived by service providers influence their behavior toward customers and other stakeholders. In this context, customers include both the client organization as a whole and its on-site managers and employees.

The first logic is that of SVs, or frontline service employees (FSEs), and is based on the SVs' past experiences and beliefs about their work. It is constructed and maintained independently by each SV. For instance, many informants believed that SVs need to have a high level of skill and knowledge and perform their work solemnly based on guidance from senior SVs in their group and past work experiences. This emphasis on skills and knowledge is fundamental to the SVs' logic. Several SVs said, "When a knowledgeable person is in charge, [customers] trust that person and think that they can entrust the work to this person" (Nakamura, Section E, No. 7). The main tasks of SVs include the delivery and installation of machines to client companies, as well as maintenance and troubleshooting after delivery. One of SVs' duties is to provide technical guidance to onsite managers and workers who manage and operate machines at client companies' plants and other facilities. Therefore, SVs who followed this approach tended to avoid other activities, such as inspecting and repairing other machines that were not part of the work contracted in advance between the customer firm and Company Z.

By contrast, some SVs performed tasks outside their assigned duties, either at the request of their clients or voluntarily. This behavior was driven by their understanding that respecting customers is one of the roles of SVs and their willingness to take on additional work. For instance, the narratives from the SVs demonstrate their willingness to collaborate with field workers, despite being prohibited from doing so in principle.

I think it is natural for me to do my job, and in addition to that, I want to be an SV who is praised by customers, and I want to be thought so by them (Kobayashi, Dept. C, No. 8).

I believe that it is only when one goes that far that it becomes guidance. I think teaching is not only showing by doing, but also doing together (Yamazaki, Dept. A, No. 21).

The second logic is that of the customers. This is not the logic that customers actually have, but the logic that customers demand and expect from SVs, focal firms, and products, as perceived by SVs during conversations and work with customers. The findings showed that SVs' behaviors were driven by the logic of the customer, such as compliance with the terms of the contract and expectations of SVs' knowledge and skills. For example, when a machine delivered by Company Z broke down and the SV visited the customer for troubleshooting, "the customer also wanted the machine to work (Takahashi, Dept. B, No. 3). For this reason, the SV arranged for the machine to be repaired at the customer's plant, and at the same time, an additional inspection was conducted at Z's internal plant, and the work proceeded quickly.

The third logic pertains to the focal firm. The third logic is that of the focal firm, which in this case is Company Z. Central to this logic are the business rules and norms of Company Z. Therefore, the SV is required to comply with the rules set by Company Z and work within the scope of the contract with the customer. The SV is not allowed to deviate from the logic of Company Z. However, it is also obvious that the SV coordinates the logic of the focal firm with other logics (e.g., the logic of the customer), as shown in the next narratives.

We (Company Z) had the restriction that we could not provide detailed drawings unless we were affiliated with a factory or specialized contractor. ...... We discussed with the customer and the factory, but it was very difficult to get things done (Suzuki, A Dept, No, 2).

The behavior of the SVs was driven by both the logic of the focal firm and that of the department to which they belonged. Because each department, such as manufacturing and sales, is part of the focal firm, this logic is considered identical to that of the firm. For instance, "if you go as an instructor, you are not allowed to physically handle or tighten the parts with a wrench" (Watanabe, D Dept, No. 5). The company expects SVs to comply with the contracts.

However, the data showed not only overlaps between logics, but also the existence of department logic that conflicts with the logic of the firm. This is manifested in the acceptance of the different ideas held by each SV. As mentioned previously, when SVs are sent as supervisors, their guidance is primarily verbal. However, the results revealed that the department did not force its SVs to follow the logic of the firm in providing verbal guidance but implicitly accepted ideas that deviated from it. This is evident in the following narrative of the team leader: The "various ways of doing things", as seen in Takahashi's narrative, suggests following the logic of the firm and provide verbal guidance, giving priority to the logic of the SVs (FSEs) and the customer, and providing guidance in cooperating with the on-site workers.

I think there are various ways of doing things, so ... I tell [my colleagues and junior team members] that they should listen to the ways of different people [in the team], make their own judgments, and then take the way they think is the most correct as their own way (Takahashi, Dept. B, No. 3).

4.2 Type of Service Providers' Behaviors

We identify four service behaviors of the focal service provider: performing, supporting, collaborating, and coordinating. The label names were derived inductively from textual data and data analysis.

Performing behavior is defined as service providers' contribution of resources, such as knowledge, skills, experience, and labor, to performing a job task assigned in advance by the focal firm. For instance, an SV assigned to instruct a client company's onsite workers in machine installation work instructs and supervises workers while monitoring their skill levels. However, since it is not in the job description for the SV to do the work, the SV does not collaborate with the workers but only instructs them. While performing contracted service activities, the SV never deviates from the content of the contract but rather plays the role of a worker who solemnly performs the work for which he or she is responsible.

> *We have an installation manual and follow it. If a customer omits that procedure, we instruct them to do it properly because it will cause problems in the future. Basically, I do not do the work myself (Saito, Dept. D, No. 16).*

We also identified supporting behaviors. *Supporting behavior* is defined as service providers' contribution to resources such as knowledge, skills, and experience in response to customer consultations and requests. For example, they provide solutions and information in response to customer consultations or requests for non-contractual services. When consulted about preventing problems with machines sold by other companies or training onsite workers, SVs actively offered advice based on their own experiences. This type of service behavior was observed not only within the scope of their duties but also outside of them. Yoshida sometimes performs work outside his duties when requested by customers. This supporting behavior is passive in that it responds to customer requests and takes on the role of a mentor by providing advice and consultations on solving problems.

> *If we do it elsewhere, if it is a standard SV contract, we only provide guidance. There was a time when I went to [the name of the country] and clients said, "This is your machine, so you have to do all the work. At that time, there was another person who went with me, and the two of us sometimes did the work without any particular help from the customers (Yoshida, Dept. E, No. 11).*

Next, *collaborating behavior* is defined as service providers' active contribution of resources such as knowledge, skills, experience, time, and effort to solve customer problems. SVs may collaborate with customers' on-site workers as part of their educational instruction. For example, when Sasaki instructs on machine installation, he feels limited by verbal instruction and works with the workers to provide more effective instruction.

> *When it comes to instructions on installation, it depends on the size of the machine, but I can just use words, such as attaching the bolts while using a laser pointer.*

But when it comes to adjustments, I felt it was difficult for them to understand if I only used words, so I would explain and instruct them in a way that was easiest for them to understand, by actually working with them and showing them what I was doing, and asking them if they would take a picture of this part (Sasaki, Dept. C, No. 13).

In contrast to the passive nature of supporting behavior, collaborative behavior is active. In the previous narrative, the SV collaborated with onsite workers to guide them effectively, and such actions were carried out at their discretion, although they were outside the scope of their duties. However, many of our informants engaged in collaborative behavior driven by the logic of the SVs, such as a desire to please their customers, or by the logic of the customers, such as requests for additional work or tasks from customers to the SVs. Therefore, SVs act as partners who share common goals and actively work with customers to achieve them.

Coordinating behavior is defined as the service providers' contribution of resources, such as knowledge, skills, experience, and relationships, to reconcile the gap in thinking between customers and other actors and communicate information about customers to other actors. To facilitate customers' value creation, SVs organize, translate, and communicate information to ensure that customer requests are accurately conveyed to the technical department, and share customer information with staff in other departments. For instance, Tanaka suggests that SVs who are in direct contact with customers can accurately understand the situation and requests of customers and communicate them to other departments. Therefore, SVs who perform coordinative behaviors that support relationship-building and agreement between actors play a mediating role.

We, SVs, visit customers from the start-up stage to learn how they operate the machines. During after-sales service, customers may request specific machine operations or explain problems and difficulties while looking at the machines together. SVs understand these requests and convey them accurately to the relevant departments in our company (Tanaka, Dept. C, No. 4).

Figure 1 outlines the typology of SVs' behaviors, which include providing various services to customers, such as machine production and installation, maintenance, and technical guidance. The findings indicate that SVs' service behaviors consist of four specific behaviors and that the collaborating behavior and part of the supporting and coordinating behavior are outside the SVs' job duties.

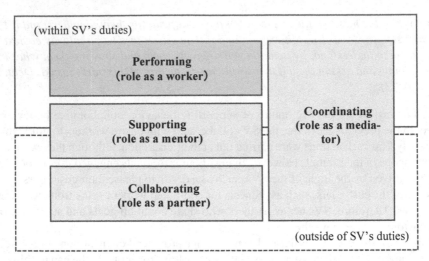

Fig. 1. Typology of FSEs' (SVs) behaviors

4.3 Value Outcomes of Behaviors

It can be inferred from the collected data that SVs' service behaviors have significant benefits for customers, SVs, and focal firms. Customers benefit from faster and more cost-effective problem resolution as well as the expertise and additional advice provided by SVs. Additionally, SVs may perform additional work to benefit their customers. For instance, one service provider noted that a client company expressed satisfaction with the timely completion of work and the start of production, despite the challenges in meeting deadlines.

> *I believe that meeting deadlines is a basic requirement, and I am sure that customers feel that it is a bit difficult to meet deadlines as they observe the work site with us. If we manage to meet the deadlines and make it to production on time, [the client company] will be grateful, and if we meet the minimum deadlines and finish the work safely, [the client company] will appreciate it (Inoue, Dept. C, No. 17).*

These value outcomes were the results of the services provided by the SV; however, in some cases, client firms valued the process rather than the results of the services. In the U.S. project in which Yamada participated, the machines provided by Company Z were incompatible with the customer's software program, making coordination between the two very difficult. Yamada completed the project through a trial-and-error process in cooperation with a client company. The client company expresses its gratitude for Yamada's response.

Value outcomes for SVs themselves were also identified. Participants perceived the benefits of gaining experience, skills, satisfaction, and esteem from others through various tasks. For example, one SV said that even if a client company asked him to perform a task outside of his job, he would be willing to accept it because it would add to his own experience. Another SV described the emotional benefits as follows:

If I go on a business trip to solve the problem, the customer may later send an e-mail to the sales representative saying, "The (Shimizu) who came to our office was very responsive." Such e-mails make me a little happy (Shimizu, Department C, No. 20).

Finally, monetary benefits such as the acquisition of other projects and additional services are extracted as value outcomes for focal companies. Yamazaki, with 25 years of SV experience, believes that proactive communication and cooperation with customer employees not only facilitates business operations but also leads to the acquisition of after-sales services. In addition to monetary benefits, there are informational benefits such as understanding the timing of part replacement and maintenance, gaining information about other companies' machines, and understanding customer issues and needs that arise in the field. SVs spend more time in contact with customer companies, site workers, and machines installed in the field than other actors in the focal firm, such as the sales department. The information that SVs bring back is a valuable benefit for Company Z, especially because the information in the field is sticky and difficult for actors other than the client company to understand.

Since SVs are in direct contact with customers and work with them for a long time, I think it is the role of SVs to do things that sales and other employees cannot do, such as directly picking up on customers' problems and communicating them to our own companies (Saito, Dept. D, No. 16).

5 Discussion

This study examines how service providers' behaviors and logic contribute to value co-creation. Service providers support customer value creation (Grönroos, 2008; Grönroos and Voima, 2013). The study identified specific service behaviors, logic, and value outcomes for each actor through data and analysis obtained from SVs. A framework (see Fig. 2) was developed to capture these findings and answer the research question.

5.1 Theoretical Implications

This study contributes to the marketing literature in several ways. First, it extends the research that has focused exclusively on service providers' behavior. This study identifies four types of value co-creation behavior: performing, supporting, collaborating, and coordinating. While existing research identifies specific behaviors such as developing and influencing (Jaakkola and Alexander, 2014) and shaping and supporting (Echeverri and Skalen, 2011), we identify service providers' behaviors and the relationship between their behaviors and the logic driving them, the specific roles of the service providers assigned to these behaviors, and the value outcomes that are generated from these behaviors. The second theoretical implication is that service providers' behavior is influenced by multiple logics. SVs, as service providers who interacted directly with customers, perceived various logics of SVs, focal customers, firm, and departments, coordinated, and selected these logics while providing services. In the field of marketing, previous research has examined how changes in corporate logic can affect salespeople's behavior (Cova et al., 2019) and how employees can adopt corporate logic (Flaherty and Schroeder, 2022). However, these studies have focused on a single logic, and few have explored the effects of multiple logics on service providers. Moreover, our finding that SVs are significantly impacted by customers' logic regarding what they want and expect from service providers is in line with recent research that applies a customer-dominant perspective (Heinonen and Strandvik, 2015; Heinonen et al., 2010) to marketing and service research.

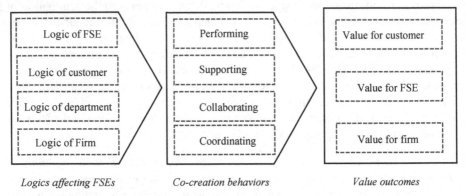

  Logics affecting FSEs   *Co-creation behaviors*   *Value outcomes*

Fig. 2. Framework of service providers' logics, behaviors, and value outcomes in value co-creation

5.2 Practical Implications

This study provides insights into the role of service providers in value co-creation. These findings suggest that frontline service employees (FSEs) perform a variety of tasks beyond their assigned duties during interactions with customers. Managers often overlook these tasks. Understanding the role and position of FSEs in value co-creation can help managers better support the value co-creation process between them and their customers. Furthermore, our research indicates that different logics influence FSE's behavior of FSEs. Therefore, it is crucial for managers to identify the logic behind their organizations. This may have affected the development of educational materials for FSEs. The framework presented is useful for comprehensively understanding the drivers, behaviors, and outcomes of value co-creation. It can be useful not only for B2B firms but also for B2C firms that have opportunities to interact directly with consumers.

5.3 Limitation and Future Research

This study has several limitations. First, although this study identified multiple logics possessed by FSEs, it is necessary to clarify how FSEs coordinate and select these logics. This analysis suggests that FSEs who focus on customer logic tend to perform behaviors outside the scope of their jobs, such as collaborating, supporting, and coordinating. Therefore, future research should expand this framework by clarifying the characteristics of each logic, the relationships among them, and the mechanisms of logic coordination and selection. Additionally, this study was limited to interviews with FSEs who interact directly with customers. In future studies, it may be possible to gain a more complete understanding of the logics and service-providing behaviors of service providers in value co-creation by interviewing managers and staff in other departments to which the FSEs relate. Additionally, interviews with clients will enable us to understand and categorize the actual value co-created.

References

Alexander, M., Jaakkola, E.: Customer engagement behaviours and value co-creation. In: Brodie, R.J., Hollbeek, L.D., Conduit, J. (eds.) Customer Engagement: Contemporary Issues and Challenges, pp. 3–20. Routledge (2016)

Becker, L., Jaakkola, E.: Customer experience: fundamental premises and implications for research. J. Acad. Mark. Sci. **48**(4), 630–648 (2020)

Brodie, R.J., Hollebeek, L.D., Jurić, B., Ilić, A.: Customer engagement: conceptual domain, fundamental propositions, and implications for research. J. Serv. Res. **14**(3), 252–271 (2011)

Corsaro, D.: Value co-destruction and its effects on value appropriation. J. Mark. Manag. **36**(1/2), 100–127 (2020)

Cova, B., Skålén, P., Pace, S.: Interpersonal practice in project marketing: how institutional logics condition and change them. J. Bus. Ind. Mark. **34**(4), 723–734 (2019)

Crosby, L.A., Gronroos, C., Johnson, S.L.: Who moved my value? Not companies create value. Mark. Manag. **11**(5), 10–11 (2022)

Dehling, S., Edvardsson, B., Tronvoll, B.: How do actors coordinate for value creation? A signaling and screening perspective on resource integration. J. Serv. Mark. **36**(9), 18–26 (2022)

Echeverri, P., Skalen, P.: Co-creation and co-destruction: a practice-theory based study of interactive value formation. Mark. Theory **11**(3), 351–373 (2011)

Echeverri, P.: Interaction value formation spaces: configurations of practice-theory elements in service ecosystems. J. Serv. Mark. **35**(9), 28–39 (2021)

Flaherty, K., Schroeder, C.S.: An institutional logics perspective on salesperson responses to environmental disruptions. J. Person. Sell. Sales Manag. **42**(4), 377–391 (2022)

Friedland, R., Alford, R.R.: bringing society back in: symbols, practices and institutional contradictions. In: Powell, W.W., DiMaggio, P. (eds.) The New Institutionalism in Organizational Analysis, pp. 232–263. University of Chicago Press, Chicago (1991)

Grönroos, C.: Service logic revised: who creates value? And who co-creates? Eur. Bus. Rev. **20**(4), 298–314 (2008)

Grönroos, C.: A service perspective on business relationships: the value creation, interaction and marketing. Ind. Mark. Manag. **40**(2), 240–247 (2011)

Hartmann, N.N., Wieland, H., Vargo, S.L.: Converging on a new theoretical foundation for selling. J. Mark. **82**(2), 1–18 (2018)

Grönroos, C., Gummerus, J.: The service revolution and its marketing implications: service logic vs service-dominant logic. Manag. Serv. Qual. **24**(3), 206–229 (2014)

Grönroos, C., Voima, P.: Critical service logic: making sense of value creation and co-creation. J. Acad. Mark. Sci. **41**(2), 133–150 (2013)

Heinonen, K., Strandvik, T.: Customer-dominant logic: foundations and implications. J. Serv. Mark. **29**(6/7), 472–484 (2015)

Heinonen, K., Strandvik, T., Mickelsson, K.J., Edvardsson, B., Sundström, E., Andersson, P.: A customer-dominant logic of service. J. Serv. Manag. **21**(4), 531–548 (2010)

236   A. Oyabu et al.

Jaakkola, E., Alexander, M.: The role of customer engagement behavior in value co-creation: a service system perspective. J. Serv. Res. **17**(3), 247–261 (2014)

Lipkin, M., Heinonen, K.: Customer ecosystems: exploring how ecosystem actors shape customer experience. J. Serv. Mark. **36**(9), 1–17 (2022)

McColl-Kenedy, J.R., Vargo, S.L., Dagger, T.S., Sweeney, J.C., Van Kasteren, Y.: Health care customer value cocreation practice styles. J. Serv. Res. **15**(4), 370–389 (2012)

Medberg, G., Grönroos, C.: Value-in-use and service quality: do customers see a difference? J. Serv. Theory Pract. **30**(4/5), 507–529 (2020)

Mikelsson, J., Sarkikangas, U., Strandvik, T., Heinonen, K.: User-defined ecosystems in health and social care. J. Serv. Mark. **36**(9), 41–56 (2022)

Thornton, P.H., Ocasio, W.: Institutional logics and the historical contingency of power in organizations: executive succession in the higher education publishing industry, 1958–1990. Am. J. Sociol. **105**(3), 801–843 (1999)

Thornton, P.H., Ocasio, W., Lounsbury, M.: The Institutional Logics Perspective: A New Approach to Culture, Structure, and Process. Oxford University Press, Oxford (2012)

Van Doorn, J., et al.: Customer engagement behavior: theoretical foundations and research directions. J. Serv. Res. **13**(3), 253–266 (2010)

Vargo, S.L., Lusch, R.F.: Service-dominant logic: continuing the evolution. J. Acad. Mark. Sci. **36**(1), 1–10 (2008)

Vargo, S.L., Lusch, R.F.: Service-dominant logic 2025. Int. J. Res. Mark. **34**(1), 46–67 (2017)

Yi, Y., Gong, T.: Customer value co-creation behavior: scale development and validation. J. Bus. Res. **66**(9), 1279–1284 (2013)

Analyze the Design Considerations of Tainan's Tourist Map and the Benefits It Aims to Achieve

Yu-Dan Pan[1], Lien-Shang Wu[1(✉)], and Yen-Yu Kang[2(✉)]

[1] Department of Geography, National Kaohsiung Normal University, Kaohsiung City, Taiwan
1741@nknucc.nknu.edu.tw
[2] Department of Industrial Design, National Kaohsiung Normal University,
Kaohsiung City, Taiwan
yenyu@nknu.edu.tw

Abstract. This study takes official tourism maps published by Tainan City as the research object. The research method adopts the general interview method, and the interviewees are map publishers (Tainan City Tourism Bureau) and map designers (illustrators). The purpose of this study is to explore the benefits to be achieved by official tourism map publishing, and the planning and considerations of illustrators when designing tourist maps.

Research findings (1) The purpose of publishing illustrated maps is to increase tourists' interest in attractions, boost visitor numbers, increase visibility, and enhance attractiveness. Factors such as the selection of illustrators, whether their styles are suitable for the map's theme, and their popularity are all considerations. The authorities hope to promote local illustrators in tourism marketing, so several maps are drawn by local illustrators from Tainan. As for how much illustrated tourist maps actually increase tourist numbers, the authorities lack statistical data to determine, but they do increase people's willingness to collect them.

(2) Official emphasis is primarily on the accuracy of tourist maps' information, especially the relative positions of attractions, with design aesthetics coming second. The attractions on illustrated maps are provided by the authorities, while the illustration style and color scheme are determined by the illustrators.

Keywords: tourist map · illustrated map · map design

1 Introduction

Subsequent paragraphs, however, are indented. Tainan, after more than 300 years of accumulation, witnessed the evolution of dynasties, in terms of cultural landscape, brings together historical monuments, religious temples, characteristic food, in terms of natural landscape, contains national parks, wetland ecology, mud hot springs and other world-class landscape, in terms of celebration activities, salt water bees, Nanying five incense, Siraya night festival, international orchid exhibition, etc., in recent years, The vitality of old houses and the revitalization of historic assets inject new vitality into Tainan and drive the development of cultural and creative tourism. Tainan shows the unique style of blending the old and the new. Tainan tourism charm is well-known.

The tourism map is the most direct contact with tourists. The official classification and arrangement of tourism resources in Tainan will be carried out by professional illustrators for drawing and design, and illustrated maps full of feel temperature and aesthetic feeling of The Times will be launched. How do these illustrated maps connect with local characteristics of Tainan? How to present contemporary beauty? Can illustrated maps really trigger travel incentives? Therefore, the tourism map published by Tainan Tourism Bureau is selected as the research object in this study, aiming to explore its aesthetic design features and the attraction of the map to users, etc. The research results can become an important reference for tourism map designers.

1.1 Research Purpose

This study takes Tainan City Tourism Bureau's tourist maps in circulation in 2023 as research samples. The categories of maps include: There are 39 inter-regional tourism maps, tourism maps based on highway route planning, film and television scene maps, feature theme maps, etc. The purpose of the research is to conduct qualitative interviews with mapmakers and designers to understand the mapmakers' considerations in mapping and design planning, as well as the aims and benefits to be achieved by issuing maps.

1.2 Research Limitations

By observing the illustrated tourist maps of Tainan City, we can find that these maps, drawing styles, color schemes, graphic layout and introduction of stories all present a unique contemporary style and are highly valuable for research. Therefore, this study takes the illustrated tourist maps still in circulation and use by the Tourism Bureau of Tainan City Government in 2023 as research samples. The data were collected from Tainan City Tourism Center and Tainan City Tourism Bureau website. Maps published by the public were not included in this study. The sample of this study is shown in Fig. 1, which can be divided into cross-region tourism map, film and television scene tourism map, Michelin three-star scenic spot tourism map, and characteristic theme tourism map according to the content.

2 Literature Review

2.1 Research Purpose

In the study of maps, the main disciplines concerned are geography and visual design. In a retrospective paper in Geography, Chun-Lan Chang (2004) explored the development trend of map research in Taiwan's master's and doctoral theses, and found that there was an increasing trend of research on GIS maps, computer maps, cognitive maps and map education during 1977–2003. Regarding the journal papers on maps, Chun-Lan Chang (2003) pointed out that from 1990 to 2002, 1997 was the peak year. In terms of map categories, the number of papers published on traditional maps was the most stable, while computer maps and GIS maps showed an increasing trend. However, although the number of papers related to ancient maps increased year by year, the number was

臺南超好玩
Tainan is so much fun

豐收之秋
Autumn of harvest

南風旺來人人安康
When the south wind blows, everyone is healthy

花海遊蹤
A sea of flowers

鮮採果漾
The fruits are fresh and rippling

西濱海party
West Coastal party

Fig. 1. Study sample travel map Image: from tainan city sightseeing tourism tourist map publishing, https://www.twtainan.net/zh-tw/media/publicationlist, browsing time: 2023/02/25.

relatively small. Published mainly in historical and cultural related journals. Kao Ching-zhen (2009) pointed out that map research on Taiwan is mostly educational and cognitive, and only partially focuses on map design and simplified content.

Geography also focuses on the research of map design, including the symbolic design, preference and cognition of thematic maps (Xu, Sheng-mo, 1975; Ching-Jen Kao, 2000, 2002), Application of gradient color in maps (Hsin-cheng Wu, 1989), Research on user cognition of map using high color (Yun Chuang, Chun-Lan Chang, 2013), Research on Internet map element design (Zhang Chunlan, 2002). In GIS, Ming-Chang Lin (2006) studied the application of GIS in spatial analysis and spatial data presentation; Chun-Lan Chan and Yin-Yu Liu (2006) discussed the application of GIS in public health in Taiwan; Ching-Lung Fan and Jinn-Guey Lay (2006) discussed the order of geographical names selection after GIS map generalization according to population density and regional characteristics.

In terms of design theory, Chun-Wen Chen and Man-Lai You (2002) discussed the visual communication design in cartography. Map production is a combination of science and art. In visual design, map design belongs to "information design". From the aspects of "visual communication", "environmental space, psychology" and "human-machine interaction", we should also pay attention to the communicability and user experience. In terms of map creation, Chen Yu (2019) discussed the creation of tourist information images of the Silver ethnic group, Huang Yi-Shuang (2015) created a cultural map of Dadaocheng district in Taipei, and Hsieh-Chun Lin (2014) created a food map of Yancheng district in Kaohsiung City.

Summary: It is known from the above literature that map design spans two fields: science and art. The study of geography pays attention to the scientific aspect, mainly focusing on the cognition, functionality and technology of map symbols, while the visual design discipline pays attention to the artistic aspect, mainly focusing on the artistic expression and creation of map, observing contemporary tourism map design. More shoulder the responsibility of marketing and promoting tourist attractions, tourist map is a purposeful art, tourist map needs to be beautiful, must have aesthetic sense in order to attract users.

3 Research Methods

In order to understand the views of the organizers, illustrators, visual design experts, art design experts and cartography experts of Tainan City Tourism Bureau on the drawing of tourism maps, the semi-structured interview method was adopted, and the interview content was mainly to understand the planning and considerations of the drawing of tourism maps, as well as the objectives and benefits to be achieved. The interviewees included: government officials of Tainan City Tourism Bureau, illustrators who have drawn illustrations of Tainan City, visual design experts and scholars, art design experts and scholars and cartography experts and scholars. A total of 10 interviewees were interviewed, including face-to-face interviews, video interviews and written interviews. The face-to-face and video interviews lasted about 1 h. The respondent code is shown in Table 1.

Table 1. Respondent code table

Title	Code	Interview method	Introduction
Government official, Section Chief Xu of the Tourism Bureau	G01	written interview	The person in charge of organizing the Tainan City Tourist Map
Illustrator 1, illustrator named Yan	I01	video interview	I have been drawing illustrations for 6 years and once drew a tourist map of Tainan City
Illustrator 2, illustrator named Da	I02	written interview	I have been drawing illustrations for 8 years. I once drew a tourist map of Tainan City
Illustrator 3, illustrator named Lin	I03	written interview	I have been drawing illustrations for 12 years and once drew a tourist map of Tainan City
Illustrator 4, illustrator named C	I04	face to face interview	I have 17 years of experience in drawing illustrations. I once drew a tourist map of Tainan City
Illustrator 5, illustrator named H	I05	written interview	I have been drawing illustrations for 10 years and once drew a tourist map of Tainan City
Illustrator 6, illustrator named S	I06	written interview	I have been drawing illustrations for 8 years. I once drew a tourist map of Tainan City
Cartography expert, Professor Lin	G01	written interview	Map experts and scholars working at universities
Visual design expert, Professor Lin	V01	face to face interview	Visual design experts and scholars working at universities
Art design expert, Professor Zhang	A01	video interview	Art design experts and scholars working in universities

Source: Researchers' tabulation

4 Research and Analysis

4.1 Benefits to Be Achieved by Publishing Tourist Maps

Why choose to design a tourist map in the form of illustration? What are the considerations and planning when issuing a tourist map? The interviewee (I04), a professional illustrator who has worked in the illustration industry for 17 years and has helped Tainan

City Tourism Bureau to draw tourist maps many times, said, "The authorities are tired of traditional tourist maps and people are not willing to ask for them. The Tourism Bureau wants to increase the public's willingness to ask for them in a new way, so it looks for illustrators to draw maps." Chief Xu (interviewee G01), who is responsible for Tainan City Tourism Map, said:

The main consideration was the popularity of illustration in 105 years of the Republic of China (2016 AD), and the Director of the Bureau at that time wanted to change the design style of folding propaganda in previous years and use illustration methods that were highly accepted by the public to design. The official thought that illustrated maps were more attractive and could arouse more topics for tourists and the general public.

The reason for choosing the form of illustration to design the tourism map is that in the year 105 of the Republic of China (2016), the then Director of the Bureau wanted to propose a new type of publicity design, coupled with the popular illustration at that time, the Tourism Bureau invited a number of local illustrators in Tainan to jointly draw an illustrated map, including "Tainan super fun", "West Coastal party", and other six special theme maps. In the case of the map "Tainan Super Fun", the illustrator takes the father with his two daughters as the protagonist, and the map is vivid and interesting. The map is like the happy memories of the father and daughter's journey. Through the introduction of this warm story, we hope to allow tourists to imagine all kinds of good memories created by travel in the illustration, so as to drive travel motivation. According to the questionnaire survey of this study, the degree of attraction of illustrated maps to users is 4.4 points, and the degree of preference of users to illustrated maps is 4.36 points. The results obtained by the questionnaire are in line with the expectations of cartographers.

What are the advantages or charm of illustrated maps compared with conventional maps? Professor Lin (respondent V01), a visual design expert and scholar who has been working in visual design for more than 15 years, said:

Illustrated maps can trigger tourist motivation and generate projections of scenic spots. Illustrated maps can give people who are not familiar with the place or local strangers the incentive to travel or come to the site, stimulate their psychology of wanting to participate, and the beauty of the environment projection, how fun and beautiful it is to go to the place, and have expectations in mind, so they will have time to explore. Therefore, most tourist maps will be placed in public transportation for people to obtain. Such as stations, high-speed rail stations, etc., mainly in attracting foreign visitors, his purpose is not to attract people in the place, look at the map of products, food, imagine that through tourism can obtain physical and mental satisfaction, the map should let people can imagination of the tourist place, otherwise why should tourists spend time traveling here?

Through the viewing Angle and unique style of the illustrator, the map depicts the image and style of Tainan, and allows the brush to outline the beautiful imagination of Tainan tourism. Tainan has a special cultural and historical status, but also carries the development history of Taiwan for nearly 400 years, whether it is rich and wonderful food and snacks, cultural heritage, cultural relics skills, historical buildings and natural scenery, etc. Through the illustrator's hand strokes, the map of illustration can make this wonderful show in front of the public in a more emotional way.

How do I choose an illustrator to draw a map? Will illustration style or audience preference be taken into account? Chief Xu (interviewee G01), who is responsible for Tainan City Tourism Map, said:

Generally, well-known illustrators will be selected from the street, of course, it depends on whether the style of the illustrator is good at and the theme of the design, for example, if you want to make a flower map, at least the object is to be good at drawing "plant" type of illustrator, but the final decision maker is of course still the head of the agency.

An illustrator with the surname C (respondent I04) who has worked with Tainan City Tourism Bureau many times said:

Can draw the official illustration map, almost famous illustrators on the Internet, everyone has their own fans, and the release of these illustrated maps, each has the signature of the illustrator, so it has led many illustrator fans to search the map, and successfully create a topic after the publication of the map, and attract attention.

According to the interview, most illustrators who draw map illustrations are from Tainan. The official will look for illustrators who are well-known on the Internet to draw tourist maps, and whether the drawing style of illustrators is in line with the map theme is also a factor for the official consideration. The illustrator's own works have accumulated a number of fans on the Internet, and the illustrator's painting charm will trigger the collection effect of fans. Therefore, finding well-known illustrators can also improve the topicality and discussion of the map. In the marketing of Tainan tourism, we can also publicize local illustrators in Tainan, achieving a win-win publicity benefit.

What benefits are expected from the release of illustrated maps? Chief Xu (interviewee G01), who is responsible for Tainan City Tourism Map, said:

The most important goals of the launch of the illustrated tourist map include: increase the number of tourists, improve attention, attraction, etc., from different themes of the folding literature, is hoping to tell the public from different angles, how to play Tainan, the tourism Bureau occasionally catch up with the current events, such as drama map (for example: Common women develop memories, want to see you, my mother-in-law how lovely, lonely taste, etc.), by integrating the introduction of scenic spots in the play, the scenic spots are further connected into suggested trips for public reference, which help to attract people and increase tourist numbers.

The expected benefits of illustrated maps include increasing the number of tourists, increasing attention, increasing attractiveness, etc. The official will design tourist maps with different themes, plan different tourist routes, and adopt different perspectives to let tourists know that Tainan has diversified and multi-oriented journey planning. When the official is looking for an illustrator, it should have already planned what customers the map wants to attract and what benefits it may bring. The illustrator will adjust the color, painting style and content according to different customer groups to achieve the purpose of attracting the tourist object. The official will also match current events, such as the recent popular idol drama "vulgar women to form a record", "want to see you", "How is my mother-in-law so cute", "lonely taste", etc., the shooting scenes are in Tainan, the scenes of the drama are connected into a tour, to facilitate the public to do tour planning, these measures to facilitate the tourist tour planning, to promote local tourism are helpful.

Has there been an increase in the number of tourists since the launch of the illustrated map? How many tourists are actually driven? Are there any statistics? Chief Xu (interviewee G01), who is responsible for Tainan City Tourism Map, said:

There are no specific statistics for this section, but people do come to the Tourism Bureau to request folio brochures for collection purposes.

Professor Lin, Visual design expert and scholar (respondent V01) said:

This part depends on whether there are official statistics, but these illustrators who draw Tainan City tourist map have a certain popularity, after the illustrator uploads the work in the fan page, these messages have a certain influence in the design circle, will cause a wave, let people want to collect, many design students begin to pay attention to the official news because of the beautiful illustrations, which is a successful topic.

Since there is no official statistics on the number of tourists driven by illustrated maps, there is no statistical data for discussion on the growth of the actual number of tourists. However, tourist maps do increase people's willingness to search for collections. Interviews with visual design experts also point out that after these well-known illustrators release their works, they will exert influence in the design circle. This in turn drives attention to official news. According to the results of the questionnaire survey in this study, users' willingness to collect illustrated maps is 4.23 points, which is consistent with the official and visual design experts' statements. Illustrated maps can indeed improve users' willingness to collect.

5   Summary

5.1   Benefits to Be Achieved by Publishing Tourism Maps

The official design of tourist maps in the form of illustrations, that illustrated maps are more attractive to users, and can arouse more topics. Through the illustrator's viewing Angle, unique style and touch, the map depicts the image and style of Tainan. As for the selection of illustrators, the official will look for illustrators who are well-known on the Internet to draw maps, among which there are many illustrators in Tainan. Looking for well-known illustrators can also improve the topicality and discussion of maps, and promote local illustrators in Tainan when marketing Tainan tourism, so as to achieve win-win benefits. Whether the illustrator's style of painting fits the map theme is also a factor in the official consideration.

The expected benefits of issuing illustrated maps include increasing tourist arrivals, increasing attention, increasing attraction, etc., providing tourism maps with diversified themes for different tourism types, so that users can know what other different ways Tainan plays. The illustrator will adjust the painting style according to different tourist groups to achieve the purpose of attracting the tourist object. The official will also be paired with popular idol dramas, the scenes of the drama will be linked into a tour, to achieve the benefit of increasing tourist arrivals.

How many visitors did the map bring? Since there is no official statistical data, it is impossible to know, but tourist maps do increase people's willingness to search for Tibet, which is consistent with the questionnaire survey results of this study. Illustrated maps can indeed improve users' willingness to collect and travel motivation.

5.2 Planning and Considerations for the Cartographer to Draw a Tourist Map

The content design, generalization degree, color matching, style, and selection of printing paper in the map of tourism illustration are determined by what considerations? Chief Xu (interviewee G01), who is responsible for Tainan City Tourism Map, said:

The content is usually provided by the agency to the illustrator, and the illustrator then draws the content design into a draft for the agency to review. Generally, the illustrator will also give suggestions on the type of paper, mainly based on the style of the publicity of the production.

An illustrator surnamed C (interviewee I04) who has drawn a tourist map of Tainan City said:

When selecting an illustrator, the official has seen the illustrator's work and finds that the illustrator's work is good and in line with the style required by the bureau. In the painting style and color matching, usually the illustrator can make decisions, but will do full communication with the owner, probably will propose two sketches for choice, the owner hopes that after the illustration is drawn, can have a topic, the map design will be put on the Internet for the public to download, so as to increase the map circulation rate, but also let the owner do not have to print all the time. Some special color printing is put forward by me, such as fluorescent color and silver special color, the official think it is good and accept my proposal. In the color, I especially like yellow, and I will use blue and yellow to show my personal style.

According to the interview, the content design of the tourism illustration Map is provided to the illustrator by the government. In terms of content design, the illustrator will make the design according to the characteristics of the scenic spots that the government wants to emphasize or the atmosphere that it wants to present. Before the drawing, some illustrators will mark all the routes and scenic spots that need to be drawn on Google Map and decide the map scope. Scale too large general adjustment. In terms of style and color matching, it is usually up to the illustrator to make the decision, and the illustrator will take the official needs as the main consideration, and design a suitable match according to different themes.

As for the design style, when selecting an illustrator, the official has first read the illustrator's works and believes that the illustrator's style meets the needs, and will only invite the illustrator to draw. The illustrator will probably provide two drafts for the official review, and the official gives the illustrator a lot of creative space, basically not changing the design style, but has special requirements for the orientation between scenic spots, such as the relativity between east, west, north and south. Most of the officials do not have much opinion on the use of color, mainly for scenic spots, text content, main roads, bus routes and symbol positions to make adjustments, the official hope that the illustrations drawn can be topical, the content should be attractive. In printing, the illustrator will give suggestions, such as special color printing, if the official thinks it is good, the illustrator's proposal will be accepted. As for the selection of paper, the illustrator will give the official advice, the official consideration is mainly suitable for the style of the paper, the paper needs to be foldable, the paper with long fiber is more suitable, the paper thickness should be moderate, too thin and broken and the light transmission will affect the reader's interpretation of the information, the cost is also an important consideration, if the printing volume is too small, the selection of too expensive paper is not in line with the benefit.

How to select tourist locations in the map? Is it up to the illustrator or the tourism bureau to decide which tourist locations to present? Who decides which attractions to present in which districts? What are the main considerations? "It's usually the tourism bureau, and the reasons for the decision are mainly marketing or cultural promotion needs," said Lin, an illustrator (interviewee I03) who has drawn tourist maps of Tainan.

Chief Xu (interviewee G01), who is responsible for Tainan City Tourism Map, said:

In terms of scenic spot selection, the tourist destinations in the illustrated map are provided by the agency in principle, and the consideration point is based on the theme of the brochure, because most of the agency's brochures are thematic in nature, such as Maozi, West Coast Religion, Shopping Flowers, parent-child mountain climbing, etc., different points will be selected according to different themes, and of course some external opinions will be consulted to make adjustments.

An illustrator surnamed S (interviewee I06) who has drawn a tourist map of Tainan City said:

Some attractions of the theme map will be proposed by the illustrator, and the official review will be carried out again, because some shops do not like to be disturbed, so they do not want to be put into the map, at this time, we must respect the opinions of the business and delete the attraction.

In principle, the tourist places in the illustrated map are provided to the illustrator by the official, and the official will provide the introduction of scenic spots, relevant cultural and historical investigation information, etc., but when the illustrator is doing information inquiries, sometimes he will find that the shop has been closed, and he will inform the official real-time information. Some themed attractions will be provided by illustrators, but the final right of review is official.

Does the official focus on functionality or artistry in the design of illustrated tourist maps? Chief Xu (interviewee G01), who is responsible for Tainan City Tourism Map, said:

In design, no matter what kind of publicity, it is the correctness of the first information, the wrong information does not need to talk about other, and then the presentation of the layout content and the design is good or not? After all, the primary purpose of these communications is to provide passengers with correct information (respondent G01).

An illustrator surnamed C (interviewee I04) who has drawn an illustrated map of Tainan City said:

To be honest, this kind of map is less practical, more emphasis on art and beauty, illustration map is not to give people to know the way, the most important thing is to arouse the interest of tourists. This year (2020) the head of the agency has changed, so we need to put photos instead, and we feel that information is more important.

The official design of the illustrated tourist map first focuses on providing tourists with correct information, and then the design is beautiful or not. In today's era of developed Google Map positioning system, the practicality of maps will soon be replaced by Google Map, and the public has become accustomed to using Google Map to plan routes. The purpose of illustration maps is not to provide travelers with directions. The map will show the relative positions of scenic spots, but the accuracy of actual distances is not so important. Illustrated maps are designed to attract tourists' interest in scenic spots and achieve the effect of attracting tourists, publicity and collection. Google Map will be used in functional requirements, and illustrated maps are more artistic.

Apart from the general indication of scenic spots, what other content can be added to the tourist map to increase the willingness of tourists to obtain, collect or visit? Chief Xu (interviewee G01), who is responsible for Tainan City Tourism Map, said:

This depends on the different themes of the literature, such as parent-child mountaineering literature, and furry child travel literature. The target audiences for these requests should be different, and the information content they may need should be placed based on these different audiences.

When planning the tourist map, the official will place information content with different needs according to different themes and different objects. For example, the Tainan pro-mountain walking trail tour map is drawn by an illustrator who loves mountaineering. Five entry trails are selected and divided into challenge type and parent-child type according to the difficulty for reference by tourists who love mountaineering. Promotional content needs to be interesting to attract people, such as parent-child travel maps, to be able to make children interested. The illustrators who create the maps already have their own fan base, which can be combined with official marketing. The launch of a series of maps will make people want to collect the whole series. Among other additional features, you can plan stamp collection activities to allow visitors to collect stamps by the map. Maps can be matched with discount activities, such as with store offers, discount rolls, etc. Maps can be printed on special materials, so that the map is at the same time silk scarves, hand towels, flags, or apply special folding methods into lanterns, paper dolls, perpetual calendars, cool cards, etc., or add design ingenuity, with baskets, hot stamping, special printing, etc., converted into different functions, generate topic, arouse public attention, and increase the willingness to collect and discuss.

How does the illustrated map create the local character of Tainan? Professor Lin Surname (G01), an expert in cartography, said, Symbols and images should be designed so that people can accurately and clearly understand the local features they represent.

Art Design expert Professor Zhang (Interviewee A01) said:

Be sure to draw familiar landmarks, iconic buildings, and easily recognizable places, such as: The shape of Pingtung Station, Pingtung Mazu Temple, Changhua Bagua Mountain Buddha, must have these people in order to determine that this is Changhua, if the lack of this landmark, people can not know the characteristics of this place, New York must have the Statue of Liberty, Paris must have the tower. Color is different, the illustration will be subjective consideration. Since it is in line with illustration, it is an artistic creation.

Visual design expert Professor Lin (Respondent V01) said:

The map should appear iconic buildings, landscapes, terrain, such as paths, properties, cultural customs, etc., such as Hakka kitchens, back-shaped buildings, villages with the same surname, etc. Attractions can be attached religion, 邊 border, etc. In terms of products, such as Guanmiao pineapple, Qishan banana, Guanshan rice, special cultural customs, such as Confucius Temple on behalf of learning, Jing character pavilion on behalf of Hakka people cherish the word, pay attention to scholars, sunny cultivation and rain reading, literary style and so on.

The illustration map needs to draw iconic buildings, landmarks, terrain, products and other contents to create the local characteristics of Tainan, so that users can accurately identify where this place is, such as Tainan Chikan Lou, Anping Castle, Chi Mei Museum, etc. The lack of representative buildings will make people unable to identify local characteristics. In terms of products, typical products such as Okjeong mango, Guanmiao pineapple, Ma Dou Wendan, Hougbi orchid and Dongshan coffee will remind you where they are. In terms of cultural customs, for example, the Confucius Temple represents the development of learning, the Wind Lion Lord connects with the history of early Anping people praying for a harvest at sea, and the sword lion represents the social environment of early Anping with poor public security, etc. When you see these illustrations, you can associate the cultural atmosphere of the place and make people see the characteristics at a glance. As for color, some illustrators will refer to the color matching suitable for Tainan, such as temples will use orange, red, coffee, etc., while some illustrators will not deliberately express Tainan colors, but draw with colors according to personal habits to show their personal illustration style. The application of colors is subject to the subjective considerations of illustrators.

Must tourist illustration maps conform to the basic elements of cartography? Such as scale, coordinate system, legend, north needle, etc. Geography expert Professor Lin (Respondent G01) said:

Illustration map (no projection, scale): focus on beautiful and easy to understand, orientation, proportional correctness is not much required. The legend depends on the need, the rest (coordinate system, scale) is difficult to apply to illustrated maps.

The illustrated map is different from the scale map, the illustrated map attaches importance to the beauty, and the accuracy of the orientation and proportion is not required. The illustrated map has limitations such as distance and size, and the map cannot be presented according to the true scale, but can only show the relativity between points. When drawing according to the scale, if the distance between two points is too short, only one point can be marked, and no illustration can be placed, and the overall space is not in line with the visual beauty of the illustrated map. Therefore, when drawing the illustrated map, the composition will be arranged according to the placement position of the illustration. Rather than taking into account actual distances, it is not necessary to conform to all elements of cartography, such as scales and coordinate systems.

What do I need to do before making a travel illustration map? Like fieldwork? Has the illustrator taken any courses in cartography or visual design? Professor Lin, an expert in cartography (respondent G01), said, "Tourist illustrated maps usually do not have projections, coordinates or scales, so cartography is unnecessary and visual design is needed."

Art design expert and scholar Professor Zhang (Interviewee A01) said:

Cartography and visual design are two different things. To draw a map with correct proportions and indicative maps, of course cartography is very important, but if it is just a guide to the direction and a guide to the goal. You don't need to have studied cartography to map a trip, just know the location and direction.

Drawing tourist illustration maps requires drawing ability and skills, and understanding of color matching and picture composition, so it is necessary to learn visual design related courses, but cartography is not necessary, because illustration maps do not pursue

100% accurate position. In terms of advance homework, the official will prepare information such as photos of scenic spots for illustrators, illustrators can usually search for supplementary information from the Internet, use Google Map to see the real sample of scenic spots, grasp the location of the point, with the help of scientific and technological tools, if you can find information on the Internet, you do not need to actually go to the scene, which can save work time.

When the illustrator wants to draw the content or direction is different from the owner's opinion, how does the illustrator overcome? An illustrator surnamed C (interviewee I04) who has drawn an illustrated map of Tainan City said:

There is usually a division of labor, with the owner responsible for the content and me responsible for the presentation. But for example, when there is a policy change (a change of the chief officer), the design will be changed, and now the chief officer wants to show a different location, he has to change. Tainan official units are more special, because they have done more, so the acceptance is higher. Generally speaking, the owner came to me just because he wanted to present something richer, so he would not have too much opinion.

When the content or direction that the illustrator wants to draw is different from the owner's opinion, the illustrator will fully communicate, understand the official needs, and explain the reasons for the different opinions. If the two sides have different considerations and the official opinions are justified, the illustrator will make modifications according to the official needs, hoping that the owners can obtain satisfactory content. When making a proposal, two different contents will be put forward for the official reference, and the official will not have too many opinions. However, when the policy changes, the way to be presented or the focus changes, the illustrator will make corrections according to the official needs. Sometimes, the illustrator will have blind spots, so he will not reject the official requirements at the beginning. We will try to adjust it to a more appropriate content with the official explanation.

Are there any difficulties in drawing an illustrated travel map? How to solve it?

The difficulties encountered in drawing illustrated tourist maps include: drawing historical attractions that have disappeared and have no photos must be drawn by imagination, but it is the function of illustration creation. Simplifying is not easy when the information being drawn is very complex. When the scenic spot is arranged according to the relative position, if the picture is not beautiful enough, it is necessary to make deformation adjustment or change the color match, so that the overall picture can be better. When the information provided by the owner is more clear and complete, there is less need to make too many corrections.

Three findings from in-depth interviews between cartographers and designers:

1. Scenic spot selection and style formulation of tourist map

In principle, the tourist locations in the illustrated map are provided by the government to the illustrator, but some scenic spots with themes will be provided by the illustrator to the government, and they will discuss with the store whether they are willing to be put on the map, but the official integration, and the final review right is in the official.

In the process of drawing, the content design is provided by the official, and the illustrator will design according to the content and atmosphere that the official wants to present. Before drawing, the illustrator will search for more scenic spot information through Google. In terms of style and color, it is usually decided by the illustrator to design a suitable match according to the official needs and different themes. In terms of style, the illustrator will provide about two drafts for the official review, and the official will give the illustrator a lot of creative space, basically will not modify the design style, but special requirements for the orientation between scenic spots, text content, main roads, bus routes and symbol locations sometimes need to be adjusted. In terms of the selection of paper, the illustrator will give the official advice, the main consideration is to suit the style of the article.

When the content or direction that the illustrator wants to draw is different from the owner's opinion, the illustrator will make full communication to understand the official needs. When the official opinions are reasonable, the illustrator will modify the official needs according to the official needs, and will not directly reject the official needs. If the change is not better, he will try to adjust the design to a more suitable one with the official explanation. The authorities have great respect for the expertise of illustrators.

2. How do tourist maps create local characteristics

Illustrated maps can create local characteristics by drawing iconic buildings, landmarks, terrain, products, and cultural customs of Tainan, and can also apply decorative illustrations to strengthen the local atmosphere. As for the application of color, there are subjective considerations of the illustrator. The map of tourism illustration does not need to conform to the basic elements of cartography, and the legend can be determined according to the situation, but the coordinate system and scale are difficult to apply to the illustrated map.

3. Map design highlights and other suggestions

The most important thing is to provide passengers with correct information, and then the design is beautiful or not. Google Maps will be used for functional requirements, and the illustrated map is more artistic. Illustrated maps are designed to attract tourists to scenic spots, to attract tourists, to play a promotional role and to make tourists willing to collect the effect.

Official tourism map planning will be based on different themes, different objects, into the information content of different needs, in other additional functions, it is suggested to be integrated into chapter activities, with discounts, or can be printed on special materials (silk scarves, hand towels, flags, etc.), or the application of special folding (lanterns, paper dolls, calendars, cool cards, etc.). Or add design ingenuity (basket empty, hot stamping, special printing, etc.), the map is converted into different functions, which can increase the willingness to collect and topic.

6 Conclusion

The results of this study are as follows:

1. The intended benefits of publishing illustrated tourist maps are to increase tourist number, increase attention and increase attraction, and the cartographer has achieved this.

   The purpose of publishing illustrated maps is to increase tourists' interest in scenic spots, increase tourist number, increase attention, increase attraction, etc. The popularity of illustrators will also improve the public's discussion on maps and willingness to search for collections. Therefore, regarding the selection of illustrators, whether the style of illustrators is in line with the map theme, whether they are well-known, and whether they are local illustrators in Tainan. Both factors are considered, and the authorities hope to promote local illustrators as well when marketing tourism.

   Officials hope to create local characteristics of Tainan by drawing iconic buildings, landmarks, landforms, products and cultural customs through the unique perspective and touch of illustrators. The official planning of different themes of tourism content, the launch of different types of maps, such as the journey with pets, suitable for a family of old and young people to travel together, specially planned for mountaineering groups, illustrator according to different customer groups, adjust the painting expression, such as the map for children will adopt a childlike style. The official will also publish maps with current affairs, while the idol drama is hot, the trend of the launch of film and television scene maps, such as: common women to form a record, my mother-in-law how lovely, lonely taste and other tourism maps, to increase the number of tourists. As for the actual increase in tourist visits, due to the lack of official statistics, it is impossible to know, but illustrated tourist maps do increase people's willingness to search.

2. The correctness of information is the first consideration in the planning of tourist map, followed by the beauty of design. The integration of illustrator's design in tourist map can effectively trigger travel motivation

   When the official publication of illustrated tourist maps, the first priority is the correctness of information, especially the relative position between scenic spots, and the second is the beauty of design. Illustrated tourist maps tend to be artistic rather than functional, and illustrated maps cannot be drawn according to the actual scale due to the limitations of drawing layout, so the basic elements of the map are not applicable to illustrated tourist maps. If tourists have functional needs, such as navigation, finding the way, etc., they will use Google Maps. The purpose of illustrated maps is not to provide tourists with way-finding, but to increase the attraction of scenic spots and promote tourism motivation.

   In drawing, the scenic spots of the map are provided by the official, while the painting style and color matching application are decided by the illustrator. The illustrator will draw according to the atmosphere that the official wants to present, and two sketches will be provided for the official to choose when proposing the proposal. The official will give the illustrator a lot of creative space and respect the professional of the illustrator. In terms of the selection of paper, the illustrator will give the official advice, mainly considering the style suitable for the article. Through the observation and interpretation of illustrators, the tourist map allows users to trigger the motivation of travel and arouse the beautiful imagination of tourist destinations through hand-drawn strokes, beautiful pictures, balanced color matching and composition.

References

Bureau of Tourism. Tainan City Government. Tainan Michelin three-star tour. Tainan Tourism Monthly, 20 (2014)

Bureau of Tourism, Tainan City Government (2021)

Tainan City Affairs-Shiguozilin Coffee. Search date. 2020/7/26. 取自https://www.tainanoutlook.com/blog/shi-guo-zi-lan-ka-pei

Bureau of Tourism, Tainan City Government. Tainan travel guide, Tainan City: Bureau of Tourism, Tainan City Government (2018)

Bureau of Tourism, Tainan City Government. Promotional leaflet publications. Search date: 2020/02/25 (2020). https://www.twtainan.net/zh-tw/media/publicationlist

Wu, H.: 吳信政 The Application of Gradate Coloring to Cartographic Presentation. National Taiwan Normal University Geographical Research (1989)

Lin, M.-C.: Apply spatial analyses and represent spatial data within a geographic information system. J. Cartography (16), 147–166 (2006). https://doi.org/10.30006/JC.200606.0011

Lin, H.-C.: Gourmet map of Yancheng Distric, Kaohsiung City. Shu-Te University Master's Thesis of Department of Visual Communication Design, kaohsiung City (2014)

Fan, C.-L., Lay, J.-G.: The study of place names selection using GIS on cartographic generalization. Bull. Geogr. Soc. China (37), 69–87 (2006). https://doi.org/10.29972/BGSC.200606.0004

Xu, S.: Research on thematic map symbol design. Geosci. Trans. **3**, 48–57 (1975)

Kao, C.-J.: A cognition research of frequently used symbols on tourist maps. Hwa Kang J. Sci. (17), Page 115–129 (2000). https://doi.org/10.6364/HKJS.200005.0115

Kao, C.-J.: A research of cartographic symbols using preference ranking test. Hwa Kang J. Sci. (19), 77–89 (2002). https://doi.org/10.6364/HKJS.200205.0077

Kao, C.-J.: Cartographic education and academic research in Taiwan. J. Cartography (19), 15–32 (2009). https://doi.org/10.30006/JC.200910.0002

Chang, C.-L.: Study of cartographic layout design for Taiwan web maps. J. Cartography (12), 17–28 (2002). https://doi.org/10.30006/JC.200207.0002

Chang, C.-L.: The analysis of cartography-related papers published in Taiwan between 1990 and 2002. J. Cartography (13), 1–11 (2003). https://doi.org/10.30006/JC.200309.0001

Chang, C.-L.: Cartographic research trends of dissertations and theses in Taiwan. J. Cartography (14), 63–70 (2004). https://doi.org/10.30006/JC.200407.0006

Chan, C.-L., Liu, Y-Y.: Research and application of geographic information systems in public health in Taiwan. Environ. Worlds (13), 57–80 (2006). https://doi.org/10.6304/EAW.2006.13.4

Youth Development Administration. MOE. Improve self-confidence into adulthood. Search date: 2021/2/6 (2014). https://www.sa.gov.tw/PageContent?n=1533

Chuang, Y., Chang, C.-L.: The perceptional influence of hypsographic color design to map reader. J. Cartography **23**(2), 41–55 (2013)

Chen, C.-W., You, M.-L.: Visual communication design in cartography. J. Des. Res. (2), 117–128 (2002). https://doi.org/10.30178/SJYJ.200207.0012

Chen, Y.: Research of Tourism Infographics Creation for the Seniors. Master's Thesis, Department of Visual Design, National Kaohsiung Normal University, Kaohsiung City (2019)

Huang, Y.-S.: Taipei Dadaocheng local cultural marketing design. Master's Thesis, Department of Visual Communication Design, National Yunlin University of Science and Technology, Yunlin County (2015)

An Interactive Visual Instrument to Address the Scoping of Bespoke Information Systems

Anelis Pereira-Vale[1]([⊠]) [iD], Tomás Vera[1,2] [iD], Daniel Perovich[1] [iD],
Sergio F. Ochoa[1] [iD], and Fabiane Benitti[3] [iD]

[1] Computer Science Department, University of Chile, Santiago, Chile
{apereira,tvera,dperovic,sochoa}@dcc.uchile.cl
[2] Zenta Group, Santiago, Chile
[3] Department of Informatics and Statistics, Federal University of Santa Catarina,
Florianópolis, Brazil
fabiane.benitti@ufsc.br

Abstract. The literature in requirements engineering recognizes the product scoping activity as an important source of risks and fails in bespoke software projects. In order to help address this activity, we designed and implemented an interactive visual instrument that allows providers and customers to jointly define the scope of bespoke software products, particularly, information systems. The instrument was formally evaluated through a qualitative study that involved three projects in Chile and three in Brazil. Real customers and providers took part in these experiences. The evaluation results were highly encouraging, showing the instrument is a serious candidate to help deal with the product scoping challenges. Customers, software providers and also software engineering researchers can also take advantage of it, by reusing and adjusting the instrument to their own reality.

Keywords: Software product scoping · interactive visual instrument · visual knowledge shared space · bespoke information systems · empirical evaluation

1 Introduction

Every new bespoke project requires that both parties, i.e., the customer and the provider, start the development activities performing the *product scope definition* (also known as *product scoping*). This activity includes determining: 1) the current features of the system to be intervened (if any), and 2) the new features to be added. These specifications are known as the "as-is" and the "to-be" of the product respectively.

The software engineering literature identifies the quality of the product scoping as a major source of problems in bespoke software projects, due to several causes related to the definition of the *as-is* and *to-be* of the product [2,6,13].

H. Mori and Y. Asahi (Eds.): HCII 2024, LNCS 14689, pp. 253–263, 2024.
https://doi.org/10.1007/978-3-031-60107-1_18

Concerning the definition of the as-is, in the best case the customer counts on some system's information to share with each new provider that intervenes in the software. Such information usually has low trustworthiness, mainly because nobody is responsible to keep it complete and updated, and the customer is not able to determine its validity [13,18]. In these cases, the provider must analyze the source code of the system to determine its structure, the accuracy of the supporting information, and the points in which the product could be intervened in order to add or modify its functionality.

Concerning the definition of the *to-be* of the product, it is also challenging since most of the systems do not count on a product owner or a product roadmap that helps determine its evolution and the way to intervene the system. Instead, there is a customer that needs to address a problem or an opportunity using a system, but who usually ignores (or partially knows) the as-is and the to-be of the product [1,18]. It generates misunderstood, omitted, ill-defined, and poorly specified requirements, including technical debts [2].

These limitations to perform suitable product scope definitions in bespoke projects has also been evidenced in a study conducted by the authors in 2020 [19]. Such a study shows the need to define solutions that help reduce the software project risks and fails, given the low cost-effectiveness of the current scoping practices.

This article proposes an interactive visual canvas and a collaborative technique that can be used by project requesters and providers, in order to define the as-is and to-be of information systems bespoke projects. This definition activity can be done at the precontract o project starting stage [15,16,19].

Next section presents the background and related work on product scoping, Sects. 3 and 4 introduce the proposed instrument (i.e., the visual canvas and the collaborative technique). Sections 5 and 6 describe the evaluation process and the obtained results respectively. Section 7 presents the conclusions and the future work

2   Background

According to a study conducted by the authors on 57 Chilean software companies, these organizations address the product scoping process by trying to involve experts in the business and technical domain of the project, which is usually difficult for most software companies given the variety of domains they have to address.

The people that lead the product scoping process usually utilize traditional requirements engineering practices and instruments, like interviews or questionnaires, and usually produce a list of customer needs or a coarse-grained requirements specification [19].

The outcome of such a process should be the shared understanding, between the customer and provider, on the goal and scope of the product (to-be) [4,8]. However, in most cases the customer and the provider have their own picture about both, what is required and what is expected for the project output.

Given the business and technical knowledge on the context, problem, and eventual solution resides in both sides, i.e., in the customer and the provider, the collaboration among them is mandatory to build a shared understanding on these structural elements.

The collaboration activities on product scoping are quite structured at high level [15]; however, it is context-aware and unstructured at low level [19]. The cost-effectiveness of this activity is usually low, except when it is performed by experts in the business and technical domains being addressed [14, 19], or eventually when this collaboration process is effective, although knowledgeable people participate in it. In this second case, the instruments and techniques supporting these people play a key role.

The literature report several instruments and techniques to support the product scoping process, for instance, pilot studies or proof-of-concepts [10], requirements engineering techniques [7], elicitations considering COTS (Commercial Off-The-Shelf) [5], and hybrid approaches (e.g., viewpoints) [3].

These techniques and tools help clarify the context and problem to address, the product's functional requirements, but not necessarily to reach a sound agreement between both parts on the project scope. In this sense, it is expected and required that any technique supporting the scoping process can guide the provider and the customer in such a road, helping them reduce the project uncertainty and make reliable estimates [14]. These techniques should deal with several constraints arisen from the conditions to perform the pre-selling of bespoke projects, which were reported in [20]:

C1: *Be feasible in a pre-contract scenario.* The personnel required to perform the product scoping should be available, and the effort required to perform the activity should be affordable for both, the customer and the provider [4, 14]. This capability of the scoping techniques is particularly relevant for small organizations, since they usually have scarce resources.

C2: *Output achieved in a short time.* Since the product scoping is usually performed under a competition situation, the software providers count on a small time window to carry out the activity [4, 14].

C3: *Low dependence of key people (particularly, experts).* There is a large variety of technical and business domains in which the project prospects can be involved in. Consequently, it is almost impossible that the providers count on experts in any combination of domains. Therefore, these techniques should help knowledgeable people to perform the activity and obtain a sound outcome [9].

Additionally, the output of this activity (i.e., product scope definition of the project being addressed) has to deal with several requirements in order to be helpful for both parts [20]. Particularly, this output should:

R1: *Accurately represent the scope of the product to be addressed (project prospect).* The product scope definition should explicitly represent the product structure (if any), its coarse-grained functionality, and also its main non-functional aspects [19]. Such a definition should be accurate enough, in a way that allows the provider to prepare a project proposal from it [12].

R2: Be understandable for regular customers and providers. Given the product
   scope definition involves at least the validation of the project output by
   the participants, it is mandatory that they understand the activity and the
   product scope representation.

R3: Be suitable as input to the estimation activity. The software providers need
   to count on the product scope to estimate the development effort; therefore,
   it has to include well-defined and agreed information to support such an
   activity.

Considering the constraint 3 (C3) and the requirement 2 (R2) we can identify a clear need to count on low entry barrier techniques and instruments to
support the product scoping activity. Next section presents the interactive visual
instrument that was designed to address the scoping of bespoke information systems. This instrument intends to deal with the stated constraints, and allows
the involved people to generate product scope definitions that deal with requirements indicated above.

3   The Interactive Visual Canvas

In order to help software companies and customer organizations conduct the
scoping of bespoke information systems, we defined a visual canvas that is used
to represent the "as-is" and "to-be" of a product. This canvas is a shared space
accessible to all the participants in a development project, and its layout embeds
the knowledge of an information systems reference architecture (Fig. 1); such
knowledge helps perform the product scoping.

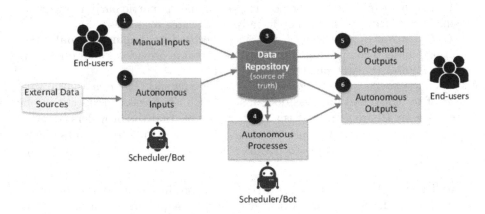

Fig. 1. Reference architecture of an information system (based on [17]).

Typically, the information systems involve four major components [17]: a
data repository and its inputs, outputs and data transformations. The inputs
consider manual and autonomous feeding components (labeled in Fig. 1 as "1"

and "2" respectively). The manual inputs are the set of components that allow a human user to update the information of the repository; for instance, a web form to perform a CRUD of a data entity represents a manual input. An autonomous input corresponds to a component that retrieves information from external data sources, without the users participation, and feeds the data repository of the information system. An ETL is an example of this component type.

The data repository (labeled as "3") provides data persistence to concepts of the business domain being addressed; for instance, in a marketplace these concepts might be: clients, articles, payments, and purchase and delivery orders. Therefore, the data concepts are an abstraction of the information stored in the repository.

The autonomous processes ("4") periodically analyze the information of the data repository in order to generate new knowledge (e.g., indicators or statistics) or perform validations. Such information is eventually delivered to end-users (e.g., through notifications).

Moreover, these systems include mechanisms that allow end-users to retrieve information on-demand ("5"); for instance, to perform queries or review indicators deployed in a dashboard. This system type eventually performs autonomous notifications to the end-users ("6"), e.g., to deliver warnings by email when required or deliver awareness information periodically.

The architecture also considers non-functional requirements of the information system; particularly, the quality requirements and constraints. In addition, the architecture includes the product goal and the user profile to be supported by the system (i.e., the end-users).

Taking into account that architecture, we designed the product scoping canvas for information systems (Fig. 2). Each section of the canvas specifies, through post-its, the as-is and to-be for each component type described above. Thus, the customer and the provider count on a shared and understandable specification of the system, which can be updated and negotiated until they reach an agreement about these two information layers; i.e., the as-is and to-be of the product.

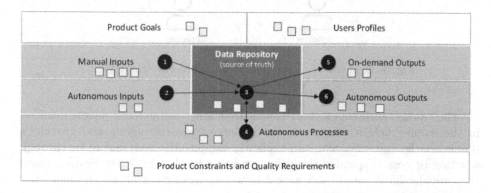

Fig. 2. Scoping canvas for information systems.

Every post-it (represented with a yellow square in Fig. 2) should be added and validated by representatives of the customer and provider organizations. These people collaborate to jointly perform and agree on this product scope definition. Next section explains how to do it.

4   The Collaborative Scoping Technique

During the working sessions, the participants instantiate each zone of the canvas using post-its, which should be explicitly agreed (through a voting process) between both parties to formally be recognized as part of the product scope. Thus, the product scope becomes explicit and easy to understand and validate for both parts.

The collaborative dynamic for using the canvas is flexible; i.e., there are activities that must be performed, but the workflow between the activities is defined at runtime according to what is required for the activity (Fig. 3). Particularly, based on the customer request, the participants analyze information and discuss to determine the features that are part of the as-is, and the envisioned to-be of the product. Each feature is specified in a post-it and located in a particular zone of the canvas (i.e., linked to a conceptual component of the system). Then, the features are evaluated and eventually agreed between both parties.

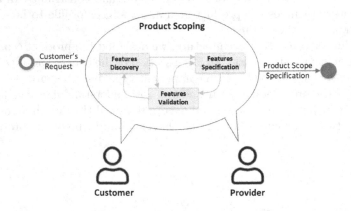

Fig. 3. Dynamic of the product scoping process (from [19]).

The canvas represents a shared space that is accessible to all people involved in the scoping activity; however, the leaders of the customer's and provider's teams are the only ones who can explicitly validate the as-is and to-be through a voting process. Typically, the scoping process finishes when the customer and the provider have voted, and have reached an agreement about the new as-is and to-be of the information system to be developed.

5 Evaluation Process

The canvas and the collaborative technique was used in 6 real software development projects. The evaluation process was qualitative, and it involved three projects in Chile (that involved three provider and three customer organizations), and three projects in Brazil (two providers and three customers). In all cases, the scoping activity was embedded in Scrum software practices that help providers address brownfield and greenfield projects. The authors acted as observers in these experiences, and the results were elaborated based on a survey and an interview performed to the participants.

The Chilean providers were small and medium-sized software companies, enrolled in the MITI consortium[1] and customers were medium-sized and large companies operating in several business domains in the country.

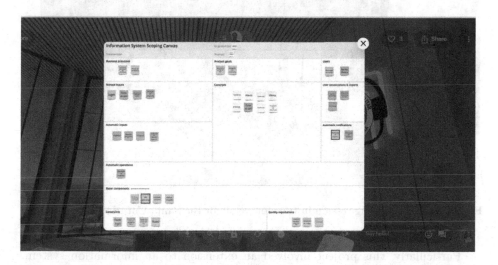

Fig. 4. Example of an information system canvas for Santa Catarina Fire Brigade.

In case of Brazil, the providers where the Bridge technology center[2] that performed two projects for the Brazilian government; one for the ministry of health and the other for ministry of education. The other Brazilian provider was the software development division of the Fire Brigade from the Santa Catarina state[3]; the customers were other firefighters divisions of the same institution. Figure 4 presents a canvas that shows the product scoping, and Fig. 5 depicts a

---

[1] MITI (Consortium of small and medium-sized software companies): https://www.miti.cl/.

[2] Bridge technology center, Federal University of Santa Catarina, Brazil: https://portal.bridge.ufsc.br/.

[3] Emergency support software development, Santa Catarina Fire Brigade, Brazil: https://www.cbm.sc.gov.br/.

product scoping session in the metaverse, performed by customers and providers of this latter institution, using the canvas. In this case the board was implemented using Miro (an online whiteboard tool) [11].

Fig. 5. Product scoping session in the metaverse for the Santa Catarina Fire Brigade.

Particularly, this project involved an extension to an information system. The yellow and white post-its represent the as-is of the product, and the green ones indicate the features to be added; i.e., the to-be.

The first step in the evaluation of the proposed instrument was to introduce the participants in the role and functionality of the canvas, and explain to them the dynamic to carry out the scoping activity in a flexible way. Then, they performed two or more scoping sessions, depending on the size, complexity and uncertainty of each project and product. This process finished when both sides felt comfortable with the result, and after voting the inclusion of the post-its.

After that, the participants filled a survey to rate the perceived usability and usefulness of the instrument. Finally, they gave us quality information about the experience of using the instrument, and assessed the cost-effectiveness of the scoping process in comparison with the techniques and tools that they previously used to perform this activity.

6   Preliminary Results and Discussion

The results of the case studies indicate the use of this instrument is quite intuitive and engaging for customers and providers. Particularly, they perceived its utilization as cost-effective to perform product scoping in short-time periods and address multiple product domains. Most scoping sessions involved less than 90 min, which was suitable according to the participants' opinion. The most valuable aspects for customers and providers were the following:

- The use of the instrument allowed them to build an explicit, shareable and understandable view of the as-is and to-be of the product. It eased the discussion, negotiation and agreement of the product scope between both sides.
- Both parties perceived that they were able to reach a clear agreement and feel comfortable, not only with their participation but also with the process output.
- The entry barrier for using the canvas was affordable for all them.
- Most participants envisioned that this instrument will help them evolve and govern the product at the short and mid-term, in contrast to their current scoping methods that produce a puzzle of functionality after a couple of product evolution projects.

In addition, various providers indicated that the use of the canvas allowed inexperienced people to focus on the product scoping, taking advantage of the know-how embedded in the board. This reduced the chances to overlook key aspects of the product to be developed.

On the other hand, some customers highlighted that due to this scoping process has an explicit output, which can be shared with other suppliers, customers can easily reduce the ambiguity and time required to communicate the request.

After these experiences, development teams in four out of five providers adopted this instrument as a regular supporting tool to perform the product scoping in bespoke information systems.

7   Conclusions and Future Work

This work proposes an interactive visual instrument, which involves a canvas and a flexible collaborative dynamic, to perform scoping of bespoke information systems. On the one hand, the canvas represents a shared space that allows customers and providers to jointly define the product scope. On the other hand, the collaborative dynamic guides the scoping process in order to help them reach an agreement on the product scope.

The instrument was used in three projects performed in Chile and three projects in Brazil. The empirical results show the instrument was perceived as cost-effective by the participants. Moreover, they think that the instrument can help them govern the product evolution in the short and mid-term.

The future work considers evaluating the proposed instrument in more software companies, and also in various evolution projects of a same bespoke information system.

Acknowledgment. The research work of Anelis Pereira-Vale has been funded by ANID - Subdirección de Capital Humano/Doctorado Nacional/2021-21211216, Chile. We want to express our gratitude to those who contributed significantly in this study. Thanks for their dedication and valuable comments.

References

1. Bass, J.M., Haxby, A.: Tailoring product ownership in large-scale agile projects: managing scale, distance, and governance. IEEE Softw. **36**(2), 58–63 (2019). https://www.doi.org/10.1109/MS.2018.2885524
2. Bonfim, V.D., Benitti, F.B.V.: Requirements debt: causes, consequences, and mitigating practices. In: The 34th International Conference on Software Engineering and Knowledge Engineering, (SEKE 2022), KSIR Virtual Conference Center, USA, July 1–July 10, 2022, pp. 13–18. KSI Research Inc. (2022). https://www.doi.org/10.18293/SEKE2022-114
3. Boulila, N., Hoffmann, A., Herrmann, A.: Using storytelling to record requirements: elements for an effective requirements elicitation approach. In: 2011 Fourth International Workshop on Multimedia and Enjoyable Requirements Engineering (MERE 2011), pp. 9–16 (2011). https://www.doi.org/10.1109/MERE.2011.6043945
4. Breiner, K., Gillmann, M., Kalenborn, A., Müller, C.: Requirements engineering in the bidding stage of software projects – a research preview. In: Fricker, S.A., Schneider, K. (eds.) REFSQ 2015. LNCS, vol. 9013, pp. 270–276. Springer, Cham (2015). https://doi.org/10.1007/978-3-319-16101-3_19
5. Carvallo, J.P., Franch, X., Quer, C.: Requirements engineering for COTS-based software systems. In: Proceedings of the 2008 ACM Symposium on Applied Computing, SAC 2008, pp. 638–644. Association for Computing Machinery, New York (2008). https://www.doi.org/10.1145/1363686.1363839
6. Cerpa, N., Verner, J.M.: Why did your project fail? **52**(12) (2009). https://www.doi.org/10.1145/1610252.1610286
7. Davis, A., Dieste, O., Hickey, A., Juristo, N., Moreno, A.M.: Effectiveness of requirements elicitation techniques: empirical results derived from a systematic review. In: 14th IEEE International Requirements Engineering Conference (RE 2006), pp. 179–188 (2006). https://www.doi.org/10.1109/RE.2006.17
8. Lauesen, S., Vium, J.: Communication gaps in a tender process. Requirements Eng. **10**, 247–261 (2005)
9. Maciel, C.P.C., de Souza, E.F., de Almeia Falbo, R., Felizardo, K.R., Vijaykumar, N.L.: Knowledge management diagnostics in software development organizations: a systematic literature review. In: Proceedings of the XVII Brazilian Symposium on Software Quality (SBQS 2018), pp. 141–150. Association for Computing Machinery, New York (2018). https://www.doi.org/10.1145/3275245.3275260
10. Mairiza, D., Zowghi, D., Gervasi, V.: Utilizing TOPSIS: a multi criteria decision analysis technique for non-functional requirements conflicts. In: Zowghi, D., Jin, Z. (eds.) Requirements Engineering. CCIS, vol. 432, pp. 31–44. Springer, Heidelberg (2014). https://doi.org/10.1007/978-3-662-43610-3_3
11. Miro: Online whiteboard tool. www.miro.com. Accessed 12 Jan 2024
12. Müller, C., Koch, M., Adam, S.: Elicitation of information needs in precontract requirements engineering. In: Joint Proceedings of Workshops, Research Method Track, and Poster Track co-located with the 21st International Conference on Requirements Engineering: Foundation for Software Quality (REFSQ 2015), Essen,

Germany, 23 March 2015, CEUR Workshop Proceedings, vol. 1342, pp. 77–82. CEUR-WS.org (2015). https://ceur-ws.org/Vol-1342/02-re4p2.pdf

13. Ochoa, S.F., Robbes, R., Marques, M., Silvestre, L., Quispe, A.: What differentiates Chilean Niche software companies: Business knowledge and reputation. IEEE Softw. **34**(3), 96–103 (2017). https://www.doi.org/10.1109/MS.2017.64

14. Oemig, C.: When analysts turn into boxers: an introduction to pre-sales requirements engineering. Complex Syst. Informatics Model. Q. **3**, 1–14 (2015)

15. Pereira-Vale, A., Perovich, D., Ochoa, S.F.: Understanding the pre-contract process of small software projects. In: The 35th International Conference on Software Engineering and Knowledge Engineering (SEKE 2023), KSIR Virtual Conference Center, USA, 1–10 July 2023, pp. 146–151. KSI Research Inc. (2023). https://www.doi.org/10.18293/SEKE2023-016

16. Savolainen, P., Ahonen, J.J., Richardson, I.: When did your project start? - the software supplier's perspective. J. Syst. Softw. **104**, 32–40 (2015). https://www.doi.org/10.1016/j.jss.2015.02.041

17. Shaw, M.: Software architectures for shared information systems. In: Technical Report CMU/SEI-93-TR-003. Software Engineering Institute. Carnegie Mellon University (1993). https://insights.sei.cmu.edu/library/software-architectures-for-shared-information-systems/. Accessed 12 Jan 2024

18. Tuape, M., Iiyambo, P., Kasurinen, J.: Organizational governance: resolving insufficient practice and quality expectation in small software companies. In: The 3rd European Symposium on Software Engineering (ESSE 2022), Rome, Italy, 27–29 October 2022, pp. 17–24. ACM (2022). https://www.doi.org/10.1145/3571697.3571700

19. Vera, T., Ochoa, S.F., Perovich, D.: Requirements engineering in the pre-contract stage: exploring the processes and practices used in small and medium-sized software enterprises. In: Proceedings of the 36th Annual ACM Symposium on Applied Computing (SAC 2021), pp. 1346–1353. Association for Computing Machinery, New York (2021). https://www.doi.org/10.1145/3412841.3442009

20. Vera, T., Perovich, D., Ochoa, S.F.: An instrument to define the product scope at preselling time. In: 2021 IEEE 24th International Conference on Computer Supported Cooperative Work in Design (CSCWD 2021), pp. 604–608 (2021). https://www.doi.org/10.1109/CSCWD49262.2021.9437717

Is This Comment More Relevant?
Understanding the Structural Aspects of Relevance in Comment Sections

Jan Steimann[ID], Markus Brenneis[✉], and Martin Mauve

Heinrich Heine University, Universitätsstraße 1, 40225 Düsseldorf, Germany
Markus.Brenneis@hhu.de

Abstract. What makes a user comment relevant for readers? In this paper, we investigate the structural aspects of user comments as they appear e.g. in the comment sections of news media websites. While other studies already have examined the deliberative quality of user comments across different media, it is not yet well understood how the structural features influence the perceived relevance of a comment. Our goal is to develop an understanding of the influence of various structural aspects like position and different kind of justifications on the perceived relevance of user comments. We approach this question by means of a user study. For this, we ask the participants to decide which of the shown user comments is more relevant in comparison with others. Our study shows that the perceived relevance follows some intuitive rules, e.g. adding more justifications increases the relevance. On the other hand, some results were also surprising, like simple statements without any insights are considered relevant by the users. Our results should support the development of proper metrics and algorithms for comment recommendation systems by providing an additional understanding.

Keywords: Recommender Systems · Comment Recommendation · Information Systems · Humand-Centered Computing

1 Introduction

Discussions in comment sections of news agencies are a popular way to participate in the public debate about a topic. Here, users have the opportunity to state their opinion about the topic of an article and, in the best case, engage in a constructive discussion about their opinion. However, this best case is fairly seldom to see and many discussions become a shouting match or an echo-chamber over time.

For this reason, users need a way to identify relevant contributions which provide new points of view or represent different arguments within the discussion. This task of news article and comment recommendation has been widely examined in the past and various studies have presented interesting and promising approaches.

H. Mori and Y. Asahi (Eds.): HCII 2024, LNCS 14689, pp. 264–278, 2024.
https://doi.org/10.1007/978-3-031-60107-1_19

However in the field of computer science, many approaches for developing new algorithms rely on labeled data-sets where the comment relevance is assessed only on the content level [6,9,11,20]. For example, in [19] the dataset contains scores for how relevant a given comment is on the content level for a specific article and these scores are then used to evaluate the performance of the model.

While these are proven and effective approaches to develop and evaluate new algorithms, assessing the relevance of a comment on the content level is a very difficult task. Each person weighs argumentation differently based on their experience, background, and political orientation. Especially in the context of comment recommendation, there is most likely more than one relevant comment that would be a good recommendation for a given discussion. This makes it even more difficult to develop a robust model that can assess the relevance of comments.

Therefore, we believe that the development of future recommendation algorithms can benefit from a deeper understanding of the structural aspects of what makes a user comment more relevant than another. Studies like [7,13] have already examined the deliberative quality of comments from the structural composition of a comment. [13], for example, has used these structural aspects to compare the deliberative quality of comments across different media and in contiguous discussions. However, it remains to investigate how these features influence the perceived relevance of a single comment in comparison with others.

Does a comment become more relevant if we add more structural features like sources or alternatives? Which features need to be present so that a comment is considered relevant at all? Do some features affect the relevance more than others?

We try to answer these questions through a user survey in which we asked participants to compare comments that state the same opinion but differ in one structural aspect. Then, they had to decide which comment is more relevant than another. For example, all comments state that they like chia seeds very much for breakfast. However, one comment justifies its opinion and we expect that the participants will assess this comment as more relevant than the other comments. With the results of this survey, we want to support the development of future algorithms by providing a deeper understanding of comment relevance backed by human intuition.

In the following section, we take a look at the previous work in this field. In the third section, we outline the different characteristics of a comment we have examined in this study. Afterwards, we explain the methods we used to conduct the survey and to evaluate the results. In the last section before the conclusion, we present the results and interpretation.

2   Related Work

The topic of online commenting has been widely studied from different fields and point of views like computer science, journalism, and computational linguistics [2,12,13,18,21].

Here, users exchange their views on the content of news articles and engage in debates with others. However, the quality and relevance of these comments varies significantly, with some comments being highly informative and insightful, while others being irrelevant or even harmful. Many studies have investigated these aspects and tried to provide an explanation when and how a comment is relevant, a high quality contribution, or harmful in the debate. One example is the tone of the debate. [4] investigates the comment section of news agencies to better understand when and why incivility occurs. The authors found that especially in discussions with a lively debate, incivility was less common. Furthermore, not all incivility is the same for every user. [10] states that people detect and approve incivility differently depending on whether it coincides with their views. This supports our argumentation from Sect. 1 that assessing comment relevance on the content level is a difficult task. Furthermore, some studies [8,13] have even shown that the quality and relevance of a comment differs between different media. In comparison comment sections on news organization sites showed a greater deliberative quality than their online presence on social media like Facebook [13].

This shows that it is worth to consider a wider range of influencing factors in addition to labeled datasets when assessing the quality and relevance of a comment. Future algorithms should consider these influences.

For example, [22] studied the effect of message factors on user comments intention and behavior. On the one hand, they found that certain factors like *aggression, incivility,* and *drifting off-topic* increase the likelihood that other users respond in a similar tone, heating up the discussion. On the other hand, deliberative discussion factors like *question* or *additional knowledge* reduce the likelihood of incivility and drifting off-topic in the discussion. This underpins our argumentation that understanding the structural aspects that make one comment more relevant than another is crucial, highlighting the need for better understanding in this area.

Previous recommendation approaches in the field of computer science use content and word-relation features focused approaches for recommending highly relevant comments [1,17,19]. [17] for example uses various textual and discourse relation features like *article length, average number of verbs per sentence,* etc. and an annotated dataset where the annotators had to judge whether a comment was relevant for the given article and whether the comment was thoughtful. [19] uses a data-set with different level of relevance for the news and comments and [1] four different categories for the comment article pair like *Relevant, Same Entities, Same Category,* and *Irrelevant.* All these approaches use an efficient and proved way for developing recommendation algorithms. However, they focus on content and word-relation features and every study uses a different dataset for the problem which makes it difficult to assess how universal there approaches are. Thus, with the results of our survey, we do not want to provide another labeled dataset, but a deeper understanding of the structural aspects of what makes a user comment more relevant than others backed by the human intuition. These aspects are separated from the content level and therefore are not affected by the context of the discussion. We believe that future approaches can develop more robust recommendation models by combining our findings with labeled datasets.

3 Relevance Characteristics for Comments

We now introduce how we model a comment to determine its relevance. We will later compare it against the human intuition of our participants in our survey. The features of this model are based on previous research on this topic [7,13].

3.1 Relevance Characteristics

We now take a look at characteristics of a relevant comment. Our definition is mostly based on [13].

Necessary Characteristics. For a comment to be considered relevant at all, we believe the following necessary characteristics have to be present.

Topic: First and foremost a relevant comment has to address the topic of the discussion. This seems rather obvious, however certain comments only address the topic of the discussion at first glance and then derive to a completely different topic, driving its own agenda. These comments are considered irrelevant by us.

We differentiate two types of topic relevance. First, the *Structuring Topic* which argues about the topic of the discussion e.g. the article addresses the expansion of wind power plants and the comment argues about the unreliability of wind power. Second, we have the *Interactional Topic* which treats a slightly different topic that is however still relevant in the context of the discussion. For example, in a discussion about nuclear power plants, arguments about other forms of power generation are often invoked and provide additional information or perspectives. *Instead of nuclear power plants, we should use wind power plants because...*

Position: Relevant comments have to express their position on a give issue, otherwise they just repeat information already stated in the article or other comments like *Solar power panels are a possibility to generate power.* Though, we want to support the public debate by presenting new point of views to think about to the user and for this the comment has to state a position towards the topic of the discussion.

Justification: Relevant comments have to justify their position. This allows others to judge *the authority of the better argument* [7]. If we only present a selection of positions to the user without any justification, the user would be unable to compare the benefits and downfalls and therefore, it would be much harder to consider the different positions.

Optional Characteristics. In our model the following characteristics are not necessary for a comment to be relevant. However, they can be used to support the justification and by this increase the relevance of the comment. We expect that the different optional characteristics do not contribute equally to the relevance of the comment. In the following, the features are presented in order of their expected relevance for the comment.

Personal Story: Comments can overcome communicative barriers by invoking personal stories. These barriers often arise through a lack of knowledge or about complex issues. A personal story helps to overcome these barriers by warping the complex issue in a more comprehensible form [14]. This is the reason why we expect the personal story to be the most relatable and therefore most relevant additional feature. For example: *I am against the reform of the administration because it will do more harm than good. I work in an administration myself and after the reform the responsibilities were unclear and no one felt responsible for the critical decisions which then have not been made.*

Example: Similar to the personal story, the example uses a concrete situation to make a complex or abstract argumentation more comprehensible. The main difference to the personal story is the missing personal aspect. Nevertheless, we expect the example to be equally relevant as the personal story. For example: *American football is not a more dangerous sport than others. It is only much more prominent in the news. For example, we don't hear about surfers drowning or climbers falling, but these sports can be much more dangerous than football.*

Alternative: Comments that attempt to provide a solution to the problem at hand by offering an alternative are considered more relevant than comments that provide additional sources because they offer another point of view on the topic. Nevertheless, we expect this characteristic to be not as relevant as the example and personal story because the alternative solution is not as relatable as a personal story or example. For example *I reject the conclusion of the article that we need to replace all old houses with more energy-effective homes. The demolition of the old and construction of a new house is far more energy intensive that just modernizing old houses that are still in good shape.*

Source: By using and referencing additional sources comments provide users with the opportunity to verify the quality and validity of their justification and by this making the comment more relevant. Nevertheless, we expect this characteristic to be the least relevant feature because sources refer to external material which the users need to consider while the other characteristics provide all their information at hand.

Remember that not all of these characteristics are necessary so that a comment is considered relevant. However, at least a comment needs to address the *topic, position,* and *justification* dimension to be relevant in our context and therefore provide new point of views on the topic of the discussion and by this fuel the public debate. The remaining dimensions support the *justification* and make a comment more relevant.

Nevertheless, we did not incorporate all quality dimensions which come to mind in terms of comment relevance like *interaction* or *asking questions*, mentioned in [13]. This is because paper like [13] focus on comments only in the context of contiguous discussions where the deliberation occurs through the interaction of participants by referring or responding to each other. However, in the context of comment recommendation such comments that refer to others are not always that relevant as in the context of the contiguous discussion they have been published. Yet, the comments we are interested in, have to be relevant in connection with the topic of the discussion while at the same time have to be understood isolated. We want to incorporate comments from various discussions and news agencies to provide multiple perspectives on the discussion. Therefore, if the comments are only understood in the context of their original discussion, they are not relevant for us.

3.2   Example

An example for a relevant comment[1] in a discussion about solar power panels as a renewable energy source could look like this:

> Everyone with their own house should install solar plant panels to power their house. (**Position and Topic**)
> You get free power all the year and during the day you power the neighborhood with clean energy helping the environment. (**Justification**)
> For example, you could install them on your garage and power your electric car with it. (**Example**)
> I had solar plant panels installed years ago, with an estimated payback of 15-17 years. However, we also acquired two electric cars and charge them at home. The savings in gasoline alone took the solar system payback down to under 3 years. (**Personal Story**)
> Additionally, as explained here: *www.somewebsite.com*, sun and wind power are not "too unreliable". The sun is only unreliable if we look from a local point of view. It is always shining on half of the earth at any given time. If the world were connected into a single electrical distribution network, the sun would be perfectly reliable all the time.(**Sources**)
> And even if you don't own a house and live in a rental apartment, you can rent portable solar panels to reduce your energy consumption from your power supplier. (**Alternative**)

4   Methods

In this section, we explain how we developed our hypotheses to check if our characteristics for a relevant comment match the perception of humans. We

---

[1] The example is based on these comments: https://nyti.ms/327zNHC#permid=107994755, https://nyti.ms/3tYGpVa#permid=107994566.

developed a questionnaire with scenarios for every hypothesis, and participants of the survey were asked to compare the displayed comments and decide which of the given comments was more relevant or most relevant. In order to achieve a higher information value for our results and to avoid any biases that might occur towards certain topics, we have used different topics with pro and contra position. For every hypothesis one topic with the pro and contra position was randomly chosen. Every participant had to answer all 14 hypothesis which results in 14 topics and 28 comments for every participant.

We selected two more neutral topics *Chia Seeds* and *Boosting the Immune System* and two more controversial topics *Solar Power Panels* and *American Football*. The reason for this is that we want to know if our relevance characteristics apply for neutral topics as well as more controversial topics where many users have a strong opinion. Even if some users assess some comments based on their personal opinion, we can still get valuable data for our hypotheses. For example, if a user is heavily biased against solar power panels and is not open to any arguments in favor of them, we have always an opposing argument for the same topic which they will most likely assess not biased.

The comments we use for our study are all based on comments we extracted from real conservation's in comment sections and have been transformed and reshaped into building blocks so that we can present the same comment that differs in exactly one structural feature to the participants. This way, we can clearly associate the results with a certain characteristic. If we would use the comments as they appeared in the comment sections, it would be difficult to present the same comment with exactly one different structural feature because these comments use them intertwined with each other. For example, a comment might combine its position towards the topic with its justification. Therefore, we would need to find a different comment with exactly the same position that differs exactly in this specific structural characteristic. However, then we could not differentiate if the results are based on the additional characteristic or the different writing style of the two comments.

Before the users started with the survey, we presented them with a definition what makes a comment more relevant than another comment. For this, the comment has to *provide a more thoughtful or elaborate perspective in the discussion than the other comment*. This definition is the essence of our definition for a relevant comment from Sect. 3. We believe that a comment becomes more relevant the more it elaborates its position on the given topic with justifications and additional characteristics like personal stories, sources, examples, or alternatives. At the same time the definition which we presented to the participants of our survey must not be too detailed to prevent us from influencing the participants to much.

The complete list of hypotheses is in Table 1. At first, we were interested in the minimal requirements for a comment to be considered relevant. Afterwards, we examined how a comment becomes more relevant, either by adding more justifications or by supporting the justification with additional characteristics. Then we asked ourselves if there exists an order between the different characteristics that support the justification. For example, do users tend to consider a personal story more relevant than supporting the argumentation with additional sources? Additionally, we asked our self if a comment becomes more relevant if we provide more supporting characteristics of the same type or if these are of lower importance the user.

As an example, we now present how Hypothesis 4 *(A comment becomes more relevant if it backs up its justification with sources, a personal story, an alternative, or an example)* has been developed and transformed in a questionnaire scenario.

We were interested whether adding a supporting characteristic like a personal story or sources to an existing comment, adds more relevance to the comment. Therefore we can assume in future metrics or recommendation models that if a comment contains an additional characteristic, it can be considered more relevant than the same comment without.

From our hypothesis, we constructed the following comments where the users should answer different questions like *Is Alice's comment more relevant than Bob's?* to determine which comment is more relevant:

Alice writes:
Everyone with their own house should install solar power panels.

Bob writes:
Everyone with their own house should install solar power panels because they provide you with free energy.

Charlie writes:
Everyone with their own house should install solar power panels because they provide you with free energy.
However, even if you don't own a house you can rent solar panels and install them on your balcony to reduce your electricity bill.

We expect that *Charlie's* comment is the most relevant one because he additionally provides an *alternative solution* for the topic at hand. We added the other comment to prevent biases in the answers.

We created the questions and scenarios for the remaining hypotheses in the same way.

Table 1. Our hypothesis about the structural aspects of relevance in comment sections.

#	Hypothesis
H1	*A comment needs to address the topic, take a position towards the topic, and provide a justification to be relevant.*
H2	*A comment with an interactional topic will be considered relevant, but not as relevant as a comment with structuring topic.*
H3	*Providing more than one justification makes a comment more relevant than one justification.*
H4	*Backing up the justification with additional characteristics like sources, personal stories, alternatives, or example makes the comment more relevant.*
H5	*Providing more than one additional characteristic makes the comment more relevant.*
H6	*Using an alternative instead of a source makes the comment more relevant.*
H7	*Using a personal story instead of an alternative makes the comment more relevant.*
H8	*Using an example or a personal story makes the comment equally relevant.*
H9	*A comment with an alternative is more relevant than the same comment with sources, but less relevant than a comment with a personal story or an example.*
H10	*Providing more than one source makes the comment more relevant.*
H11	*Providing more than one personal story makes the comment more relevant.*
H12	*Providing more than one alternative makes the comment more relevant*
H13	*Providing more than one example makes the comment more relevant.*
H14	*A comment with an example is equally relevant as a comment with a personal story. But example and personal story are more relevant than an alternative.*

5   Results

In the following section, we present our results of the survey. For the evaluation, we used the method presented in [3] where we report the p-value for the null hypothesis H_0 that *Our expected answer is not the most frequently (relative frequency) given answer.*[2]

We conducted the survey with Amazon Mechanical Turk. We are well aware that MTurk needs to be treated with caution due to bots and randomly clicked answers by the workers. For this reason we used several carefully developed control questions to ensure that only qualified worker participate in our survey. Of the 82 participants of our survey, only 36 answered enough control questions correctly to meet our quality standards. These 36 workers had an median age of 30–39 years, and 15 men and 21 women participated.

Furthermore, we should note that our sample of worker is not representative for the US population, and even less world wide and the sample size is insufficient to assert the universality and representatives of our findings. Consequently, we cannot completely generalize our results and have to use them with caution. Nevertheless, the insights we gathered offer valuable contributions to enhance the understanding and develop an intuition regarding the structural aspects of relevance for future studies and recommendation algorithms.

However, our results confirmed our most important hypotheses and we also made some surprising findings. In the next section, we will talk about the hypotheses that were confirmed and afterwards, we discuss the remaining results. Additionally, a figure of our results can be found in our data repository[3].

Before proceeding, as we explained in Sect. 4, we ensured that there is no bias due to the chosen topics. To validate the absence of such a bias, we computed the average percentage of expected answer for all hypotheses and questions related both neutral and controversial topics.

Our analysis revealed no significant differences between the results obtained from the controversial and neutral topics. The average percentage of expected answers for neutral topics was 52%, while for controversial topics, it was 50%. These results underscore the consistency of our results and reaffirm its suitability for drawing unbiased conclusions.

5.1 Results that Confirmed Our Hypotheses

In hypothesis H2, we wanted to investigate how user assess the relevance of a comment that states a position with an interactional topic in comparison with a comment that provides a structuring topic. An interactional topic addresses a slightly different topic, which is still relevant in the context of the discussion, while a structuring topic matches the subject of the discussion. For H2, the expected answer was given by 56% of the participants with a p-value of 0.02. This strongly supports our hypothesis that the interactional topic is considered more relevant than a comment that just states a position towards the topic and

---

[2] We used an intersection-union test [16] with a one-tailed z-test on the variance of the two multinomial proportions [5,15], i.e. H_0 is that the differences of the relative answer frequencies between the expected answer and the other answers is not greater than 0.

[3] https://github.com/hhucn/Comment-Relevance-Survey-Results.

slightly less relevant than a comment with a topic that is a little bit more on point.

An essential aspect for us was to understand if we can make a comment more relevant by additively adding more structural aspects to the comment or if the relevance is perceived in a different way that does not allow an additive consideration.

To check this property we started with hypothesis H3, where we investigated if a comment becomes more relevant if we add more than one justification to the comment. The expected answer was given by 61% of the participants (p<0.001), which strongly suggests that our hypothesis is true.

Afterwards we tried to understand what makes a justification more relevant. For this, we have explored if a comment becomes more relevant if the justification is supported by additional characteristics like a personal story, alternative solution, sources, or an example (H4), or if the users do not perceive these as separate building blocks and focus only on the content of the comment. 61% provided us with the anticipated answer (p = 0.006), which confirms our hypothesis that a comment becomes more relevant if we support the justification with additional characteristics.

The logical step is to investigate if the idea of hypothesis 3 applies also to the justification and we can make it more relevant by additively adding more characteristics to the justification (H5). This was confirmed (58%, p = 0.001).

Following, we have investigated the additional characteristics in more detail. We wanted to find out if the users recognise more than one additional characteristic of the same type as separate entities or just as a larger single entity. This would have different consequences for the perceived relevance of the comment because e.g. providing different examples for a justification gives a comment more credibility than just a single example. First, we provided more than one additional source (H10) and received the expected answer by 61% (p < 0.001) which confirms our hypotheses with a high confidence. Next, we investigated if providing more than one personal story makes a comment more relevant (H11), which was confirmed (55%, p-value = 0.012). Afterwards, we did the same for the alternative (H12) with 52% providing the expected answer (p-value = 0.034).

5.2   Unexpected Results

After we have discussed the results that confirmed our hypotheses, we now examine the results that surprised us or where further investigations are needed.

First and foremost in our survey, we wanted to understand if there exists a structural threshold from which a comment can be considered relevant. Our hypothesis was that a comment needs to contain certain features to be considered relevant (H1). First, the comment needs to address the topic of the article and state a position towards it and second it needs to justify its position. We thought that especially the justification is crucial for a comment to be considered relevant because it allows users to judge the different argumentations. However, the expected answer was given only by 39%; whereas 58% considered the comment that just states a position towards the topic relevant. This indicates that the users set the threshold for a relevant comment much lower than we expected. Thus, it is still necessary to examine in more detail at what point users classify a comment as relevant at all.

Subsequently, we investigated the additional characteristics for the justification. As we explained in Sect. 4, we wanted to understand if there exists an order of relevance for the different additional characteristics like personal story, example, alternative solution, and sources. For example, is a personal story more relevant than sources because the personal story helps the users to comprehend a complex issue by wrapping it in a relatable story? However, the results indicate that the users did not perceive some additional characteristics more relevant than others. In H6, we investigated if a comment with an alternative is more relevant than a comment with sources. Here, only 31% selected the alternative as the most relevant comment. In H7, we investigated if a personal story is more relevant than an alternative (expected answer by 43% for the personal story). In H8, we expected that a personal story and an example are equally relevant. However, only 38% gave the expected answer. In H9, we directly compared the personal story, alternative, and sources, and supposed that the personal story is the most relevant comment, the alternative the second most relevant, and the sources the least relevant of the three comment. However, only 30% gave the expected answer. In the last hypothesis (H14), we put the personal story in direct comparison with an example where we assumed that they are equally relevant because they only differ in the personal component (expected answer by 21%). However, the results indicate that the comment with the personal story is perceived as the most relevant (51%) which is contrary to the results of hypothesis H9 where the comment with the personal story was not the most relevant one. Therefore, a more detailed investigation here is needed.

The last hypothesis which was not confirmed was H13. Here, we investigated if a comment becomes more relevant if we provide more than one example. Here, only 47% considered the comment with two examples more relevant, though, 47% indicate that the comment was indeed perceived slightly more relevant.

6 Discussion

After examining the results of the survey, many hypotheses were confirmed. First and foremost, it could be confirmed that we can increase the relevance of a comment by additively adding more structural features like sources, personal story, etc. independent of the content of the comment. We also gained a deeper understanding how additional characteristics like sources, personal story, example, or alternative solution influence the perceived relevance of a comment. For example, we can confirm that the user perceive a comment as more relevant just by adding more than one personal story or source.

However, some results were unexpected and need further investigation. The most unexpected result is that users perceive the threshold for when a comment is relevant much lower than expected. Many user considered a comment as relevant even if it only addresses the topic of the article. We assumed that a comment needs to state a position towards the topic and justify it to be considered relevant. This is a very interesting result and needs to be investigated in more detail to find out where the user draw the line for when a comment is not considered relevant any more or whether this is to subjective to have a threshold here.

Most of the other not confirmed hypotheses focus much more on the details of the structural characteristics like if a personal story is more relevant than sources. Here, we expected that e.g. a personal story is considered more relevant than sources because the personal story wraps a complex issue in a comprehensible format that can be processed more easily.

Still, most of our key hypotheses were confirmed with a high significance. Our main point was to see if we can increase the relevance of a comment by adding more structural features like one or more justifications or making a justification with e.g. a personal story more compelling.

As explained in Sect. 5, we are well are that our results are not completely generalizable due to our limited worker sample and artificial setting. However, we still gathered some valuable insights which help to develop a better intuition regarding the structural aspects of comment relevance.

7   Conclusion and Future Work

In this study, we have conducted a survey with human participants about the structural aspects of comment relevance in news agency comment sections. Our results help to deepen the understanding of comment relevance and provide an additional angle for the development of more sophisticated machine learning and recommendation models. Most of our important hypotheses were confirmed and we showed that we can increase the relevance of a comment additively by adding more structural aspects like justifications. We were also able to improve the justification of a comment by adding additional characteristics like personal story, alternative, example, or sources.

However, some of our hypotheses were not confirmed, e.g. the threshold when a comment is considered relevant is much lower as we expected. Second, we tried to understand if there is an order between how much relevance the additional characteristics could add to the relevance of a comment. For example, we assumed that a personal story makes a comment more relevant than sources.

Nevertheless, this does not automatically mean that there is no just order, but more research is needed here. In future work, we will refine our results and investigate the hypotheses that were not confirmed. Here, it will be of great interest to understand if there exists a threshold for a comment to be considered relevant or if this is too subjective. Another interesting aspect will be to investigate the additional characteristics in more detail.

Yet, with the results that confirmed our hypotheses, we can use these new insights in comment relevance for the development of future comment recommendation algorithms that consider both content and structural aspects for the recommendation.

References

1. Alshehri, J., Stanojevic, M., Dragut, E., Obradovic, Z.: Stay on topic, please: aligning user comments to the content of a news article. In: Hiemstra, D., Moens, M.-F., Mothe, J., Perego, R., Potthast, M., Sebastiani, F. (eds.) ECIR 2021. LNCS, vol. 12656, pp. 3–17. Springer, Cham (2021). https://doi.org/10.1007/978-3-030-72113-8_1
2. Ben-David, A., Soffer, O.: User comments across platforms and journalistic genres. Inform., Commun. Society **22**(12), 1810–1829 (2019)
3. Brenneis, M., Mauve, M.: Do I Argue Like Them? A Human Baseline for Comparing Attitudes in Argumentations. In: Fazzinga, B., Furfaro, F., Parisi, F. (eds.) Proceedings of the Workshop on Advances in Argumentation in Artificial Intelligence 2020, pp. 1–15. No. 2777 in CEUR Workshop Proceedings, Aachen (Nov 2020). http://ceur-ws.org/Vol-2777/paper21.pdf
4. Coe, K., Kenski, K., Rains, S.A.: Online and uncivil? patterns and determinants of incivility in newspaper website comments. J. Commun. **64**(4), 658–679 (2014)
5. Franklin, C.H.: The 'margin of error' for differences in polls (2007). https://abcnews.go.com/images/PollingUnit/MOEFranklin.pdf
6. Gao, M., Do, H.J., Fu, W.T.: Burst your bubble! an intelligent system for improving awareness of diverse social opinions. In: 23rd International Conference on Intelligent User Interfaces, pp. 371–383 (2018)
7. Habermas, J.: The structural transformation of the public sphere: An inquiry into a category of bourgeois society. MIT press (1991)
8. Hille, S., Bakker, P.: Engaging the social news user: Comments on news sites and Facebook. Journal. Pract. **8**(5), 563–572 (2014)
9. Hoque, E., Carenini, G.: Convisit: Interactive topic modeling for exploring asynchronous online conversations. In: Proceedings of the 20th International Conference on Intelligent User Interfaces, pp. 169–180 (2015)
10. Muddiman, A., Stroud, N.J.: News values, cognitive biases, and partisan incivility in comment sections. J. Commun. **67**(4), 586–609 (2017)
11. Mullick, A., Ghosh, S., Dutt, R., Ghosh, A., Chakraborty, A.: Public sphere 2.0: targeted commenting in online news media. In: Azzopardi, L., Stein, B., Fuhr, N., Mayr, P., Hauff, C., Hiemstra, D. (eds.) Advances in Information Retrieval: 41st European Conference on IR Research, ECIR 2019, Cologne, Germany, April 14–18, 2019, Proceedings, Part II, pp. 180–187. Springer International Publishing, Cham (2019). https://doi.org/10.1007/978-3-030-15719-7_23
12. Reimer, J., Häring, M., Loosen, W., Maalej, W., Merten, L.: Content analyses of user comments in journalism: a systematic literature review spanning communication studies and computer science. Digital Journalism, pp. 1–25 (2021)
13. Rowe, I.: Deliberation 2.0: Comparing the deliberative quality of online news user comments across platforms. J. Broadcast. Electron. Media **59**(4), 539–555 (2015)
14. Ryfe, D.M.: Narrative and deliberation in small group forums. J. Appl. Commun. Res. **34**(1), 72–93 (2006)
15. Scott, A.J., Seber, G.A.: Difference of proportions from the same survey. Am. Stat. **37**(4a), 319–320 (1983)
16. Silvapulle, M.J., Sen, P.K.: Constrained statistical inference: Order, inequality, and shape constraints. John Wiley & Sons (2011)
17. Swapna, G., Jiang, J.: Finding thoughtful comments from social media. ACL (2012)
18. Weber, P.: Discussions in the comments section: Factors influencing participation and interactivity in online newspapers' reader comments. New media society **16**(6), 941–957 (2014)

19. Wei, H., Zheng, W., Xiao, Y., Dong, C.: News-comment relevance classification algorithm based on feature extraction. In: 2021 International Conference on Big Data Analysis and Computer Science (BDACS), pp. 149–152. IEEE (2021)
20. Zhou, M., Shi, R., Xu, Z., He, Y., Zhou, Y., Lan, L.: Design of personalized news comments recommendation system. In: Zhang, C., et al. (eds.) ICDS 2015. LNCS, vol. 9208, pp. 1–5. Springer, Cham (2015). https://doi.org/10.1007/978-3-319-24474-7_1
21. Ziegele, M., Johnen, M., Bickler, A., Jakob, I., Setzer, T., Schnauber, A.: Male, hale, comments? factors influencing the activity of commenting users on online news websites. Stud. Commun. Media 2(1), 110–114 (2013)
22. Ziegele, M., Weber, M., Quiring, O., Breiner, T.: The dynamics of online news discussions: effects of news articles and reader comments on users' involvement, willingness to participate, and the civility of their contributions. Inform., Commun. Society 21(10), 1419–1435 (2018)

A Study to Prevent People from Using a Smartphones at Bedtime with ASMR

Madoka Takahara[1]([✉]), Shunsuke Nishimura[1], and Shun Hattori[2]

[1] Ryukoku University, Kyoto, Japan
takahara@rins.ryukoku.ac.jp
[2] The University of Shiga Prefecture, Hikone, Japan

Abstract. With the widespread use of smartphones, smartphone addiction has become a social problem. In addition, people who are absorbed in cell phones, e-mail, and games after going to bed wake up and stay up late. Therefore, in this study, we developed a system that restricts smartphone usage before bedtime using an independent sensory climax response (ASMR) to prevent the use of a smartphone before bed to address the above problem. This study investigated the effectiveness of this system in preventing smartphone use before bedtime.

Keywords: ASMR · Smartphone-in-bed · Smartphone Addiction

1 Introduction

A "Smartphone-in-bed" or bedtime smartphone refers to a smartphone used before sleeping. Many people use their bedtime smartphones to engage in activities such as reading e-books, watching videos, or browsing social media content before going to bed. Smartphone addiction causes sleep disorders such as "not getting enough sleep" and "waking up at night" (1). In addition, in March 2014, the Ministry of Health, Labour and Welfare of Japan issued a sleep guideline for health promotion, stating that after going to bed, people who are absorbed in cell phones, texting, or playing games wake up, and after going to bed, light stimulation for a long time can promote wakefulness and cause people to stay up late, so it is important to pay attention to these factors. Frequent late-night waking can cause a shift in the body clock, leading to irregular sleep schedules and nighttime sleep (2). It is important to be mindful of screen time and to consider implementing strategies to promote a healthier sleep routine.

To address this problem, this study developed a system that restricts smartphone use before bedtime using an Autonomous Sensory Climax Response (ASMR) to improve sleep duration, sleep quality, and prevent sleep-smurfing before falling asleep. The effectiveness of the system in preventing smartphone use before bedtime was also investigated.

H. Mori and Y. Asahi (Eds.): HCII 2024, LNCS 14689, pp. 279–288, 2024.
https://doi.org/10.1007/978-3-031-60107-1_20

2   Conventional Method

2.1   ASMR

ASMR (Autonomous Sensory Meridian Response) is an abbreviation for "Autonomous Sensory Meridian Response," and refers to a tingling sensation that occurs in the scalp, back of the neck, and sometimes other parts of the body due to visual and auditory stimulation by specific sounds and videos. The term 'tingling sensation' refers to a feeling of relaxation and well-being. This sensation is widely reported to be accompanied by a sense of relaxation and happiness (4). (4) Uchida et al. (2021) analyzed the effects of ASMR on brain activity and mood states using Profile of Mood States (POMS), an electroencephalogram (EEG) measuring device, and reported that when ASMR sensation was felt, the mood state decreased in liveliness, the tense region increased in the EEG, and the relaxation and sleepiness values decreased. The ASMR used in this study is a type of ASMR used to measure the mood of the brain and the brain activity of Subjects. (5) The ASMR used in this study contains an element of "1/f fluctuation.

In a study by Arai et al. (2019), physiological measurements have demonstrated that the throaty sounds produced by cats have a relaxing effect on people. In this study, the relaxation effect will be used to promote falling asleep before going to bed.

2.2   1/f Fluctuation

It is known that intermittent sounds in nature, such as heartbeats and raindrops, which appear to have a fixed interval, are not constant but have irregular deviations. The power spectrum of these fluctuations, which is inversely proportional to the frequency, is called 1/f fluctuation. This 1/f fluctuation is said to have a healing effect by producing brain waves (alpha waves) that appear when people relax. In this study, it was considered that the 1/f fluctuation was effective in inducing sleep based on the above effects.

2.3   Fitbit and Sleep Efficiency

Fitbit is a watch-type activity meter manufactured by Fitbit, Inc. That measures the number of steps taken, calories consumed, sleep status, heart rate, and so on (Fig. 1).

Fig. 1. Smart watch "Fitbit".

In this study, in addition to sleep information such as sleeping time, the HF/LF ratio, which is a stress index, was obtained using heart rate data, and the effects of cat's purring sound on the body and mind were observed.

In this study, sleep efficiency was used as experimental data. Sleep efficiency was calculated as "actual sleeping time ÷ time spent in bed × 100," which is the ratio of time spent in bed to the time slept.

2.4 Stress Index LF/HF

The HF (High Frequency) wave is related to respiration and has a period of about 3–4 s, while the LF (Low Frequency) wave is related to blood pressure variability with a period of about 10 s, called Mayer wave, and is related to sympathetic nerve activity.

Stress is defined as the state of balance between sympathetic and parasympathetic nerves. Based on this, it is possible to assess the balance between the sympathetic and parasympathetic nervous systems from the heart rate, and to grasp the state of stress and relaxation.

In this study, LF/HF is calculated using the heart rate measured by Fitbit, and whether the user is relaxed or not is determined by ASMR.

2.5 Related Works

Ichikawa and Nishida (2015) proposed the following application to prevent people from using smartphones before going to bed (3).

The application is a using a smartphone before going to bed when all the following four conditions are met: the time is nighttime, the surroundings are dark, the smartphone is being operated, and the posture is that of a sleeper in bed. By creating a calendar that visualizes the results of the judgment of sleeping smart phones and the user's physical condition, we proposed an application that displays a warning when the user is sleeping on a smartphone and makes the user stop sleeping on a smart phone, informs the relationship between whether the user is sleeping on a smart phone and the user's physical condition the next morning, and encourages the user to acquire knowledge about sleeping on smart phones. An application that pro-motes the acquisition of knowledge regarding using a smartphone before going to bed is proposed.

Also, the purpose of this study is to promote the induction to sleep by adding a cat's purring sound to the judgment result of the sleeping with smartphone. In addition to the warning display, we also aimed to introduce the cessation of smartphone use due to emotions toward cats by playing a sound as ASMR that cats dislike (threatening sound).

3 Proposed Method

3.1 The Structure of the Proposed System

An image of the proposed system structure is as shown in Fig. 6. The proposed system includes a function to prevent sleeping smart phone, a function to play ASMR (Fig. 2).

The principle of the concept of sleep-smartphone prevention using cat sounds is described below.

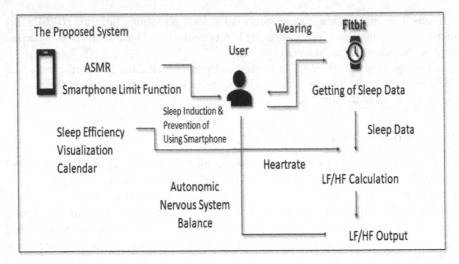

Fig. 2. An image of the system structure.

- **Sleep Smartphone Prevention**

    While the user is using the application, the cat's voice advises the user to use the smartphone, thereby restricting the use of the smartphone and preventing the user from using the smartphone before going to bed.

- **Support for falling asleep**

    While the application is advising the user to use a smartphone, it plays a cat's purring sound to calm the user's heart rate and help the user fall asleep.

    The following figure is the image of the proposed system.

3.2 The Application of the Proposed System

3.2.1 Sleeping Smartphone Prevention Application

This is an application created with Swift UI and usable on iPhone. From the title, you can navigate to five screens. Each screen is described below.

This screen plays the "cat's purring sound" and restricts the use of the smartphone. The smartphone's tilt is detected using the smartphone's gravity acceleration sensor to detect whether the smartphone is being lifted or not.

If the system determines that the smartphone is not being lifted, it plays a "cat's purr" sound. If it determines that the smartphone is being lifted, the background of the screen turns red and a cat's warning sound is played along with the words "Do not use the smartphone" (Figs. 3 and 4).

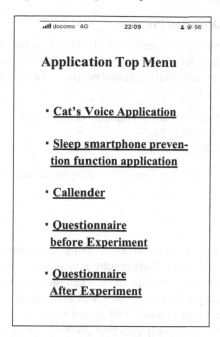

Fig. 3. An image of the proposed system.

Fig. 4. An image of the proposed system when the user use the smartphone.

3.2.2 LF/HF Ratio Calculation Program

We created a Python program to measure LF/HF based on the heart rate measured by Fitbit. It measures the state of relaxation and excitement based on the heart rate fluctuation and observes the effects of cat's purring sound on the body and mind.

The output LFHF ratio is:

o Low value: 0 to less than 0.8 (parasympathetic dominance)
o Standard value: 0.8 to less than 2.0
o High: 2.0 to less than 5.0 (sympathetic dominance)

The standard value is 0.8 to less than 2.0 (parasympathetic predominant).

4 Experiment

In this study, an experiment was conducted using the proposed system under the following conditions with the aim of preventing people from sleeping on their phones.

We conducted a comparison experiment between the case of using the screen of the application to prevent sleeping smart phones and the case of using the screen of the cat's voice to investigate two questions: "Did the cat's purring sound encourage users to fall asleep" and "Did preventing sleeping smart phones shorten the time until users fell asleep".

4.1 Participants

Participants: 6 male and 6 female (4 males in their 20 s, 1 female in her 20 s, 1 female in her 50 s).

4.2 Experimental Period

The experiment was conducted for three weeks.

4.3 Experimental Rules

- **Definition of facilitating users' falling asleep**
  Based on the results of the questionnaire obtained after the experiment, the following questions were asked: "Did the user feel it was easy to fall asleep?"; "Did the cat's purring sound shorten the time to fall asleep?" by comparing Fitbit sleep data; "Was the LF/HF ratio value low? The results were evaluated according to whether the LF/HF ratio was low and how many low values were obtained.
- **Definition of whether the time it took users to fall asleep was reduced**
  The results of the post-experiment questionnaires were used to evaluate "whether the user felt the effect of the sleep smart phone prevention" and the sleep time data obtained from Fitbit were used to evaluate "whether the time until falling asleep was shortened".

4.4 Experimental Results

4.4.1 "Was the Cat's Purring Sound Able to Promote Users to Fall Asleep?"

In the post-experiment questionnaire, two Participants (Participant 1 and Participant 5) answered that they went to bed using the "cat's voice" application in response to the question, "Which of the three bedtime methods did you find easiest to fall asleep with? In addition, three Participants answered, "Sleeping with the cat's voice" in response to the question "Which of the three bedtime methods made it the most difficult to fall asleep?

In the post-experiment questionnaire, two Participants (Participant 1 and Participant 5) answered "Sleeping with the cat's voice application" in response to the question "Which of the three sleeping methods made it easiest for you to fall asleep? The Participants who answered that they went to bed using the "cat sound" application gave the following reasons: "Because it made me feel safe" and "Because I felt it was easier to fall asleep than in the silent state", while the Participants who answered that they went to bed without using the application gave the following reasons: "Because it is the same as usual", "Because it is the same as usual", "Because it is stress-free", and "Because it is the same as usual". The reasons given by the Participants who answered, "Sleep without using applications" were "Because it is the same as usual" and "Because it is stress-free.

In addition, three Participants (Participant 2, Participant 3, Participant 4, and Participant 6) answered "Sleeping with the cat's voice" in response to the question "Which of the three sleeping methods did you find the most difficult to fall asleep? Although there were Participants who felt that the cat's purring sound gave them a sense of security, the most frequent response was that it was the most difficult to fall asleep (4 Participants), and all Participants responded that it was "noisy" or "uncomfortable".

In the comparison of the time to fall asleep, all the Participants answered that sleeping with the "cat sound" application was longer than sleeping with the "sleeping smartphone prevention" application, and in the LF/HF ratio results, sleeping with the "cat sound" application was longer than sleeping with the "sleeping smartphone prevention" application. Therefore, the cat's purring sound disturbed sleep induction users rather than encouraging them to fall asleep.

The median time to fall asleep for the "Sleeping with 'Cat's Voice' application" and the "Sleeping with 'sleep smartphone prevention function' application" were compared on a weekly basis, and the results showed that the recordings for the "Sleeping with 'Cat's Voice' application" exceeded those for the "Sleeping with 'sleep smartphone prevention function' application" for all Participants. The results showed that the median sleep time was higher than the median sleep time for all Participants.

Figure 5 shows the results of a comparison of the median values of the "LF/HF of time to fall asleep" between "sleeping with the 'cat's voice' application" and "sleeping with the 'sleep smartphone prevention function' application," based on Fitbit sleep time records for each week.

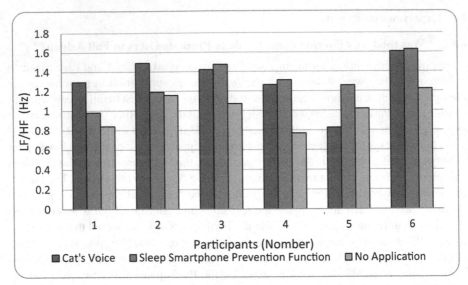

Fig. 5. Graph comparing the average "LF/HF of time to fall asleep" of "going to bed using the "Cat's Voice" application" and "going to bed using sleep smartphone prevention function application", ", and "sleeping without the application" per week.

4.4.2 "Did Preventing Sleeping with Smartphones Shorten the Time Until Users Fell Asleep?

The result of the answer to the question "Did you feel the effect of preventing sleeping smart phones?" in the questionnaire after the experiment was completed was "Yes, a little" for five Participants (Participant 1, Participant 2, Participant 3, Participant 4, and Participant 6), and "Yes, a lot" was selected by one Participant (Participant 5).

Figure 5 shows the results of a comparison of the median values of the "time to fall asleep" between "sleeping with the 'cat's voice' application" and "sleeping with the 'sleep smartphone prevention function' application," based on Fitbit sleep time records for each week.

All Participants answered the question "Did you feel the effect of the anti-sleeping with smartphone?" in the post-experiment questionnaire. As for the fact that the time to fall asleep was not shortened only for Participant 6, he answered "No" to the question "Do you use your smartphone when you go to bed? We believe that this is because they do not usually use a smartphone in their sleep, and the effect of preventing sleeping smart phones was not readily apparent in the results.

This suggests that the sleep smartphone prevention was effective in inducing sleep onset for users who routinely use their smartphones when falling asleep.

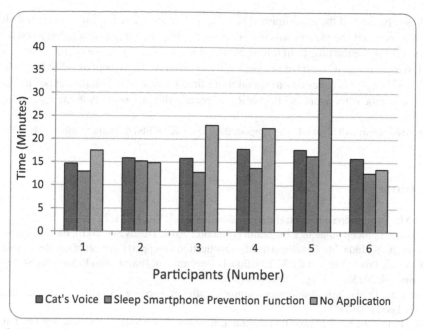

Fig. 6. The graph compares the average time to fall asleep per week for the three sleeping methods: "Sleeping with the application 'Cat's Voice'", "Sleeping with the application with sleep smartphone prevention function", and "sleeping without the application".

5 Discussion

5.1 About the Time Before Falling Sleep

As for the result of the number of days on which sleep time increased after the system was introduced compared to before the system was introduced, we believed that the time spent on the smartphone before the system was added to the sleep time as well as the time before falling asleep, which was reflected in the results.

5.2 About Sleep Efficiency

Although the time until falling asleep decreased, since sleep efficiency was calculated based on the time spent in bed, the time spent in bed after waking up was included in addition to the time until falling asleep. Therefore, the time spent in bed after waking up after the introduction of the system was longer than before the introduction of the proposed system, and the results of this study are the result of the introduction of the system.

6 Conclusion

In this experiment, we developed a system to restrict smartphone use before bedtime using ASMR to prevent and eliminate the time spent sleeping on smartphones before falling asleep.

A comparison of the experimental results, such as time until falling asleep and sleep time, showed that the system was able to prevent sleeping smartphones, lengthen sleep time, and improve the time until falling asleep, which was the purpose of this experiment.

However, because we have not been able to observe the effects of ASMR on sleep, mind, and body, it is necessary to spend more time on research in future experiments to demonstrate the effectiveness of ASMR and review the proposed system.

Acknowledgments. This work was supported by JSPS KAKENHI (grant number 20K13787).

References

Kajita, M.: Smartphone addiction (Internet addiction). Sci. Vis. **34**(3), 73 (2013)

Uchiyama, M.: Sleep guidelines for health promotion 2014. Trends Sci. **20**(6), 68–71 (2015)

Ichikawa, A., Nishida, M.: Development of an application to support the habit of not sleeping smart phone. In: Proceedings of the 77th National Convention of Information Processing Society of Japan, vol. 2015, no. 1, pp. 4-887–888 (2015)

Barratt, E.L., Davis, N.J.: Autonomous sensory meridian response (ASMR): a flow-like mental state. PeerJ (2015)

Uchida, I., Fukutsuka, S., Yano, T., Yoshimura, K.: Effects of ASMR on brain activity and mood states. J. Sci. Technol. **10**(2), 179–184 (2021)

Automated Diagnostics and Its Advantages of AI in Mental Health

Min Yang$^{(\boxtimes)}$ and Hirohiko Mori

Tokyo City University, 1 Chome-28-1 Tamazutsumi, Setagaya City, Tokyo, Japan
{g2291404,hmori}@tcu.ac.jp

Abstract. In a fast-paced urban life and an increasingly competitive environment, social pressures are increasing and people cannot help but put the pressure on themselves. When the external pressures and the internal expectations are too great, it becomes difficult to strike a balance between the two, and the depressive factors in the body become activated. If the bad mood can be resolved in time or medical attention can be sought, recovery is quick, but if it is left unchecked, it often leads to tragedies such as self-harm or suicide. The advent of the big data era has enabled the processing and application of large amounts of data on the Internet and the application of natural language processing technology, and there is a trend toward further developing psychological health diagnostics in the face of this booming technology. This paper is about the prospects for automated diagnostics in mental health with AI and its advantages. Examples of chatbots created in the past for detecting signs of depression. And it gives examples of existing AI application scenarios in mental health and their benefits.

Keywords: Mental health · Automated diagnosis · AI · Artificial Intelligence in Psychology · Benefits of Artificial Intelligence in Psychology

1 Background

1.1 Preface

In today's global society, where technology is developing rapidly, it can be said that the Internet has become one of the most important tools in people's lives. People cannot stay away from the convenience brought by the Internet. Through the Internet, people can obtain various knowledge necessary for their daily lives and studies, and people also keep in touch with each other and exchange information through the Internet. The advent of the big data era has enabled the processing and application of large amounts of data on the Internet and the application of natural language processing technology, and there is a trend toward further developing psychological health diagnostics in the face of this booming technology [1].

Especially since the New Crown epidemic, secondary disasters at the psychosocial level have attracted widespread attention, and the demand for psychological counseling, psychological intervention, and psychological assistance has skyrocketed. In conflict with the vast market demand, there is an extreme shortage of existing mental health

© The Author(s), under exclusive license to Springer Nature Switzerland AG 2024
H. Mori and Y. Asahi (Eds.): HCII 2024, LNCS 14689, pp. 289–299, 2024.
https://doi.org/10.1007/978-3-031-60107-1_21

treatment resources at home and abroad. In the face of such a social problem that affects the mental health of many people, can the power of science and technology play a role? If artificial intelligence intervenes in the field of mental health, what possibilities and changes will it bring? [2].

This paper is about the prospects for automated diagnostics in mental health with AI and its advantages. In this paper we will discuss the mental health issues towards the current society and the role of using AI in mental health and will give examples of current applications in psychology.

1.2 Research Background

In a fast-paced urban life and an increasingly competitive environment, social pressures are increasing and people cannot help but put the pressure on themselves. In particular, many white-collar workers in companies and firms, as well as students preparing for higher education or employment, are said to be more prone to depression. Depression is becoming a modern social disease. When the external pressures and the internal expectations are too great, it becomes difficult to strike a balance between the two, and the depressive factors in the body become activated. If the bad mood can be resolved in time or medical attention can be sought, recovery is quick, but if it is left unchecked, it often leads to tragedies such as self-harm or suicide.

According to the "Patient Survey" [3] conducted every three years by the Ministry of Health, Labor and Welfare on medical facilities nationwide, the total number of patients with depression and other mood disorders increased from 433,000 in 1996 to 1,041,000 in 2008, a 2.4-fold increase in 12 years. In 1998, the number of suicides, which had been hovering in the low 20,000s per year until then, exceeded 30,000. Since then, the number has remained at a high level exceeding 30,000 [3]. The current situation is that those who are potentially depressed and, moreover, those who have some mental problems but are unable to make appropriate responses are not being adequately addressed. On the other hand, in order to improve mental illness, it is necessary to rely on specialists such as doctors and counselors, but the current situation of insufficient resources of specialists in relation to the number of workers requires new means of self-help for everyone to reduce stress at the same time.

2 Related Research

2.1 About Mental Health

Mental health, also known as spiritual health, refers to a state of psychological happiness and tranquility, "the psychological state of a person whose emotions and behavioral adjustments are operating quite well" [4]. From a positive psychology or holistic perspective, mental health also includes a person's ability to enjoy life and achieve a balance among various activities and efforts in life to achieve psychological flexibility.

According to the definition of the World Health Organization (WHO), mental health includes "subjective well-being, a sense of personal efficacy, autonomy, interaction with other people, and the ability to realize one's intellectual and emotional potential" [5].

The World Health Organization further states that personal happiness includes realizing one's abilities, being able to overcome the stress in daily life, working productively, and contributing to the group [6]. Cultural differences, subjective assessments, and many related professional theories all affect the way "mental health" is defined [5]. Another definition of mental health was proposed by psychoanalyst Sigmund Freud: "the ability to work and love" [7].

2.2 About AI

AI is an abbreviation for Artificial Intelligence. Computers analyze data and make inferences (obtaining new conclusions based on knowledge), judgments, optimization proposals, problem definition and solutions, and learning (finding knowledge that can be used in the future from information), etc. refers to technology that imitates the intellectual abilities of people. AI receives information from sensors, images, text, sounds, etc., and processes it using algorithms that mimic intellectual abilities [8].

There is no clear definition of AI (artificial intelligence) in market and industrial products, but research on artificial intelligence can be broadly divided into two categories. One is "research aimed at creating machines with human intelligence," and the other is "research aimed at making machines do what humans do using their intellectual abilities." Most of the research being conducted is said to be the latter [8].

3 Research Objective

The argument of this article is the role of AI in mental health treatment and consultation, and lists the current applications at home and abroad and our own research system. The systematic justification of our own research is not based on medical findings (CONTENTS) as in the past, but more on signs that can be detected from the content and style of users' writing. For example, depressed people use too many negative mood words, especially negative adjectives and adverbs; depressed people use a lot of first-person singular pronouns. All these can be seen as the writing style of depressed people. It can be seen as a major characteristic of depression, in this case indicating less interest in others. The objective of this study is, therefore, to automatically extract the signs of depression from the chat texts, and to use these features to detect signs of depression from the chat texts. The chatbot detects predictive signs of depression through the user's writing style in daily conversations with the user, we aim to enable people with signs of depression to be advised to see a doctor at an early stage.

4 Artificial Intelligence in Psychology

4.1 Therapeutic Video Games

Video games can be used for mental health care purposes such as skills training, behavioral modeling, and therapeutic distraction. Therapeutic benefits include increased patient engagement and improved adherence to treatment. Therapeutic video games can also help adolescents improve their self-confidence and problem-solving skills. AI technologies have appeared in many commercial video games and have recently been applied to online and social networking games. AI and machine learning technologies applied to video games have enhanced the realism of the games, making them more interesting, challenging, and entertaining. For example, Brigadoon.

Brigadoon. Brigadoon is a virtual environment in Second Life designed for people with autism spectrum disorders that allows users to interact with in-game avatars in order to learn and practice social skills in a non-threatening environment [14].

4.2 Chatbot

A chatbot is a computer program that converses through dialogue or text. They can simulate human conversation and have passed the Turing Test. Chatbots are systems that automatically respond to text or voice input from humans. The first chatbot in history was ELIZA [9]. ELIZA was an attempt to create a program that would imitate a clinical treatment psychologist and make it seem as if a live person was chatting with another human being.

The mental health field utilizes advanced technology to help patients in need, and chatbots (chatterbots) are one example. A chatbot is a computer program that engages in conversation via dialogue or text. In the mental health field, a chatbot is a program that allows users to access therapeutic or emotional support services. It has been used for psychosocial support for refugee populations, often using the principles of Cognitive Behavioral Therapy (CBT). For example, Woebot and Detecting Signs of Depression for Using Chatbots.

Detecting Signs of Depression for Using Chatbots. In this system, we believed that by using SNS, which is used as a communication tool in daily life, users do not need to download a separate application, and by using a chatbot, we could give users a sense of being talked to and interested in others. We thought that we could use chatbots to give users a sense of being talked to and a sense of interest in others. Therefore, a predictive depression detection system provided as a chatbot using the SNS platform WeChat [10] (Fig. 1).

In this system, we collect online conversation data of depressed patients and speech data of depressed patients and build a corresponding knowledge base, where the user's session enters the knowledge base, the semantically closest answers also get matching, and the answer replies are extracted, which is called a depression We're designing a chatbot system for predictive disease detection. In a dialogue with the user, keywords are extracted from the user's utterances. The system extracts keywords from the user's utterances and draws conclusions by matching them with predictive signs of depression in the knowledge base and draw conclusions in correspondence with the knowledge base of predictive signs of depression [10].

The argument of this system is not based on medical findings (CONTENTS) as in the past, but more on signs that can be detected from the content and style of users' writing. For example, depressed people use too many negative mood words, especially negative adjectives and adverbs; depressed people use a lot of first-person singular pronouns. All

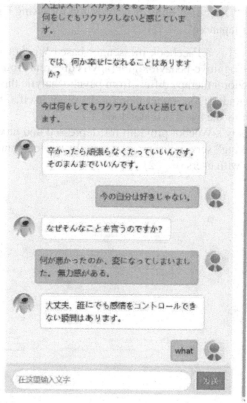

状況

うつ病の予兆を持つ確率: 0%

うつ病の予兆がない

アンケートとチャットの一致率 69%

Fig. 1. Detecting Signs of Depression for Using Chatbots

these can be seen as the writing style of de-pressed people. It can be seen as a major characteristic of depression, in this case indicating less interest in others. The objective of this study is, therefore, to automatically extract the signs of depression from the chat texts, and to use these features to detect signs of depression from the chat texts. The chatbot detects predictive signs of depression through the user's writing style in daily conversations with the user, we aim to enable people with signs of depression to be ad-vised to see a doctor at an early stage [10]. For a detailed description of this system, please see the paper "Detecting Signs of Depression for Using Chatbots-Extraction of the first person from Japanese".

Woebot. Woebot [12] is a Facebook messenger-based Woebot is based on cognitive behavioral therapy. Cognitive-behavioral therapy is different from psychoanalytic therapy. Cognitive-behavioral therapy differs from psychoanalytic therapy in that it focuses on how the event is understood, rather than on the event itself. The focus is not on the event itself, but on how the event is understood.

Stanford University's Woebot program for depressed and anxious college students offers a "mood tracking" service to improve mood symptoms and can engage in text-based conversations with users (Fig. 2).

Fig. 2. Woebot [13]

4.3   Psychological Aids to Diagnosis

Psychological disorders are a common group of mental illnesses, such as depression, anxiety, and obsessive-compulsive disorder. Traditional psychological diagnosis usually requires the judgment and experience of a doctor. However, with the development of artificial intelligence technology, more and more algorithm-based psychological diagnostic tools are appearing in the market. These tools usually automatically recognize the user's emotional state and characteristics based on the user's input information, such as self-assessment questionnaires, and provide appropriate suggestions and support. For example, the Detecting Signs of Depression for Using Chatbots mentioned earlier can assess whether the user's psychological state is an omen of depression through the daily dialog between the user and the robot, and provide corresponding emotional support or guide the user to a psychiatrist for more in-depth diagnosis and treatment.

4.4 Wristwatch Wearable Devices

Various parameters can be calculated from the data acquired by each sensor. For example, acceleration, number of steps, calories consumed, amount of conversation, sleep duration, sleep quality, and pulse rate can be obtained. The measured data is automatically uploaded to the cloud, analyzed, and sent to a medical institution. For example, SWIFT system.

SWIFT System. The "SWIFT System" aims to provide an objective indicator for the diagnosis of depression by comprehensively evaluating various biometric and activity data obtained from multiple sensors mounted on the device to evaluate depressive symptoms, which have been difficult to assess with a single indicator [11]. The device used in the SWIFT System, "Silmee," is a wristwatch-type wearable device sold by TDK Corporation [11] (Fig. 3).

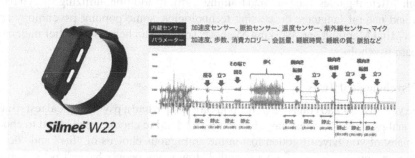

Fig. 3. Example of acceleration data acquired by Silmee [11]

4.5 Mental Health and Complementary Therapies

Artificial intelligence can be used to assist in mental health assessment and treatment. For example, through voice and text sentiment analysis, AI technology can help psychologists assess a patient's mental state and provide personalized treatment recommendations. Meanwhile, virtual reality technology combined with AI can create virtual environments for exposure therapy and cognitive-behavioral therapy to help people overcome fear, anxiety, and other psychological disorders.

4.6 Attention and Cognitive Enhancement

By utilizing techniques from artificial intelligence and machine learning, tools can be developed that can assist with attention and cognition. For example, AI technologies can use biofeedback to help people train and improve concentration, or adaptive systems to optimize the learning process by providing customized learning materials and feedback based on an individual's learning style and needs [15].

4.7 Emotion Recognition and Emotional Intelligence

Artificial intelligence technology can help recognize and understand human emotional states. By analyzing voice, facial expression and physiological data, AI can identify human emotional states, including mood, psychological stress and anxiety. This technology has potential for psychological research, clinical diagnosis and the development of emotionally intelligent systems.

4.8 Popularization of Psychological Knowledge

The popularization of mental health awareness and the dissemination of psychological knowledge have always been important goals in the field of psychology [16]. Artificial intelligence technology has also played an important role in this regard. For example, some psychology educational apps based on AI technology, such as CogniFit Brain Health Platform and BrainHQ, can improve users' cognitive and emotional abilities through different games, quizzes, and trainings [16]. In addition, utilizing speech recognition and natural language processing technologies, some popular psychology apps, such as Mind Mapping and Working Memory Trainer, can help users better understand and learn psychology.

4.9 Psychological Tests

Maybe you haven't had counseling, but odds are you've had a psychological test. But the traditional psychological test has a fatal bug – it's hard to choose, really hard to choose. How many of you haven't gotten lost in the ambiguous choices of "fits" and "doesn't fit", "doesn't quite fit" and "fits very well"? How many people haven't been confused by these ambiguous options? Such a rigid and dogmatic approach to psychometric tests not only makes it difficult to choose, but also makes it difficult to believe that the results are accurate and true.

The one who knows you best is not necessarily this kind of stereotypical psychological test, but most likely it is the "chatting partner" beside you who has nothing to say. Experiments have shown that psychometric scenarios constructed over time through conversations are more accurate, and that's what intelligences do best [17]. You don't need to deliberately recall your own action track, you don't need to rack your brain to judge whether it fits or doesn't fit, you just need to chat with the intelligent body more often, and it will be able to make more accurate judgments through semantics.

5 Benefits of Artificial Intelligence in Psychology

5.1 24-Hour Immediate Response

I'm afraid it's difficult for even the closest of relationships, not to mention counselors, to be on call 24 h a day. But AI can. AI intelligences can provide 24/7 psychological support, instantly responding to the user's needs and establishing a strong "connection" with the person. Whether it is late at night depression, the intelligent body can give users the timeliest feedback, by judging the semantics of the user, to give the most accurate "customized psychological guidance". Thus, those late-night feelings that have no place to rest have a place to return to from now on.

5.2 Breaking Down Psychological Barriers for Users

The biggest controversy about the application of AI in the field of mental health is that, after all, AI is not a real person and cannot have human empathy. But on the other hand, not being a real person is exactly where AI intelligences have an advantage. Patients in the face of counselors, out of shame, often will not dare to reveal their true selves, but also afraid of counselors will reveal their secrets. Many patients have said that they will habitually disguise themselves as a "good boy" in front of the counselor, not daring to show their inner darkness [17]. However, in the face of the intelligent body will not have such concerns, the user can completely let down their guard, show their true self, which is also conducive to the follow-up intelligent body and counselor according to the actual situation, to provide more accurate guidance program. At the same time, through the encryption and desensitization of data, there is no need to worry about the intelligent body will leak, to protect the user's privacy and security.

5.3 Provide More Stable Services

Another advantage of artificial intelligence is that there will be no negative emotions. As a psychological counselor who needs to face different visitors every day and receive negative emotions from different directions, the psychological pressure must be enormous. When the counselor suffers from too much negative emotions but is unable to channel them, it will also affect the visiting patients, resulting in a vicious circle. However, artificial intelligence is not affected by negative emotions, which means it can provide more stable services.

5.4 Get More Customers at a Low Cost

The same AI can serve thousands of consultants at the same time. This will not only solve the structural problem of imbalance between supply and demand, but the service price will also be significantly lower than the traditional model, which will be more easily accepted by the majority of patients and stimulate the vitality of the demand side. Counselors are expected to receive more customer orders, the demand side and the supply side to achieve a virtuous cycle, in order to solve the dilemma of the mental health industry.

6 Conclusion

In summary, artificial intelligence has made great progress in psychology research. With the continuous application of AI, the advantages it brings will be more and more reflected in psychology. Through the application of AI technology, psychologists and therapists can diagnose and treat psychological disorders more accurately, manage and discover a large amount of data on psychological disorders more effectively, and find breakthroughs and innovations from it step by step. It can help clinical psychologists make more accurate diagnoses and provide better treatment plans for patients. In the future, AI has a broader development prospect.

Overall, AI has great potential in mental health treatment and counseling. Through automation, intelligence and personalization, AI brings many new opportunities and challenges to the mental health field. As the technology continues to evolve and improve, it is believed that AI will be able to better serve the mental health needs of users. Artificial Intelligence is not an illusion; it is deeply integrating with mental health service scenarios. Looking to the future, perhaps more people who were originally struggling with psychological difficulties will find inner strength in the company of intelligent bodies. The harmonious integration of technology and human nature will also continue to open up new possibilities for mental health services.

7 Future Tasks

There are several important aspects to the future challenges of AI and psychological health.

1. Protection of personal information and ethical considerations: When AI is used in the field of psychological health, it is extremely important to protect patients' personal information and privacy. Furthermore, from an ethical perspective, patients' interests and well-being must be given top priority.
2. Reliability and accuracy: When AI is used to aid in diagnosis and treatment, its reliability and accuracy are essential. Inaccurate information or diagnosis can harm patients. Therefore, the development and operation of AI systems requires rigorous testing and monitoring.
3. Collaboration with humans: AI can be a powerful tool in the medical field, but collaboration with human experts is essential. Human insight and empathy can make up for what AI lacks. Therefore, collaboration between AI and humans is important.
4. Bias and diversity: AI systems can be biased if the training data is biased. In the field of psychological health, biases against people from different cultures and backgrounds are highly influential. Therefore, efforts must be made to minimize bias by training with diverse datasets.

Addressing these challenges will allow AI to be used more beneficially in the field of psychological health and contribute to patient care.

References

1. Zheng, X., Lu, Y., Deng, H., et al.: Study on chat robot based on crowd-sourcing. Inf. Technol. 4(19), 102–103, 109 (2017)
2. https://baijiahao.baidu.com/s?id=1772913560738790166&wfr=spider&for=pc
3. MHLW. https://www.mhlw.go.jp/seisaku/2010/07/03.html. Accessed 20 Jan 2023
4. Mental Health. WordNet Search. Princeton University (2017)
5. The World Health Report 2001. Mental Health: New Understanding, New Hope (PDF). WHO (2017)
6. Mental Health. World Health Organization (2014)
7. Freud, S.: Das Unbehagen in der Kultur, p. 101. Internationaler Psychoanalytischer Verlag Wien (1930)

8. AI. https://www.keyence.co.jp/ss/general/iot-glossary/ai.jsp
9. Weizenbaum, J.: ELIZA—a computer program for the study of natural language communication between man and machine. Commun. ACM **9**(1), 36–45 (1966)
10. Yang, M.., Mori, H., et al.: Detecting signs of depression for using chatbots--extraction of the first person from Japanese. In: Human Interface and the Management of Information, pp. 660–671 (2023)
11. Development of a Wearable Device to Support Objective Diagnosis of Depression: A Case Study of Collaboration with i2medical, LLC and Keio University School of Medicine. https://fbo-sumitomo-pharma.com/ja/collaboration/i2medical.html
12. Woebot. https://baike.baidu.com/item/Woebot/20844627?fr=aladdin. Accessed 20 Jan 2023
13. Woebot Health. https://woebothealth.com/covid-19/
14. AI and Mental Health. https://mp.weixin.qq.com/s?__biz=MzA3NzIxNDQ3MQ==&mid=2650323526&idx=3&sn=be7f37cad21a644f3fe8e9fd41d0ec02&chksm=87597c2eb02ef5383eceb6c9f86a7b06adfaa52458c5c8cfc801b399ee1ed130bc16184b41de&scene=27
15. Artificial Intelligence as an Interdisciplinary Field of Application in Psychology. https://baijiahao.baidu.com/s?id=1774201465267369862&wfr=spider&for=pc
16. The Use of AI in Mental Health. https://wenku.baidu.com/view/ea3a0c22306c1eb91a37f111f18583d049640ffb.html?_wkts_=1706371063370&bdQuery=ai%E5%9C%A8%E5%BF%83%E7%90%86%E5%81%A5%E5%BA%B7%E4%B8%AD%E7%9A%84%E5%BA%94%E7%94%A8
17. AI+Mental Health. https://baijiahao.baidu.com/s?id=1772913560738790166&wfr=spider&for=pc

Proposal on the Application Design Method of Aging-Friendly Smart Home System Based on User Experience Under Health Needs

Jiaqi Zhang[1], Keiko Kasamatsu[1], and Takeo Ainoya[2]([✉])

[1] Tokyo Metropolitan University, 6-6 Asahigaoka, Hino, Tokyo, Japan
22964602@ed.tmu.ac.jp
[2] Tokyo University of Technology, 5 Chome-23-22 Nishikamata, Ota City, Tokyo, Japan
marcoux.aude_marie@courrier.uqam.ca

Abstract. Smart home systems provide a lot of convenience for contemporary people's daily lives, and the popularity of smart homes is increasing yearly. However, the experience design of existing smart home systems for elderly users is still deficient, and the current age-friendly smart home systems lack user experience design guidelines for application design. Therefore, this study conducted an in-depth investigation of existing application design application roaches by investigating the overview of theories related to smart home systems and user experience elements, an in-depth study of the five-layer model of user experience elements, as well as combining the systematic application characteristics of smart home applications, and collecting user needs through user interviews, and dividing the needs of elderly users from strategic to performance layers through the user experience elements model. Finally, a competitor analysis was conducted to understand the problems that users have with similar products and to help establish the strategic positioning of the product. The study will provide new user experience design guidelines from different perspectives of application design. The study will improve the developers' design efficiency and further enhance the users' experience, thus creating a comfortable, safe, and free smart home life mode for the elderly.

Keywords: User Experience · Aging-Friendly · Health Needs

1 Introduction

A smart home refers to a residence furnished with a communication network, sensors, household devices, and appliances that can be remotely identified, accessed, monitored, and controlled, these devices can provide services and respond to the residents' needs either autonomously or upon user intervention [1].

Continuous breakthroughs in artificial intelligence technology have led to the introduction of more and more smart home products, and more and more users are slowly accepting smart homes. Smart home products are usually designed to allow users to control and collect data by exchanging information with their

H. Mori and Y. Asahi (Eds.): HCII 2024, LNCS 14689, pp. 300–313, 2024.
https://doi.org/10.1007/978-3-031-60107-1_22

smartphones. Currently, there are two main types of smart home products: the first is a traditional product that has been updated through the implantation of digital technology, and the second is a completely new product designed to fulfill a specific need. These two types of user experiences are completely different; the first improves existing habits, while the second provides a new way of operating and creates a new user experience [2]. This paper focuses on the second type of smart home products, such as smart home security products, smart home monitoring products, smart switches, smart lamps and lanterns, and other products. The market penetration of smart homes has been steadily increasing over the past few years due to the many conveniences that smart home products bring, with the global smart home market generating revenue of $20.38 billion in 2020 [3]. Although the smart home industry is constantly moving forward, but the product itself has not yet fully realized automatic control, APP is still an important way to control the use of smart home products. In terms of the author's own experience of use, the interactive interface of the app is too complex to operate. An interface that pursues more and more functions is unable to directly and quickly reach the functions that the user wants to use, and the fault tolerance rate is low. Young people are prone to frequent errors in the process of using the app, not to mention the elderly. Population aging has become one of the biggest social and economic challenges in the 21st century [4]. Advances in medicine and the popularization of the concept of public health services have increased the overall life expectancy of human beings, and in the next 50 years, the proportion of elderly people in the population will grow from the current 10% to 22% [5].

Smart homes allow the elderly to stay in the comfort of their home environment instead of expensive and limited medical facilities, healthcare professionals can also get real-time insights into the overall health of the elderly through the feedback from the smart home system, which not only provides feedback and support from a remote facility, but also provides more autonomy, efficiency, and ease of day-to-day operations for the user.

2 Background

2.1 APP of Smart Home System

APP is A mobile app (or mobile application) is a software application developed specifically for use on small, wireless computing devices, such as smartphones and tablets, rather than desktop or laptop computers. is a mobile application developed for user services [6] . With the rapid development of the Internet of Things, smart home product apps are also constantly being introduced to provide users with smarter and more convenient services.

2.2 Age-Friendly Smart Home System Apps

The new crown epidemic that began in 2020 has made more and more elderly people realize the importance of smart home systems, and some scholars have conducted research on the user interface of smart home product apps on the interaction mode. China's Liao Qinglin [7] and others through the emotional interaction experimental research, questionnaire analysis, comprehensive analysis of the data that the degree of emotional interaction between the user and the smart home products determines the degree of anthropomorphism of the smart home assistants, the degree of anthropomorphism of the voice assistant of the smart home products is directly proportional to the user's satisfaction. Zhou Wenxiang [8] analyzes the characteristics of communication and dialogue between people and puts forward the method of intelligent voice emotional interaction design, one is to perceive the user's emotional state, and the other is that the device automatically substitutes into the corresponding situation and gives the corresponding response, and through the above method, it provides the user with matching services and contents, meets the user's personalized needs, and improves the user experience.

Gavrila Cristinel [9] et al. utilize the combination of health detection devices and typical smart home products, and select smart TVs as the main interaction point to construct the initial architecture of health detection devices in home environments; Choi Yong K et al. [10] propose a voice-interactive smart home platform based on the feedback from older adults on future improvements or desirable features for health maintenance to support healthy aging and provide a strong support for the health of the elderly; Ferrero Renato [11] et al. analyzed the use of RFID technology with natural language interaction to enhance the product identification of smart refrigerators and integrated the Google Assistant development framework to allow the interaction of a smartphone with a smart refrigerator device, allowing connected devices to improve the daily problems of the home kitchen environment; and Zahid Muhammad [12] et al. in order to solve the important and common problem of human health detection, new materials such as textiles are applied to wearable devices, making sensor devices easy to integrate into daily life and suitable for integration with smart detection devices; Kailas Patil et al. [13] in the context of the increasing environmental degradation and keeping up with changes in the needs of the smart home, have proposed to smart systems that use renewable energy to monitor the health of the home environment.

Smart home products for the elderly and various IoT sensors have also been used in the home care of the elderly, sensors like cameras [14,15], floor sensors [16], and accelerometers [17,18]have been frequently used in previous studies to detect falls in the smart homes of the elderly. Biomedical sensors such as electrocardiogram (ECG) [19,20], body temperature [21,22], and galvanic skin response (GSR) [23,24]have also been used in smart homes to provide telemedicine monitoring for the elderly.

By organizing the study of age-appropriate smart home system apps, age-appropriate smart home system apps under health needs are slowly transitioning from a single product to a multi-product cross-use, and the elderly are interested in the scenario-based use of smart home systems, but the physiological, psychological, and behavioral and cognitive specialties of the elderly lead to more barriers to the use of smart home systems by the elderly. To improve this problem, this paper proposes a design method for apps of age-appropriate smart home products, which makes up for the lack of research in this direction and provides a reference for exploring the interaction of apps of age-appropriate smart home systems under health needs.

2.3 Elements of User Experience

Jesse James Garrett, in his book "Elements of User Experience", proposed a five-layer element model of user experience [25] (see Fig. 1.), from low to high, bottom up is the strategic layer, scope layer, structural layer, framework layer, and performance layer respectively [26], from the strategic layer to the performance layer of the division of the APP product from the abstract to the concrete a design process. The design of UX elements at each level corresponds to part of the scope and content of the APP design.

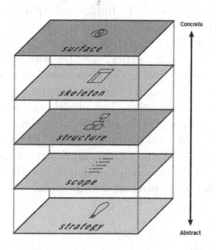

Fig. 1. Five-layer model of user experience elements

The user experience element model is divided into five layers, which are as follows:

- Strategy layer: Determine the product design goals and user target requirements.
- Scope layer: analyze the design goals and user requirements proposed by the strategy layer, and generate design opportunities.
- Structural layer: Setting up the distribution pattern of product information architecture and overall interaction design requirements.
- skeleton layer: Optimize the product's functions and operation flow.
- Performance layer: refine the final visual design according to the positioning of the overall product requirements.

Garrett's UX elements model has been widely used in the field of product design. For example, Zhang Ting and Peng Li [27]applied the model in the design of a non-heritage APP to enhance the value, reliability and ease of use of user experience; Xie Jiaying and Yuan Hao et al. [28] utilized the theory of the five elements of user experience to study the design strategy of a job search APP and carried out a specific design in practice, which provided a reference for similar applications; and Qian Xiaosong and Yang et al. [29], based on the principle of universal design, conducted a demand analysis on the Five Elements of User Experience conducted a demand analysis and designed a fully automated driving experience strategy for special user groups such as the elderly and the disabled, which not only provides theoretical support for automotive companies to enhance product competitiveness and social value, but also provides a reference for similar user experience design.

This model is refined based on the experience in Internet project development, and its five elements cover the entire product creation process from idea to realization. The model also unifies and integrates all stages of the product design process from strategy, scope to implementation, establishes clear design goals and processes, helps the development team avoid arbitrariness, and ensures that the functional design of the product meets the desired goals. This model not only helps design the product experience, but also effectively integrates the entire product design cycle. This model is refined based on the experience in Internet project development, and its five elements cover the entire product creation process from idea to realization. The model also unifies and integrates all stages of the product design process from strategy, scope to implementation, establishes clear design goals and processes, helps the development team avoid arbitrariness, and ensures that the functional design of the product meets the desired goals. This model not only helps design the product experience, but also effectively integrates the entire product design cycle.

3   User Research

3.1   Research Purpose

The purpose of the research in this paper is to understand the behavior and living habits of elderly users through the use of existing smart home system apps by the elderly, to obtain the user needs, and the problems of the current smart home products.

Research the four aspects of sensory characteristics, cognitive characteristics, emotional characteristics, and personality characteristics of the elderly to accurately locate the needs of elderly users.

Scenarios and problems encountered by elderly users when using smart home apps, and Factors Affecting Users' behavior Usage Preferences of Elderly Users

3.2   User Interviews

User interviews are used as one of the methods of user research, and through a semi-structured interview program, not only can we collect first-hand data from users, but also understand their needs in a more targeted manner, with a higher degree of authenticity.

Target Users

pre-screening, the author will target users as 50–65 years old middle-aged and elderly people, four men and one woman, are more or less being used or before the use of various types of smart home systems, etc., and then on the five users were interviewed, the basic situation of the interview is as follows (Table 1).

Table 1. Analysis and arrangement of key points of user interview results

USER BASIC INFORMATION	NUMBER	1	2	3	4	5
	Age	55	60	65	63	57
	Career	retire	retire	retire	retire	retire
	Income	1 . 2w	1.02w	1.4w	1.8w	1.37w

(INCOME IS EXPRESSED IN RMB PER MONTH)

BEHAVIOR	WHICH BRAND TO USE	MIJIA	ALEXA	HUAWEI	APPLE HOME	MIJIA
	Why you choose this app?	Friend recommends	Buy it myself	cheaper	Trusted Brands	cheaper
	Is it used by family members?	Yes	Yes	Yes	Yes	Yes
	Equipment purchase channels	Shopping Mall	Internet	Gift	Shopping Mall	Internet
	Frequently used features?	Always	Sometimes	Often	Often	Sometimes
	What other functions are used?	Mall and Community	Community	Instructional Videos	Guidance notes	Community and Instructional Videos

4   Competitive Product Analysis and User Research Summary

4.1   Competitive Product Analysis

Competitive Analysis (CA) is a term that originated in the field of economics, which is used to evaluate the strengths and weaknesses of existing or potential competing products, and to formulate product development strategies from them. In the UX industry, Competitive Analysis tends to analyze products with the same attributes and functionality, and is not limited to the analysis of competing products, especially the analysis of specific page interactions and visuals, etc. There are many smart home system products, based on the market share, we have selected "Mijia" from China, "Alexa" from Japan, and "Home" from the United States. In order to compare and analyze the advantages and disadvantages of three different countries' smart home system APPs, the specific analysis is shown in Table 2.

Table 2. Competitive Product Positioning Functional Analysis

Home screen icon	🔲	alexa	🏠
Product Name	Mijia	Alexa	Home
Product Position	Mijia is a home smart hardware management platform that creates Xiaomi smart homes and creates an APP for smart appliances and life services. It is also a future-oriented smart appliances brand and a high-quality smart home life e-commerce platform.	It is Alexa's unified management platform for IoT smart devices and the experience entrance to the Alexa Echo smart home ecosystem. It can discover and connect terminal products that comply with the Alexa Echo connection protocol, and create a grounded and smart new life experience scenario	Is Apple's smart home management platform for iPhone, iPad, HomePod, Mac An APP such as "Home" apps can easily and safely control HomeKit-enabled accessories, and combine them into scenes to achieve intelligent joint control.
Common	The three products are basically the same in terms of the main functional services they provide, and they all provide the core function of adding smart devices to achieve smart control. • However, looking at its positioning, Mijia is to create a big IOT era where everything is connected in the Xiaomi ecological chain, and to provide mid-to-low-end products at favorable prices; • Alexa e provides products that connect brands to cooperate to achieve common intelligent linkage, and is committed to the mid-to-high-end market; • Home is the smart home APP with the most exquisite interface at this stage. Like Apple products, it has strict permission management. However, most of the smart accessories are international brands and the price is not advantageous. It is difficult to occupy the home market.		

Through Table 3 users' feedback of using the above three software, combined with Table 4 users' needs obtained through user interviews, the needs of elderly users were summarized based on the user experience element model:

Table 3. Benefits and Disadvantages Analysis Of Users Using Competitive Product

	Mijia	Alexa	Home
Benefits Point	1. Refreshing interface, complete basic functions 2. ecological chain products cover a wide range of third-party platform access manufacturers, and Good shared family function	1. Full functionality 2. Single interface design, you can get started more quickly to use	1. There is a whole set of system scenarios set 2. There are instructions to learn how to use the system 3. High automation level
Pain Point	1. Less intelligent scene recommendation 2. There are many third-party platforms, but fewer traditional big manufacturers. 3. Only one administrator is allowed in the shared home.	voice recognition is very difficult to use, only English or Japanese is supported Not friendly to the elderly	Expensive accessories

Table 4. Analysis of design elements of the user experience element model of personalized diet recommendation

Layer	Elements	Principles of Design
Strategy	User needs	Elderly users need apps that are designed to be more concise and easier to operate
	Product objectives	Attracting more users by analyzing their needs and meeting their diverse needs
Scope	Functional specifications	Need to rationalize the book order of content to ensure the integrity of the design requirements
	Content requirements	The need to prioritize the needs of older users can be better met with accuracy
Structure	Interaction design	Need for actionable areas to be more visible and for timely feedback
	Information architecture	Intuitive information architecture needs to be designed so that users can easily find the functionality they need
Skeleton	Interface design	App interface design needs to be designed in a simple and atmospheric style Need to ensure the smooth transmission of information
Surface	Sensory design	Aging-friendly smart home system APP needs to be perfected in terms of page layout, color scheme, and enhancement of senses.

5 Proposal of User Experience Model of APP for Elderly Smart Home System Based on Health Needs

5.1 Construction of the Strategy Layer of APP for Elderly Smart Home System Based on Health Needs

Product Objectives

At the first strategic level of user experience (UX) design, product goals need to clearly reflect the core vision and purpose of that product. For an app design about an age-appropriate smart home system, the product goals may include the following aspects:

Firstly by improving the quality of life of older people, the focus should be on increasing the independence and comfort of older people's lives through smart technologies, for example by simplifying household tasks through automation features; and from an ease of use and accessibility design perspective, product goals should include developing intuitive, easy to understand and use interfaces that reduce complexity, taking into account the physical and cognitive challenges that older users may face.

As older persons may experience loneliness and isolation, product goals should include facilitating interaction and communication among family members, enhancing social connections and considering long-term sustainability, including ease of updating and adapting to changing technology and user needs.

These goals should guide the design and development process to ensure that the final product meets the specific needs and expectations of older users.

User Needs

Through the preliminary literature survey and user interviews, the needs of the elderly were statistically analyzed and the elderly user needs were summarized:

(1) The way of linking APP and smart home products needs to be simpler, and the way of operation more intuitively can be shown.

(2) When problems occur during the use of smart home products, it is hoped that more timely feedback can be provided, and the problem description is more detailed, and the tutorial for solving the problem is also hoped to be more detailed.

(3) Due to the different needs of family members, I hope that there is another interface for the elderly, simple, colorful, do not want the interface is black and white gray.

(4) In the process of using, the content can be displayed through a page, minimize the possibility of turning up and down the page, or turn the page with consistency, there will be a previous page of tips.

5.2   Construction of the Scope Layer of APP for Elderly Smart Home System Based on Health Needs

Needs Analysis

Elderly users have a certain sense of unfamiliarity with existing smart home apps, and elderly users need to be analyzed in four aspects: sensory characteristics, cognitive characteristics, emotional characteristics, and personality characteristics, according to the special needs of the elderly, with the growth of age, the sensory functions of the elderly appear to be declining phenomenon, and the decline in vision is one of the most common manifestations [30]. Along with the physiological decline of the elderly, the psychological condition also changes, affecting the daily life of the elderly. The personality characteristics of older adults are the psychological characteristics when facing themselves or the outside world [31], and the classic Big Five personality theory proposes five personality dimensions-extraversion, easygoing, conscientiousness, neuroticism, and openness [32], and the personality of older adults is altered by the synergistic effects of life experiences, the environment they live in, and other factors, and the personality characteristics presented by each individual vary [33].

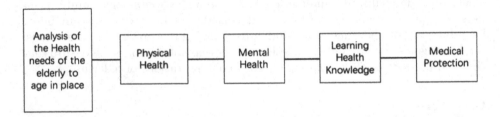

Fig. 2. Needs classification of the elderly living at home

5.3   Construction of the Structure Layer of APP for Elderly Smart Home System Based on Health Needs

Interaction Design for App Interface of Age-Appropriate Smart Home System

The criteria for interaction design are not only limited to usability, i.e., the product's functions are designed to meet the user's goals and needs. For elderly users, on this basis there is also to find a way to resonate with the elderly users and simple to use, and through the user's behavioral motivation, whether it can make the elderly users simple and easy to understand the completion of the established instructions, and through the mobilization of the user's motivation, so that the elderly users can be sustained use. The interaction design of the interface can be designed with large touch targets for easy finger operation, especially for users with poor hand dexterity. Voice control and voice feedback options are provided to support the needs of different users.

Ease of Use

As a smart home app that can be used by the elderly, the most important thing is ease of use. Based on usefulness, ease of use is to fully consider all aspects of the user's operation process to establish a clear and clear task module and content structure. Clear information framework and clear logic between pages allow users to understand each module of the APP at a glance and switch freely [34]. The pages of the APP need to be unified, and the design style and operation logic of the whole application should be consistent to minimize the difficulty for users to learn new interfaces and functions.

Information Architecture

In terms of the layout of the App, it should follow the usage logic of elderly users and make the information architecture of the App simple, intuitive and easy to understand through an intuitive layout. For elderly users, it is important to reduce the cognitive burden. Menu items and functions should be logically grouped and easy to find and use. And prioritize the main functions: put the most commonly used and important functions (e.g. emergency call, health monitoring, home security) on the home page or in an easily accessible place.

5.4 Construction of the Skeleton Layer of APP for Elderly Smart Home System Based on Health Needs

The page design of the APP should divide different functions (e.g. health monitoring, emergency response, home automation) into the following independent modules, which are easy to maintain and expand, and protect user data security and privacy with encryption and secure authentication mechanisms.

Health monitoring: integrates various health monitoring devices (e.g. heart rate monitor, blood pressure monitor) and ensures real-time data synchronization.

Emergency Response System: In case of emergency, the system can automatically notify family members or healthcare providers.

User education and support: Built-in tutorials and help: Provide easy-to-follow user guides and tutorials to help older users familiarize themselves with the app.

5.5 Construction of the Surface Layer of APP for Elderly Smart Home System Based on Health Needs

From the perspective of the sensory and cognitive characteristics of elderly users to a certain extent, the construction of the APP performance layer can allow the elderly group to overcome geriatric physiological problems to a certain extent (Tab 3), solving the troubles of elderly users due to slow movement and slow reaction.

First, in terms of visual design, use large fonts and high-contrast colors. Icons and buttons should be designed to be intuitive and easy to understand, avoiding overly complex or abstract symbols, and too many menu items or buttons.

Table 5. Analysis of needs arising from physical changes in the elderly

Categorize	Body Programs	Major changes associated with aging	Standard data (data setting values for smart devices)
Perceptual limitations	Hearing	frequent short-term hearing loss, insensitivity to high-frequency sounds	
	Vision	significant loss of visual acuity and color recognition, significantly narrowed field of vision, increased likelihood of disease-related blindness	
	Memory	instantaneous and long-term memory loss, less change in short-term memory	
Chronic Disease Related	Blood pressure	aging and hardening of blood vessels, increasing the risk of cardiovascular disease.	Systolic blood pressure > 21.3 kPa (160 mmHg) Diastolic blood pressure > 12.6 kPa (95 mmHg)
	Blood glucose	decreased ability to respond to glucose stimulation, decreased blood glucose levels, predisposition to diabetes	
	Lipids	cholesterol accumulates in the body and blood viscosity increases, leading to high blood lipids.	
	Heart rate	susceptible to cardiovascular diseases such as arrhythmia.	Normal heart rate ranges from 60 to 100 beats per minute
	Lungs	Decreased lung function and dyspnea leading to insufficient oxygen supply to organs	Lung capacity decreases by about 150 ml in 10 years
Restricted mobility	Muscle strength	reduced muscle elasticity, weakened contractility, muscle weakness and fatigue	
	Bones and joints	decreased bone elasticity and toughness and cartilage deterioration.	

Ensure that important functions such as emergency help and health monitoring are directly accessible and conspicuous, making them easier to read for older users. This can also be done by offering a choice of different interface layouts to accommodate users with different vision and operating abilities.

Secondly, through intuitive navigation, users can easily find the functions they need. And give older users clear feedback on the operation of the design, such as visual or audible feedback when a button is clicked, to ensure that older users understand that the operation has been performed. Provide confirmation steps for important actions (e.g., changing settings).

Finally, the design should take into account multiple usage scenarios, such as visibility in different lighting conditions. Provide different modes for indoor and outdoor use (e.g. night mode). And ensure the compatibility of the APP with assistive technologies to provide convenience for older users with weaker vision.

With the above design, the presentation layer of the APP for age-appropriate smart home systems based on health needs will be more friendly and easy to use, which will help elderly users to better manage their health and home environment.

6   Conclusion

The main objective of this study is to systematically propose user experience guidelines for designing and implementing future age-friendly smart home systems. Through a literature review of previous studies, the design of age-friendly smart home systems based on user experience is technically more oriented toward developing sensor technology and studying interaction design methods for elderly users. However, there is still more space for designing and thinking about the holistic design of the smart home app system from the physiological, psychological, and emotional perspectives of the elderly.Compared to previous studies, the main contribution of this study is to propose a user experience guide for the future implementation of an age friendly smart home system APP. For example, the method based on user experience element models divides the needs of elderly users. In addition, due to the current interface design of the APP being unfriendly to elderly users, So this article also provides specific suggestions for the information architecture or interaction design of the APP interface when designing elderly users. Finally, it emphasizes the need for the APP to increase compatibility with auxiliary technologies to better protect and assist elderly users in different usage scenarios.

It is crucial for developers to understand user experience design, especially for elderly users, which requires more efforts from developers to ensure that user can use the program to meet their highest expectations and acceptance. Although there have been many scholars based on the user experience methodology proposed application program design, but suitable for the elderly smart home system still lacks a complete user experience design guidelines, at the same time, broaden the user experience design research field, for the smart home system application design to provide practical reference ideas, focusing on the value of practical use. However, there are still shortcomings and limitations in the article's research, and it is necessary to consider the user service scenarios and optimize the user's emotional experience in depth, to find out more detailed and in-depth needs, and to discover more entry points for the design method.

In conclusion, in today's technological development, we need to continue to improve and think about the ways and means of interaction between users and smart home system apps, to provide users with more convenient and convenient use of the experience.

References

1. Balta-Ozkan, N., Davidson, R., Bicket, M., Whitmarsh, L.: Social barriers to the adoption of smart homes. Energy Policy **63**, 363–374 (2013). https://doi.org/10.1016/j.enpol.2013.08.043
2. Yichen, W., Pillan, M.: From respect to change user behaviour. Research on how to design a next generation of smart home objects from User Experience and Interaction Design. Design J. **20**(sup1), S3884–S3898 (2017). https://doi.org/10.1080/14606925.2017.1352891
3. Statista. Total Market Value of the Global Smart Homes Market in 2014 and 2020 (in Billion U.S. Dollars). http://www.statista.com/
4. Zhou, Z., et al.: A real-time system for in-home activity monitoring of elders. Engineering in Medicine and Biology Society, 2009. EMBC 2009. In: Annual International Conference of the IEEE. IEEE (2009)
5. Aging, can we stop the clock?', Wellcome Trust Report. http://www.wellcome.ac.uk/
6. Techtarget. https://www.techtarget.com/whatis/definition/mobile-app
7. Qing-lin, L., Mei, W., Zhan, F.: Voice interaction design of smart home products based on emotional interaction. Packag. Eng. **40**(16), 37–42 (2019)
8. Wen-xiang, Z.H.O.U.: Emotional design for intelligent speech interaction: showcasing the emotional design and solutions to Xiaoduzaijia under music scenes. Comput. Sci. Appl. **9**(3), 638–643 (2019)

9. Gavrila, C., et al.: Health monitoring in a smart home environment: digest of technical papers-IEEE International Conference on Consumer Electronics, v 2022-January

10. Choi, Y.K., Thompson, H.J., Demiris, G.: A voice interaction-mediated smart home to support aging in place: a new paradigm to engage with health-related data. Innov. Aging 3(Supplement1), S442–S442 (2019)

11. Ferrero, R., et al.: Ubiquitous fridge with natural language interaction[J]. In: 2019 IEEE International Conference on RFID Technology and Applications, RFID-TA 2019, pp. 404–409 (2019)

12. Zahid, M., et al.: Recent developments in textile based polymeric smart sensor for human health monitoring: a review. Arab. J. Chem. 15(1) (2022)

13. Patil, K., et al.: A consumer-based smart home with indoor air quality monitoring system. IETE J. Res. 65(6), 758–770 (2019)

14. Min, W., Cui, H., Rao, H., Li, Z., Yao, L.: Detection of human falls on furniture using scene analysis based on deep learning and activity characteristics. IEEE Access 6, 9324–9335 (2018)

15. Sehairi, K., Chouireb, F., Meunier, J.: Elderly fall detection system based on multiple shape features and motion analysis. In: Proceedings of the 2018 IEEE International Conference on Intelligent Systems and Computer Vision (ISCV), Fez, Morocco, 2-4 April 2018; pp. 1–8 (2018)

16. Daher, M., Diab, A., El Badaoui El Najjar, M., Ali Khalil, M., Charpillet, F.: Elder tracking and fall detection system using smart tiles. IEEE Sens. J. 17, 469–479 (2017)

17. Yacchirema, D., De Puga, J.S., Palau, C., Esteve, M.: Fall detection system for elderly people using IoT and ensemble machine learning algorithm. Procedia Comput. Sci. 130, 603–610 (2018)

18. Sucerquia, A., Lopez, J.D., Vargas-Bonilla, J.F.: Real-life/real-time elderly fall detection with a triaxial accelerometer. Sensors 18, 1101 (2018)

19. Chan, A.M., Selvaraj, N., Ferdosi, N., Narasimhan, R.: Wireless patch sensor for remote monitoring of heart rate, respiration, activity, and falls. In: Proceedings of the 2013 35th Annual International Conference of the IEEE Engineering in Medicine and Biology Society (EMBC), Osaka, Japan, 3-7 July 2013 6115–6118 (2013)

20. Perego, P., Standoli, C., Andreoni, G.: Wearable monitoring of elderly in an ecologic setting: The SMARTA project. In: Proceedings of the 2nd International Electronic Conference on Sensors and Applications, MDPI, Basel, Switzerland, 5 November 2015 S3001 (2015)

21. Milici, S., Amendola, S., Bianco, A., Marrocco, G.: Epidermal RFID passive sensor for body temperature measurements. In: Proceedings of the 2014 IEEE RFID Technology and Applications Conference (RFID-TA), Tampere, Finland, 8-9 September, pp. 140–144 (2014)

22. Boano, C.A., Lasagni, M., Romer, K., Lange, T.: Accurate temperature measurements for medical research using body sensor networks. In: Proceedings of the 2011 14th IEEE International Symposium on Object/Component/Service-Oriented Real-Time Distributed Computing Workshops, Newport Beach, CA, USA, 28–31 March 2011, pp. 189–198 (2011)

23. Kim, J., Kwon, S., Seo, S., Park, K.: Highly wearable galvanic skin response sensor using flexible and conductive polymer foam. In: Proceedings of the 2014 36th Annual International Conference of the IEEE Engineering in Medicine and Biology Society, Chicago, IL, USA, 26-30 August 2014, pp. 6631–6634 (2014)

24. Guo, R., Li, S., He, L., Gao, W., Qi, H., Owens, G.: Pervasive and unobtrusive emotion sensing for human mental health. In: Proceedings of Proceedings of the ICTs for Improving Patients Rehabilitation Research Techniques, Venice, Italy 5–8, 436–439 (2013)
25. (U.S.) Jesse James Garrett: Elements of User Experience, translated by Fan Xiaoyan, Beijing: Machinery Industry Press (2011)
26. Li, X., You, Y.: Kano model analysis required in app interactive design based on mobile user experience. Int. J. Multimed. Ubiquit. Eng. 11(11) (2016)
27. Meng, P.: Research on Personalized Diet Recommendation Service Based on Eating Behavior. Shaanxi Normal University (2016)
28. Wyskida, K., Zak-Gołab, A., Łabuzek, K., et al.: Daily intake and serum concentration of menaquinone-4 (MK-4) in hemodialysis patients with chronic kidney disease. Clin. Biochem. 48(18), 1246–1251 (2015)
29. Gao, B., Xu, X.: Research progress on the relationship between dietary factors and human trace element balance. J. Baotou Med. Coll. 2010, 26(3), 136–138 (2016)
30. Qiong, W.U.: Planting Design of Nursing Homes Based on Physiological, Psychological Characteristics and Dem- ands of the Elderly. Southeast University, Nanjing (2018)
31. Zheng, C.-Y.: Product operation feedback design based on the elderly people's sensory characteristics. J. Mach. Design 31(1), 116–119 (2014)
32. Jian-chun, Z.H.U.: Interpretation of intelligent product design based on cognitive characteristics of the elderly. Indust. Design 8, 145–146 (2018)
33. Rui, G.U.O.: Research on Information Service for the Elderly Based on Cognitive Process. Heilongjiang University, Harbin (2019)
34. Rust, J., Golombok, S.: Modern Psychometrics: The Science of Psychological Assessment. Li, S.-Y., Miao, J.-J., Translated. Beijing: China Renmin University Press (2011)

Author Index

Seto, Kazuki   III-217
Shan, Junjie   II-24
Shima, Shigeyoshi   II-238
Shimohara, Katsunori   III-366
Shiozu, Yurika   III-366
Shirahige, Koki   III-148
Steimann, Jan   I-264
Stephens, Michael   II-3
Sugio, Nobuyuki   III-16
Sunayama, Wataru   III-178
Symanzik, Jürgen   II-65

T
Tahara, Yuya   II-249
Takahara, Madoka   I-279, III-16, III-178
Takashima, Kinoka   II-262
Takasu, Mone   III-230
Takatsu, Taiyo   III-118
Takeba, Ryo   I-12
Takemura, Toshihiko   II-238
Taniai, Nono   II-276
Taniguchi, Chizuru   III-197
Tasaki, Sakie   II-292
Teixeira, Ana Rita   I-51
Theis, Sabine   II-35, III-275
Tomoto, Takahito   II-95, III-3, III-148, III-338
Tsukatsune, Kenta   II-304

U
Uchida, Misaki   II-292
Uwano, Fumito   III-245

V
VanderHoeven, Hannah   I-60
Vanderplas, Susan   II-140
Vera, Tomás   I-253, III-382
von Kurnatowski, Lynn   II-121
Vu, Kim-Phuong L.   III-44

W
Wang, Fan   II-189
Wang, Jianmin   I-81
Wang, Yuchen   I-81
Watanabe, Tomio   I-3, I-42, III-309
Wende, Gerko   I-162
Wiederich, Tyler   II-140
Wu, Lien-Shang   I-237

X
Xie, Haoran   I-99
Xu, Wei   II-175

Y
Yamamoto, Michiya   III-59
Yang, Min   I-289
Yang, Xi   I-99
Yang, Yeqing   II-157
Yoshida, Satoko   III-366
You, Fang   I-81

Z
Zarefard, Motahareh   III-397
Zhang, Jiaqi   I-300
Zhang, Jing   I-223, II-175, III-261
Zhang, Sirui   II-320
Zhao, Lijuan   II-175

Printed in the United States
by Baker & Taylor Publisher Services